Also by Carolly Erickson

THE RECORDS OF MEDIEVAL EUROPE

CIVILIZATION AND SOCIETY IN THE WEST

THE MEDIEVAL VISION

BLOODY MARY

GREAT HARRY

THE FIRST ELIZABETH

MISTRESS ANNE

OUR TEMPESTUOUS DAY

BONNIE PRINCE CHARLIE

TO THE SCAFFOLD:
THE LIFE OF MARIE ANTOINETTE

Carolly Erickson

Crown Publishers, Inc.
New York

Published by Crown Publishers, Inc., 201 East 50th Street, New York, New York 10022. Member of the Crown Publishing Group.

Random House, Inc. New York, Toronto, London, Sydney, Auckland
CROWN is a trademark of Crown Publishers, Inc.
Manufactured in the United States of America.

Design by Nancy Kenmore

Library of Congress Cataloging-in-Publication Data

Erickson, Carolly, 1943–
    Great Catherine / Carolly Erickson.
        p.   cm.
    Includes index.
    1. Catherine II, Empress of Russia, 1729–1796.   2. Empresses—
Russia—Biography.   3. Russia—History—Catherine II, 1762–1796.
I. Title
Dk170.E75 1994
947'.063'092—dc20
[B]   93-44164
                                                                                  CIP

ISBN 0-517-59091-3

10 9 8 7 6 5 4 3 2 1

First Edition

To Lillian Cunningham
and the Windward Writing Retreat

Aloha nui loa

Chapter One

THE SMALL, LIVELY, RATHER PLAIN LITTLE FOUR-YEAR-OLD girl walked up to the king and reached up to tug at his jacket. She had been taught to kiss the garments of older people, as a sign of reverence, but the stout, red-faced man who watched her approach with a severe expression was wearing a jacket that was too short, and this made it difficult for her to do what her mother had ordered. A look of disapproval, almost of disdain, crossed the child's regular features. Her unusually large, wide light blue eyes, bright with intelligence and sensitivity, looked fearlessly into his sternly imposing face. Then she turned and walked back to where her mother and great-aunt were waiting.

"Why does the king have such a short jacket?" the little girl demanded in a voice that carried well even in the grand salon with its high painted ceiling and thick hangings. "He's rich enough to afford a longer one, isn't he?"

Her mother, intensely uncomfortable and only too aware that the watchful dignitaries, military officers and titled ladies—not to mention the court chamberlain with his broad-bottomed wig and long staff, the elegantly dressed ladies of honor and chamber gentlemen, the solemn footmen in their velvet liveries—and her grandmother, the duchess, were all waiting for her to respond to the child, was silent.

1

The king wanted to know what the little girl had said, and what Frederick William of Prussia wanted to know, he found out.

Someone repeated to him the child's words. The courtiers held their breaths, the mother turning very red, her distress apparent.

Then, to her amazement, he laughed. The king, who carried a cane to beat his soldiers with when they didn't march fast enough to satisfy him or when they deviated from his strict and detailed orders, actually laughed.

"The little one is impertinent," he was overheard to remark. Then he turned away, and the tension in the room was broken.

The child, Sophia Augusta Fredericka of Anhalt-Zerbst, was precocious and active, with an excess of energy that made her brash and often headstrong. She chattered endlessly, she was full of questions and she noticed and remembered things that made no impression on duller children. She learned to read at a very young age, and before she was four she was reading French, at least after a fashion, and writing names and dates. She knew that she was not a pretty child—and she sensed that that was all her mother cared about—but she also knew that she was clever, and that her animated conversation, high energy and cheerful disposition could bring a smile of pleasure to the faces of the adults about her, just as her impertinent question had made King Frederick William laugh.

She was a princess of the insignificant but honorable principality of Anhalt-Zerbst, one of the three hundred or so independent political entities where German was spoken. In the year of her encounter with the Prussian king, 1733, these three hundred scattered principalities, Free Cities, bishoprics and dukedoms were bound only by the loosest of political ties, a vague and largely ceremonial union under the greatly decayed authority of the Holy Roman Emperor. Much more real than the emperor's shadowy aegis was the power of the king of Prussia, who had at his command one of the largest and most highly disciplined armies in Europe and whose territorial ambitions threatened the integrity of the smaller states that bordered his kingdom.

Anhalt-Zerbst was among these states, a few hundred square miles of pine forests, pastureland and bog nestled between the Electorate of Saxony on the south, the Archbishopric of Magdeburg on the west and Prussia on the north. Since the early thirteenth century Anhalt had been proudly independent, but over the centuries its princely dynasty had branched out in so many directions that all its princes were impoverished, the tiny state lacking the resources to support a populous ruling house. For several generations the Anhalt princes had avoided destitution by serving in the army of the Prussian king, and Sophie's father, Prince Christian August, had followed this tradition, leading troops into battle against the French and the Swedes, devoting his young manhood to the advancement of Prussian arms though he had neither the talent nor the inclination to distinguish himself as a leader of men.

At the advanced age of thirty-seven Christian August had married a relatively poor but well-born princess, Johanna of Holstein-Gottorp, and had taken her to live in the bleak garrison town of Stettin on the Pomeranian border, where he and his regiment were stationed. Johanna was only sixteen, a pretty, shallow girl accustomed to being spoiled by her grandmother the duchess and dismayed by the sparse social life of Stettin, where the leaders of society were grimly correct provincial military officers and tedious tradesmen's wives. Johanna and Christian August rented a house from a local businessman, settled in, and soon Johanna was pregnant.

This at least gave her hope. If she had a son, he might inherit the principality of Anhalt-Zerbst, for the current ruler, a cousin of Christian August, was childless and likely to remain so, and Christian August's older brother Ludwig was unmarried. The birth of a son would liberate Johanna from Stettin, and might liberate her husband from having to live in thrall to the Prussian king.

But the child was a girl—Sophie—and in giving birth to her Johanna suffered terribly. Her labor nearly killed her, and for five months she barely clung to life, in pain and no doubt resenting the disappointing child whose arrival had brought her to death's door. Sophie was put into the care of a nineteen-year-old wet-nurse, then when she was weaned she was turned over to a governess, Madeleine Cardel, who did her best to curb the little girl's overactive energies and tried to turn her into a quiet and docile child—at least for as long as she and her rather fawning governess were within her parents' view.

Johanna, once she recovered, was soon pregnant again and this time she was determined to have a son. When Sophie was eighteen months old, her brother Wilhelm was born, and immediately he became the center of Johanna's world. Sophie was cast into the shade and neglected, while the new baby received all his parents' attention, all the more so as it became apparent that one of his legs was weak and shriveled, making it impossible for him to develop normally. Doctors were consulted, folk remedies tried; the boy was prayed over, taken to bathe in mineral springs and subjected to every kind of therapy. But little Wilhelm did not thrive, and Johanna suffered yet another severe disappointment as she watched the son she had hoped for grow up a cripple.

Christian August now benefited from the influence of his wife's family and found himself appointed governor of Stettin. Apart from the increase in honor and status, this meant more pay (though the parsimonious general remained tightfisted with money, to the disgruntlement of his rather profligate young wife) and more dignified quarters in the four-square, gray stone castle that dominated the town. An entire story in one wing of the castle, adjacent to the chapel with its tall bell tower, was given over to Christian August and his household. Now when the family knelt for morning and evening prayers they heard the tolling of the chapel bell, and its mournful sound was to haunt young Sophie's childhood.

When Sophie was four years old, Madeleine Cardel left Christian August's service to marry an advocate, and her sister Babette took over as governess to the princess. Babette was a treasure: clearsighted and full of common sense, she neither spoiled nor bullied Sophie but treated her with gentleness and patience, attending to the cultivation of her exceptional mind while restraining her boisterousness. Babette was good-tempered, Sophie remembered when she came to write her memoirs many years later, a "model of virtue and wisdom."* Her father, a Huguenot refugee, was a professor in Frankfurt and Babette had been well educated. She may or may not have had some grounding in the Greek and Latin classics, but she certainly knew the classics of French drama, and taught Sophie to recite long passages from Molière and Racine. In a household where conventional Lutheran piety and a rather grim sense of duty were all-pervasive, Babette represented rationality, tartness and a touch of the acerb.

"I had a good heart," Sophie wrote of herself as a child, "I was full of common sense, I cried very easily, I was extremely flighty." Full of physical daring but with an overdeveloped sense of shame—the product of overzealous religious teaching—she was easily frightened and often hid to avoid undeserved punishments she feared would fall on her. Her mother was quick to blame her and slow to recognize when she herself had been wrong; consequently Sophie had more than her share of slaps and blows, which wounded her sense of justice and left her fearful.

Liking to run up and down stairs, jump on the furniture and dash headlong from room to room, Sophie was bound to hurt herself. Once she was playing with scissors and the point of one of the blades went into the pupil of her eye; fortunately her sight was undamaged. Another time she was playing in her mother's bedchamber where there was a cabinet full of toys and dolls. She

---

*Catherine the Great wrote at least seven versions of her autobiography, beginning the first of them when she was in her late twenties. The various versions differ in detail, and their author was neither modest nor unbiased, but their six hundred-plus pages are a rich lode of narrative lore and an incomparable aid to the biographer.

reached up to unlock it—and in doing so she inadvertently pulled the entire heavy cabinet over on top of her. By this time the doors had opened, however, and she eventually crawled out unscathed.

When Sophie was five years old Johanna gave birth again, this time to another son, Frederick. Two years later she had a fourth child, also a boy, but he lived only a few weeks. Wilhelm, the crippled heir apparent to the Anhalt-Zerbst dominions, continued to preoccupy his mother, who sent him to take the waters at Aix-la-Chapelle, Karlsbad and Teplitz, and worried over him and his brother to the neglect of her daughter.

Brittle bones seem to have plagued the family, for at the age of seven even the normally robust Sophie threw her spine severely out of alignment when a violent fit of coughing caused her to fall on her left side, and for weeks she was bedridden with severe pain. The cough persisted, along with shortness of breath, and when after nearly a month the child was allowed to get up, she was so crooked that she looked deformed, her right shoulder being much higher than her left, her spine zigzagging down her back in the shape of a letter Z.

Johanna's first reaction was one of chagrin; she felt mortified enough having a crippled son, a disfigured daughter was an embarrassing liability she did not need. Sophie's condition was kept secret from all but Babette and a few trusted servants. No one knew what to do; severe dislocations were no rarity in the early eighteenth century—they were often inflicted deliberately on tortured prisoners—but the only man in the vicinity of Stettin who was versed in treating them also served as the local executioner, and Johanna did not want it known that she had hired him to treat her daughter.

In the end, in the greatest secrecy, the executioner was smuggled into the castle. He examined Sophie and gave his recommendations: first, that a young virgin be found who would spread her spittle over the princess's back and shoulder every morning, and second that Sophie wear a brace on her back, a torturous contraption like a stiff corset that kept her in one position night and day and that she was not allowed to remove except to change her underwear.

Johanna, who invariably exhorted her daughter to "suffer her illness patiently" and became cross when Sophie moaned and complained, insisted on this regimen of saliva and corsetry; when after many months the executioner allowed the stiff brace to be removed, Sophie's torso had returned to normal.

But it was not enough to train her limbs; her intellect too had to be carefully straitjacketed, lest it grow in awkward directions. Babette Cardel remarked that Sophie had an "esprit gauche"—an eccentric and highly individual turn of mind. She was opinionated and contrary, and she "resisted all resistance," as she herself put it later, remembering what she had been like at five and six. Sophie had "a perverse spirit which took all that was said to her in the opposite sense," and in an age when all children, and most especially little girls, were expected to be obedient and submissive, her "perverse spirit" presented her teachers with a challenge.

Besides Babette, who knew how to govern the young princess with reason and gentleness, Sophie had a German teacher, a French dancing-master, a music teacher and a Calvinist schoolmaster who taught her calligraphy. The schoolmaster she dismissed as "an old weak-head who had been an idiot in his youth," and the unfortunate music teacher, "the poor devil Roellig," as she called him when she remembered him later, made himself ridiculous by going into raptures over the booming tones of a bass singer he always brought with him to her lessons who "roared like a bull." Having no ear for music herself, Sophie envied those who did, but had no respect for Roellig or the other inferior provincial pedants who were put in charge of her.

Toward Herr Wagner, however, who taught her religion— along with a smattering of history and geography—Sophie had more complicated feelings. Herr Wagner was an army pastor who saw it as his duty to impress on the flighty, cheerful princess the seriousness of life, the wickedness of the world and the dread of hell. He presented her with a large German Bible with hundreds of verses underlined in red ink and told her to memorize them. Hour after hour she sat with the book on her knees, repeating to herself phrases about the wages of sin and the mighty armor of God and the heart as "deceitful above all things, and desperately wicked." Messages about grace and mercy were mixed in her child's awareness with visions of torment and divine vengeance—and in fact the vengeance of the Lord may well have become confused with the vengeance of Herr Wagner, for when Sophie stumbled over a word or forgot a verse, he punished her harshly and conveyed a degree of disapproval that made her feel not only that she had failed but that she was well nigh worthless.

Tragedy, evil and sin were Herr Wagner's themes, and he did his best to implant in Sophie a lively sense of pessimism toward earthly life and a lively fear of the Last Judgment, when God would mete out a terrible retribution to those who had not gained his mercy. Sophie took Pastor Wagner's messages very seriously indeed, and wept bitterly and privately over her shortcomings. When it came to the logic of history, however, and the teachings in the Book of Genesis about the creation of the world, her curiosity and natural argumentativeness outstripped her piety.

She argued with her instructor "heatedly and in a very opinionated way" about how unjust she felt it was for God to damn all those who lived before the birth of Christ. What of those wise philosophers of antiquity, Plato and Socrates and Aristotle, whose sagacity had been prized for several millennia? she asked. Was not God deficient in fairness in condemning them? Herr Wagner quoted chapter and verse, but Sophie continued to defend Aristotle and Plato. Finally the pastor went to Babette and demanded that she give Sophie a good beating to make her see the truth and obey her elders.

Babette gently explained to Sophie that it was not appropriate for a child to express a contrary opinion to an older authority such as Herr Wagner, and told her to submit to his view. But before long teacher and pupil were at odds again. This time Sophie wanted to know what came before the biblical creation.

"Chaos," Herr Wagner announced with what he hoped was finality. But what was chaos, Sophie demanded, and would not be satisfied with what he told her.

Exasperated beyond endurance, and no doubt angry at Babette for refusing to beat the recalcitrant princess, Herr Wagner once again threw up his hands and called in the governess, whose intervention restored peace until the next point of debate arose, over the unfamiliar word "circumcision." Sophie naturally wanted to know what it was, and Herr Wagner was naturally reluctant to tell her. Babette too told her to stop asking, though it took all her art to persuade the persistent child to be content with ignorance, and it was not lost on Sophie that Babette found the situation amusing.

Herr Wagner's examinations were nearly as terrifying as the Last Judgment. "I was horribly, persecutorially questioned," Sophie remembered years afterward. Worst of all was the burden of having to learn by heart what seemed an infinite number of Bible verses as well as long passages of poetry. To help her concentrate on what she was learning, at the age of seven all her toys and dolls were taken away. (She didn't miss them much; she preferred the active rough-and-tumble games the boys played and had never liked dolls, amusing herself at odd moments by playing with her hands or folding a handkerchief into fanciful shapes.) "I believe it was not humanly possible to retain all that I had to memorize," she recalled many years later. "Also I do not think it worth the trouble."

The strain on her nerves was great; eventually she began to despair. When autumn came, and the days grew very short in the far northern town of Stettin, and the mournful chapel bells tolled at twilight, she took to hiding behind the hangings and crying as though her heart would break. The tears were for her sins, and for the errors she made when she recited her lessons, and the love she missed. Babette found her in her hiding place, got her to admit at least some of what was troubling her, and went to the pastor to complain. She told him that his methods were making Sophie overly melancholy and frightened about the future, and asked him to be less severe. Neither Babette nor anyone else addressed the more serious problem that was troubling Sophie: the knowledge that her mother did not love her, and her resentment of the crippled, pampered Wilhelm, who, in her view, often deserved the slaps and blows that she received.

Inwardly Sophie was in despair, but outwardly she shone—when in the presence of others. Her brash cheerfulness, her innate tendency to "chatter on boldly and endlessly" in adult company, her striking intelligence combined to make a strong impression on those outside her family circle. She became accustomed to being praised for her cleverness. When her mother took Sophie to Brunswick to visit her great-grandmother the duchess, she was coaxed into reciting the long dramatic pieces she had memorized, and was stroked and complimented so that she came to see herself as unusual. "I heard it said so often that I was smart, that I was a big girl now, that I really believed it." King Frederick William, who had had his first taste of Sophie's precocity when she was four, continued to encounter her as she grew older and followed her progress, asking after her whenever he was in Stettin or when Christian August went to Berlin.

When the princess was eight, Johanna took her to Berlin for the first time. They stayed for several months, and Sophie went to court, dressed like a miniature lady in a gown with a long train. Her spine no longer zigzagged down her back, her shoulders were level and she held her proud little head straight as she passed through the halls of the royal palace—which, in truth, was less grand than her great-grandmother's establishment at Brunswick. The king renewed his acquaintance with her, and the queen invited her to dine with her and Crown Prince Frederick, then a young man of twenty-five. Both were charmed by her and impressed with her, and Frederick, who like Sophie possessed an outstanding intellect and a spirit of questioning, was to remember her well.

That her eight-year-old daughter should eclipse her was irksome to Johanna, in whose rather limited understanding girls had value only insofar as they were beautiful—or at least reasonably attractive. Sophie, Johanna thought, was ugly, and no matter how intelligent she was, her ugliness could not be disguised. Johanna did not broadcast her opinion outside the family circle, but her sensitive daughter was well aware of it. Besides, Sophie was growing up in a social environment where a woman's value was determined by her beauty. Everyone knew that ugly little girls grew up to be plain women, and plain women did not find husbands. They languished in their parents' houses, or in convents where they lived in secluded luxury, not taking religious vows but boarding with the nuns in their own well-appointed apartments. Every family, including Sophie's, had several of these unfortunates in it, superfluous women for whom no other place could be found. In Johanna's view, Sophie was in danger of growing up to be one of them.

Highly intelligent, pleasing, but plain: such was the verdict on Sophie of Anhalt-Zerbst. The child did what was expected of her, observed her world through her large, bright eyes, asked a thousand questions, and awaited her chance to shine.

Chapter Two

F ROM THE AGE OF EIGHT ON, SOPHIE SPENT LESS AND LESS time in the cold and dreary backwater of Stettin and more and more time at the active, vital courts of Brunswick and Berlin. Johanna joined her grandmother's court for three or four months each year, and spent the long northern winter in Berlin, and she took Sophie with her.

Christian August did not object to his wife's being away for months at a time. He was now in his fifties, she in her mid-twenties; they were dissimilar in personality, he serious and austere, and liking solitude, she witty and vivacious and teasing, at her best when surrounded by admiring friends. Johanna, her daughter recalled years later, was considered to be the more intelligent of the two, but Christian August "was a man of rectitude, and solid judgment," acquainted with many subjects because of his wide reading. He and Johanna cannot have been very good company for one another. Christian August was beginning to age, his circulation was poor and he could not have kept up with the ceaseless round of hunting parties and balls and promenades that court society demanded.

So Johanna went off with Sophie and the other children, and took her place among the minor notables surrounding King Frederick William, reminding herself that, though her husband was only a very obscure prince, she herself came from a family closely allied to royalty. Her great-grandfather was Frederick III, King of Denmark, her late father had been Prince Bishop of Lübeck and her cousin Karl Frederick was married to Anna, daughter of Emperor Peter the Great of Russia. Karl's son and namesake, nine-year-old Karl Ulrich, was heir to the thrones of Sweden and Russia. Johanna's late brother Karl August had been betrothed to Peter the Great's younger daughter Elizabeth, but had died on the eve of his wedding.

To be sure, Johanna's royal connections had not brought her wealth, and she had married beneath her. She was only the fourth daughter of the prince bishop, among the least significant of his twelve children, and apparently estranged from her own mother for reasons history does not record. Yet she had hope that her own children would do better than she had. Possibly because she had not succeeded in advancing herself very far, Johanna was intensely ambitious for her children. If boldness and pride could push them to the forefront of society, then push she would. She consulted mediums and fortune-tellers in hopes of discovering what lay in store for each of them, though when it came to the homely little Sophie, Johanna was inclined to wince at her prospects, no matter what any self-professed visionary said.

Among the other children at the court of Brunswick was little Princess Marianne of Brunswick-Bevern, whose attractive features bore in them the promise of beauty. Johanna liked her and singled her out for praise. Now, there's a little girl who'll win a crown one day, she said, or words to that effect—in the hearing of the ill-favored Sophie. Also within earshot was a clairvoyant monk, a member of the entourage of the Prince Bishop of Corbie. The monk hastened to correct Johanna's prediction, telling her that he saw no crowns in Marianne's future but that there were three crowns visible over Sophie's head.

Sophie treasured that brief triumph, and connected it with another fragment of information that had come to her from her father's mentor and friend Bolhagen, who had lived in close proximity to the family since before Sophie was born and had spent a good deal of time with the children. Once when Bolhagen was reading the newspaper he told the children about a notice he saw there concerning the forthcoming marriage of Princess Augusta of Saxe-Gotha with the eldest son of King George II of England. "Well now," he remarked, "that Princess Augusta was much less well brought up than ours; she isn't a bit pretty, and there she is destined to become the Queen of England. Who knows what our princess will become?"

German princesses were in demand at foreign courts. There seemed to be an inexhaustible supply of them, and if they did not bring large dowries, at least their fathers were too unimportant to drive hard bargains with prospective bridegrooms. Many European ruling houses sent representatives to the German courts to examine their princesses in person, and to request portraits to carry back home with them.

Reluctantly at first, Johanna began to see that Sophie might be a commodity in this bride-market—a marginal commodity, to be sure, yet not entirely without value. As Sophie grew older she became slightly less ugly, and much more impressive in her ability to learn and to discuss ideas. Many people admired her original turn of mind, and complimented her mother on Sophie's pleasing personality. Johanna remained skeptical about Sophie's prospects, but saw to it that her daughter made the right friends and remained within the circle of familiars around the Prussian royal family—just in case.

Johanna loved Berlin, and was at her happiest when in residence there. A small, picturesque city with wide streets and many fine houses—a number of them built by the king himself, who had a penchant for knocking down small and inferior structures and ordering better ones erected at his own expense—Berlin was dominated by its military population. Some twenty thousand soldiers were quartered in the homes of the inhabitants; every fourth or fifth person one met in the street was a soldier. Between campaigns, especially during the winter, these men were largely idle, and free to attend masquerades and fetes. Johanna, pretty and unencumbered by her husband, was an attractive ornament at these gatherings.

When the balls were over, however, Johanna had to return to her responsibilities. Her chief concern, as always, was the ill health of her eldest son Wilhelm. His leg hung uselessly, he had to be carried everywhere. His temper, if Sophie's account in her memoirs is to be trusted, was irritable if not savage. Johanna hovered over him, calling in every physician she knew of, accompanying her son to bathe in the health-giving waters of mineral spas. She began to worry over her younger son Frederick as well, looking on him as more and more precious as Wilhelm declined.

Sophie's vibrant good health must have seemed almost an affront to her more delicate brothers. She was big for her age, and strong. She amused herself by seeing how fast she could run up and down steep staircases and by playing boys' games. At night she was put to bed quite early; wakeful and full of energy, she feigned sleep and then, when her women left her alone, jumped up and arranged her pillows like a saddle and galloped astride them until she was exhausted.

In the course of taking Wilhelm to consult physicians and bathe in mineral springs, Johanna stopped to visit various relatives and in-laws. Her aunt Marie Elizabeth was abbess of the Protestant convent of Quedlinburg, where her own older sister Hedwig was provost. The two women, aunt and niece, quarreled incessantly, sometimes contriving not to see one another for years at a time, though they occupied the same set of buildings and walked the same grounds. Johanna did her best to make peace between them, and sometimes succeeded, but the reconciliations were invariably brief; clearly the enmity that bound Marie Elizabeth and Hedwig gave a focus to their lives, and neither was about to give that up.

Hedwig was short and grossly fat, and passionately fond of animals. Though her room at the convent was small she kept there sixteen pug dogs. Many of them had puppies, and all of the dogs, adults and puppies, slept, ate, and relieved themselves in the one small room. Hedwig employed a young servant girl to do nothing but clean up after the dogs. She was kept busy from dawn to dusk doing nothing else, but despite her efforts the room stank like a kennel and to add to the odor Hedwig kept a good many parrots that flew from rafter to rafter, twittering and screeching and driving visitors mad. Whenever Hedwig went riding in her carriage, at least one of the parrots and half a dozen dogs rode along with her; the dogs went with her even to church.

Another maiden aunt of Sophie's, her father's sister Sophie Christine, also loved animals but had a somewhat more balanced life. She was past fifty when little Sophie knew her, very tall and painfully thin yet inordinately proud of her spare figure— probably in compensation for her unsightly face. As a girl, she told her niece, she had been beautiful, but a tragic accident had marred her beauty permanently when a little cape she was wearing caught fire and the lower part of her face was burned. The scarring was quite hideous, and put an end to her hopes of marrying well.

A poor deformed thing herself, Aunt Sophie Christine took in crippled and injured birds, and looked after them until they healed. Young Sophie described her aunt's winged menagerie as she remembered it: a one-legged thrush, a lark with a broken wing, a one-eyed goldfinch, a chicken attacked by a cock, its head halfway bitten off, a nightingale paralyzed on one side, a legless parrot that lay on its belly, and many other such creatures, all of which roamed free about the room. Sophie Christine's compassion made less of an impression on her niece than her anger when young Sophie left one of the windows open and half the birds escaped.

It must have seemed to Sophie that spinsters inevitably fell prey to eccentricity. Without a husband to obey, children to worry over or in-laws to placate, they devoted themselves to animals or to nurturing petty quarrels. Or to superstition.

One of Johanna's attendants was Fräulein Kayn, a woman of

mature years who believed in ghosts and claimed to see them often. ("I was a Sunday child," she told Sophie. "I have the second sight.") When Sophie was eleven years old, she shared a bedroom with Fräulein Kayn one night while she and her mother were on a journey to Brunswick. The room had two beds. Sophie went to sleep in hers but was awakened in the middle of the night when she felt someone crawl into bed beside her. She opened her eyes and saw, by the dim light of a candle, that Fräulein Kayn had joined her. She asked her why.

Speaking with difficulty, for she was trembling with fright and could hardly utter a sound, the older woman whispered, "For God's sake leave me alone and go to sleep quietly!"

Sophie was persistent, and pressed her to explain why she had left her own bed.

"Don't you see what is going on in the room and what is there on the table?" Fräulein Kayn said—and drew the covers up over her face.

Sophie looked around the room, but could neither hear nor see anything odd, only two beds and a small table with a candle, pitcher and basin. She told Fräulein Kayn what she saw, and succeeded in calming her somewhat. But neither of them could sleep, and shortly afterwards the fearful Fräulein crawled out of bed and over to the door, checking to see that it was locked. Sophie managed to go to sleep again but her companion was wakeful; the following morning she looked as if she hadn't slept a wink and her anxiety was evident. Again Sophie questioned her, but Fräulein Kayn was tightlipped.

"I cannot say," she murmured portentously and refused to be pressed further. But it seemed clear to Sophie that she thought she had had a brush with the occult.

Fräulein Kayn often frightened Johanna with her talk of apparitions, "white ladies," and other appearances from the beyond, and Sophie could not help but be affected by these stories and by the folk tales about witches, goblins and spirits repeated within her hearing. But counteracting the general climate of superstition was the bastion of reason, manned by Babette Cardel. Babette held every belief up to the light and scrutinized it.

"That is not common sense," Babette said whenever she heard something farfetched. Sophie too came to revere common sense, and she listened with interest when Babette's friend Monsieur de Mauclerc came to call and the two of them discussed the commonsensical English approach to law, religion and government. Monsieur de Mauclerc was engaged in editing a history of England written by his father-in-law, and through listening to him talk with Babette Sophie encountered concepts of social equality, popular representation and political reform—while learning to scorn credulity and prize rigorous debate.

At the age of eleven Sophie was taken to Eutin in the ducal state of Holstein to meet her second cousin Karl Ulrich, the promising boy who was heir to two thrones and who had just become the object of a great deal of excitement in the family. Karl Ulrich's father, Johanna's cousin Karl Frederick, had just died, and his son had inherited his ducal title and his claim to the throne of Sweden. And since through his late mother the boy was also the grandson of Peter the Great, he had a strong claim to the sovereignty of Russia as well—a sovereignty tenuously held by his aging childless relative Empress Anna Ivanovna, his mother's cousin.

Karl Ulrich was a year older than Sophie, a pale, thin, delicate-looking boy who could put on pleasant manners when he chose. Sophie's uncle Adolf, Johanna's brother, was in charge of looking after him and guiding his education, and a number of family members gathered to witness the boy's investiture with his ducal honors and to try to benefit from his prospects. The matriarch of the Holstein family, Johanna's mother Albertine, was present along with Sophie's Aunt Anna and her Uncle Augustus.

Sophie had been brought to Eutin for the express purpose of matchmaking. Given the role Karl Ulrich seemed destined to play on the world stage, a wife would have to be chosen for him soon, and a wife from among his near relations, one whom he had met and with whom he felt familiar, would be a safe choice. Sophie was not told directly that she should try to please her cousin, but her uncles and aunts, along with Karl Ulrich's chamberlain, a Swede named Brümmer, let fall a great many hints that a betrothal between them would be gratifying to the family.

Sophie's first impression of Karl Ulrich was that he was good-looking and courteous. She liked the idea that, if they married, she would be Queen of Sweden, and although he paid much more attention to her mother than to her, his inattention did not bother her. Possibly she remembered the prediction of the soothsaying monk and thought that marriage to this pale boy would fulfill it. As for Karl Ulrich's response to Sophie, it was limited to one overwhelming reaction: he envied her her liberty.

The young duke was clearly miserable. Surrounded by flatterers, he was smothered by handlers and pedagogues who watched him day and night. He chafed under their restraints and it soon became evident to his visiting relatives that beneath his polished manners lurked an irritable temper.

He had had an unnatural upbringing. His mother died when he was two months old, and his father, a rather feeble, sickly man, passed on to his son little besides his title and his attachment to Holstein. From infancy the boy had been the center of a grand and numerous household; though constrained by a thousand restrictions he had been at the same time indulged and spoiled, with the result that his recalcitrance and fiery temper had never been curbed. He did what he liked and said what he thought. He was not unintelligent, but his behavior was so incorrigible that his teachers could not teach him anything. He hated most of the men in charge of him, especially when they tried to prevent him from enjoying his wine at meals. All too often, he drank too much, and could hardly get up from the table. It seemed to Sophie that he showed affection to only two people, of all those around him. They were his valets de chambre, a Livonian named Cramer and a loutish Swede, Roumberg, an ex-soldier with whom he could play military games.

Sophie came away from her meeting with Karl Ulrich convinced that everyone expected her to marry him. Yet other eligible princes also came forward, among them King Frederick's intelligent and promising brother Prince Henry, to indicate an interest in Sophie. At twelve and thirteen she was physically mature—"larger and more developed than one is ordinarily at that age," as she expressed it in her memoirs—and already ripe for marriage.

Another distant cousin, Wilhelm of Saxe-Gotha, sidled into her life. He was lame, but attentive; he sat beside her in church, pestered her with his conversation and ultimately declared himself intent on marrying her. But Christian August put him off and suggested that he marry Johanna's sister Anne instead. Apparently Wilhelm was not too particular. He gladly married the thirty-six-year-old Anne and the two disappeared into obscurity together.

In the year that Sophie turned thirteen, Christian August had a stroke that left him temporarily paralyzed on his left side. He recovered, and was able to return to his work of soldiering and governing, but the stroke was a reminder of mortality and a worry to Johanna, who was pregnant once again and also more concerned than usual about her eldest son.

Wilhelm was growing weaker. All the doctors, remedies and mineral baths were of no avail now. He lay in his bed, limp and feverish, with his distraught mother keeping vigil beside him. Wilhelm had been her dearest treasure since his birth, and everyone in the family knew it. Now he was slipping away. When he died she was inconsolable. All her relatives, even the aged Albertine, came to stand by her in her grief, but her son's death left a void in her heart that nothing and no one could ever fill.

The ruling prince of Anhalt-Zerbst now died and Christian August and his brother Ludwig inherited joint rulership of the little principality. Frederick (or Fritz), Christian August and Johanna's second son, became the designated heir. Even Sophie inherited an estate of her own, at Jever on the North Sea coast.

Christian August resigned his military duties and moved with his family to the medieval town of Zerbst, a quaint walled community with dark winding streets, ancient narrow houses and a charming palace. Johanna still grieved for her son, but she had some consolation in her grief. She had attained her ambition, she and Christian August now had their own miniature domain, with a tiny royal household, a modest royal income, a troupe of guardsmen and subjects who bowed in reverence when the carriage of the prince and princess passed by. Never mind that Anhalt-Zerbst was so small that a swift horseman could ride across it in a single day; it was, in a very unassuming way, a sovereign power, and within its boundaries Johanna was the highest lady in the land.

When Sophie was fourteen, the family traveled to the estate at Jever, and there Sophie encountered a woman she was to remember all her life.

The Countess of Bentinck was thirty years old when Sophie met her, a strapping, mannish woman with an ugly face, a hearty manner and an exuberant physicality. She was intelligent, she knew a good deal and she seemed to have an utter and joyous disregard for respectability. Married to the Count of Bentinck, who was nowhere in evidence, she lived on her mother's estate, in the company of another woman who was most likely her lover. She also had a three-year-old son whose father, Sophie discovered, was one of her mother's footmen.

But it was the countess's spontaneity and self-directedness as much as her unconventional living arrangements that Sophie found compelling. With childlike abandon she took Sophie by the hand and swept her into a peasant dance, the pair dancing so lustily that a crowd gathered to watch them. She rode expertly— "like a courier," Sophie thought—galloping off on her own in a way that Sophie had never seen any woman do before. And the countess managed to persuade Christian August to agree to let her take Sophie riding too, all around the grounds of the estate. "She gave a new boost to my natural vivacity," Sophie recalled.

For Sophie the hours spent in the countess's exhausting company were exhilarating. "From that moment," she remembered many years later, "riding became my dominant passion and remained so for a long time thereafter." That her parents, especially Christian August, were disconcerted by the bold countess only added to her allure for Sophie, and she continued to contrive ways of visiting her for several days, risking severe punishment each time. The countess took her to her private apartments. On one wall was a portrait of a very handsome man, whom the countess identified as her husband.

"If he hadn't been my husband," she told Sophie confidentially, "I would have been madly in love with him."

Christian August and Johanna left Jever sooner than they had meant to, largely in order to tear Sophie away from her newfound friend. But the countess's charm and fascination had a lasting impact. For weeks afterward, Sophie basked in the recollection of this free spirit who did what she liked and had no fear of disapproval. The Countess of Bentinck had kicked over the traces of other people's expectations. She was married, yet independent of her husband. She slept with her servants, and was intimate with another woman. Her speech was as free as her actions, and, most important, she seemed comfortable with herself and her choices. All in all, the Countess of Bentinck, Sophie thought, had a uniquely enviable life.

"This woman had made some noise in the world," Sophie recalled. "I think that if she had been a man, she would have been an exceptional one." Sophie, an exceptional child, and one whom the countess recognized as a kindred spirit, must have begun in those few days at Jever to realize that she too could grow into an exceptional woman, one who might make some noise in the world.

Chapter Three

A T FOURTEEN SOPHIE WAS A SLIM AND VITAL GIRL, WITH A slender waist and womanly curves. Her manner was serious and decided, and at the same time ingratiating. There was nothing comely about her face—her nose was too long, and too wide at the bottom for prettiness, her chin was pronounced, her mouth was narrow, and she held her lips primly together, as if declaring her unapproachability. Her large, wide eyes, the left one straying disconcertingly from alignment with the right, had something feral about them; her gaze was piercing and made people uncomfortable. She was much more challenging than demure, though she was learning how to hide her feelings and keep her opinions to herself when necessary.

One of Johanna's waiting women, the Baroness von Prinzen, knew Sophie well and described her as having "a serious, calculating and cold personality." Intelligent and wary she certainly was. Calculating, perhaps. But not cold. Here the baroness misread her. Sophie had a warm heart and it was about to be awakened to the transports of infatuation.

Johanna's entire family was gathering at Hamburg to celebrate a major event: Johanna's brother Adolf, Prince Bishop of Lübeck, was about to become King of Sweden.

Empress Anna Ivanovna of Russia had died, and after a brief

interval of chaos the throne had passed to her cousin Elizabeth, younger daughter of Peter the Great and erstwhile sister-in-law to Johanna and her siblings. The new empress felt a strong tie to the Holstein-Gottorp clan into which, save for the untimely death of her fiancé, she would have married. She had recently decided to name her sister's son, Sophie's cousin Karl Ulrich, as her heir. And since that meant that he would renounce the Swedish succession, Elizabeth decided to extend another mark of her favor to the Holstein-Gottorp family by nominating Adolf to wear the Swedish crown.

The ceremonies at Hamburg were impressive. Members of the Swedish Estates arrived to greet Adolf and escort him to his court across the Baltic, and they and their numerous suite were entertained at balls and assemblies over a period of weeks. Swedish Senators, envoys of foreign courts, diplomats and other notables mingled in an endless round of social events. Attending the festivities was Johanna's young brother Georg, a good-looking cavalry officer with an ebullient, outgoing personality not unlike Sophie's. He lacked his niece's pensive side, he was not at all intellectual but he was cheerful company and he was so handsome—and, at twenty-four, so much more worldly than she was—that Sophie was quite captivated by him. She thought that he had lovely eyes.

Uncle and niece spent a great deal of time together. Georg came to Sophie's room to talk to her, tease her, and secretly woo her. He interfered with her lessons, much to Babette Cardel's annoyance and alarm. They became inseparable, and Johanna, who might under other circumstances have objected, was only too happy to indulge her favorite brother by letting him charm her daughter. She saw what was happening, and knew that Georg was becoming interested in Sophie, not just as a bright young relative, but as a prospective wife.

Johanna had not entirely given up hope that Sophie might marry Karl Ulrich, now grand duke, and that hope was nourished when, at two different times, emissaries from Empress Elizabeth's court came to ask for Sophie's portrait to carry back with them to Russia. Clearly the empress was considering Sophie, along with other suitable girls, as a candidate for becoming grand duchess of Russia. But now that Karl Ulrich had become such an exalted personage Johanna could no longer assume that Sophie's chances of marrying him were good; the empress might well decide on a young woman of higher rank. For that reason she could not afford to neglect whatever other opportunities presented themselves for Sophie to marry. Marriages between uncle and niece were not unknown, the Lutheran church sometimes permitted them.

Besides, if Sophie married Georg, Johanna would have one less worry. She was still mourning the loss of her elder son, and had a new baby to be concerned about, a girl she had named Elizabeth in honor of the family's imperial benefactress in Russia. Christian August's precarious health was a continuing cause of anxiety, and she herself had begun to suffer from stomach pains. So she let the flirtation continue.

Sophie must have been flattered by her uncle's attention, beyond enjoying his companionship. And his was not the only attention she received at Hamburg. One of the party of distinguished Swedes who had come to escort the new king to his realms, Count Gyllenburg, singled Sophie out for praise. He was impressed with how well read she was, how she was conversant with philosophy and political ideas and could discuss them without the shyness he expected in a sheltered princess. He observed how Johanna slighted Sophie, and reprimanded her. Her daughter was very precocious, he said, and accomplished far beyond most fourteen-year-olds. Johanna was wrong to undervalue her.

Basking in Count Gyllenburg's praise, and perhaps savoring the rebuke to her neglectful mother, Sophie continued to enjoy her uncle's company. "We were inseparable," she later wrote. "I took it to be friendship."

But Uncle Georg took it to be love, and showed every sign of lovesickness. He dogged Sophie's footsteps and followed her with his beautiful eyes. Every moment out of her presence was agony to him. When the ceremonies at Hamburg were complete and Johanna and Sophie left for Brunswick, Georg was desolate, knowing that he would see less of Sophie there. He told her so, and she asked him why.

"Because it would lead to gossip better avoided," he said.

"But why?" Sophie demanded, unaware that her friendship with her uncle could be misconstrued by others. He didn't answer her, but when they reached Brunswick, and he no longer had so many opportunities to spend time alone with her, he became visibly distraught. Sophie noticed that he was not himself, now moody and dreamy, now full of chagrin. He confronted Sophie one night in her mother's room and complained bitterly of his lot in life and of the pain he was in. Another time he confided to her that what aggravated him most was the fact that he was her uncle.

Sophie was astonished to hear this, and quickly asked him why, what had she done? Was he angry with her?

"Far from it," he said. "The reason is that I love you too much."

When she tried to thank him for his affection, he interrupted her angrily.

"You're a child, I can't make you understand!" he burst out, and Sophie, disconcerted, pressed him to tell her what he meant by this, and why he was so distressed.

"Well then, is your friendship for me strong enough to give me the comfort I need?"

She assured him that it was.

"Then promise me that you will marry me."

Sophie was thunderstruck. She had never imagined that her uncle was in love with her.

"You can't be serious," she managed to say. "You are my uncle, my father and mother wouldn't want us to marry."

"Nor would you," he said morosely. Just then Sophie was called away, and the astonishing conversation came to an end.

But Georg renewed it as soon as he could. His wooing took on a new urgency and he pressed Sophie hard to accept him, telling her in impassioned tones how much he loved her and wanted her to be his. She had recovered from her original amazement at his proposal and was beginning to get used to the idea of becoming his wife. He was exceptionally handsome, they were used to one another, he knew and accepted her moods; she liked basking in his melting gaze. "He began to please me and I didn't run away from him," Sophie recalled in her memoirs. She agreed to marry him provided her parents put no obstacle in their way.

Once she gave him her promise Georg gave free rein to his passion. He lay in wait for her, stealing kisses when and where he could, arranging things so that they could be alone together, losing sleep, forgetting to eat, so great was his all-consuming obsession with Sophie. His sighs and groans were baffling to Sophie, eventually he lost all his good humor and became tiresome. And for reasons of his own, he failed to ask Christian August for her hand in marriage. Perhaps he was only out to seduce her. Or perhaps he did want to marry her, but feared that she was still too young. Possibly he was worried about being rejected in favor of Prince Henry or even Karl Ulrich. The time came for Johanna to leave Brunswick and Georg wrung from Sophie a promise not to forget him. No doubt she expected to see him again before long.

But a few months later, in the first week of January, 1744, Georg's chances were superseded.

A swift courier from Berlin came riding into the courtyard of the palace at Anhalt-Zerbst, with a packet of letters for Johanna. As this was a very unusual event, the entire family, just then sitting at the dinner table, became curious and Johanna asked a servant to bring her the letters immediately. She opened them then and there, and Sophie, sitting next to her, tried to read them over her shoulder. She recognized the handwriting of Karl Ulrich's tutor, Otto von Brümmer, and the words "the princess your eldest daughter." A duller girl than Sophie would have realized at once that the letters had to do with her betrothal to Karl Ulrich, yet Johanna was secretive about their contents.

For three days nothing was said. Finally Sophie confronted her mother.

"So, you're anxious, you're dying of curiosity," Johanna said.

"Yes! But I can guess what your letters say."

"Well then, what?"

Instead of saying straight out what she thought she knew, Sophie played a game. "I'm going to make my prediction," she announced, imitating a woman they both knew who claimed she could guess the name of a woman's beloved from the letters of her own name.

"Let us see what you will guess."

Sophie went away and worked out an elaborate acrostic, using the letters of her own name. It prophesied that she would marry Karl Ulrich, who on being baptized into the Orthodox Church had taken the new name Peter.

Johanna stared at her daughter, then laughed. "You are a little minx, but you won't find out any more."

Later Johanna explained that, although Sophie had guessed correctly that overtures had been made about the possibility of a betrothal, she and Christian August were having second thoughts. Count Brümmer had invited Johanna and Sophie to come to St. Petersburg, an arduous and dangerous journey of nearly a thousand miles. No guarantees were being made. If Sophie was not to the empress's liking, she would be sent home again. Russia was too far away, Christian August thought, there was too much risk associated with the journey. Both parents were reluctant to send Sophie off to spend her life at an impossibly distant court—and they were in fact on the point of writing to Brümmer and telling him their decision when Sophie demanded to know just what was in the letters.

"What do you think?" Johanna asked her.

"Since it doesn't please you, it would be ill-advised for me to wish it."

"It seems that you don't find the idea repugnant."

It was not repugnant, it was exciting. Sophie had ambition, she had never forgotten the prediction that she would wear three crowns. Yet now that she faced the prospect of actually going to Russia, it daunted her. Realizing that if she agreed to marry her cousin she might never see her parents again, Sophie began to cry. She was tenderly attached to her father and could not bear the thought of leaving him. Christian August joined in the conversation, kissing Sophie and telling her that he would not think of insisting that she go to Russia. Johanna ought to go alone, he said, to thank Empress Elizabeth in person for all that she had done for the Holstein-Gottorp family. If Sophie did want to go along, she could, but she would be under no obligation to stay on and marry Karl Ulrich—or rather Grand Duke Peter, as he now was. She could return home again and would always find a welcome.

"I was dissolved in tears," Sophie wrote in her memoirs, recalling the conversation. "It was one of the most affecting moments of my life. I was agitated by a thousand different feelings: gratitude for my father's goodness, fear of displeasing him, the custom of blind obedience to him, the tender affection which I had always felt toward him, the respect he deserved—truly no man ever had more merit, the purest virtue guided his steps."

In the following days Sophie managed to resolve her conflicting feelings and persuaded her parents to let her accept Count Brümmer's invitation. No doubt Johanna's ambition for her family and her daughter reasserted itself, and everyone, even Christian August, must have been overawed by the great honor that beckoned from afar. Uncle Adolf was King of Sweden, but Sophie was being invited to occupy a far higher rank at a far more imposing court. Johanna did have a twinge of discomfort over how the decision would affect her favorite brother. ("What will my brother Georg say?" she asked Sophie. "He could not but wish me good fortune and happiness," was the tart reply.) So much for infatuation.

Trunks were hastily packed and preparations made. Sophie's wardrobe was modest—three rather plain gowns, none of them cut in the elaborate style Russian court etiquette required, a few changes of underwear, a dozen handkerchiefs and six pairs of stockings. Even if her parents had wanted to outfit her sumptuously, there was no time to order new gowns and petticoats. And besides, Count Brümmer had been most insistent in his letter that Johanna and Sophie should travel incognito, keeping the purpose of their journey and their destination secret. Had extensive preparations been made, with new gowns and other finery, the servants would have guessed what was going on, and the secret would have been out. Sophie had to content herself with buying a new pair of gloves. In addition, her paternal uncle Johann gave her a length of beautiful blue and silver brocade fabric woven in Zerbst, which could be made into a gown later.

Sophie went to Babette Cardel to say goodbye, telling her, as she told all the palace servants and officials, that she was going to Berlin. She had to mask the pain she felt at the leavetaking, for it was essential to disguise her true destination even from her beloved governess. Babette guessed that there was more to this journey than Sophie was admitting—the servants gossiped endlessly about it—and demanded to be told the truth. But all Sophie would tell her was that she was sworn to secrecy, and could not reveal anything. Babette was annoyed and angry. Hadn't she been, in many ways, a surrogate parent to Sophie? The one who had formed her mind and helped to mold her feelings, the person who knew her best and with whom she had spent the most time? There was no dispelling the bad feeling, yet both women cried as they embraced, each sensing that she might not see the other again.

To lend plausibility to the story that Johanna and Sophie were going no farther than Berlin, Christian August accompanied them there. King Frederick II was also in Berlin at the time, the brilliant, eccentric successor to his father Frederick William, who had died four years earlier. Frederick was thirty-two, a formidable soldier who was at the same time well-read and cultivated; an Anglophile, he had once tried to escape his punitive father by running away to England.

Frederick knew all about the journey that Johanna and Sophie were about to make to Russia. His ambassador at St. Petersburg, Baron Mardefeldt, kept him informed of all that transpired at Empress Elizabeth's court, and in particular about the empress's choice of a wife for her nephew and heir.

The selection process had taken many months. Choosing a bride for the heir to the throne was a political decision, and Empress Elizabeth's officials and advisers were divided in their political loyalties. One faction, headed by the Chancellor Alexei Bestuzhev, favored closer ties with Austria, Britain, and the lesser powers within their orbit. The other, which included the Prussian ambassador Mardefeldt, the French ambassador Chetardie, many of the more influential Russian nobles and Empress Elizabeth's physician and trusted friend Armand Lestocq, favored Prussia and her political partner France. Accordingly, Bestuzhev proposed that Peter marry a Saxon princess, while Mardefeldt, Chetardie, and the others recommended a French princess. Sophie, Elizabeth's own preferred candidate, was forgotten in the factional battles that resulted.

To break the deadlock Frederick was consulted. Would he consider sending one of his sisters to St. Petersburg to marry Peter? Certainly not, he said, but he suggested the names of several compromise candidates, including Sophie. As it happened, the French ambassador had been in Hamburg at the time that Johanna's family gathered there to congratulate the departing King Adolf. He had seen Sophie, and, like most who saw her, he had been impressed. He declared himself in favor of Sophie, which pleased Elizabeth and satisfied the others, except for Bestuzhev, who was outmaneuvered by his enemies. Sophie it was.

Now Frederick wanted to meet Sophie, his compromise candidate, and he sent an invitation to Christian August, Johanna and Sophie inviting them to dine at the palace. At first Johanna refused to let Sophie go, but when the king insisted she had to give way. Frederick seated Sophie next to him at the dining table and talked to her all afternoon, asking her questions, discussing the theater, literature, opera—"whatever thousand things one could ask a girl of fourteen," she remembered many years later. Frederick did not ask Sophie anything about Peter, or the Empress Elizabeth—whom he privately thought to be a woman of "sybaritic tastes," unfit to govern a realm—or about what she knew of Russia. But he sampled her mind and her understanding, and made her blush with his gallant compliments.

"In the beginning I was very timid with him," Sophie recalled, "but gradually I became accustomed to him, until by the end of the evening we were on the most cordial terms—so much so that the entire company was wide-eyed in amazement to see Frederick in conversation with a child."

On another occasion Frederick talked to Johanna, telling her bluntly that he had been instrumental in bringing about Sophie's good fortune and striking a bargain with her: if Johanna would serve as his eyes and ears at the Russian court, promoting Prussian interests there and acting in concert with his ambassador Mardefeldt, then he, Frederick, would ensure that Johanna's rotund sister Hedwig would become Abbess of Quedlinburg. Christian August, with his goodness and his devotion to virtue, Frederick did not approach.

Johanna and Sophie set out on their secret journey in three coaches, taking only a minimum number of servants: a gentleman of the chamber, M. de Lattorf, four chamber women, a single valet de chambre, several lackeys, a cook, and, as companion and chief lady-in-waiting to Johanna, the superstitious Fräulein Kayn. On the orders of Count Brümmer, Johanna adopted the name "Countess Rheinbeck," and swore her servants to secrecy about her true identity and the actual purpose of the journey. Christian August rode with his wife and daughter as far as Schwedt on the Oder, then he went on toward Zerbst, while they turned north. Sophie embraced her father for the last time, cherishing the letter of advice he gave her and remembering his caution that she should never, under any circumstances, abandon the Lutheranism in which she had been raised for the religion of the Orthodox church.

The brief, frigid days were at their shortest. A pallid yellow sun rose late and lay just above the horizon for only a few precious hours, illuminating trees and fields glistening with frost. The first snowfall was late that winter, but icy winds and hard, pelting rain swirled around the swaying coaches as they lumbered over the rutted post road, sinking suddenly into deep ditches and coming perilously close to overturning. Ordinary travelers never used the post road, they went by sea, and then almost never in winter; storms and ice made the Baltic unnavigable between December and April, when sensible people stayed home. Lone couriers braved the post road in all seasons, but they took their lives in their hands, for robbers haunted the bleak outlands and no search parties went out to look for couriers who lost their way or froze to death before they could reach shelter.

The frosts grew thicker, the cold more biting as they reached Danzig on the Baltic coast. Huge chunks of ice floated on the frigid sea, the rocky shoreline was frozen, the dunes covered with ice. Johanna and Sophie, bundled in layers of wool, had to wrap woollen scarves around their red, swollen faces to protect them from the fierce wind. Black and blue from being tossed about and jolted in the coach, they longed for nightfall when the outriders would lead them to a posting station—or better still an inn with a huge earthenware stove where they could warm their hands and feet and thaw their stiff, bruised bodies. Inns were few and far between, however, and generally filthy. No special quarters were available for Countess Rheinbeck and her entourage; they had to join the innkeeper's children and livestock in the cluttered common room.

Inn parlors were pigsties, Johanna complained to her husband in a letter written on the road. Dogs, hens and cocks rooted in the layers of straw and ordure on the floor, babies bawled in cradles, older children huddled together for warmth, "lying one on top of the other like cabbages and turnips" on ancient tattered featherbeds drawn up close to the stove. The food was terrible, there were bugs and rats and sometimes the wind howled through holes in the roof or walls, making sleep impossible. Sophie, trying to wash down her dinner with large quantities of the local beer, became sick to her stomach. Johanna, having satisfied herself that neither the innkeeper nor his numerous children had smallpox, ordered a bare plank brought for herself and lay down on it, fully clothed, in an effort to sleep.

Once the travelers reached Memel both inns and post houses ceased. The impossible roads grew more rutted and at times disappeared altogether. Frozen marsh gave way to lakes covered with a treacherous crust of ice, thin in some places and thick in others. The coachmen hired local fishermen to test the firmness of the ice before venturing across, knowing that if the brittle crust gave way the coaches and their occupants would not survive their plunge into the chill black water. Where ice-clogged rivers flowed into the sea, the coaches were loaded onto wooden ferries and poled across. There were long delays to repair broken axles and take on fresh provisions, and when the horses grew tired, the servants were sent out to bargain with peasants for fresh teams.

By the end of the third week of travel, with the cold becoming more and more severe and Sophie's feet swelling so badly from frostbite that she had to be carried in and out of the coach, she must have been having second thoughts about her impulsive decision to present herself to Empress Elizabeth. As she ate her unpalatable supper while a servant tried to rub life back into her painfully swollen feet, her thoughts must have turned to Karl Ulrich, her irritable, recalcitrant cousin who would one day be emperor of Russia. The boy, now on the threshold of manhood, who would, if all went well, become her husband. She must have recalled his pallor and his delicacy, his battles with Count Brümmer and his affection for his loutish valets, his liking for Johanna and his insatiable appetite for wine. She must have wondered, as she struggled to compose her miserably cold body for sleep, whether it might have been wiser to marry Uncle Georg and settle into obscurity.

Chapter Four

WEEK AFTER ARDUOUS WEEK THE TRAVELING PARTY crawled northward along the shores of the Baltic, into the teeth of the bitter wind. As they passed through each village, peasants wrapped in layers of rags came out to stare at the coaches, crossing themselves and murmuring prayers. Each evening the travelers bedded down where they could, and listened to the wolves howling outside. Along the mist-enshrouded Latvian coast the villages thinned out, and the blanched landscape took on a wearying sameness. At night, however, the sky was lit by the spectacular glow of a comet. Sophie was enraptured. "I had never seen anything so grand," she wrote in her memoirs. "It seemed very close to the earth."

Comets were portents of disaster, as Fräulein Kayn no doubt pointed out to her companions. And there was a disaster in the making, or so it seemed to Sophie's relatives once Christian August revealed to them that his daughter was en route to Russia. He wrote to Johanna, telling her of the all but universal outrage expressed by her sisters and aunts and cousins when they learned the news. They had wanted Sophie to marry Karl Ulrich when he was Duke of Holstein. But the last thing they wanted was for her to marry him now that he was Peter, Grand Duke of Muscovy, living at a court notorious for its political instability and barbarity. She would be at the mercy of the empress, she could be murdered or shut away in a dungeon or worse. Her very soul would be in peril, amongst the heathen Russians who would be sure to persecute her for her Lutheran faith.

Johanna was not surprised by her relatives' reactions. She had expected a whirlwind of opposition, she wrote to her husband. But Providence had determined that Sophie would go to Russia, and Providence could not be denied, even by Aunt Marie Elizabeth and sister Hedwig in Quedlinburg. "We can be certain that the Omniscient brings to fruition His plans which are hidden from us," she wrote piously, praying that the Omniscient would continue to provide fresh horses and edible food and would not let them lose themselves in a blizzard.

They were nearing the Russian border. Dense silver-gray marshes spread themselves on all sides, glowing faintly in the pale light of midday. Out of the emptiness a figure rode toward them. It was a courier, sent to meet them and then to ride back the way he had come, spreading the word that their arrival was imminent. Soon another rider approached, Colonel Vokheikov, and escorted them across the frontier and on to the town of Riga.

It seemed as though the entire population of the town had turned out to greet the frozen visitors from Anhalt-Zerbst. Cannon thundered, bells pealed, and one of the empress's ambassadors, Semyon Naryshkin, made a speech of welcome. The vice-governor Dolgorukov was present with an escort of soldiers from the garrison, and there were generals and civic officials galore.

Johanna's head was turned by all the pageantry. She could now abandon her alias and assume her own honored name, as a parade of nobles lined up to bow to her and kiss her hand. For two days the display of honors continued, with guardsmen at attention and trumpeters announcing every move the visitors made. Johanna and Sophie were given warm sable coats sewn with gold brocade, fur collars and a fur coverlet, along with letters of welcome from the empress and Count Brümmer.

Sophie let her extroverted mother take center stage in all the festivities, though she knew that she, as the future grand duchess, was the important one. Her mind was already at work, observing the behavior and tastes of their Russian hosts. She asked one of the generals to tell her about the imperial court, who the key personalities were and what they were like. Her political sense was already aroused, she knew she would need to inform herself as fully as possible in order to adapt.

Sophie must also have thought a good deal about Peter, recalling his pale good looks and his incorrigible behavior, his liking for her mother, and the boorish valets who were his favorite companions. She must have wondered how much he had changed in the years since their meeting at Eutin, and whether his exalted position had gone to his head.

Deep snow now blanketed the fields and marshes, and the travelers abandoned their uncomfortable coaches for a capacious and warm sleigh provided from the empress's personal carriage house. It was less a vehicle than a small house on wheels, so large and heavy that a dozen horses were needed to draw it through the snowdrifts. The sleigh was equipped with a stove, mattresses and snug fur-lined bedding, indeed the very walls were covered with fur and Sophie, Johanna and Fräulein Kayn lay on silk cushions to sleep at night. To protect them on this last stage of their journey they had a squadron of cavalry and a detachment of footsoldiers, plus the sleighs of a number of Russian nobles and officials.

Another four days of travel brought them to St. Petersburg, the city built a generation earlier by Empress Elizabeth's father, Peter the Great. Here, as at Riga, cannonades and extravagant peals of bells announced the arrival of the important German visitors and a huge crowd gathered on the outdoor staircase of the Winter Palace to greet them. The empress and most of the courtiers were in Moscow, four hundred miles away, but the Chancellor Bestuzhev and a number of other courtiers greeted Johanna and Sophie and escorted them to their lavishly appointed rooms in the grand and opulent structure the Italian architect Rastrelli had built for Elizabeth.

After six weeks of exhausting travel, Sophie and Johanna must have craved rest and peace, but peace was denied them. They had to meet dozens of courtiers and dignitaries, they had to be shown the principal landmarks of the extraordinary city that the great Emperor Peter had erected on a remote and unpromising marsh. They had to attend the winter carnival, to ride down a snowy hill on a toboggan—which the tomboyish Sophie thoroughly enjoyed—and to attend elaborate dinners and suppers. The chamberlain Naryshkin presented the newcomers with an exotic spectacle. Fourteen elephants, a gift to the empress from the Shah of Persia, were led into the courtyard of the Winter Palace and made to perform.

In the intervals between entertainments, Johanna was closeted with the Prussian ambassador Mardefeldt and the French ambassador Chetardie. Both instructed her on how best to ingratiate herself with the empress, and reminded her that it was the Chancellor Bestuzhev who represented the greatest obstacle to her interests and Sophie's. Bestuzhev, the ambassadors said, was strongly opposed to having Peter marry Sophie. Such a marriage would symbolize the union of Russia and Prussia (since Sophie was Frederick's nominee) and all of Bestuzhev's efforts were directed toward preventing such a union. Chetardie recommended that Johanna cut short her stay in Petersburg and try to reach Moscow by the tenth of February (by Russian reckoning; in Russia the Julian calendar still prevailed, and the date was ten days behind that of Western Europe), which was Peter's birthday. The empress would be certain to appreciate this gesture.

Still weary from their long and grueling journey, Johanna and Sophie got back into the empress's fur-lined sleigh for the trip to Moscow. They were joined by four of Elizabeth's ladies of honor, and all six women, plus Fräulein Kayn and the other attendants from Zerbst, braced themselves for four hundred miles of swaying and bouncing and general discomfort. A great many officials joined the cortege, there were thirty sleighs in all, each requiring ten horses.

Stopping only when the horses were spent, the procession moved forward through the night, relying on bonfires tended by shivering peasants to illuminate the way. Crowds gathered to glimpse the long train of sleighs. Sophie heard shouts and asked her Russian companions what they meant. "It is the fiancée of the grand duke who is being escorted!" people were saying.

With the horses galloping at breakneck speed over the frozen snow, and the drivers at times blinded by sleet and wind, there were bound to be accidents. Passing through a village the sleigh in which Johanna and Sophie were riding turned sharply and ran into a house. The collision wrenched loose one of the heavy iron bars supporting the roof of the sleigh, and it fell heavily on Johanna's head and shoulder. Sophie was unhurt.

Johanna, shocked and smarting from the blow, thought she was dying. The entire procession came to a halt in the village while her injuries were examined. One by one the thick layers of fur came off and no blood or bruises were revealed. Johanna angrily insisted that she had been grievously wounded but eventually conceded that the furs had protected her. After a delay of several hours, the sleigh was repaired and the journey continued.

On the third day, some five miles outside of Moscow a courier approached with a message from the empress. She wanted the visitors to delay making their entrance into the city until after nightfall. They halted and waited, then proceeded after dark. Sophie's first view of Moscow was of a dim and dingy place with narrow crooked streets and scurrying inhabitants muffled in furs. Presently they came to a torchlit mansion where the empress's adjutant general, the Prince of Homburg, was waiting with the entire glittering court. The newcomers were welcomed with far less fanfare than they had been at Petersburg and were subjected to thorough scrutiny. Sophie, who had put on a pink silk gown with silver trim, must have felt very conspicuous as the prince escorted her from one grand, high-ceilinged room to the next.

She heard him murmur the names of people they passed—
courtiers who bowed low—but the hundreds of faces and names
must have blurred.

Then she saw Peter, taller and better looking than he had been
when she saw him last, with small eyes and delicate features in a
thin face.

"I couldn't bear the last hour of waiting for you," he told
Johanna ingenuously. "I would have liked to harness myself to
your sleigh and pull it along faster." His boyish effusiveness was
encouraging. He stayed with Sophie and Johanna for several
hours, while they waited in their rooms for the summons to meet
the empress. Finally, late in the evening, it came. Armand Lestocq, the empress's physician and one of her most trusted political
advisers, came to tell Johanna and Sophie that his mistress was at
last ready to receive them.

She met them at the entrance to her bedroom, a strikingly tall,
heavy woman with a plumply beautiful face, bright blue eyes and
a warm smile. Her auburn hair was elaborately arranged and
sparkled with diamonds and a single long black feather; her
gown, with a wide hoop skirt, shimmered with silver and gold
lace. To the fourteen-year-old Sophie she was a vision of beauty
and magnificence.

The empress hastened to embrace Johanna, and looked critical-
ly, then approvingly, at Sophie. Vanity was among Empress
Elizabeth's besetting sins, and she had chosen Sophie as a prospective bride for her heir in part because it was clear from
Sophie's portraits that she would never be a beauty. Elizabeth
needed to outshine those around her, she couldn't stand having
other pretty women nearby. At thirty-four, she was as striking as
ever, though very fleshy, but there were lines at the corners of her
lively blue eyes and her pink cheeks had faded. She relied on
cosmetics to restore her look of youth, and she had developed a
sharp eye for potential rivals.

The most beautiful woman at Elizabeth's court, Countess
Lopukhin, had felt the wrath of the empress. Pink was Elizabeth's

favorite color, and she had made it an unwritten rule of the court that she and she alone could wear it. The countess had dared to ignore this edict and had worn a pink gown. Indeed she had gone even further and copied the empress's hair style, adding a pink rose to her coiffure. Incensed, Elizabeth commanded the countess to kneel, and while the entire court watched, she cut the rose from her hair (and some of the hair with it), then slapped her smartly on both cheeks. She took the further vindictive step of banishing the countess's lover to Siberia, and hounded the countess herself, finally accusing her formally of plotting against the throne.

Sophie, curtseying in her pink and silver gown, was ignorant of the story of Countess Lopukhin, yet she was aware that the empress was staring at her, she felt her scrutiny along with her affability. The empress was scrutinizing Johanna too, and suddenly she saw something in Johanna's face that made her rush from the room. When she returned sometime later it was evident that she had been crying. Johanna looked very much like her late brother Karl August, Elizabeth's long-dead fiancé. Seeing Johanna brought back tender memories of Karl August, and the sentimental empress had been overcome.

That evening Peter dined with Sophie and Johanna, and Sophie, listening to him talk, was astonished at how childlike he was. Though older than she was—he was to turn sixteen the following day—Peter still had the interests and passions of a ten-year-old. It was not just that he had led a sheltered, tethered life: Sophie had observed that for herself, and could make allowances for it. But beyond that, there was something essentially unformed about this very boyish young man, physically slight, with a thin chest and thick waist and underdeveloped muscles. Something essential to manliness had been left out of his makeup, he chattered on about soldiers and uniforms and drill in a puerile way that Sophie found disconcerting. Still, he had a guileless charm and fair good looks, and everyone said that he was a young man of great promise. Distrusting her uniquely skeptical judgment, Sophie decided to be pleased with him.

The rituals of Elizabeth's very large and grand court put a distance between the empress and the visitors from Zerbst. Sophie caught sight of Elizabeth only briefly as she walked briskly along the wide corridors or through the crowded reception rooms on her way to attend official functions. She was a gleaming icon, glimpsed from afar.

Sophie began to find out more about her. That she was the daughter of the venerated Emperor Peter the Great she already knew. That Elizabeth owed her beauty to her mother, a peasant woman who had been Peter's second wife, she now found out, along with the fact that Elizabeth had been born out of wedlock. The empress's physical vigor was evident, as was her fondness for expensive finery and for unrestrained eating. She loved to ride and hunt, she wore her ladies out with her energetic stride and her fast gallop. She was capricious, moody, temperamental.

Sophie knew that Elizabeth had not been educated or trained for rulership. Her father had not intended that either of his daughters should succeed him, and Elizabeth spent much of her childhood and young womanhood away from the court, living in the countryside and interesting herself in the lives of the peasants on the imperial estates. While her earthiness and hearty physicality were nurtured in this rural existence, her mind remained uncultivated, and though intelligent and shrewd, she was mentally lazy.

Elizabeth had courage, certainly—and much boldness. When the throne passed to a distant relative of her father's, the infant known as Ivan VI, Elizabeth had allowed herself to be persuaded to seize it from him. Encouraged by a small circle of advisers, including her physician Lestocq, and being assured that she had the full approval of the French and Swedish courts, Elizabeth went to the barracks of the Preobrazhensky Guards in Petersburg and appealed to them to back her in a coup. She put her fate in the guardsmen's hands—and they did not fail her. The infant Emperor Ivan was deposed and, with his parents and siblings, imprisoned.

Young Ivan was still in prison, and Elizabeth continued to be apprehensive about him. So long as he lived he could be used by conspirators as the figurehead of a plot to depose her. Yet she could not bring herself to order the child's execution, opposed as she was to all judicial executions. As a result, she lived in fear, her nerves taut, a victim of insomnia. She was afraid to close her eyes, knowing that anyone, even one of her trusted servants, might betray her.

Two years before Sophie's arrival in Russia one of the empress's manservants, Turchaninov, tried to assassinate her by placing a barrel of gunpowder under her bed. Luckily the deed was discovered and Turchaninov was imprisoned. Under torture he refused to name his accomplices, but some were eventually brought to light and punished—though not with execution, only maiming.

The empress had no peace of mind. Not long after the discovery of the barrel of gunpowder some hotheaded young officers of the guard were overheard to threaten her and had to be exiled to Siberia. The court, Elizabeth knew only too well, was full of plotters and opportunists, servants whose loyalty could be bought and officials who could not be counted on. She ordered additional men recruited for the dread secret police and had all conversation at the palace monitored. People suspected of having divided loyalties were watched at all times. Yet vigilance alone could not prevent disaster, and the knowledge that her throne was far from secure continued to vex and plague the empress.

And now there was another vexing problem: the succession.

Elizabeth had decided, for reasons Sophie was never to discover, that she would not make a political marriage of the kind arranged for her in her teens. Instead, she made a secret morganatic marriage to the tall, dark, divinely handsome Alexei Razumovsky, a Ukrainian whose extraordinary singing voice won him an appointment to the palace chapel. Razumovsky, whose father was a farmer and who as a youth had tended sheep on a rural hillside, did not try to dominate the empress; a soulful man with melting black eyes, he cared a great deal for music and dancing and his beautiful wife but was indifferent to politics. In marrying Razumovsky Elizabeth chose personal happiness over dynastic duty. She would bequeath her throne to her nephew Peter, and he and his children would carry on the line.

Yet Peter was proving to be a disappointment. He looked puny and girlish. He offended people. His health was poor and his personality odd and disturbing. Elizabeth disliked him, and probably regretted having made him her heir. Worst of all, Peter seemed bent on rejecting, with contempt, every aspect of Russian culture. He spoke German and resisted learning Russian. He despised Russian servants and surrounded himself with Germans and Swedes, preferring the company of his boyhood favorites, the valets Cramer and Roumberg. He had formally converted to Orthodox Christianity—indeed his becoming heir apparent was contingent on this—but he showed his disregard for the church at every opportunity, displaying scant reverence and laughing and joking during the long services conducted in the palace chapel and in the soaring, candlelit cathedrals of Moscow and Petersburg. This flamboyant irreverence was particularly displeasing to Elizabeth, who spent hours in prayer and was punctilious in her religious observances, regarding Orthodox worship as the foundation of a moral life.

Peter was a disappointment—and a liability. With her necessary overconcern about the security of her throne, the empress was only too aware that the plotters and potential plotters around her looked on Peter and took heart. He was not winning the loyalty of any of the courtiers, and it was hard to imagine him growing into a commanding, feared ruler. He had no political skills and Elizabeth, whose own political astuteness was modest, was not teaching him how to acquire them. He continued to assert, to anyone who would listen, that he was a German and not a Russian and that German ways were in every respect superior to Russian ways. He offended the Russian soldiers by wearing the uniform of an officer in the Prussian army, and he thoroughly enjoyed their discomfiture, smiling and laughing at them until they all but bared their teeth and wanted to reach out to throttle him.

The festivities at court for Peter's sixteenth birthday surpassed any splendor Sophie had ever witnessed. The sprawling wooden palace with its hundreds of rooms and thousands of servants was filled to overflowing with guests, all of them eager to see the princess imported from the West. They thronged the staircases and stood on chairs, the women's movements impeded by their wide hoop skirts, the long jewelled swords of the men a hazard in the crush.

Johanna and Sophie made their appearance, a thousand eyes on them as they exited their apartments. The empress summoned Johanna, and Sophie was left waiting, displayed like a bijou in a jeweller's shop, scrutinized from all angles, whispered about and openly discussed. Eventually she too was summoned and made her way to Elizabeth's private rooms, nodding and smiling to all those who lined the corridors and galleries along her route.

A gracious Elizabeth, elegant in a gown of dusky silk embroidered in silver, with jewels at her neck and waist, received Sophie and presented her with the ribbon and star of the Order of St. Catherine. Johanna too was invested with her ribbon and star and afterwards Elizabeth's chamberlain, the Prince of Homburg, paid Sophie a compliment on her grace and winning manners. She was glad to hear that she had been found pleasing "both to the empress and the nation." She had passed her test.

Ordinarily talkative, she consciously restrained herself and said little. Yet the courtiers whispered to one another that she was highly intelligent and a brilliant conversationalist—convinced by their own expectations that it was so. Her smiles and nods had made a good impression on the courtiers, who, having expected her to be haughty and full of pride, were delighted at her warmth and affability. One of them remarked to her that she greeted the chancellor and the servant who was stoking the stove with the same degree of openness and respect.

Lent began, the six-week period before Easter during which the church prescribed self-denial, penance and prayer. The empress set off on a pilgrimage to the Troitsky monastery forty-five miles outside of Moscow. She wanted Sophie to begin instruction in the Orthodox faith while she was gone.

Sophie had known that a formal conversion would be required of her before she could marry Peter. She also knew that her father had been adamant in his opposition to her forsaking the Lutheran faith, and the knowledge of his opposition may have weighed on her. Before she left Zerbst he had given her a thick scholarly book setting out the differences between Lutheranism and other Christian theologies, along with a long list of instructions, repeatedly insisting on the importance of her maintaining the creed into which she had been born. As a child Sophie had associated religious teaching with anxiety and trauma, and she must have heard with some trepidation that Simon Todorsky, Archimandrite of the Orthodox church and sometime student in the German university of Halle, would be her instructor.

Todorsky was a cultivated man and an intellectual. He was able to present theological concepts in a way that intrigued Sophie's agile mind and could answer her questions as Pastor Wagner never had been able to. Yet though she studied long and eagerly, Sophie was troubled by her change of religion. The lonely tearful evenings she had spent in Stettin, pondering the torments of hellfire, now came back to her, and led, when she was with people she trusted, to fresh floods of tears. Her father's letters, brought by courier along the frozen roads from Zerbst, added to her distress.

"Do not take this difficulty lightly," he cautioned her. "Question yourself scrupulously to discover whether your heart is led by inspiration or whether perhaps, unawares, your conversion has been influenced by the approval of the empress and others in her service." Christian August reminded his daughter that God "searches the heart and our secret desires," and that nothing she might do could deceive him.

Adjusting to a harsh new climate and to life at the imperial court, studying for her lessons with Todorsky, struggling to learn the unfamiliar Russian words of the creed, all the while trying to imagine herself married to the callow Peter all combined to strain Sophie's constitution. She became seriously ill.

At first it was feared that she had come down with smallpox, which was frequently fatal, or else a grave disease of the lungs. The servants gossiped to one another that the Saxon ambassador had found a way to poison Sophie so that Peter would have to marry the Saxon Princess Marianne. The empress's Dutch physician Boerhave diagnosed pleurisy and recommended that Sophie be bled, but Johanna, mindful that her brother Karl August had been bled almost at once when he arrived in Russia seventeen years earlier and had died, was afraid that bloodletting would kill Sophie too. Johanna complained to Boerhave, who continued to insist that bleeding was the sovereign remedy. Sophie's blood was inflamed, he explained, as a result of the rigors of the rough journey and the terrible cold of the roads. Unless she was bled at once, she would die.

Facing an impasse, Boerhave ordered ointments applied to Sophie's chest—Johanna did not complain about that, at least— and wrote to Lestocq, who was at the Troitsky Monastery with the empress. The princess would not survive long without bleeding, he said. Lestocq told Elizabeth, who immediately ended her devotions and rushed back to Moscow to deal with the emergency.

She took charge, ordering the anxious Johanna to stand aside and taking Sophie in her arms while the surgeon pricked a vein in her foot and let several ounces of blood flow into a basin. Almost at once Sophie recovered consciousness, and looked up into the plump, concerned face of Empress Elizabeth. She was dimly aware of the others in the room, the doctors and officials, and Johanna, greatly upset and worried. But she soon lapsed into unconsciousness again.

The surgeon continued to bleed his royal patient at frequent intervals, every six hours or so, and Johanna, whose hand-wringing and complaints became intolerable, was ordered to stay in her apartments. Days passed, a week, two weeks, and still Sophie lay in a stupor, hardly aware of anything save the murmuring of voices and the rustling of skirts. The empress came to sit by her every day, and began to feel maternal and possessive about her. It was like Elizabeth to want to monopolize people's attention and emotions, and during Sophie's illness she became jealously bonded to the girl she had chosen to marry her nephew. Stepping into Johanna's role, and wanting to supplant her, Elizabeth began to find excuses to blacken Johanna in her daughter's eyes, claiming that Johanna's opposition to having Sophie bled was a sign of her indifference and lack of affection. Relations between mother and daughter had never been smooth, Sophie had never felt greatly valued or loved. Now the empress was intervening to make them worse.

Unconscious or at best semiconscious, unable to eat and growing weaker by the day, Sophie lay in her sickbed, all but inert. A message was brought to her from her mother. Would she like to see a Lutheran pastor? No, she said faintly. She would see the archimandrite instead.

Simon Todorsky brought the frail girl the comforts of the church, and the empress was pleased. Now if Sophie died, she would at least die having turned in her heart to the Orthodox faith.

More days passed, and gradually, thanks to her innate robustness, Sophie began to recover. She coughed up quantities of pus, her fever gradually abated, and Boerhave and Lestocq began to smile.

Easter was approaching, and Johanna, who had been consistently kept away from Sophie, made the miscalculation of asking Sophie for the length of brocade fabric her uncle had given her before leaving Zerbst so that she could have a new gown made from it for herself. Sophie, still convalescent, readily agreed. But when Elizabeth heard of the request she condemned

Johanna as heartless and selfish, and ordered two lengths of more costly fabric in the same color sent to Sophie to replace her loss. Earlier, after Sophie's first bloodletting, the empress had sent her a pair of diamond earrings and a cluster of diamonds. She was demonstrating her love for Sophie in countless ways, while doing her best to stir up resentment against Johanna.

As Sophie recovered she heard nothing but tales of petty quarrels and disputes, little animosities and slights that rippled through the court like a contagion. No one, it seemed, could be trusted to be free of intrigue; no words could be relied on, no act or gesture of kindness was what it seemed. Though the empress spread tales about Johanna's selfishness, she continued to smile at her in public and show her favors, sending her jewels, giving her a special and honored status in the midst of the other courtiers. And Johanna, for her part, while professing the utmost gratitude and loyalty to Elizabeth, was meeting with the Prussian and French ambassadors, corresponding with King Frederick, doing her utmost to be useful to the clique that intended to topple the chancellor Bestuzhev and his anti-Prussian policies. Spies and informers listened at keyholes, slipped in and out of private rooms, watched for secret letters and messages. All was reported to the empress, who bided her time.

Sophie, who was becoming accustomed to thinking of Elizabeth as a second mother of sorts, sat up in bed, ate heartily, and began once again to study her Russian and her theology. Her cheeks grew pink again, and Elizabeth, gazing fondly at her, pronounced her almost well. It had been twenty-seven days since the onset of her illness. The first signs of spring had arrived, though snow still lay thick on the ground and cold winds invaded the drafty palace. Sophie wrote to her father, apologizing for her shaky handwriting and asking him to give her his permission to adopt the Orthodox faith.

Unknown to her, King Frederick was also using his influence on Christian August, trying to convince him, disingenuously, that the differences in theology between the Greek Orthodox

church and the Lutheran church were slight. Frederick, who cared
little about religion, had no qualms about misrepresenting matters
of faith, while the devout and dutiful Christian August was in
anguish. ("Meine Tochter nicht griechisch werden!" he cried
again and again. "My daughter cannot become a Greek!") He was
torn. His superior King Frederick, to whom he was indebted in
countless ways, the man who had promoted him to field marshal,
was asking him to go against his conscience. His daughter too had
become convinced that she wanted to convert to Orthodoxy. His
wife, never very scrupulous, took a neutral position. "I leave it to
Sophie to decide," she told him bluntly, knowing as well as he did
that in the end Sophie would either have to make her formal
profession of faith in the Orthodox church or return home to
Zerbst having lost her chance to become grand duchess.

While Christian August wrestled with his conscience and
Sophie waited for his reply, the court witnessed a memorable
display of the empress's wrath. Countess Lopukhin, the foolhar-
dy beauty who had dared to wear pink despite the empress's
prohibition, had been convicted of plotting to dethrone her mistress. She was one of several accused conspirators who had been
found guilty of conducting an intrigue with the Austrian ambassador. She was sentenced to execution, along with her husband,
yet the empress, ever squeamish when it came to taking life, gave
other orders.

The courtiers joined a large crowd assembled in an open square
where a broad wooden platform had been erected in the snow. It
was very cold, a sea of fur hats and coats stretch away on all sides
of the scaffold. Thousands of ordinary citizens looking forward to
a spectacle thronged the edges of the open space and waited
patiently for the solemnities to begin. Presently the count and
countess, their hands tied, were dragged onto the platform by
muscular guards, the countess struggling violently, appearing
almost demented. Her clothes were torn, she tossed her head,
screaming in fear. She had believed until moments earlier that she
would be decapitated—now she was told that her life would be

spared, she would be tortured instead. With her was the wife of the chancellor's brother Michael Bestuzhev, her closest friend and, in the judgment of her accusers, her fellow-conspirator.

One by one the victims faced their punishment. Count Lopukhin was tied to a rack, his wrists and ankles secured with strong ropes, and then the rack was slowly stretched until all his bones cracked and broke, while his sobbing, writhing wife stood nearby, in the grip of her captors. When her turn came she was forced to kneel and submit to repeated blows with a thick wooden stick. Gasping and crying for mercy, she endured only a few clouts before she fainted, her back a mass of welts and bruises. When the beating was finished the executioner seized the countess by her hair and reached into her mouth to cut out her tongue. Blood flowed from her mouth. The spectators, having savored every frisson of horror, and satisfied that the traitors had gotten what they deserved, shouted their approval.

The work of barbarity was over. No one noticed that, in the last moment of her friend's suffering, Madame Bestuzhev managed to drop a costly diamond cross into the executioner's hand. He gave no sign, but later, when the criminals were on their way to exile in Siberia, Countess Lopukhin discovered that she could still talk.

Chapter Five

I N THE WOMBLIKE DIMNESS OF THE PALACE CHAPEL, WHERE thousands of flickering candles cast a pale light on the gleaming mosaics and paintings on every wall and pillar, Sophie knelt to repeat her confession of faith. She was quite overawed by the dozens of golden chandeliers, the tall candlesticks, the precious icons in their jewel-studded frames and the wealth of decoration that seemed to cover every colorful surface. Her senses all but overpowered by the acrid odor of incense, the resonant music of the choir that vibrated and echoed in the vast sanctuary, the kaleidoscope of vivid hues and flashing gold, she seemed to drowse as she knelt, swaying slightly as her knees sank into the soft silken cushion.

She had been fasting for three days in preparation for the ritual to come, cleansing herself before offering her confession of faith. She felt dizzy and faint, yet her mind was keen enough to recall the Russian words she had painstakingly memorized, parrot-fashion, with the coaching of her Russian teacher Vasily Adadurov. Learning by rote was a skill she had mastered as a young child, when Pastor Wagner had hounded and threatened her and she had spent hours hunched over her German Bible.

The confession of faith she had memorized for this day had been written for her by Simon Todorsky. He had had it translated into German so that she would know what she was saying, yet she had to repeat it in Russian at this ceremony of confirmation, along with the Orthodox version of the Nicene Creed. In all, she had memorized some fifty handwritten pages of Russian, and she hoped that she would be able to repeat the words with conviction if not with understanding.

The empress had dressed her herself earlier that morning, in a gown which was the exact duplicate of her own gown of crimson brocade trimmed in silver. The two women had grown close, Elizabeth treated Sophie more and more like her own daughter and kept her nearby for much of each day. Since Sophie's illness they had traveled together, eaten many meals together, attended balls and concerts and plays together. Sophie viewed the empress at that time "as a divinity," she later wrote in her memoirs, "exempt from all fault." She had witnessed Elizabeth's sudden anger and savage capriciousness at first hand, yet she basked in the older woman's warmth and maternal tenderness. Her respect and gratitude knew no bounds; she was still somewhat timid toward Elizabeth yet her affection for her was strong.

She began her long recitation, striving to keep her voice audible and distinct, taking pains with her pronunciation following her tutor's instructions. Johanna, standing in the recesses of the chapel, watched her daughter with pride. "From the moment she entered the church until the end of the ceremony," Johanna wrote to Christian August, "she carried herself with the utmost nobleness and dignity. Even if she had not been my daughter I would have been forced to admire her."

Sophie's strong, low-pitched voice carried well in the vast chapel, filling every fold and niche in the high stone walls with its resonance and echoing among the painted pillars. A huge crowd had gathered, and many who listened to the voice were moved to tears.

When Sophie finally came to the end of her recitation, she faced her godparents, who conferred on her her baptismal name, the name by which she would from then on be known: Catherine Alekseyevna.

Sophie, the Lutheran Princess of Anhalt-Zerbst, had become Catherine of Russia, a daughter of the Orthodox church. She had made her choice, ensuring the displeasure of her father for the sake of pleasing her new parent, the empress.

And Elizabeth did seem very like a mother to her, overwhelming her with attention and solicitude, showering her with gowns and jewels, treating her with familial tenderness and affection. Her conversion was pleasing to Elizabeth, and so was her new name—which was also the name of Elizabeth's mother. Catherine she would proudly be from now on, as Catherine and not Sophie she would become betrothed to Peter.

That night the empress, with Catherine and Peter, were lodged inside the Kremlin, the immense white-walled fortress that dominated Moscow. To Catherine and her servants was assigned a suite of rooms high in an upper story of the old brick Terem Palace, abandoned for decades and now in a sorry state of disrepair yet made habitable for this one important night, the eve of Catherine and Peter's betrothal. If Catherine felt any qualms she did not remember them years later, when she recalled the experience in her memoirs. What she remembered was the view from the small windows, a panoramic view of the fortress and its many golden-domed churches and state buildings, and the city stretching away to the distant hills. She was so high that the people walking along the Kremlin wall far below were hard for her to distinguish, they looked like ants marching in winding columns toward unseen destinations.

It was the end of June, the sun lingered above the horizon until late in the evening and darkness seemed never to fall. Catherine, the center of all concern and attention, about to exchange solemn betrothal vows with the heir to the Russian throne, must have been wakeful with excitement. Besides, she had just concluded a taxing ceremony and had not eaten in three days; her fast may well have heightened her air of nervous expectation.

The following morning messengers arrived bearing gifts for Catherine. First the empress sent her a portrait miniature of herself in a diamond-studded frame, and shortly afterwards a miniature of Peter was delivered in a similar costly frame. The empress, resplendent in her imperial crown and mantle of state, walked ahead of the betrothal couple across the square and into the cathedral, past ranks of guardsmen who held back the crowds. Elizabeth walked under a massive silver canopy held by eight officers, but when she entered the church she abandoned this formality to take Catherine and Peter by the hand and lead them onto a velvet-covered dais in the middle of the sanctuary. There the Archbishop of Novgorod presided over the long, intricate betrothal ceremony, while the choir sang and the worshipful onlookers knelt and stood and knelt again. After four hours the empress handed Peter and Catherine their jewelled betrothal rings, which they exchanged, and stood by while Catherine was addressed for the first time by her new title of grand duchess.

The rest of the afternoon and evening was devoted to public rejoicing. Bells rang, cannon were fired time and time again, all normal life stopped while the city was swept into celebration. The empress held a dinner to which everyone of rank was invited, and afterwards a lavish ball. Catherine, much admired and con-gratulated, did her best to smile at everyone and be gracious. Now that she was grand duchess she had to become accustomed to being treated with elaborate deference. No one except the empress and Peter dared to sit in her presence, or to enter or leave a room ahead of her. People bowed or knelt and murmured "Your Imperial Highness" when addressing her, and stepped aside with a bow to let her pass.

That Catherine was, after the empress herself, the highest rank-ing woman at the court was a fact not lost on Johanna, who suddenly had to kneel and kiss her daughter's hand like everyone else. What respect she had commanded as Catherine's mother now evaporated, for Catherine no longer needed her, she was a titled lady in her own right. Johanna was merely the Princess of

Anhalt-Zerbst, a lowly German aristocrat lost in the sea of aristocratic ladies in the grand duchess's entourage. She could not walk near her daughter in the betrothal procession, but had to keep to the rear with the other women of low rank. At the wedding dinner she was informed that she could not sit with the other women present, but would have to find a humbler and lower seat. She protested—as did the British ambassador, who also felt insulted by the place assigned to him—and in the end the two of them dined together, at a special table off to the side, in exile from the festivities.

Johanna was humiliated, and at the same time thwarted. She had come to Russia on an important mission, to advance the interests of Prussia and Prussia's allies at the Russian court and to undermine the anti-Prussian policies of the Chancellor Bestuzhev. But she had failed dismally. Only four weeks earlier she had discovered just how formidable an enemy the chancellor could be.

Bestuzhev had been keeping himself informed of all Johanna's activities ever since her arrival in Russia, and, through his spies, had intercepted the dispatches of the French ambassador Chetardie and had read there full details of Johanna's intrigues. The dispatches quoted the Princess of Anhalt-Zerbst saying many unflattering and critical things about the empress, and revealed a pattern of hypocrisy and political machination in her behavior. Gathering his evidence carefully, Bestuzhev presented it to Elizabeth, then stood back and waited for the explosion.

Furious that this German woman whom she had enriched and honored and treated like a close relative had shown her such disloyalty, Elizabeth was so enraged at Johanna that she threatened to call off the betrothal and send both Johanna and Catherine back home. She ordered Johanna brought before her and shouted at her accusingly, reducing the frightened Johanna to tears. For two hours the empress stormed and the princess suffered, doing her best to plead her case and beg for forgiveness. Too late Johanna realized that her clumsy and transparent maneuvering had placed her daughter's great prospects in peril. Ultimately Elizabeth relented, and agreed not to send either Johanna or her daughter away, though Chetardie was banished. But the incident had placed Johanna in more or less permanent disgrace, and her snubbing at the betrothal banquet was only one of many incidents designed to remind her of this.

Terrified of the empress, snubbed and denied respect, forced to abnegate herself before her exalted daughter, Johanna became petulant. Her bad humor made her impossible to talk to, she refused to be placated and took petty revenge on servants and minor officials—anyone with whom she could quarrel without risk of retribution. She spent her time with the Prince and Princess of Hesse-Homburg, who were sympathetic to her and gave her a refuge. Her relations with Catherine became more strained than ever, and Catherine, overwhelmingly eager to ingratiate herself with the empress, trying her best to please everyone, struggled in vain to please her difficult mother.

And there was another cloud on Catherine's horizon as well.

Peter, who had shown her a genuine if childlike friendship, now developed an attitude of swaggering antagonism. He was learning from his valet Roumberg how wives ought to be treated, and was practicing asserting his authority. Roumberg told Peter that a wife must be kept in constant fear of her husband, scarcely daring to breathe without his permission. Peter was to demand complete and unquestioned obedience from Catherine, never allowing her to express or even formulate views of her own on any subject; she was to be his to mold, use, and chastise. He would have to beat her from time to time, Peter told his fiancée. Roumberg recommended it, and he considered it good advice.

Peter became at once menacing, with his talk of beatings and subjection, and distant. Catherine did not expect fidelity from him, he had confided to her his infatuations with various women of the court and she knew that men were rarely faithful to their wives—her conscientious, virtuous father being a notable exception. Yet she must have begun to feel apprehensive about her future. What would Peter be like once they were married? Before she left home her father had given her a letter of advice, which she reread from time to time. He told her to look to Peter as "her

Lord, Father, and Sovereign." "His will is to govern all," Christian
August had written, and she had taken the phrase to heart. But what
if Peter, willful as he was, became capricious and decided to mistreat
her? Could she rely on the empress to protect her?

Women had very low status in Russia, as Catherine was beginning to find out. Until very recently, in the time of Elizabeth's
father, Peter the Great, they had been kept in Oriental confinement in terems, or upper rooms, of Russian houses. In these
women's quarters they lived out their lives, kept away from all
men other than their relatives, shielded from prying eyes and
from the temptations of the world, to which they were believed
to be far more susceptible than men. The higher a woman's social
class, the more complete her confinement was; only the poorest
peasant women, whose labor was necessary to the survival of the
family and whose living conditions did not permit segregation,
were allowed to mingle freely with men.

Emperor Peter had done his best to put an end to the terem,
though his female subjects resisted his efforts and clung to their
familiar confinement. In his daughter's reign, however, they were
becoming emboldened, and were accustoming themselves to
joining in public life. But though women were no longer kept
physically confined, at least in Moscow and Petersburg where the
impact of Emperor Peter's reforms was greatest, they were still in
thrall to the teachings of the church, which viewed them as weak,
vapid and prone to sin, especially sexual sin, and were still subject
to the constraints of the law, which virtually enslaved them to
their husbands and fathers and threatened them with barbarous
punishments if they failed to be obedient to their natural masters.

When a young woman married, it was customary for her father
to touch her lightly with a whip, and then to pass the whip on to
the husband he had chosen for her—a reminder that she was
exchanging one form of physical subjection for another. During
the wedding ceremony itself the bride demonstrated her subjuga-
tion by prostrating herself before her husband and touching her
forehead to his feet. While she lay at his feet he covered her with
one of his garments in token of his obligation to care for her.

Later, as he led her away to her new home he struck her gently with the whip, saying with each stroke, "Forget the manners of your own family and learn those of mine." When the couple entered their bedroom together for the first time, the groom ordered the bride to take off his boots. She knelt to remove them, and discovered in one of them a whip, yet another reminder that, in the words of the Russian proverb, "the wife is in the power of her husband."

Throughout her married life a wife could expect to be on trial, constantly in danger of being sent away if she displeased her husband. The Orthodox church permitted a man to divorce his wife by sending her to a convent, where she became as one dead to the world, entombed among other rejected women and wives who had run away from their abusive husbands. The husband was then free to remarry. Many husbands took advantage of this expedient to rid themselves of unwanted spouses, but many more took out their frustrations on their hapless wives by beating them, frequently and brutally. Peter's valet was giving conventional advice when he told his master to give Catherine a few blows to the head from time to time. Such punishment was mild compared to the beatings some men administered, hanging their wives by their hair and stripping them naked, then beating them until their flesh was raw and their bones broken.

Though many women died under such punishment, the law did not view their husbands as guilty of any crime. Should a wife turn on her tormentor and kill him, however, the law was severe: a pit was dug in the earth and the guilty woman was buried in it, with only her head above ground, and left to die of thirst. Nor was this cruel punishment rare; one visitor to Russia in the early eighteenth century wrote that he often saw such burials and that the women he observed sometimes took seven or eight days to die. An even more common sight were women who had had their noses cut off for offending their husbands.

To a young woman as strong-willed, intelligent and opinionated as Catherine, the thought of being subject to the callow Peter must have made her shudder. Yet her desire to please the empress was overwhelming, and it was Elizabeth's pleasure that Catherine marry Peter. Besides, if not Peter, some other man would one day claim mastery over her, unless she chose to live like the outlandish (though enticing) Countess of Bentinck, free of all conventions and viewed with horror by nearly everyone. And she could not, except in fantasy, envision that.

Now that she was grand duchess Catherine was given her own household, with three chamberlains, three chamber gentlemen, three waiting maids and, as mistress of the household, Countess Maria Rumyantsev, once mistress of Peter the Great and a commanding personality. All but one of her menial servants were Russian, and among them was a girl only a year older than Catherine who quickly became a friend. Like Catherine herself the girl had extremely high spirits, and loved to have fun. The friendship was limited to giggles and horseplay and dumb show, since, as Catherine recalled later, she still knew very little Russian. But it was genuine enough, even without words, and it brought relief from the tensions of court life.

Johanna, smarting and raw from the empress's rebuke and indignant over being reduced to insignificance in her daughter's entourage, attacked the innocent friendship between Catherine and the young Russian girl in an effort to reassert her importance. Johanna lectured Catherine on the unsuitability of showing special favor to her inferiors—something Catherine was prone to do— and insisted that she treat all her woman servants with the same degree of distant affability. Catherine protested, but in the end, chastened, she complied.

Meanwhile Johanna, elated by her one small success, sought others. Having won over Catherine's chamber gentleman Count Zernichev, and relying on him to do her bidding, she insinuated herself into every small intrigue and ongoing quarrel in Catherine's establishment and where there was harmony, introduced discord. Slighted by many of the courtiers, she continued to find a haven with the Prince and Princess of Hesse-Homburg, and confined herself to their circle. Spiteful gossip said that she found

more than a haven there. The princess's handsome brother Ivan
Betsky was a frequent visitor to the Hesse-Homburg apartments,
and Johanna was attracted to him. Ignoring the letters that arrived
periodically from Zerbst, in which Christian August urged his
wife to return home immediately, Johanna lingered at the imperial court, determined to stay on as long as she could, unwilling
to leave before Catherine's wedding though it was clear that no
one, apart from Catherine herself, the Hesse-Homburgs and
probably Count Betsky, would mind a bit if she did.

Summer had arrived with its long, hot days and warm scented
nights. Elizabeth, as was her custom in warm weather, became a
nomad, camping in the countryside and playing at peasant life.
Her mother, Peter the Great's second wife, had been a Lithuanian
peasant, radiant, flower-faced, buxom, and unaffected, to whom
the pretenses and artificialities of court life were foreign. Elizabeth
took after her, and was at her happiest when away from her
palaces, exploring the sparsely populated hinterlands, living as she
had in her childhood among the villagers who made up the vast
majority of her subjects.

And where the empress went, the court followed. Hundreds of
carts, piled high with trunks, boxes and chests of clothing and
provisions, trundled along freshly repaired roads to the vicinity of
where the empress was staying. Thousands of weary, dust-
covered servants clung to the carts or walked along behind them,
coughing and wheezing and slapping at the thick black clouds of
gnats that rose up from the dust and seemed to attack everything
that lived. Elizabeth never traveled without her court and household, and she never left anything behind. Her enormous wardrobe (with four thousand fewer gowns than usual—they had been
destroyed in a huge palace fire earlier in the year), her linens and
plate and woven hangings, her icons and chapel furnishings, her
dogs and hunting mounts and hairdressers all followed her, as did
each member of the government and each household officer, no
matter how menial.

Like a swarm of locusts the migration of the courtiers spread

itself out over the countryside, engulfing every available horse
and cart in its path, devouring sheep and chickens by the
thousands and commandeering every sackful of stored grain.
Two thousand gallons of wine, beer and honey were needed each
day to quench the thirst of the travelers, and uncounted thousands
of pounds of meat and cheese, eggs and vegetables to satisfy their
insatiable hunger. Provisioners rode ahead of the main columns of
riders, stopping in each village to strip barns and granaries of their
contents, leading away horses and seizing carts, all but stealing the
unripened crops from the fields.

The villagers endured these visitations without outward complaint, gaping open-mouthed at the parade of dignitaries and
liveried retainers as they rode by in all their dusty splendor,
dropping worshipfully to their knees or prostrating themselves
when the empress came into distant view.

To them the empress was a divinity, yet a divinity of a remarkable sort. She passed among them quite without hauteur, taking a
kind and sincere interest in their crops and their children, talking
to them knowledgeably about their fruit trees and their breeding
stock. She liked to stride from cottage to cottage, impulsively
entering one after another to sample the housewife's blinis and
cabbage soup and pickled pork. She drank kvass with the men and
went mushrooming with them, leaving them in no doubt as to
how much she enjoyed their company and basking in their un-
abashed admiration.

For in truth she preferred handsome, lowborn men to aristocrats, and she flaunted her opulent charms, gratified when she
attracted gazes that were more than worshipful from her admiring
subjects. Elizabeth was well aware that, should her passion for her
morganatic husband Alexei Razumovsky wane, she could easily
find a replacement for him. As she made her swift way through
the villages, ordering cottages renovated and new ones built,
instigating new agricultural ventures with a wave of her imperial
wand, she kept an eye out for attractive men.

For the first month of the summer the empress contented
herself with her rural rambles, driving her troika at a reckless pace

along the narrow roads, her head thrown back and her whip flicking over the lathered backs of her fleet horses, hunting wolves and hyenas, putting flowers and ribbons in her hair and dressing in peasant costume to join in the dancing at local festivals. Folk songs delighted her, she had her court musicians write them down and attempted to compose at least one herself.

But when August came she put her hunting and dancing clothes aside and became a pilgrim. Without her customary finery, with boots covering her sturdy, fleshy legs she set out to walk to her favorite shrines, keeping a fast pace while an entourage of hundreds followed in her wake in case she should have need of a drink of water or a change of boots or a frugal meal. She walked for hours, covering seven or eight miles before halting to rest, eventually reaching a monastery where she would stay several days and make her devotions.

The entire court did as the empress did, though most people did not follow her example to the extent of descending from their carriages to tramp the roads on foot. Towns offered hospitality— Serpukhov, Tula, Sefsk, Glukhov, Baturin, Negin. They stayed for three weeks at Kozelsk, where Razumovsky had a huge mansion, and there, Catherine recalled, they enjoyed constant music, balls and gambling for high stakes. The monasteries and convents at which the travelers halted sometimes put on entertainments, mounting ballets and comedies, mock battles and grand fishing scenes. After many hours of such spectacles Elizabeth grew weary, and commanded the actors to quit the stage. Even so more entertainments followed: banquets and masquerade parties, magnificent albeit dangerous fireworks displays, expeditions to local landmarks and visits to churches.

The summer's peregrinations gave Catherine the opportunity to see more of the country over which her husband would one day rule. Thick forests of birch and pine, so dense they seemed never to end; fields of yellow wheat and rye stretching to the horizon; fresh meadows, full of blooming daisies, lilac and cornflowers, their grasses tall and ready for harvest; cool lakes bordered by stands of sycamore and willow; marshy swamps, overgrown with brown reeds and waist-high sedge: all this she drank in, her eye caught by tiny deserted churches, farmsteads and millponds, villages whose wooden houses, black with age, leaned at crazy angles and huddled together as if for protection against the surrounding emptiness. The holy city of Kiev inspired her awe, with its splendid churches and whitewashed, slate-roofed monasteries, their golden cupolas shining in the warm sunlight, their well-watered gardens in full summer bloom.

The vastness of Russia, and the vastness of the empress's entourage, dwarfed Catherine despite her newly acquired stature. She was but one among thousands in the great imperial household, one more mouth to feed, one more young body requiring shelter. That she was now grand duchess did not stop Peter from teasing her roughly about how he would have to keep her in line once they were married, nor did it stop Johanna's persistent incivilities and irritating moodiness. Johanna, who had not wanted to come along on the summer wanderings of the court because Ivan Betsky was not included, took out her irritation on her daughter, and on Peter, coming close to slapping him when he provoked her, and on the ladies in waiting, with whom she quarreled constantly.

Riding in her carriage with the irascible Johanna, sharing a tent with her, and trying to keep peace between Johanna and Peter put Catherine under a constant strain. The empress, who had been keeping Catherine by her side and sending her costly presents each day, grew more distant, caught up in her hunting and her strenuous devotions. Elizabeth could not in any case protect Catherine from the rancor of those closest to her, she could only offer her own warmth and ebullience to counteract it. As the long summer's ramble drew to its end, and the first frost chilled the air, Catherine took her place in the huge procession returning to Moscow, feeling more keenly than ever that she was young, vulnerable, and alone.

Chapter Six

I N OCTOBER PETER TOOK TO HIS BED WITH A DRY COUGH and pains in his side. His doctor watched him closely, and forbade him to exert himself, but his symptoms evoked no great concern as he had been ill many times before and this episode appeared to be no worse than the others. Catherine, perhaps relieved to be free of her fiancé's teasing and rough play, sent him notes and went on happily without him.

She had found new friends to replace the Russian girl Johanna had sent away. They were Praskovia and Anna Rumyantsev, daughters of her chief lady-in-waiting Maria Rumyantsev. Close to Catherine in age, the two girls shared Catherine's taste for energetic games and silliness, and in their company she was able to forget the worries that beset her and lose herself in boisterous pleasure. Maria Rumyantsev let the romping and dancing in Catherine's apartments go on, she thought it harmless enough. The empress, who continually told Catherine how pleased she was with her, how she loved her "almost more than Peter," did not inquire too closely into what went on in the grand duchess's apartments. Johanna, who only a few months earlier had stepped in to destroy the burgeoning friendship between her daughter and her young waiting maid, did not intervene this time, preoccupied as she was by her growing involvement with Count Betsky and housed at the Winter Palace in rooms distant from Catherine's.

Night after night, when the balls and parties were over, Catherine went back to her rooms and invited Praskovia to sleep in her bedchamber—sometimes in her bed—"and then the whole night went in playing, dancing, and foolishness," she wrote in her memoirs, "sometimes we only went to bed toward morning, there was no end to our mischief."

Weeks went by, and Peter developed chickenpox. Now alarm spread through the court, and fears for his safety. At the same time there were rumors of scandal. People were saying that Johanna's increasingly turbulent affair with Count Betsky had led to complications, and that she was pregnant. Whether or not Catherine believed these rumors, and whether or not she knew the actual truth about her mother, a cloud of dishonor hung over both Johanna and herself, and once again she had reason to be anxious about her situation. If Johanna disgraced the family, or if Peter should die, Catherine would be shipped back to Anhalt-Zerbst at the earliest opportunity.

Winter closed in, another brilliant season of parties and entertainments preoccupied the court, with Catherine drawing admiration for her slender figure, smooth fair skin and long elegant neck. She spent and far exceeded the allowance the empress gave her on gowns and finery—along with expensive gifts for her friends—and, like the other courtiers, developed a consuming passion for French styles. When Peter at last began to improve and was able to join the others at evening gatherings, Catherine was greatly relieved. At the end of November they both appeared at a masquerade, Peter slightly wan-looking but clearly recovered, Catherine brimming with vitality and charm, wearing an expensive gown and looking happier than she had for months.

But this interval of contentment was not to last. Several weeks later, as the court was migrating to Petersburg for Christmas, Peter again became unwell. Two hundred and fifty miles from Moscow the cortege halted while he rested, Dr. Boerhave hovering over him. His fever grew worse, he lay inert, hardly able to move, gripped by stomach pains. A day later skin eruptions appeared, the dreaded indicators of smallpox.

At once Boerhave took extreme precautions. No one was to be allowed in the room with Peter except himself and a few expendable servants. Within hours Catherine and Johanna were in a sleigh on their way to Petersburg, where Catherine would be kept in seclusion, and in ignorance of Peter's condition. A messenger was sent to the empress, who was already in the capital, to inform her of the disastrous turn Peter's illness had taken. She came in haste to his bedside and insisted upon nursing him herself.

The cold, dark Christmas season was made somber by the gravity of Peter's illness. Catherine, shut away for six weeks, applied her agile mind to the study of Russian and, with her tutor's help, produced several letters that were sent to the empress and that pleased her. Catherine had begun to understand and speak the language; now she learned, imperfectly, to write it. She saw few people other than her servants during January, as Johanna was kept away from her, even at meal times. The empress had given orders that Johanna be ignored and treated with coldness. Probably she hoped that Johanna would decide to return to Anhalt-Zerbst. But Johanna, as stubborn as she was angry, refused to be accommodating. She clung to her rights, as she saw them, determined to stay in Russia until her daughter was married, which would not be for many months. And in defiance of Elizabeth's severe chastisements, she continued to write to Emperor Frederick and to carry on ineffectual intrigues with Frederick's diplomats and others.

Despite his history of chronic illness, Peter proved to have a hardy constitution. He survived his attack of smallpox, and at the end of January 1745 was back at court. Yet he was not himself: his face was misshapen and so swollen that his features were distorted. The marks of the pox made him repulsive, as did the huge wig he wore, his own hair having been shaved off.

"He had become hideous," Catherine wrote in her memoirs. "My blood ran cold at the sight of him." This repulsive creature, his once good-looking face altered beyond recognition, was to be her bridegroom. He supped with her every night, and she, desperately eager to please, swallowed her revulsion and endured his company, but secretly she longed to run away, back to Germany, to someplace where she would not have to face the horrifying prospect of becoming his wife. The closer the date of the wedding came, the more she longed to forget all that had happened in Russia and go home.

In March Elizabeth declared that the wedding would take place in the first ten days of July. Catherine shuddered at the announcement. "I had a very great repugnance to hear the day named," she wrote in her memoirs, "and it did not please me at all to hear it spoken of." She had a presentiment of disaster, she felt more and more certain that she was about to make a very bad marriage. Yet she had too much pride to let anyone see her fears and thought of herself as an embattled heroine, steeling herself to endure what was to come. She knew that Peter did not love her, that at best he showed her a fitful brotherly affection and a qualified friendship, which was clearly to be maintained only at his suffrance; his broad flirting with the empress's maids of honor upset her and made her uneasy, but she knew that to complain about his behavior would be the height of folly, and would do no good besides.

She hid her inner trepidation when in public, but among those closest to her, her maids of honor and personal servants, it was difficult to mask her qualms. She tried to dispel her fears by throwing herself into playing vigorous games and tiring herself out striding through the gardens of Peterhof, but her dark moods always returned. "The closer my wedding day came," she wrote looking back on these events many years later, "the more I became dejected, and often I began crying without knowing why." Her women were aware of her crying spells and tried to cheer her up, yet their efforts only lowered her spirits further. She feared that to give in to tears was a mark of weakness, and would lay her open to scorn.

To make matters worse, Peter seemed to become more withdrawn, seeing less of her than previously and treating her with callous disregard. The empress too was for the moment remote and inaccessible. And Johanna, her capabilities as a mother never very high, was too self-absorbed to provide her daughter with comfort. To solace her own bruised ego she resorted to histrionics.

One spring morning Catherine went to visit her mother in her apartments, and came upon a frightening scene. Johanna, who may or may not have known that her daughter was coming to see her, was stretched out on a mattress in the middle of her room, apparently unconscious, her frantic attendants rushing here and there and Dr. Lestocq bending over her, looking very perplexed. At the sight of her Catherine cried out in alarm and wanted to know what had happened. No one, it seemed, could give her a coherent account, but eventually she gathered that Johanna had felt the need to be bled and had summoned a surgeon. The man was so inept that, having been unable to draw blood from her arms, he attempted to cut into veins in both of her feet, whereupon Johanna, for whom being bled was always a fearsome ordeal, had fainted. Eventually she revived, but instead of being pleased to see Catherine nearby, she told her irritably to go away, bringing tears to Catherine's eyes and reminding her of all that estranged them from one another.

Preparations went forward as the wedding day approached. Many nobles, in anticipation of the coming celebrations, had already ordered sumptuous finery for themselves and elegant livery for their servants. Some had sent orders to master wagonmakers in Paris and Vienna for new carriages, all were awaiting shipments of fine fabrics from Europe, Naples silk and English brocade, along with soft gloves and satin slippers from France and golden saddles and stirrups from the armorers of northern Italy. The empress dictated that those belonging to the highest grades of the nobility were to be attended by no fewer than twenty footmen, runners, pages and other servants during the wedding festivities, and that all the servants had to be expensively turned out in velvet coats and breeches with metallic trim, fine bag-wigs, silk stockings and lace cuffs.

Elizabeth had made up her mind to stage the most splendid

wedding ever seen at any European court. Taking as her model the wedding of the French dauphin, the son of Louis XV, she wrote to Versailles for details of the ceremony and aimed to surpass them. It was a lofty ambition, for the French court at that time was a gilded fairyland of ornament and bauble and decoration. There were said to be five hundred goldsmiths in Paris, all of them engaged in producing exquisite jewels and trinkets to embellish the wardrobes of the aristocracy. Hundreds of skilled craftsmen devoted their labors to carving wood and shaping metal, hundreds more turned out fine china, delicate furniture and objets d'art. The extravagance of Louis XV's courtiers was becoming legendary, and they had outdone themselves in celebrating the dauphin's wedding.

Renewed warfare in Europe threatened to involve Russia but Elizabeth resisted the pleas of her chancellor that she turn her attention from wedding preparations to affairs of state. Emperor Frederick, whose incursions against Austria had begun five years earlier, was once again attacking the territories of the young Empress Maria Theresa and he had captured Prague. Bestuzhev was urging Elizabeth to face the danger to Russia which Frederick's aggression implied, and to send Russian troops to Maria Theresa's aid, but to his infinite frustration she all but ignored the Prussian onslaught. When in May 1745 the armies of Prussia's ally France won a stunning victory over the Austrians and their British allies at Fontenoy, Elizabeth was bemused—but fleetingly. She soon immersed herself in the wedding once again, and let the chancellor do her worrying for her.

The effort to create in Petersburg an opulent and magnificent spectacle akin to that of Versailles led to difficulties. Not all the shipments of goods from the Western capitals arrived on time, workmen were slow, there were not enough seamstresses to cut and stitch the elaborate gowns or embroiderers to sew on the thousands of beads and jewels and seed pearls. No matter how keenly the empress supervised the renovations and repairs to the Winter Palace, the decorating of the cathedral, the plans for the

banquets, balls and other entertainments to be attended by the
wedding guests, things went wrong, and there were unavoidable
delays. The date of the ceremony had to be changed, not once but
twice. And still it was not certain that all the boatloads of foodstuffs arriving from the south would reach the capital in time, or
that there would be enough fresh meat for all the guests, or that
the actors, singers and dancers hired to put on operas and plays
would be ready to take the stage.

All but lost in the maze of arrangements were the future bride
and groom. Peter, recovering his strength and his volatile temper,
able to abandon his ill-fitting wig as his pale hair grew in once
again, had a new obsession: his role as Duke of Holstein. He was
emerging from the unwanted tutelage of Brümmer, asserting his
ducal authority, strutting through his apartments with a look of
hauteur and giving orders. A troupe of Holstein soldiers had been
sent to him, and he became their drill master, marching the men
up and down for hours, making them stand at attention and
perform guard duty, lecturing them in his high voice and playing
at warfare. He no longer had his valet Roumberg at hand to advise
and teach him; the empress had had Roumberg sent away to
prison. But his newfound experience of command was teaching
him how to govern a wife, and he included Catherine in his
military games, instructing her to obey him as his Holsteiners did.

Catherine, miserable and alone, often in tears, followed his
orders, outwardly submitting to his newfound authority. She still
found it hard to look at him. Though the swelling in his face had
gone down, he was marked for life with the scars of the pox, his
skin was a mass of slowly healing sores and his small eyes seemed
even smaller now behind his pale lashes. Narrow-shouldered,
with thin arms and legs and a fleshy belly, Peter was a poor
specimen of manhood. Expensive jackets, fine lace and diamond
buttons did nothing to improve him, and even in the German
uniforms he loved to wear he looked puny and boyish, as if
dressed for a role that did not suit him.

To imagine him as a husband must have made Catherine

cringe. Lacking experience, completely innocent of instruction about sex, Catherine brought up the subject of the difference between men and women in the privacy of her chamber, among her ladies. The wedding was only weeks away, and she was full of curiosity and dread. Not surprisingly, her attendants claimed to be as ignorant as she was. All of them had observed the coupling of animals, yet when it came to human anatomy and to that mysterious and sacred union between husband and wife, their imaginations could only take them so far.

Catherine approached Johanna, and asked her bluntly about what happened on the wedding night. With her question she evidently touched a nerve—probably the sensitive nerve of marital fidelity—and instead of answering her Johanna scolded her severely. Far from recognizing any duty to dispel Catherine's ignorance, Johanna became suspicious, and on another occasion accused Catherine of having gone in search of sexual adventures one night when she stayed out late in the palace gardens with her women. Catherine protested; the accusation was unjust, she said, there had been no men present, not even a valet. But Johanna castigated her more harshly than ever before, leaving Catherine wounded and resentful—and as ignorant as before.

At last the final, definitive date for the wedding was named: August 21. Catherine's wedding gown, made of thickly embroidered cloth of silver with patterns of leaves and flowers on the slender, low-cut bodice and yards of gold trimming the hem of the wide skirt, received its final fitting. The streets of Petersburg rang with the trumpeting and shouting of heralds, announcing the coming festivities. Drums beat, calling the populace to attention. The route the wedding procession was to take, from the Winter Palace to Kazan Cathedral, was cleaned and swept. In the palace kitchens, the baking and stewing, roasting and frying went on day and night. Barrels of wine were emptied into the fountains, bells rang, horses were groomed and carriage wheels polished.

On the night before the wedding, Johanna softened and attempted to offer Catherine her advice and help. The two had "a long and friendly talk." "She exhorted me concerning my future duties," Catherine recalled in her memoirs, "we cried a little together and parted very tenderly." Love triumphed over injured feelings, mother and daughter prepared themselves for the momentous change that the morrow would bring.

Elizabeth, resplendent in a gown of rich brown silk and glittering with jewels, came to dress Catherine very early on the wedding morning. One by one the layers of undergarments and petticoats were put on and tied in place, then the shimmering silver wedding gown, thick and stiff with metallic embroidery, drawn so tight at the waist that Catherine could hardly breathe. On a whim Catherine had had her bangs cut short and her valet Timofei Ievrenef brought out a hot iron to curl them. The empress became enraged, and shouted at Ievrenef, insisting that Catherine could not wear her crown over a puffy mound of curls. She stomped out of the room, and it took all the tact of the valet and of Catherine's household mistress Maria Rumyantsev to bring her back. In the end Catherine's curly brown hair, left unpowdered, was gathered back off her face and the diamond crown secured in place. Having created a scene, Elizabeth grew calmer, and surveyed the attractive, slim-waisted sixteen-year-old bride with approval.

The empress was a great believer in cosmetics, and Catherine may have been understandably pale that morning; pots of rouge were brought out and artfully applied to Catherine's long face with its broad jaw and strong chin. Finally Elizabeth offered Catherine all her jewels, letting her choose for herself strands of diamonds for her throat, sparkling earrings, bracelets and rings. A long cloak of silver lace floated over her shoulders.

Tall and graceful, smiling yet virginal, Catherine was an enchanting sight, and as she walked toward the waiting coach beside the empress and Peter she did her best to conceal her discomfort. The magnificent silver gown weighed nearly half as much as she did; in it she felt more like a knight in armor than a carefree young bride, and each step cost her an effort. And in any case she was far from carefree. Peter, never comfortable at public functions, walked stiffly beside her in his silver doublet, no doubt wishing that the whole distastefully Russian ceremony were over so that he could go back to his Holsteiners. She sensed his unease, and was acutely aware of her own misgivings. But there was no turning back. Fate had chosen her, and she had accepted the challenge, blindly but courageously. She would see it through, even though she could hardly bear to glance at the odd, disfigured boy she was about to marry.

The new painted carriage Elizabeth had ordered, with panels that were works of art and wheels that gleamed with gold foil, pulled by six fine horses wearing jewel-studded harnesses, led the long procession of one hundred and twenty coaches that took three hours to wind its way from the Winter Palace to the cathedral. An immense crowd had formed to ogle the splendid parade. People stared open-mouthed at the gorgeous carriages with their gilded cherubs and flashing mirrored wheels, and did their best to catch sight of their resplendent occupants, for the lords and ladies inside each sumptuous coach were nearly as beautifully dressed as the empress and the bridal pair. The delicate pale silks and gems of the women, their pearl-studded gowns and waving plumes, the men in suits of embroidered brocade or rich caftans trimmed in gold, silver and diamonds, were a feast for the eyes to rival any in recent memory. "Of all the pompous shows in Russia," wrote an English traveler who was present, "the appearance made upon the great duke's marriage, in clothes and equipage, was the most magnificent."

The religious ceremony in the huge echoing cathedral took three hours, and long before its end Catherine, weighed down by her tight and bothersome dress, must have been weary. The Archbishop of Novgorod droned on and on, exhorting the couple to love and cherish one another, exhorting the deity to grant them long life and many children, while delicate openwork crowns were held over their heads and the rich resonance of the choral voices filled the dimness. At one point one of the court ladies,

Countess Chernyshev, whispered something in Peter's ear, and Peter in turn whispered to Catherine that the countess had cautioned him not to turn his head while standing before the archbishop. According to an old superstition, when the bridal couple stood before the priest, whichever of them turned his or her head first would be the first to die. Catherine thought this a rather ghoulish sentiment for a wedding, but let it pass. (Later she learned that what the countess had really said was "Get on with it, what nonsense!" It had been Peter's whim to bring up the old superstition.)

When the ceremony finally ended, and Catherine and Peter had exchanged rings and received the archbishop's blessing, they returned to the palace. But the tiring day was far from over. They were to be guests of honor at a lavish banquet, attended by all the dignitaries who had been present at the wedding. In addition there were fireworks, music and dancing, a long parade of boats on the Neva, all of them decorated with bright banners and painted sails.

Outside, in Admiralty Square, tables had been spread for the citizens of Petersburg. Wine bubbled up in the fountains and in the taverns, men toasted the bride and groom until they fell into a drunken doze. Work was suspended while the entire city enjoyed a long holiday. This, the wedding day itself, was only the beginning; there would be nine more days of celebration, during which food and entertainment would be supplied in abundance.

In the long banqueting hall, the wedding guests drank deeply of the empress's wine, and stuffed themselves with her viands. Wearily Catherine complained to Countess Rumyantsev that the heavy dress and crown were giving her a headache. Would the countess be willing to remove the crown, just for a moment? Maria Rumyantsev refused, saying it would be a bad omen, but she was willing to carry Catherine's request to the empress. Elizabeth sent back word that the grand duchess could remove her crown temporarily. But Catherine barely had time to take it off before she had to put it on again, for the ball had begun. For yet another hour Catherine sat and listened as the court musicians

played polonaise after polonaise—no livelier dances were permitted on this night—and tried to look alert and cheerful.

At last the ball ended and Catherine was able to retire to the
bridal chamber. It had been newly redecorated under the
empress's supervision, the walls covered with crimson velvet and
the great high bed with its embroidered coverlet decorated with
posts of carved silver. The bedchamber women took off Catherine's heavy wedding gown and put on her soft, lace-trimmed
nightgown. They brushed out her long brown hair and put her to
bed, leaving only a dim light burning in the room. All was in
readiness for the bridegroom.

Suddenly apprehensive, Catherine pleaded with the Princess of
Hesse to stay with her for a while, but the latter refused. It would
not be seemly for Peter to come in seeking his bride and not find
her alone. Everyone left, and Catherine lay in bed, waiting, tense
with anticipation, unable even to doze yet uncomfortable in her
wakefulness.

An hour passed, then two hours, and still she was alone. What
could have happened? Ought she to get up or stay in bed? Confused and nervous, she listened for the sound of approaching
footsteps in the corridor outside. Finally she heard them. But
when the chamber door opened it was not Peter who came in, but
Catherine's new attendant, Madame Kraus, who informed her
with much suppressed merriment that her husband was still waiting for his supper. After he ate, he would join her.

Catherine lay on the bed, listening for the clocks to strike
midnight, her mind a maze of speculations and worries. After
what seemed an eternity the door opened once again, and there
stood Peter, swaying uncertainly in his silver doublet, a drunken
grin on his disfigured face. He lurched toward the bed, clawing at
his clothing to loosen it, and collapsed beside her. In no time at all
he was snoring, and Catherine, more bewildered than relieved,
closed her eyes and attempted to go to sleep.

Chapter Seven

UNPREDICTABLE, SUSPICIOUS, VORACIOUSLY APPETITIVE, magnificent even in her stoutness, Empress Elizabeth bestrode the Russian court like a colossus and kept everyone around her in a constant state of fear. That she could be generous and sympathetic, even affectionate, did nothing to dispel this fear, for her discrepant nature was at the heart of her power; no one knew when her charm and sunny disposition would be replaced by violent anger leading to savage reprisals.

Every time she did something unexpected, the courtiers trembled. If she did not arrive on time for the start of a ball, they watched for her, keenly aware of the passing of time and increasingly nervous, speculating among themselves about why she was late. Was she interrogating someone who had displeased her? Was she instructing Bestuzhev to send someone to Siberia? Thousands had already been banished there, and more were sent off every month. Was she investigating some plot, real or imagined, to dethrone her? And if so, who would fall under suspicion next?

When she traveled, any departure from her scheduled itinerary was taken as an indication that something, most likely something unpleasant, was afoot. On a journey in 1746, on her way to Riga accompanied as usual by most of the imperial household, she suddenly ordered the entire gigantic procession to halt. No one knew why. Alarm spread among the servants, the officials, the nobles along the route of march. Hours passed. Eventually her carriage was glimpsed, racing along the road in the direction of Petersburg. Why had she suddenly decided to turn around? Many anxious hours later, it was whispered that she had received a mysterious warning from a Lutheran priest. Assassins waited for her at Riga, he said. If she did not turn back she faced certain death. Immediately everyone fell under suspicion, and the journey was aborted.

It was impossible to predict Elizabeth's moods, or anticipate her whims. As suddenly as she changed her mind about visiting Riga, she changed her mind about other plans, upsetting careful preparations and leaving her frustrated household officers agape. On an impulse the empress frequently ordered the entire court to follow her into the country for a picnic, or to camp overnight; horses and carts were hastily assembled, tents ordered, food cooked. Yet as often as not, the area where she wanted to camp was found to be ankle-deep in mud, the tents were late in coming, and a sudden rainstorm washed the picnic away.

The women of the court were Elizabeth's particular victims. She subjected them to minute scrutiny, taking particular note of any complexion more radiant than her own, any pair of eyes more entrancing than hers, any bosom more ample and alluring. To challenge her attractions was to feel her wrath: she was not above ordering a woman with a beautiful dress to leave the room and remove it immediately, and in time all the women of the court had to learn the art of dressing just well enough not to outshine the empress. At the same time, however, they knew that she was capable of being moved by an almost maternal tenderness; she liked to single out a pretty woman, cup her face between her hands and murmur compliments to the blushing object of her admiration, showering her with gifts and privileges.

In the winter of 1746 the empress suddenly issued an order that all the women of the court must shave their heads. Weeping and wailing, they did as she commanded, not knowing why, and bitterly lamenting the loss of their crowning glory. It had come to Elizabeth's attention that in the western monarchies, black hair was the height of fashion. She was determined that her court would follow this fashion, and so she sent her women black wigs to wear over their shorn heads, and wore one herself. All season long the plague of black wigs struck balls and social gatherings. They clashed with the pastel silks and damasks that were the prevailing mode, and clashed even more with the fair-skinned coloring of most of the Russian women. Even temporary visitors to court had to follow the imperial dictate and hide their hair under coarse coal-black wigs. But the empress was content. She had created an oasis of taste amid the rustic wasteland of Russia, her court was in style with the sophisticates in France. The black wigs, badly combed and ill suited to their wearers, lasted until spring when, with the empress's permission, the women were allowed to take them off and be seen in their own gradually lengthening hair again.

The empress was bewilderingly inconsistent, especially when it came to such basics as food, clothing and sex.

Where food was concerned she gave in to the most outrageous gluttony, stuffing herself with pickled pork and French pâtés and rich breads and pastries. She imported chefs from France and kept them busy supplying her table with fattening delicacies. Loving fresh peaches and grapes, which were only grown in the southerly reaches of her kingdom, she ordered a special road built to connect Moscow and Astrakhan. Along its twelve-hundred-mile length swift riders passed, carrying fruit specially packed in wicker baskets. Yet her gluttony often gave way to abstinence, and when the church prescribed fasting Elizabeth deprived herself severely and grew furious when those around her failed to emaciate themselves by living on mushrooms and water.

No one knew how many expensive gowns there were in the empress's measureless wardrobe. By one estimate, she had fifteen thousand of them, each wrapped in lengths of silk and kept in a large leather trunk. Dressmakers amassed fortunes in Elizabeth's service, though she was always in debt to them and often kept them waiting years for their payments. Still, she spent lavishly, as if there were no end to her resources, on satin trims and lengths of frothy lace, delicate embroidery and chains of satin rosebuds. To match her countless gowns she had countless pairs of high-heeled slippers, trunks of silk stockings and gloves and chests of jewels and ornaments for her hair. Yet in matters of dress she could suddenly turn austere, appearing in the plain stark black of mourning or castigating her women for failing to adopt more simple modes. Her dress followed her moods, sometimes reflecting a gossamer lightness of spirit, sometimes flamboyant passion, at other times a somber piety, and no one could sense in advance how their own dress might clash with her current mood, resulting in an outburst of imperial temper.

When it came to men the empress indulged her appetites without restraint. Black-haired, black-eyed Alexei Razumovsky, supremely handsome and unfailingly amiable, was not enough for her. She had had lovers since the age of fourteen, and as empress, she favored many men with an invitation to share her bed. All were well rewarded afterward. When her courtiers strayed from marital fidelity, however, her response was unpredictable. Sometimes she turned a blind eye, and sometimes she was harshly critical. Beneath her sensual exterior was a wide puritanical streak, and from time to time she was overcome with righteous wrath when confronted with evidence of immorality. She strode energetically through the halls of her palaces, seeking out all those who pursued illicit liaisons, persecuting courtesans and other "worthless" women and ordering her officials to imprison them. Like the Austrian Empress Maria Theresa, whose own personal life was above reproach and who set up a Chastity Commission to regulate the morals of those who served her, Empress Elizabeth appointed a commission to discover and penalize adulterers, and though her efforts in this direction were sporadic they added to her fearsomeness.

Observers were puzzled by Elizabeth's quixotic temperament. To Emperor Frederick, who had never met her but who was kept well informed about her by his ambassador, she appeared to be "secretive but amenable, loathing work, unfitted for governing." Lady Rondeau, wife of the British ambassador to the Russian court and a perceptive judge of character, found the empress to be a lovable but fissured personality. "In public she has an unaffected gaiety, and a certain air of giddiness," Lady Rondeau wrote in her memoir of Russia, "that seem entirely to possess her whole mind; in private, I have heard her talk in such a strain of good sense and steady reasoning, that I am persuaded the other behavior is a feint."

Catherine too thought that the empress had an impressive intelligence, well disguised by her surface pleasure-seeking and capriciousness. "Laziness prevented her from applying herself to the cultivation of her mind," Catherine wrote. Indeed Catherine was convinced that laziness and vanity were the vices that controlled Elizabeth, and made her a slave to self-indulgence and to the flatterers who surrounded her. Elizabeth's beauty, which in another woman might have led to self-confidence, only made her feel rivalry and jealousy, especially as she advanced into her thirties and her coloring began to fade. Her hair was still a lovely natural reddish-brown, but her cheeks needed rouge, her lips had lost their vivid red and her eyes, which Catherine described as "like those of a merry bird," were a softer blue than they had once been.

It was partly in an attempt to deny that time was passing and robbing her of her attractions that the empress sought oblivion in frenetic activity. From the time she rose, generally in the late morning, until the time she went to sleep—which was often not until dawn—Elizabeth kept herself busy with time-consuming pastimes and pleasures. Always on the move, she threw herself into riding, hunting, going on journeys, visiting monasteries, attending to her devotions and, in the evening, presiding at grand banquets and balls. She went to church services at least three times a day, more often in the frequent seasons of fasting, and spent many hours in prayer. She spent many more hours at her toilette, having herself gowned and coiffed and painted, and still more time with her dressmakers and jewelers. And while all this was going on, the empress gave grudging attention to the urgent matters her chancellor brought before her, gathered support from informants for her everpresent suspicions and vented her fury on those who fell out of favor.

Her nights, especially the long nights of winter, were the worst, for then she wound down, her bulky body sought rest and it was harder for her to distract herself from the darker realities of her life. Fears and suspicions crowded in, she remembered that there was war on Russia's western border and that, on the grand chessboard of European politics, Russia and her allies were for the moment losing. Despite her extreme resistance to serious work, Elizabeth was not entirely deaf to Bestuzhev's pleas that she give thought to Russia's predicament; it haunted her, as did the question of her successor.

Her blighted, pockmarked nephew Peter continued to disappoint her. Having made him her heir, she did not feel more secure, as she had hoped to, for he seemed to have a talent for alienating people. He was not improving as he grew older. Marriage had not matured him; on the contrary, instead of taking his responsibilities seriously he was retreating more and more into juvenile fantasies and showing no capacity for governance. As for his wife, the German Catherine, Elizabeth was dissatisfied with her. Rather than becoming pregnant right away, as was her clear duty, Catherine was still as slim as a reed, and was growing more disturbingly attractive by the day. She was not the robust, obedient breeder Elizabeth had expected her to be, but something else altogether: she was entirely too clever, too sociable, too shrewd a judge of people and too quick to learn. She made Elizabeth uncomfortable.

Elizabeth was afraid—of the dark, of being alone, of being overthrown or murdered while she slept. She herself had come to the throne through a conspiracy to overthrow her predecessor Anna Leopoldovna, regent for the infant Emperor Ivan VI, carried out one night while Anna was sleeping. It could easily happen again.

Every night Elizabeth sent her women to seek a room where she could sleep in safety, and prepare it for her. She rarely slept in the same room for more than one night, hoping that if she kept moving it would help to foil lurking assassins. Once she was installed in her temporary bedroom, she was still much too afraid to sleep, and so she gathered her drowsy women around her and made them talk to her, telling her every piece of gossip that was circulating at court, no matter how minute, recounting their love affairs and confessing their innermost dreams. While they talked they tickled the soles of her feet, to keep her awake and amused and to distract her from her fears.

At the foot of her bed, on a thin mattress, lay her bodyguard, the powerfully built Shulkov, a former stove-stoker with thick muscular arms and a fierce scowl for anyone who came too near his mistress. Shulkov had protected Elizabeth ever since she was a child, and she relied on his strength. Yet she knew that even Shulkov, armed and intimidating as he was, would be no match for a clever band of assassins who might steal in in the quiet of the night and surprise him. So she stayed wakeful until dawn, examining the shadows and listening for the muffled footfalls that might mean that the end of her reign was near.

Catherine, ever in the fearsome empress's orbit though rarely, in the months following her marriage, in her good graces, trembled and worried like everyone else and struggled to avert Elizabeth's wrathful whims. She suffered continually from terrible headaches, fevers, and sore throats brought on by being dragged from one drafty, uncomfortable set of apartments to another and on long tiring journeys. She endured the anxiety of knowing that she was under constant suspicion, and that among the scheming deceitful courtiers, who, as she wrote in her memoirs, "all hated each other cordially" and were perpetually engaged in murky intrigues, she was the subject of infinite gossip and accusation. She realized that the empress suspected her of working to subvert her purposes, of being a spy as Johanna had tried to be, of disobedience and disloyalty. And she knew that the empress not only bestowed blows freely on those whom she distrusted—her women, her officers, even her friends and lovers—and occasionally did real injury, but that she frequently sent them to the dreaded Fortress of Peter and Paul, from which no one ever emerged except to go into exile. Knowing all this, and knowing too that Elizabeth was watching her closely for early signs of pregnancy, Catherine tried to behave herself and keep her distance.

Treachery surrounded Catherine, she hardly knew whom to trust. Servants were bribed or blackmailed into acting disloyally; those whom she could rely on most were sent away at the empress's orders. Her faithful valet Timofei Yevrenev stayed on, at Elizabeth's sufferance, but each month others were dismissed, usually those to whom Catherine had become most attached, and she was forced to bear their loss in silence. Rumors and accusations abounded. Malicious people approached Catherine with stories of Peter's infidelities: Count Divier told her that Peter was in love with one of Elizabeth's maids of honor, and later that he had discarded his first love for yet another woman in the empress's inner circle. Stories reached Peter and Elizabeth that Catherine was flirting with this or that gentleman of the court, that she was arranging secret rendezvous, that she was deliberately frustrating Peter's efforts to win her affection, that she was cold and calculating and would not do what was expected of her. "Traitor" was the word whispered most often behind her back, and she knew it.

Before her marriage Catherine had been able to put aside the tensions under which she lived when in the company of young friends. Now, however, her new household mistress Madame Kraus forbade such foolishness. She was isolated, secluded for many hours at a time, kept from joining in her favorite pastimes because the empress did not want her to take even the slightest physical risk. At least, that was the kindest interpretation of the strict rules imposed on her, and she tried to keep it in mind when she sat indoors, alone, on hot summer afternoons, wishing that she could be hunting with the rest of the royal party and missing the long rides she loved.

Every week throughout the autumn and winter there were two masked balls, one at the palace and one at the home of some prominent subject. The balls were formal, ceremonious affairs, the few guests were stiff with self-consciousness behind their masks and desperate to demonstrate their importance and their ability to follow protocol. The empress enjoyed making a grand entrance at these balls, pausing in the doorway to strike a pose in her flowing robes, with all the bejewelled Orders of the empire gleaming on her breast. Often she left the salon and returned again two or three times in the course of the evening, having changed her gown each time.

Catherine had no choice but to attend these balls, and to try to act as if she were enjoying herself, despite the dreariness of the company and her husband's tiresome flirtations. "One pretended to amuse oneself," she recalled many years later, "but deep down one was bored to death." Boredom dogged her. At a court where only half the nobles could read (the women, on the whole, being better educated than the men) and perhaps a third could write, where ignorance abounded and wit and the art of conversation were cultivated by only a few, Catherine was starved for congenial company. Once in a long while a cultivated visitor such as the Swede Count Gyllenburg would come on the scene and raise the intellectual tone. But for the most part, Catherine wrote, "there was no sense trying to talk about art or science, because everyone was uneducated. Insults passed as clever remarks."

When not protecting herself from the malice of others, or being subjected to disquieting scrutiny, Catherine was neglected and filled with ennui. "No amusement, no conversation, no nurture, no kindness, no attention sweetened this tedium," she wrote, looking back. It was no wonder she cried, and cringed when her women caught her crying, and called the doctor.

Dr. Boerhave, an educated man who was not unaware of the strains and deprivations Catherine was forced to endure, was sympathetic when he was summoned to attend her. He knew that her headaches and insomnia, her weeping and low spirits were brought on as much by fear as by any physical weakness, and that the more she went without sleep the more likely she was to contract measles—which she did, twice—and to succumb to respiratory infections. During the severely cold winters she suffered from "twelve handkerchief a day" colds, she spat blood and the doctor worried that her lungs might be infected. He examined her head one morning before the hairdresser came in and discovered that, even though she was seventeen years old, her skull bones were still in an unformed state, like those of a six-year-old. Her headaches, he said, resulted when cold air was allowed to reach the fissure in her skull.

Her teeth hurt. Often when in a state of misery, her temples throbbing and her jaw clenched in pain, she had to endure a long evening of brittle courtesies, wishing and praying that she could leave and nurse her wretchedness in privacy. For many months one of her wisdom teeth gave her particular agony until, with great trepidation, she agreed to have it pulled.

The court surgeon, inept and no doubt very frightened of what might happen to him if his work displeased the empress, grasped his tongs and asked the grand duchess to open her mouth. She braced herself for his assault, sitting on the wooden floor with one of Peter's valets holding one of her arms and Dr. Boerhave the other. The cruel tongs went in, the surgeon turned and twisted them while the victim screamed in pain, tears flowing from her eyes and nose "like tea from the spout of a teapot." With a final terrible wrench the surgeon drew out the tooth—and a large chunk of bone along with it. Now blood gushed forth like a river, soaking Catherine's gown and staining the floor, and her whole face felt as if it were on fire.

Just at that moment the empress appeared in the doorway, and at the sight of Catherine's suffering she began to cry too. The doctor told her what was being done, and Catherine herself, as the bleeding began to subside, told Boerhave that the surgeon had only managed to pull out half the tooth—one of the roots was still in her wounded jaw. The petrified surgeon tried to feel for it with his finger, but Catherine wouldn't let him.

Servants brought basins and hot cloths and an herbal poultice to lay on the wound, the surgeon paced anxiously, and after a few hours Catherine was able to lie down and rest. In a day or two she was able to eat again. The great pain in her tooth was gone, though her jaw and chin were black and blue for weeks afterward and her headaches and insomnia continued.

One source of pain Catherine was determined to avoid. She made up her mind within days of her marriage never to allow herself to fall in love with her husband. "Had he been lovable, even the least bit, I could have loved him," she wrote, looking back. "But I said to myself, 'If you love that man, you'll be the most unhappy creature on the face of the earth.'" She lectured herself sternly, advising herself to remain detached from the pitiable, at times malicious boy to whom she was now yoked. "He hardly takes any notice of you," she told herself, "he talks only of dolls . . . and pays more attention to any other woman than to you." Hardheaded and clearsighted, Catherine was fully aware of how futile it would be for her to attach herself to her husband. He would be a friend to her at most, never a cherished love.

And indeed their married life was hardly conducive to love. There was no sexual intimacy between them, Peter appeared to be utterly indifferent to Catherine as a sexual being, and, in her hearing, told his servants that her attractions were far inferior to those of his current love, Fräulein Karr. ("He was about as discreet as a gunshot," Catherine wrote in her memoirs.) They kept separate apartments, and though Peter slept in Catherine's bed each night, he insisted upon dressing and undressing in his own rooms, and lived as independently as he had before their marriage. He seemed to feel no urgency about fathering an heir; though he knew perfectly well that his aunt expected him to have children with his new wife he ignored her expectations—perhaps because he knew that Catherine would bear the blame for her childless state. He may have been impotent. He was often ill, his doctor came frequently to his rooms to bleed him, and early in 1746 he caught a severe fever that lasted nearly two months.

Once again, while the grand duke struggled to recover from a major illness, the empress became panicked about the succession. If Peter should die before Catherine became pregnant, all of Elizabeth's painstaking plans over several years, all the wedding preparations, the entire sequence of events that had been meant to culminate in the birth of a child to carry on the Romanov dynasty, would have been for naught.

Peter's fever abated, but more months passed and still Catherine showed no sign of pregnancy. After nearly a year of marriage, she was barren. Elizabeth believed she knew why.

The whispering had been going on for a long time. The grand duchess, it was said, was in love with Andrei Chernyshev, one of Peter's valets. She had been discovered alone with him in a compromising situation. Her heart was his; gripped by her love for him, she could not be a wife to Peter, and so she was childless.

All the whispers reached the empress. She collected them, sifted them during the long wakeful hours of the night, and pondered what form of punishment might be a suitable response to Catherine's treachery. She ordered both Catherine and Peter to go to confession, and instructed the priest to question Catherine pointedly. Had she kissed Chernyshev? Catherine denied it vigorously. The priest relayed her denial to the empress, along with his opinion that the grand duchess was sincere. But the whispers continued, and the empress's suspicions grew until finally, tired of waiting for nature to take its course, and convinced that

Catherine was endangering the very kingdom by her faithlessness, she took action.

She strode into Catherine's apartments unannounced, and discovered the girl with her arms in bandages. Catherine had been suffering a severe headache for several days, and the surgeon had been bleeding her in an effort to alleviate it. At the sight of the empress, whose expression was ferocious, the surgeon and all the servants fled, leaving the bewildered Catherine to face Elizabeth on her own.

Catherine, who described the scene in her memoirs, recalled being so frightened that she was sure Elizabeth would beat her. She had rarely seen such a fearsome display of anger, and she felt helpless as the empress paced back and forth in front of her, then pinned her against the wall, accusing her in thunderous tones of having betrayed Peter with another man.

"I know you love someone else!" she raved over and over, working herself into such a state of rage that Catherine's servants, who were cowering on the other side of the door, became convinced that their mistress was in mortal danger. Madame Kraus, not knowing what else to do, ran into Peter's rooms and got him out of bed, telling him to come quickly to rescue his wife.

Peter threw on a robe and came as quickly as he could. As soon as he entered the room where the two women were the atmosphere changed. Elizabeth backed off and Catherine was able to move away from the wall and begin to catch her breath, wiping her tearstained face, her chest still heaving. Abruptly the empress addressed herself affectionately to Peter, speaking in a normal tone of voice, ignoring Catherine entirely. She stayed on for a few more moments, never looking at Catherine, and then left.

The alarming scene was over—for the moment. Peter went to his bedchamber to dress for the evening meal, and Catherine, badly shaken, sat down and tried to recover her presence of mind. She bathed her eyes and dressed, knowing that word of the terrible incident would have reached everyone in the palace by the time she emerged from her apartments to go to dinner. She felt, she later wrote, "as though the knife were in her breast," yet she managed, with supreme self-control, to eat her dinner in outward calm.

After dinner, still very upset, she threw herself down on a sofa and tried to read. But she could not concentrate, the words blurred on the page. In her mind's eye she kept seeing another image, that of the fierce-eyed, red-faced empress, shouting at her and shaking her fist, saying again and again that it was her own fault that she had no child.

Chapter Eight

CHANCELLOR BESTUZHEV WAS SEVERELY DISPLEASED. NOT only had the empress disregarded his advice in choosing the Princess of Anhalt-Zerbst to marry her nephew and heir, but she was tolerating the intolerable: that the princess was not yet pregnant.

In the chancellor's view, Peter and Catherine were two wayward, spoiled children who needed badly to be taken in hand. The best way to do this, he decided, was to appoint new, strict guardians to discipline them. He drew up instructions to be given to these disciplinarians, once they were appointed, and presented them to Elizabeth in May of 1746.

The instructions for Catherine's new guardian stressed the primary importance of the grand duchess's reproductive obligations. Catherine must be made to understand, Bestuzhev wrote, that she had been elevated to imperial rank solely to provide the empire with an heir to the throne, and nothing must interfere with her swift accomplishment of that goal—not personal friendships or trifling with "the cavaliers, pages, or servants of the Court," not clandestine meetings with representatives of foreign powers, certainly not familiarities or flirtations. A pattern of conduct must be set for the grand duchess by her new chaperon, one in which all frivolity and shallowness was avoided and seriousness cultivated, along with wifely devotion and allegiance.

At the same time, Peter's new guardian must reverse the ill effects of his bad upbringing, Bestuzhev's instructions insisted. Peter must be compelled to mature, his embarrassing habits must be restrained. Now that he was a married man, he must be made to see that he had new and serious obligations. He must be kept from spending his time with vulgar dragoons and uneducated lackeys, forced to give up his regiments of wooden soldiers and made to adopt a dignified posture and civil manners.

Bestuzhev's instructions reveal just how odd a creature Peter was, his arms and legs constantly jerking and twitching, his scarred face a grotesque mask of scowls and frowns and clownish expressions, his speech foul and his favorite diversion pouring wine over his servants' heads at the dinner table. There was a manic quality to Peter's pastimes: he giggled and chortled while disrupting church services and provoking dignitaries by telling them dirty jokes. His pronounced cruel streak had more than an edge of lunacy to it. People said that he was mad, or would soon go mad, and averted their fear-filled eyes from his sometimes wild ones.

The chancellor made his written recommendations to the empress, and the empress, after two weeks, finally read them. She decided to appoint to the post of Catherine's guardian her first cousin Maria Choglokov, a handsome young woman in her early twenties who, though somewhat thick-witted, had a strong sense of propriety and was not likely to be susceptible to Catherine's charm or to be diverted by her wiles. Humorless, unimaginative, and inclined to be spiteful, Maria was nonetheless a model wife who adored her good-looking young husband and had already given him several children. More than any of her other qualities, it was her fruitfulness that appealed to Elizabeth; Maria was perpetually pregnant, and the empress hoped that by placing her in charge of Catherine, some of this fruitfulness would be passed on to her.

Where Peter was concerned the problem was more difficult. The grand duke's tutors and his governor Brümmer, who had endeared himself to Catherine and "loved her like a daughter," were not easy to replace. Elizabeth chose Prince Repnin, a cultivated aristocrat whose refined tastes, she hoped, would in time elevate Peter's aberrant ones. Witty, gallant and sociable, the prince was also a military man, a general, and had a soldier's candor and sense of loyalty. Whether Repnin could control, let alone transform, the willful grand duke was an open question. But for the moment it was Catherine who drew all the empress's attention.

There was yet another purge of Catherine's and Peter's servants, with the favored ones sent away. In the aftermath all the remaining servants were upset and anxious, Catherine wrote in her memoirs, and she and Peter indulged in "some sad reflections."

That very afternoon the chancellor came to visit Catherine, bringing the pregnant, dour Maria Choglokov with him. As soon as Catherine saw her she burst into tears. "This was a thunderclap for me," she recalled. Not only was Maria a slavish partisan of the inimical chancellor, but she was known to be mean-spirited and rancorous, and Catherine, who had been suffering under the "Argus eyes" of Madame Kraus, now foresaw that she would come under worse scrutiny—edged with malice.

Catherine's tears began to flow even more heavily when the chancellor announced that the empress had named Maria Choglokov to be grand mistress of her household. The two women crossed swords almost at once, though Catherine, through her tears, gave assurances that "the empress's orders were an immutable law" to her, and that she would of course be obedient to this change in her household. Conveying Elizabeth's sentiments, Maria told Catherine that she was obstinate. Catherine demanded to know what she had done to deserve that accusation, and Maria retorted tartly that she had said what she had said at the empress's orders and that was that.

It was a bad beginning, and things rapidly got worse. Maria Choglokov rarely let Catherine out of her sight, and Catherine became her prisoner. They spent hour after hour together, the dully correct, leaden chaperon and the mercurial, energetic, clever grand duchess, who was now denied the company of her preferred companions and was forced to endure the tedium of Maria's constant corrections. Often Catherine had nothing to do but read, and she retreated gladly into her books, marking the days by the swelling of her chaperon's belly, praying that Maria would be delivered soon so that she, Catherine, could have a few days of respite from her ceaseless vigilance and harsh tongue.

Catherine was allowed to spend time with Peter, but her contact with all others was severely limited. Maria prohibited the members of Catherine's household from conversing with her. "If you say more to her than yes or no," the guardian told them individually, "I'll tell the empress that you are intriguing against her, for the intrigues of the grand duchess are well known." Fearing the empress's wrath, the people in Catherine's suite were eager to avoid giving even the appearance of disloyalty, and so they served their mistress in silence, deepening her isolation.

No one could speak to Catherine without arousing Maria's suspicions, and even brief compliments aroused her distrust. "That winter," Catherine recalled in her memoirs, "I spent a good deal of time on my appearance. Princess Gagarin often said to me furtively, hiding from Madame Choglokov—for in her view it was a terrible crime for anyone to praise me, even in passing— that I was becoming prettier by the day." In her isolation, denied her usual recreations, Catherine spent more time in front of her mirror, and engaged a skilled hairdresser, a young Kalmuk boy, to arrange her hair twice a day. Catherine's hair was enviably thick and curled attractively around her face. Elizabeth had exempted her from having to shave her head and wear the ubiquitous black wig, and her hair flowed luxuriantly down her back—the envy of other women—and she left it unpowdered, its rich chestnut color eliciting universal admiration.

Flattery reached Catherine's ears, if only in whispers. Someone told her that the Swedish ambassador Wolfenstierna judged her to be "very lovely," which made her embarrassed when, on rare occasions, she was allowed to address him. ("Whether from modesty or coquetry I don't know," she wrote later, "but the embarrassment was real.")

Catherine was blooming, but Maria was there to put frost on her bloom, to dampen her spirits and rein in her enthusiasms. "I'm going to make my report to the empress!" Maria announced whenever she sensed a hint of frivolity or disorder (and, as Catherine wrote, she called "everything that was not total boredom, disorder"). To induce a more serious mood, Maria enforced the empress's wish that both Catherine and Peter add to their attendance at daily mass two more religious observances: matins and vespers. And she did her best to ensure that whenever they left the royal palace, whether to attend a social event or to follow the peripatetic empress on her sojourns through the countryside, they didn't lapse into their old lighthearted ways.

Catherine remembered one particularly dismal journey, when for nearly two weeks she was stuck in a carriage with Maria and Peter and her uncle August, Johanna's wearisome, rather insipid brother who had been appointed by the empress to look after Peter's Holstein estates. (Johanna herself had departed, sent away in disgrace by Elizabeth soon after Catherine's wedding.) Uncle August was not very lively company. A short, dull-witted man who dressed shabbily and had pronounced views on the subordination of wives—views which he aired frequently for Peter's benefit—August ventured on one inconsequential topic after another. Each time, however, Maria interrupted him to say "Such discourse is displeasing to Her Majesty," or "Such a thing would not be approved of by the empress." Conversation was all but impossible, and Maria succeeded in "spreading tedium and desolation throughout our carriage," Catherine wrote.

When they stopped for the night, the chaperon's censorship of their conversation continued; the travelers were not even allowed to discuss the inconveniences caused by their flooded tents and the freezing weather. Day after day the dreariness continued, with Maria harassing the servants and alienating everyone. Catherine tried to sleep as much as possible, both during the day and in the evenings, to avoid her vexing husband, her boring uncle and the everpresent, funereal Maria.

Once they arrived at their destination, and were installed in a country house, the scene brightened somewhat. Prince and Princess Repnin, who were not insensitive to the excesses of the overbearing Madame Choglokov, steered Catherine away from her as often as they could and led her to softer and more affectionate companions, among them Countess Shuvalov and Madame Ismailof, the empress's most sympathetic waiting women. For her part, Maria was distracted by the card games that went on from morning until night in the antechamber of the imperial bedroom. There was, Catherine recalled, a "crazy furor" at court for games of chance that season, and Maria was an avid participant who became very angry when she lost. She became immersed in her cards, and forgot to supervise Catherine closely— though even so Catherine did not dare to stray out of her sight.

The tyranny of Maria Choglokov, along with the empress's oft-repeated threats to disinherit Peter, drew Peter and Catherine together, despite the radical differences in their temperaments.

"Never did two personalities resemble one another as little as ours," Catherine wrote, recalling her early years of marriage. "We had different tastes, our way of thinking and understanding things was so dissimilar that we could never have reached agreement on anything had I not compromised."

There were times when Peter sought Catherine out, and talked over with her whatever was bothering him, but only when he was in distress. ("He was often in distress," she remembered, "because he was quite a coward at heart and he had a weak understanding.") When the empress scolded him, or sent away the valets who were his favorite drinking companions, he crumpled inwardly and went in search of his ever-indulgent wife, who humored him and treated him like a petted child.

"He knew or sensed that I was the only person he could talk to without risking committing a crime by saying the least thing. I saw what his situation was like and I took pity on him. I tried to give him consolation." Though she was frequently bored by his visits, Catherine covered her boredom with an agreeable facade, even when he stayed for hours and wore her out with his incessant talk of styles of epaulets and artillery maneuvers and punishments for disobedient soldiers.

"He talked of military details, minutiae really, and never could come to the end of them," Catherine wrote in her memoirs. "He never sat down, and perpetually walked or paced, with very large steps, from one corner of the room to another, so that it was hard work keeping up with him." But keep up with him she did, even on long afternoons when her head was splitting, or her teeth aching, knowing that for the moment she was his only friend and talking to her his only permitted form of amusement. Sometimes, after hours of pacing and prattling, Peter's energy flagged and he agreed to sit down and read. Catherine got out her current book—the letters of Madame de Sevigné was among her favorites—and Peter found an adventure novel or a story about highwaymen to help him pass the time.

Many times Catherine submitted to her husband's whim and let him turn her into a soldier, giving her a musket and making her stand sentinel at the door of his room with the heavy gun on her shoulder for hours at a stretch. She stood there, a tall, slim girl in a silken gown, doing her best not to slump though the musket gouged a dent in her shoulder and her feet and legs were tired from hours of immobility, until Peter decided that she had served long enough and allowed her to leave her post.

But her training did not end there. He taught her to march and countermarch, to obey field commands and take orders like a veteran. "Thanks to his pains," she wrote, "I still know how to do the complete musket exercise with as much precision as the most seasoned grenadier."

Every summer Peter and Catherine stayed for a time at Oranienbaum, the magnificent estate near Peterhof just outside of Petersburg which the empress had given them as a summer residence. There the grand duke had an opportunity to bring his military fantasies to life on a larger scale, with Catherine observing from the sidelines. All the household servants—maids, sweepers, cooks, turnspits, valets, chamberlains, pages—were assembled into a regiment, along with the gardeners, grooms and huntsmen. Each became a soldier, and was issued a uniform of sorts and a musket. Peter drilled his troops every day, rain or shine, calling out commands in his high voice and threatening to punish the disobedient. The mansion itself became a guard house, its lower floor a guard room where thc troops passed their days when they were not on parade. At midday the mock soldiers had to eat at the mess and in the evening, still wearing their makeshift uniforms, they had to attend balls devised by Peter, where Catherine and a half-dozen of the women of her suite and Peter's waited to dance with them.

At these balls, Catherine wrote, "among the women, there were only me, Madame Choglokov, Princess Repnin, my three waiting women, and my chamber women. So the ball was very thinly populated and badly arranged. The men were harassed and in a bad humor because of their continuing military exercises."

Everyone fumed, grew irritated, bored and restless. All except Peter—who was in his element.

But Peter had in mind even more ambitious schemes. While pacing the floor in her room he shared with Catherine his vision of building a fanciful monastery where they and their servants and courtiers could live, dressing as monks and nuns in plain habits of coarse brown cloth. They would need little in the simple life he envisioned, only the most basic foodstuffs, which they could fetch themselves, riding on donkeys to the nearest farm.

It was a dream of simplicity, peace and ease, the dream of a troubled young man besieged by the opulence and hothouse atmosphere of his aunt's brilliant court. Like Marie Antoinette a generation later, Peter yearned for authenticity amid artificiality. Antoinette built her rustic refuge on the grounds of the palace of Versailles. Peter, however, could not muster the tenacity to build his, though he kept Catherine busy drawing sketches for the building itself. Or perhaps he was tenacious, but in the end was thwarted by the implacable empress.

By the time she and Peter had been married for two years, Catherine felt that she had earned a good deal of affection and trust from him. He came to her in tears when he felt bereft, he sought her out when the empress chided him, he looked to her for consolation. It was to Catherine that Peter confided that his great love, a Mademoiselle Lapushkin, had been snatched from him when her mother was exiled to Siberia. It had been Mademoiselle Lapushkin that he had wanted to marry, losing her had broken his youthful heart. But he had resigned himself to marrying Sophie, because she was his cousin, she had German blood—a great benefit in his eyes—and besides, he liked her.

Touched at times by Peter's ingenuousness and candor, and full of pity for him, Catherine felt an unmistakable tenderness toward her peculiar husband, though it was more maternal than wifely. She endured his mistreatment, and was tolerant of his whims, she encouraged his love of music (he had a good ear, and Prince Repnin engaged violin teachers for him), she played billiards with his chamberlains while he drank and disported himself in an adjacent room with his serving men. She sat patiently while he put on plays in his marionette theater ("the spectacle was the most insipid thing in the world," she later wrote), and conspired with his valets to bring him meat to eat during Lent, when he was supposed to be eating only mushrooms and fish.

Despite the tensions inherent in her situation, her worries over her unconsummated marriage, the constant scrutiny of her chaperon and of Madame Kraus, and the anxiety caused her by the empress's increasing disapproval, Catherine managed to find times of quiet domesticity and fleeting intimacy with Peter. Once in a while a troupe of young people, among them Count Pierre Divier, Alexander Galitzyn, Alexander Trubetskoy, Sergei Saltykov, and Pierre Repnin, Prince Repnin's nephew, would come bounding into her apartments, led by Peter, flushed with wine and in high spirits. There would be an impromptu party, with none of the guests over thirty years old. The wine flowed freely, Catherine joined happily in the games and horseplay and dancing, and she and Peter both were able to forget for a few hours the burdens that weighed on them and the responsibilities that they were failing to fulfill.

Or Peter came alone to Catherine's rooms, bringing a gift or a game for them to play. He once brought her a wriggling black puppy, only six months old. "It was the most amazing little beast I ever saw," she remembered, for it liked to walk on its hind legs and dance absurdly around the room. Her servants fell in love with it, and named it Ivan Ivanovich. They dressed it in mobcaps, shawls and skirts and watched with delight while it pranced and jumped.

Such scenes were rare, however, and became rarer with each passing month, while occasions of abuse and humiliation increased. Peter gave Catherine much more discomfort and pain than pleasure, keeping a dozen of his hunting dogs confined next to her bedroom so that their revolting smell made her gag all night long, quarreling with her and threatening her, tormenting her with his infatuations—no longer confined to the ladies in waiting, but now including middle-aged women old enough to be his mother—and flaunting his amours before the whole court, causing the gentlewomen to smile behind their fans or shake their heads in pity when Catherine walked by. He even occasionally struck Catherine when other forms of torment failed to elicit a satisfying response, though he did this most often after a long evening spent with the bottle.

Peter's drinking was at best a source of embarrassment, at worst a menace. He drank at the empress's table, he drank at balls and suppers and concerts, he drank with his menials, and when they lost their wits to such an extent that they treated him as one of themselves, he beat them. He drank in secret, in private, and hid his bottles in old cupboards and behind screens. He liked to go riding when tipsy through the Preobrazhensky woods on one of his fine horses, wearing the uniform of a Prussian general. Immense crowds gathered to watch him, hoping to catch a glimpse of their future emperor, only to be repelled by the sight of him, swaying from side to side on his horse, grimacing and twitching like an idiot.

Though he had made his best effort, Prince Repnin had not succeeded in taming the grand duke and making him into something resembling a polished, cultivated nobleman. Bestuzhev and the empress were not satisfied. Another guardian had to be found.

Maria Choglokov's husband, Nicholas, who had joined Peter's household with the rank of chamberlain some months earlier, was now appointed to be his guardian. Handsome in a heavy, ponderous way, and tremendously proud of having married the empress's cousin, Nicholas Choglokov strutted through Peter's apartments, his cuffs dripping with lace and his shoe buckles gleaming with diamonds, making empty remarks and imagining that they were received with admiration, his one decoration—the Order of the White Eagle—conspicuously displayed on his puffed-up chest.

"He thought himself extremely handsome and witty," Catherine wrote. "In fact he was conceited, foolish, full of self-importance, disdainful and at least as malicious as his wife." Choglokov imagined that Peter could be controlled by sheer brute force, and in fact he succeeded in making himself feared. But Peter, who was far cleverer than his new guardian, continued to find ways to get around him and, at nineteen, was too old to be tamed.

Life went on as before, with Maria keeping Catherine in tow and Nicholas issuing orders to Peter, both Choglokovs making themselves universally disliked. Yet their joint efforts were in vain. For all their vigilance, smothering and brute coercion, they had not been able to bring closer the empress's greatly desired goal: that Catherine should become pregnant.

The seasons came and went, the court moved from Moscow to Petersburg, and from Petersburg to Moscow again. During one lull between official celebrations Peter planned a diversion, a masquerade ball, to be held in Catherine's apartments even though Catherine was feverish and had a severe headache. He ordered his long-suffering servants and Catherine's servants to put on costumes and masks, and made them dance around the sofa on which she reclined while he scratched away on the violin. He too danced, carried away by his own playing and exhilarated at having created a miniature, toylike world, a court ball in microcosm.

But Catherine, who had put on a masquerade costume to placate her husband, stayed where she was on her sofa, too ill and dispirited to join in. She was weary of her role as playmate and nursemaid, weary of serving as Peter's whipping boy and scapegoat while struggling to keep her dignity as grand duchess.

She had recently been wounded to the quick when news arrived from Anhalt-Zerbst that her beloved father, Christian August, was dead. The news upset her far more than anyone around her had anticipated it would. Christian August, that upright, limited but honest princeling, as remote in temperament and character from the eccentric Russians as his principality was from the Russian Empire, was no longer there for Catherine to turn to. Johanna had been gone for many months, and Maria no longer allowed Catherine even to write to her. Now her father too was denied her, not by her malicious guardian but by an unkind fate.

"They let me cry for eight days as much as I wanted," Catherine wrote in her memoirs, recalling the painful time after she learned of her father's death, "but at the end of the eight days Madame Choglokov came to tell me that I had cried enough, that the empress ordered me to end my tears, that my father was not a king."

She answered, through her tears, that even though he was not of royal rank he was still her father, and she grieved for him. Maria was adamant.

"It is not appropriate for a grand duchess to cry longer than eight days for a father who was not a king," she insisted, and ordered Catherine to end the isolation she had imposed on herself and re-enter court society. She was allowed to wear mourning, but only for six weeks; after that she would have to conduct herself as if her loss had never happened.

During her weeks of mourning the chancellor stirred up trouble by having one of his servants spread a false tale about Catherine. According to the rumor, the grand duchess had been insulted when she did not receive formal letters of condolence from all the foreign ambassadors at Elizabeth's court. The story put Catherine in a bad light, making her seem haughty and arrogant. When the empress heard it she summoned Maria and ordered her to scold Catherine, and the latter, spent with grieving, had somehow to muster the stamina to defend herself. She was able to expose the tale—and the talebearer—and in the end the empress saw that she had been deceived.

But the damage was done, and even though the lying servant came to Catherine and apologized, it was too late to assuage the injury. And in any case, Bestuzhev and his petty incursions were pinpricks compared to the deep sorrow that now assailed Catherine and weighed her down. The bulwark of her childhood, her father, the narrow, upright soldier who had always told the truth and done his duty manfully, and who had hesitated to send her so far away from home, was no longer there to run to. In the throes of her grief Catherine must have reflected that her late father had been everything that the perfidious, treacherous court of Empress Elizabeth was not: straightforward, blunt, authentic. How she must have longed for his bluff yet comforting presence as she reclined on her sofa, drained and disheartened, watching her reckless husband cavort like one demented at his make-believe ball.

Chapter Nine

"I WAS NEVER WITHOUT A BOOK, NEVER WITHOUT SORROW, but always without happiness." So Catherine described her life as she ended her teens and entered her early twenties. "My situation was assuredly not among the most happy; I was as it were isolated from the world of the court. However, I had grown used to it." She had her reading, and books were her salvation, forming her mind and fortifying her temperament. She had her health, despite bouts of depression and hypochondria and long hours spent in unheated churches from which she returned frozen and miserable, "blue as a plum." Her sense of the absurd bubbled up at the oddest times, often in the midst of the most crushing sadness, and observers often saw merriment in her untamed blue eyes.

Quicksilver shifts of mood, from playfulness to sober concentration to the most poignant grief, allowed Catherine to adapt to the bizarre emotional polarities in her environment, and gradually the world began to seem less bleak. By 1750, when she was twenty-one, she was aware that she was crying less than in previous years, and that her "cheerful humor" served her well. "I am a philosopher as much as I can be," she wrote in a letter to Johanna—a forbidden letter, which had to be smuggled out of Russia—"and I will not give in to my passions."

Day to day she continued to be trapped in a stifling round of dreary encounters with dull people, spending her mornings reading and studying, reading more while her hair was dressed by Timofei Ievrenef or one of the other servants, paying a brief visit to Peter or receiving one from him—gritting her teeth all the while, and wishing it were over—and then, at eleven-thirty, dressing for the public part of the day. In her antechamber were her maids of honor and the decorative, often shallow men whom the empress placed in her suite as "cavaliers in service." Catherine sought out Princess Gagarin, who was witty and amusing, but was gracious to the others, even though their companionship was far from scintillating through the course of the long midday meal. Maria and Nicholas Choglokov presided over the dinner table, "taking great pains to ensure that the conversation didn't stray" and squelching all entertaining diversions; frequently Peter upset all the diners by starting an argument or provoking the Choglokovs with some outrageous prank.

The afternoon was devoted to more reading, walking in the gardens or whiling away time with Princess Gagarin and Maria Choglokov. Maria had softened considerably toward Catherine and now cultivated her friendship. The princess was lively and could follow the course of Catherine's agile mind, but she was constantly reminding Catherine of her predicament. Princess Gagarin had another drawback: she was avid for luxury and the hothouse society of Moscow and Petersburg, while Catherine preferred the country with its simplicity and peace and its opportunities for recreation.

When evening came Catherine had supper with the same group of courtiers who had bored her at dinner, after which she went to her apartments and read until she retired. Peter still came to her bed, often quite drunk, occasionally antagonistic and abusive. But he never tried to make love to her, and she was growing more and more certain that he was unable to. Adept though he was at humiliating her by his infatuations, she was convinced that he was incapable of physical love, at least for the present, and this made his incessant amours hollow, even grotesque.

There was an element of farce in his intense passion for the tiny, hunchbacked Duchess of Courland, Elizabeth's chief maid of honor, in 1750. With her small distorted body, dark complexion and heavy German accent, the duchess was hardly a beauty and could not compare to the tall, robust Catherine whose dazzling white skin and slender grace were much admired. Yet Peter, as Catherine had observed for years, was never put off by physical deformity—in this he reminded Catherine of her uncle Adolf, King of Sweden, who "never had a mistress who wasn't hunchbacked or one-eyed or lame"—and he was so enamored of the duchess that he dogged her footsteps, fixed his gaze on her and praised her to the skies, especially when Catherine was there to hear him.

Catherine did her best to shrug off her husband's remorseless insults but admitted in her memoirs that they began to undermine her vanity and her sense of self. That the misshapen, monstrous little Duchess of Courland should be preferred to her seemed an outrage, and though she tossed her head and tried to ignore Peter's goads—and her own servants' expressions of shock and anger on her behalf—she could not help but feel wounded. Meanwhile Peter, not content with one love object, carried on a second flirtation when the hunchbacked duchess was out of sight. He cornered a young Greek maid ("as pretty as a heart," Catherine thought) in a room adjacent to Catherine's bedchamber and remained closeted with her there for the whole of one day and part of the night, quite aware that Catherine lay in her bed on the other side of the thin wall, tossing with fever and hearing every sound they made.

"This was a passing attachment," Catherine wrote later, "and didn't go beyond the eyes." She got over her fever, Peter got over the Greek maid and the Duchess of Courland, and life went on. Catherine became "very cheery," laughing at her Finnish servant Catherine Voinova who put a cushion under her skirt and wad-

dled heavily through the room in a convincing imitation of the
ever-pregnant Maria Choglokov. Catherine herself developed her
gift for mimicry and made everyone, even the self-important
Nicholas Choglokov, laugh when she snuffled like a pig and
screeched like an owl. Her noisy antics drew a crowd, she
warmed to the applause and carried on even more noisily. Maria
Choglokov's brother-in-law, Count Hendrikov, who had been
away from court for a year, remarked on the change in the grand
duchess and told her that her performance "quite turned his
head." Starved for approval, Catherine took the compliment to
heart and repeated it for days afterward.

Catherine's exuberant physicality helped to buoy her spirits.
Though pent up over the long winter months, except for toboggan rides and indoor games, in the summer she was able to
exercise her muscles and vent her energies in a variety of pastimes.
No longer subject to the close scrutiny of the empress, who for
the most part followed her own pursuits and only fitfully intruded
into Catherine's life, she was able to go riding as often and for as
long as she liked, sometimes spending all day galloping across the
fields.

"I was passionately fond of riding and I was indefatigable,"
Catherine wrote, recalling her early twenties. Her hypochondria
retreated, she woke each day eager for sport. She liked to hunt
hares at Nicholas Choglokov's estate near Moscow, galloping at
full tilt along the edge of the swampy meadows in pursuit of her
prey. She had her tailor make her silk riding habits with crystal
buttons, and with them she wore a black hat trimmed with
diamonds. The costume did not wear well; the silk wilted and
cracked when it rained, and became faded when exposed to the
hot sun. The tailor complained that new riding habits were always being demanded of him, and chided the grand duchess, but
nothing could make Catherine give up her glorious hours in the
saddle.

"In truth, I didn't care at all for hunting," she wrote, "but I
loved passionately to get up on my horse. The more violent the

exercise was, the more I loved it, so much so that if a horse ran away, I galloped after it and brought it back." She was so agile that she became adept at jumping up onto her horse's back, letting her split skirt fall into two mounds of silk on either side. It was a trick that made the empress cry out in astonishment, and praise her niece's athleticism. "One would swear she was on a man's saddle," Elizabeth muttered, and in truth Catherine found a way to convert her sidesaddle so that she could ride astride most of the time.

Catherine found a worthy rival in one Madame Arnheim, who rode superbly and could jump into the saddle with nearly as much grace and aplomb as Catherine could. The two women competed, each eager to outdistance the other, and when their day of riding was over they carried their competition onto the dance floor. Madame Arnheim was an even better dancer than she was a horsewoman, and one evening she and Catherine had a friendly wager over who could go on dancing the longest. The evening wore on, Catherine and her rival went on jumping and turning and curtseying, until at last Madame Arnheim became exhausted and fell into a chair. Catherine, however, was still spinning and leaping, and by the end of the long night she had put all the other dancers in the shade.

From the empress's point of view, all of Catherine's vigor and stamina, her gritty cheeriness and hardihood, and in particular the charms of her fit, taut body mocked the court. What use were her gifts when the only role that mattered—motherhood—still eluded her? People smirked and tittered and whispered that she was still a virgin; Chancellor Bestuzhev shook his head and threw up his hands; the empress stamped her foot and swore that Catherine must have some secret "deformity of structure" that prevented pregnancy. She ordered Maria Choglokov to have Catherine examined by a midwife and Peter by a doctor, to find out once and for all why they had not followed nature and produced a child.

But the empress's irritable threats were as empty as they were rare. She appeared to take scant interest in the succession, avoiding her abhorrent nephew whenever possible and throwing herself headlong into pleasurable diversions. Thinking about the succession forced her to think about her own mortality, and she dreaded that. It reminded her that she was aging, that her plump cheeks were growing pale and her lovely hair was streaked with gray.

Thick rouge could no longer conceal the dark hollows under her eyes or the lines that creased her sagging skin; she still possessed vestiges of her former beauty, but they were fast disappearing, while her body took on unhealthy bulk. Her thousands of gowns had to be altered to accommodate the rolls of fat that now encircled her bloated waist and belly, yet she continued to stuff herself past satiety. Her body rebelled in a dozen ways, her stomach was colicky and her bowels compacted. Yet she drove herself on, even when pain doubled her over and her physicians pleaded with her to rest and take her medicine. The courtiers shuddered at the sight of her, acutely ill and pale, riding in her carriage, her mouth set in a grim line, determined to follow the hunt.

Elizabeth continued to exasperate her chancellor by avoiding business and fleeing responsibility. Sometimes she balked at signing an important paper because, having placed the paper beneath her favorite relic of St. Veronica, her heart told her that it would be better not to sign it. Sometimes she refused to read a document because a fly landed on it, and she took this to be a bad omen. She shut her eyes to political pressures, and did her best to ignore reports of unrest within her realms. When three thousand serfs mutinied, armed themselves and overthrew a regiment of dragoons, she shrugged off the news and appeared to disregard the alarming fact that six regiments were needed to put down the rebellion.

Such incidents could not be helped, and she left it to local officials to deal with them and relied on her Secret Chancery to root out those who stirred up discontent. Agents of the Secret Chancery were everywhere, listening at keyholes, gathering information from paid informants, worming their way into every government bureau and sniffing through the records of every case at law. They had only to come out of the shadows and invoke the empress's supreme authority—"By the word and deed of the sovereign!" was their battle cry—to strike terror into the hearts of the empress's subjects. It was the business of the Secret Chancery to uncover treason, and to this end they arrested, tortured and punished anyone whose name came to their notice—even those who were demonstrating their loyalty by providing information.

At the head of the Secret Chancery was Alexander Shuvalov, brother of the empress's new favorite Ivan Shuvalov. Elizabeth's morganatic husband, Alexei Razumovsky, had been superseded, and had withdrawn gracefully into the background. Ivan Shuvalov now reigned. But Shuvalov too had rivals, for the empress, as she aged, surrounded herself with many good-looking young men, clutching them to her as if in the belief that some of their glow and youthfulness could restore color to her cheeks and vigor to her gait. She had the young cadets of the Guards regiments stage Russian tragedies at court, and brought them into her private apartments where she picked out their costumes and applied their makeup with her own hands.

The cadets were exceptionally handsome, Catherine recalled, with eyes as blue as flowers and soft smooth faces. One lovely young man named Trebor came in for more attention than the others. The empress put rouge on his cheeks, dressed him in her favorite colors, and continued to keep him near her even after the tragedies were ended. Trebor became a kind of erotic pet, the empress's special mascot; she fondled him like a lapdog and heaped gifts and favors on him.

Though she did not often see the empress Catherine did her best to keep herself informed from day to day about the state of Elizabeth's health. Dr. Lestocq was gone, the empress had become suspicious of him and banished him to Siberia, but other doctors and priests were reliable sources of information and

Catherine's most trusted servants went to them—or to their servants—for news.

In February of 1749 Elizabeth failed to make her customary
court appearances for several days and rumors began to fly. The
doctors announced that she had retired to her apartments suffering from constipation, but more days passed and still there was no
sign of her. Peter came to Catherine in great trepidation. What if
the empress were really gravely ill? What if she were to die? What
would become of them? Would Peter be acknowledged as the
next ruler, or would others attempt to kill him and seize the
throne? He was so frightened, Catherine remembered, that "he
didn't know which saint to vow to."

Catherine, in some anxiety herself, tried to reassure her husband. The apartments they occupied just then were on the ground
floor; if they were menaced by assassins or political kidnappers,
she told him, they could escape by jumping out the windows
into the gardens. They were not friendless, Catherine reminded
Peter. They were assured of the loyalty of at least a few Guards
officers. And there was Zachary Chernyshev, Catherine's erstwhile admirer and household officer. He would come to their
aid, and could rally others to join him.

Catherine tried to put heart into Peter, and their sense of shared
danger no doubt brought them closer, if only temporarily. But in
truth they were very much captives of their situation; kept in
official ignorance of the actual state of the empress's health, confined to their rooms, not told of important decisions that were
being made and important discussions that were going on in
secret. Amid the general uncertainty and apprehension, not
everyone was guarded. Things leaked out. Catherine found out
shreds of telling gossip, she and her servants caught glimpses of
Chancellor Bestuzhev and the empress's other current adviser,
General Stepan Apraxin, hurrying along the palace corridors
looking purposeful and worried. Word of clandestine meetings
reached her, though she could only guess at what might be said or

planned. Agents of the Secret Chancery were suddenly everywhere, watching everyone, noting down any suspect word or
deed that might be construed as treasonous.

One thing was clear. The empress was very ill, quite possibly
fatally ill, and arrangements were being made for the imminent
transfer of power in the event of her death.

For several weeks the suspense and tension continued to grow.
If the empress was on her deathbed, Peter and Catherine
reasoned, she would not be likely to confide in them or help Peter
secure his position as heir. She was displeased with Peter. She told
Ivan Shuvalov, "My nephew is a horror, may the devil take him!"
She felt cheated, angry at Peter for not having had a son. For all
Peter and Catherine knew, the empress had made secret arrangements for the imprisoned Ivan to succeed her, under the guidance
of a regency council. Or conspirators were at work plotting to
make it appear as if Elizabeth had changed her mind about the
succession, forcing the half-conscious, dying woman to give her
consent to their schemes.

When after several weeks the empress emerged from her long
isolation, looking paler than usual but otherwise much as before,
Peter and Catherine felt tremendous relief. Yet they knew that her
return to relative health was bound to be transitory. Elizabeth's
brush with mortality did not make her more prudent or
abstemious, rather the reverse; almost at once she resumed her
unhealthy habits, and her stomach pains and digestive upsets
came back just as before. No one knew when another episode of
"constipation" might carry her off.

There came a change in the temper of the court. The succession
dominated all, and both Catherine and Peter were made aware of
the extent to which they were pawns in others' plans.

One day while on a hunt, away from the searching eyes of the
Secret Chancery agents, Peter was approached by several of his
huntsmen, who told him that an admirer was eager to meet him.
He agreed, and sometime later saw a young guardsman ride up, a

lieutenant in the Butyrsky regiment. The young man gave his name as Yakov Baturin, then dismounted, went down on his knees and vowed that from that moment on he considered Peter to be his "sole master" and that he was prepared to "carry out all his orders."

Peter, who had been giving make-believe orders to make-believe soldiers for years, now quaked in his boots. Something in the reckless young man's manner told him that Baturin was an adventurer, a rash and dangerous character and a political opportunist. Without waiting to hear more, Peter rode off in search of Catherine, and still frightened, stammered out the whole story to her.

By this time Lieutenant Baturin had been arrested, along with the huntsmen who had helped him gain access to the grand duke. The men of the Secret Chancery had learned of Baturin's elaborate plot to kill the empress, burn the Golovin Palace, and, in the confusion, muster a rebel army of soldiers and laborers who would put Peter on the vacant throne. Even under torture and the threat of death, the conspirators did not betray their idol the grand duke. They said nothing of Baturin's meeting with Peter during the hunt and so Peter escaped suspicion and the empress's retribution. Baturin was imprisoned, and Peter, still quaking, managed to keep his mouth shut and survive the incident.

At about the same time Catherine became the target of a more sinister plan. Perhaps because she had so far failed to become pregnant, but more likely because her intelligence and astuteness were perceived as a threat to those who hoped to control Elizabeth's successor, an attempt was made to infect Catherine with smallpox—which was usually fatal, particularly for young women. Catherine had never had the pox, and so was highly susceptible. She was invited to General Apraxin's house and entertained in a room where the general's infant daughter had recently died of the disease. Throughout the evening she was led in and out of this highly infectious room, in the hope that she would contract it. To the plotters' dismay, she remained healthy, though when she learned later about the fate of the general's daughter and the danger to which she herself had been exposed she knew she could never feel entirely safe again.

Clearly, both Catherine and Peter had enemies. Even those who wanted to support them and advance their interests were a danger to them. If only Catherine could become pregnant and bear a healthy child, the danger would recede, though it might never vanish entirely.

In the late spring of 1752, when Catherine was twenty-three and the court was in residence at the summer palace, she noticed that one of the chamberlains, the dark, suave, very handsome Sergei Saltykov, was more assiduous than usual in attending every function and social gathering. She could not help noticing him, he was "handsome as the dawn" and he stood out in contrast to his older brother Pierre, a hideous man whose pop eyes, snub nose and gaping mouth gave him the air of an idiot. Sergei and Pierre were of high birth and good breeding. Pierre was a tale-bearer, Sergei had a reputation as light-minded and narcissistic. Sergei's wife Matriona Balk was well known to Catherine, for she was among the women who devoted their time to making clothes for Catherine's clever little dog, Ivan. Eventually the dog became so attached to Matriona that Catherine made her a present of him.

In personality Sergei and Pierre were completely overshadowed by their constant companion Leon Naryshkin, a chamber gentleman barely out of his teens who was a natural clown. Leon was a big, corpulent, clumsy man who looked out of place in the resplendent garb of the court and whose grin and perpetual comic patter were disarming. "He was among the most singular people I've ever met," Catherine wrote in her memoirs, "and no one ever made me laugh harder. He was a Harlequin born, and had he not been born of high rank he could have made his living through his comic talents."

Among Leon's gifts was the ability to deliver a convincing lecture on any subject, whether he knew anything about it or not. He went on and on about anything and everything, from painting to chemistry to architecture, "using technical terms and going on for a quarter of an hour and longer, and at the end neither he nor anyone else had the faintest idea of what he was talking about." Everyone, especially Catherine, was reduced to helpless laughter.

While Leon Naryshkin was distracting the company with his inspired nonsense, Sergei Saltykov was ingratiating himself with the Choglokovs. With all the surface charm of a twenty-six-year-old man of the world, he insinuated himself into their circle, flattering the vain Nicholas Choglokov by telling him he had a gift for writing music, and turning all his solicitude on the pregnant Maria, who was often unwell. Catherine noticed what was going on, but did not mind. She liked looking at the man Petersburg society called, with a hint of disdain, "le beau Serge." His black hair, black eyes and rugged-looking dark skin seemed manly compared to her husband's adolescent pallor. Sergei remarked self-deprecatingly that, dressed in the prescribed white-and-silver "uniform" worn for court days, he looked like "a fly in milk." But Catherine found his looks compelling—as he thought she might—and could not take her eyes off of him.

Sergei was honey-tongued and full of compliments. It was obvious to Catherine that he wanted something—no one would deliberately seek out the companionship of the dull Choglokovs for their own sake—but she couldn't see clearly what that something was. Night after night Maria invited Sergei, along with Catherine, Leon Naryshkin, Pierre Saltykov, Catherine's friend Princess Gagarin and others, to join her in her apartments. There Sergei would amuse himself by drawing Nicholas Choglokov off into a corner near the stove and entreating him to compose a song—which preoccupied Nicholas for the remainder of the evening. (His songs, Catherine recalled, were quite pedestrian; he was, after all, "the most dull-witted man, without an ounce of imagination.")

With Nicholas out of the way, and Leon entertaining the assembled company with his hilarious absurdities, Sergei proceeded to attend to his deeper purpose. Night after night he displayed his wit, his savoir-faire, his self-deprecating charm. He knew full well that he had no equal in looks; now he showed his polish, his urbanity, the debonair manner that had always, until this moment, won him the prize he sought.

Then one night, choosing his time with great skill, he turned to Catherine and told her candidly that she was the reason he came to the Choglokov's apartments every night. She and she alone was the object of his desire.

At first she didn't answer him. Quite possibly she was genuinely taken aback by his words, and feared to acknowledge by whatever response she gave that she was attracted to him. He persisted, however, and would not leave her in peace.

What could he possibly hope to gain from a liaison with her? Catherine asked Sergei boldly. Just how far did he think it could lead?

It was the opening the deft seducer had been waiting for. He began to pour out his fantasies to her, drawing her in by confessing to her the depths of his ardor, the joy he would know when she was his at last. "He set himself to paint a picture of the happiness which he promised himself," Catherine wrote years later. "Actually it was rather laughable, as laughable as it was passionate." Laughable or not, Catherine was clearly vulnerable, and Saltykov knew it.

"I said to him, 'And your wife, whom you loved to the point of madness—as she loved you—and married only two years ago? What will she say about all this?' "

Here Sergei bent to his task. Handsome head down, eyes averted, he confided to Catherine that what appeared to the world to be a loving marriage was only a sham. He was in torment. Every day he paid a heavy price for the one heedless moment of blindness when he had deceived himself into thinking he loved Matriona.

"I did everything in the world to make him give up this idea," Catherine recalled. "I really thought I could succeed." But he elicited her pity; she listened, she succumbed.

Sergei knew how to play on a woman's emotions, and how to hide the calculating cynicism that lay behind his words. His honey-tongued glibness got around her defenses. His dark eyes, when he lifted them to her face, melted what resistance remained.

Catherine had been warned against him. Princess Gagarin disliked "le beau Serge," and Catherine usually listened to her. But in her unguarded state, her better judgment deserted her. There in the Choglokov's salon, warmed by wine and the heat of her youth, the philosopher who had sworn never to give in to her passions was caught in the silken snare of courtly love.

Chapter Ten

THE MINUET OF SEDUCTION LASTED FOR SEVERAL MONTHS.
Sergei advanced and Catherine retreated. She saw him nearly
every day, and as often as he could he told her how he dreamed of
her and longed for her. She kept him at a distance, trying to avoid
being alone with him, all the while feeling the delicious tension
between them, the lure of the forbidden and the dangerous promise of delights to come.

There is no hint, in Catherine's own accounts of her liaison
with Sergei, that she held back from encouraging him out of fear.
The climate had changed: the Choglokovs were now so impatient
to see that Catherine became pregnant that they were ready to
persuade her to take a lover. The empress had altered their man-
date. Where before they had been watchdogs, they were now to
be matchmakers. Elizabeth could no longer afford to let the realm
drift toward disaster; her nephew had to have a son and heir, and
if, as everyone said, he could not father one, then his wife must
become pregnant by another man. The Choglokovs were to make
certain that this desired outcome occurred, and soon.

Who better to play the role of lover to the grand duchess than
the handsome Sergei, who had made himself so agreeable and
who was evidently enamored of Catherine? Maria spoke to
Catherine, urged her to put aside her scruples concerning marital

fidelity and yield to Saltykov. Meanwhile Nicholas, who had been in disgrace for seducing one of the waiting women, Mademoiselle Kosheliev, had begun to flirt with Catherine himself.

Peter was complaisant; he liked Sergei, and was enough of a voyeur to enjoy watching the suave courtier pursue his wife. He was not in the least possessive, and although the succession was not a matter of complete indifference to him, how his heir was begotten apparently was. He stood by and let events unfold.

So Sergei continued his suit, and, for a time, Catherine held firm, treating Sergei with neither more nor less courtesy than anyone else, teasing him when he gave her no peace with his ceaseless declarations of love. "How do you know I don't have my heart set on someone else?" she asked him, but instead of discouraging him this only made him more urgent in his pursuit.

Summer came, and the Young Court, as the grand duke and grand duchess's circle was known, began its peripatetic rounds. Nicholas Choglokov gave a hunting party on an island in the Neva, and a select group of courtiers, including Sergei, was ferried across to spend the day in the fields. As Catherine remembered it afterwards, Sergei "seized a moment when the others were off hunting hares and approached me about his favorite subject." She listened with more patience than usual while he spun out his plan for their secret happiness, and he, noting that for once she did not raise a thousand objections, took advantage of her silence to show her how much he loved her.

For an hour and a half, isolated in their quiet refuge, Catherine listened to Sergei, while the chill wind swept up from the river and swirled around them. He begged her to let him believe that she was not entirely indifferent to him, and she, while feigning amused tolerance, was lulled to acquiescence by his words. "He pleased me," she wrote, even though she laughed at his vanity and found his ceaseless wooing somewhat wearying. Probably she was curious about love; after seven years of sham marriage, living amid sexual intrigue that seemed to touch everyone but her, reading romances and observing the unrestrained eroticism of the empress, Catherine must have yearned to be initiated into the mysteries of sexual passion.

"At heart I was convinced," she confessed in her memoirs, though she was still sufficiently in command of herself to tell Sergei to go "because such a long conversation could be suspect. He told me that he wouldn't go, unless I told him that I found him acceptable."

"Yes, yes, but go away!"

"I consider it settled then," Sergei said as he spurred his horse and rode off.

"No, no," she called out after him.

"Yes, yes," he shouted, his voice fading.

"So we parted," Catherine wrote, though it was with mixed feelings that she returned to the hunting lodge on the island to face Peter and the others. "A thousand worries filled my head that day and I was very cross with myself and discontented. I had thought that I could govern and discipline his head and my own, and now I understood that both our inclinations were difficult if not impossible to govern."

The elements too were wayward. As the company was eating supper the wind increased, and a storm blew in from the Baltic. The waters rose, the entire island was flooded and the lower floor of the hunting lodge was inundated, waves lapping at the staircase. Servants and masters alike were forced to take refuge in the upper story and wait for the storm to die down—which it finally did toward dawn.

Sergei, stranded with his beloved, was exultant. "The heavens themselves are favorable!" he declared, and strutted gleefully among the bedraggled courtiers, the image of the triumphant lover. The meaning of his elation was not lost on Peter, who commented to his valet soon afterward that Sergei and Catherine were "fooling Choglokov" and carrying on behind his back. Peter's current love was Catherine's waiting woman Martha Shafirov, and it could not have escaped his shrewd notice—as it did

Catherine's—that Sergei was carrying on more than one intrigue, pursuing both Peter's wife and Martha's sister Anna at the same time.

Sergei Saltykov's seduction of Grand Duchess Catherine was not merely tolerated but welcomed. The Choglokovs, realizing that Catherine might soon become pregnant with her lover's child, took steps to ensure that the child could be passed off as legitimate. To silence the rumors that Peter was still a virgin, Maria found an accommodating widow, Madame de Groot, who taught him what he needed to know. Peter's initiation into sex was publicized, and the stage was set for Catherine to ensure the succession.

Some time in the fall of 1752 Catherine conceived a child. Her memoirs are silent about these early months of her affair with Sergei—who was almost certainly the child's father. Whether love brought her elation, fulfillment, anguish, or perhaps disillusionment we cannot know. She did record that Sergei did not prove to be a steadfast, devoted lover; he was at times moody and distracted, he was only sporadically attentive to her (his romantic attentions were after all divided, as Catherine was later to discover), and his arrogance and conceit annoyed her. When she told him so he spouted a stream of persiflage and, drawing himself up to his full aristocratic height, accused her of failing to understand him. She was, after all, only a minor German princess by birth while he was a highborn Russian nobleman.

In mid-December the empress ordered the court to travel from Petersburg to Moscow. Catherine prepared to make the journey, but Sergei stayed behind with Maria Choglokov, who had just given birth and would not be fit to travel for several more weeks. Catherine had reason to suspect that she herself was pregnant, but decided to risk the rough roads to Moscow anyway. The going was hard, the road was cratered with deep ruts and jutting rocks. Instead of taking an easy pace, the drivers whipped the horses to a gallop and sped onward, day and night. Catherine was violently

shaken and jostled, and when the traveling party reached the last
coaching station before the capital she was seized with cramping
pains. She lost the child.

Her recovery was lonely and uncomfortable. Lodged in Moscow in a new and carelessly built wing of the Golovin Palace,
where the scuffling of rats kept her awake at night and water
dripped ceaselessly down the panelled walls, making the rooms
steamy with humidity, she tried to console herself for her loss and
to think kindly of her absent lover. When Sergei at last arrived
from Petersburg, he avoided her. Moscow was a large city, Sergei
told Catherine; he had many friends and relatives to see there, and
they lived at great distances from one another. Sergei was practiced at dissimulation, and he succeeded in throwing Catherine
into confusion. "To tell the truth," she wrote in her memoirs, "I
was afflicted, but he gave me such good and plausible reasons that
when I saw him and spoke to him my dire thoughts vanished."

Having just suffered a miscarriage, and aware, however much
she tried to deny it to herself, that her lover's ardor was cooling,
Catherine suffered through the dark winter days, ordering screens
put up in the room she shared with her seventeen waiting women
in order to create at least an illusion of privacy. She read, she
endured Peter's unwelcome intrusions and complaints, she
watched the rats scurry in and out of the worm-eaten wainscot-
ting and waited for Sergei's occasional visits.

She knew that she was more vulnerable than ever, now that she
had—albeit for the best of reasons—betrayed her marriage vows.
She needed a protector, and turned to the aging Chancellor
Bestuzhev.

Much had changed since Catherine's initial encounters with the
chancellor, when she first came to Russia nine years earlier. Then
Bestuzhev had seen Catherine as a pawn of the pro-French faction
at the imperial court, a young and dangerously precocious girl
whose elevation to the rank of grand duchess he opposed. Now
he saw her as an intelligent, potentially valuable political ally,

handicapped by her failure to have a child yet astute beyond her
years thanks to wide reading and shrewd observation.

And the chancellor stood in need of allies. He clung to his post
though the empress was at best lukewarm toward him and her
current favorites, the Shuvalovs, were doing their best to maneuver him out of office. When the empress died he would need the
approbation of her successor, and if Peter succeeded her then
Bestuzhev would value the support of Peter's wife, who was
likely to be a dominant force in the new regime. It was clear to the
chancellor, as it was to the grand duchess, that they stood in need
of one another; both welcomed a rapprochement.

Bestuzhev granted the benefit of his aid and protection to
Catherine and Sergei, becoming "very intimate with us," as
Catherine wrote, "without anyone else knowing anything."
Throughout the winter, while the courtiers spent themselves at
balls and masquerades, in pursuing petty rivalries and romantic
intrigues (Nicholas Choglokov embarked on a dangerous attempt
to seduce the ailing empress while Maria Choglokov carried on an
affair with Prince Repnin), Catherine met with Bestuzhev and
drew him surreptitiously into her circle.

There were many diversions that winter. Apart from the usual
ice sledding and sleighing parties, toboggan races and skating on
the frozen lakes and ponds, there was at least one near-fatal duel
and numerous accidents. Fires broke out all over Moscow.
Catherine recalled looking out the palace window and seeing
three, four or even five blazes going on in different quarters of the
city at the same time. The empress narrowly escaped serious
injury while on one of her pilgrimages to a nearby convent.
Lightning struck the main church and the ceiling fell in; fortunately Elizabeth had left the main sanctuary and was worshiping at a
smaller chapel on the convent grounds at the time.

The empress developed a new interest. When one of her chamber lackeys went mad, foaming at the mouth and raging, she
turned him over to Dr. Boerhave and instructed the doctor to

house him in a special room in the palace. From then on, when she heard of anyone who was similarly afflicted, she had that person brought to court and made a part of her small asylum. By the end of the winter she had quite a collection of lunatics: a major in the Semenovsky guards who confused the Shah of Persia with the deity; two other guards officers who had lost their reason; a monk—possibly a religious fanatic—who had cut off his genitals with a razor, and several others. The Semenovsky officer interested her the most, for apart from his delusion concerning the Shah he seemed quite sane. Elizabeth decided to take him out of Dr. Boerhave's care and turn him over to the priests. When the latter declared that he was possessed by a demon and performed the ritual of exorcism, the empress attended it, and was disappointed when the major, seemingly unaffected, continued to cling to his error.

Some said that the grand duke belonged in the imperial madhouse. He drank more heavily than ever, beat his servants mercilessly and lived in his own puerile world. He stayed away from Catherine, he complained about her and insulted her freely, yet he relied on her to help him administer his Holstein lands and to keep his servants in line. It irritated him, Catherine wrote, that he could not make himself obeyed even when he thrashed those who served him, while Catherine's servants carried out her commands without having to be told twice.

One day Catherine went to Peter's apartments and was struck by the sight of a huge rat hanging from a makeshift gallows erected inside a cupboard. The rat, Peter informed his wife, had committed a criminal act and, under the military code, deserved execution. It had chewed its way into one of Peter's toy fortresses and had eaten several of the tiny soldiers on parade there. The laws of war were harsh, Peter said. They demanded that the rat be captured, hanged, and left on the gallows for three days as an example to other rats who might be tempted to harm the ducal host.

Spring came, and in May Catherine was once again pregnant with Sergei Saltykov's child. With the arrival of good weather the Young Court left Moscow for Labritza, an estate some eight or nine miles away. The empress had recently given the property with its rundown stone mansion to Peter, and he had ordered a new wooden wing added to the crumbling stone of the old house. But the new addition was not yet ready, and so the guests slept in tents on the grounds.

Catherine, it seems, took only slightly more care to safeguard this pregnancy than she had her previous one. She lodged in a drafty tent, her sleep interrupted before dawn each morning by the sawing and hammering of workmen, her days spent following the hunt in an open carriage. On her return to Moscow a few weeks later she drowsed her way through the long summer days, but stayed up at night attending balls and suppers, and did not spare herself when it came to either food or recreation. As a result she was seized with sudden pains in her lower back, and when Maria Choglokov brought a midwife to examine her the midwife predicted that she would miscarry.

Once again Catherine lost her child, but this time the physical consequences were severe. The embryo was expelled, but part of the afterbirth remained, and for several weeks it was feared that Catherine might not survive. The gravity of her condition was kept from her, but she must have guessed that something was very wrong; the empress, that distant, disapproving being whom she rarely saw, suddenly appeared at her bedside with her most cherished relics in her hand and a look of concern on her jowly face.

The succession—and for a time, Catherine's life—hung in the balance, yet both Peter and Sergei stayed away, and after her initial visit so did the empress. For a time prayers were said and candles lit at the altars of Moscow's churches, but when the crisis passed and the grand duchess did not die she was left very much alone.

"During my six weeks of enforced rest," Catherine wrote in her memoirs, "I died of boredom. I had only Maria, and she came rarely, and a little Kalmuk, whom I loved, because she was amiable. I often cried from boredom." The days were unbearably hot, the nights fretful. Ill and full of ennui, in pain a good deal of the time, Catherine craved relief, stimulation, attention. She may have felt keenly the loss of contact with her mother, who following the death of Christian August had gone to live in Paris. She was forbidden to communicate with Johanna, but once in a long while she managed to find a traveler who would carry a letter to her in secret, and occasionally a visitor from the West smuggled in a reply. A year earlier, in 1752, Johanna had managed to send Catherine several lengths of rich fabric from Paris, but Maria had confiscated them immediately—leaving Catherine speechless with anger—and had sent them to the empress.

By fall 1753 Catherine was out of bed and restored to health, but her spirits were no brighter. She had failed twice to carry a child to term, and at great cost in security and peace of mind. She had let the callous Sergei toy with her emotions, trusting him and then discovering that he was unreliable, moody and at times alarmingly cool. The game of courtly love was proving to be sordid and anguishing, bruising to the heart and damaging to the ego. Yet Catherine had to continue to play it, she had no choice. There had to be an heir, and Sergei had to provide it.

Catherine was sitting in the Choglokov's salon in the Golovin Palace one chilly afternoon in November when she heard shouting in the corridor outside. Sergei and Leon Naryshkin burst in, yelling that a wing of the palace was on fire.

Catherine jumped up and ran to her own rooms, where her servants were rushing to remove as many of the furnishings as they could. Thick choking smoke was rapidly filling the hallways and anterooms, and the balustrade of the grand staircase, only twenty feet from Catherine's apartments, was already on fire. Room after room was consumed, flames devoured the rotting wood and made a terrible searing heat. As Catherine watched, thousands of black rats and gray mice filed in orderly fashion down the staircase and out to the safety of the courtyard.

Maria Choglokov and Catherine picked their way among the rats and mice and ran out of the palace, taking refuge in a carriage belonging to the Spanish singing master while they watched the terrible destruction. It had been raining for days, and the palace courtyard was ankle-deep in mud. Coughing servants struggling under the weight of trunks, boxes, beds and piles of linen staggered out into the open air and dropped their burdens into the mire, grateful to be out of danger. Catherine watched her domestics salvage her clothes, her jewels, a few of her desks and tables. She was worried about her books. For two years she had been reading Bayle's Dictionary, that monument to irreverence and sharply reasoned skepticism written in the last years of the previous century, and had been savoring each entry as she had once savored the astringent rationalism of Babette Cardel. She possessed four volumes of the dictionary, and feared to lose them to the flames. To her delight, her servants brought her the beloved books unscathed, and she felt immense relief.

Much was saved, but much more was lost. Paintings, hangings, priceless plate, furniture of inlaid wood and marble, jewel-studded gowns and untold finery fed the hungry blaze, until the entire palace was consumed. Peter's lackeys managed to save some of his chests of uniforms and trunks full of toy soldiers. His dozens of cupboards, stuffed full of empty wine and liqueur bottles, now lay in heaps exposed to the rain, their doors ajar to reveal the grand duke's private horde.

For three hours the flames burned high. The empress, who had been in another palace when the fire began, hurried back to survey the damage and supervise the vain attempt to extinguish it. "With all the coolness of mind imaginable," wrote one who saw her there, Elizabeth gave orders, clutching her relics and icons and praying for divine intervention. Her prayers were in vain. Most of her valuables were reduced to ashes, and it would be months, perhaps years, before they could be replaced.

Night fell but the orange glow of the fire made a false twilight that lingered in the vicinity of the palace for many hours. As each blackened timber collapsed, showers of red sparks rose into the dimness, until of the once splendid structure nothing but charred embers remained. The sharp stink of burned wood hung in the air, acrid and pungent, clinging to the clothes and hair and faces of those who had escaped the fire as they went about the task of salvaging what they could from the ruins. While they worked, the rats and mice swarmed in chattering hordes over the sodden goods in the courtyard.

For Catherine, her spirits low and her energies depleted, the burning of the royal palace may have symbolized a larger tragedy. She had been in Russia for nine years, and in all that time she had achieved little. Like the great palace, her life was in a state of collapse, her marriage a farce, her affair with Sergei Saltykov a betrayal of the love that still eluded her, her attempts at mother-hood a disaster. As she watched the massive structure burn, she must have been tempted to see in the blazing destruction the wreckage of all her hopes.

Chapter Eleven

Six weeks after fire destroyed the Golovin Palace in November of 1753, Empress Elizabeth presided over a grand New Year's banquet at a new palace she had had built in the interim. She had ordered workmen to take the great wooden beams from three other mansions and use them to erect a suite of apartments into which she moved in the last days of the old year. Moscow carpenters were accustomed to building rapidly; when the empress commanded, they obeyed. The structure was raised, walls of fresh green wood fitted into place, stoves installed, kitchens and storerooms constructed, furnishings brought in. By New Year's Day the palace was fit for holding court, and the empress sat in state under the royal canopy, her plump figure glittering with jewels, with Peter and Catherine beside her.

Elizabeth was "very cheerful and garrulous" on that afternoon, Catherine recalled in her memoirs. Though she had been suffering from a bad cough and had largely lost her appetite, she managed to conceal her illness, and looked better than she had in some time. She could no longer dance a minuet without having to lie down and rest for a long time afterwards, and climbing stairs had become too much for her. Special lifts were constructed that took her from one floor of her palaces to another, and when she visited the mansions of her wealthiest subjects, these had to be fitted out with mechanical devices to haul her from the entry hall up to the ballroom. But as long as she remained seated, the weakness in her legs was not apparent, and on this New Year's Day it was easy to forget that only recently her life had been despaired of and preparations had been made for an imminent change of reigns.

Long trestle tables filled the grand salon, and hundreds of courtiers sat in rows on hard benches, dining and drinking, with the empress's sharp eyes upon them.

"Who is that thin woman there?" she asked Catherine at one point, indicating where the woman sat. "The ugly one, with the long neck like a crane." The question was disingenuous; the empress knew perfectly well that the woman was Martha Shafirov, Peter's mistress, whom she herself had placed among Catherine's waiting women. One of her attendants informed her of the woman's name. She burst out laughing and leaned over toward Catherine. "That reminds me of a Russian proverb," she said. "Long necks are only good for hanging."

"I couldn't help but smile at this example of the imperial malice and sarcasm," Catherine recalled later. "It didn't go unnoticed; the courtiers overheard it and it got repeated so often that by the time I got up from the table I discovered that many people had already heard it."

Tweaking Catherine about Martha Shafirov gave the empress pleasure. She knew that Peter had been dallying with Martha—and, given her army of spies, she may well have known that Sergei Saltykov was carrying on an affair with Martha's sister, behind Catherine's back—and the reference to hanging was a very pointed one. Elizabeth enjoyed reminding people of her power, and indeed there was hardly a soul at the New Year's banquet who did not feel the oppressive weight of her authority and her potential vindictiveness.

On her good days, the empress was still formidable. She controlled her ministers, setting them against each other and keeping them off balance while profiting from their labors and their advice. Despite her distaste for the work of governing she kept herself more than adequately informed; she knew, for example, that her revenues were increasing, and that the gold and silver mines in Siberia were producing ore at a great rate. It seemed to her that there was more than enough money to pay for the enormous new Winter Palace she had ordered her Italian architect Bartolomeo Rastrelli to begin work on, and for the hundreds of new gowns she had bought to replace those lost in the fire. On her good days, Elizabeth reveled in her power, her wealth, her young lovers. On her bad days, however—and they now far out-numbered the good—she was full of fears.

For the Young Court was gaining influence. Everyone knew that Elizabeth's power, however awesome, was on the wane, and that of the grand duke and grand duchess was slowly rising. All the personnel of the court, from the most exalted ministers to the lowliest clerks, were aware that when the empress died, the new rulers would make sweeping changes in the government and the royal household. And they wanted to protect themselves and their positions by gaining the favor of the powers that were soon to be.

Foreign ambassadors residing at the Russian court speculated in their secret dispatches on precisely how and when the new regime would take over once the empress was out of the way. They assumed that Catherine would play a major role in that new regime—unless her husband found a means of ridding himself of her. Catherine, not Peter, was the obvious choice to succeed Elizabeth. She had intelligence, shrewdness and common sense; she had an evident stubbornness and force of will that made Peter look frail by comparison. But she had one overwhelming dis-advantage: she was still childless.

Within weeks after the New Year's banquet, however, Cather-ine was once more pregnant by Sergei Saltykov, and this time she was determined not to lose the baby. The empress gave orders that Catherine was to be protected and sheltered. Yet she sent her to live in an ancient drafty house with huge porcelain stoves so old that their walls were almost transparent and so full of holes that, when they were lit, sparks flew out and started small fires. Only constant vigilance on the part of the servants prevented a major disaster. Ill with morning sickness, her eyes smarting and burning from living in smoke-filled rooms, Catherine began her pregnancy with a constant sore throat and high fever. Boredom compounded her suffering, and she spent many a dull afternoon and long evening waiting in vain for a visit from Sergei, who seemed to have deserted her.

Toward the end of April Nicholas Choglokov died, his end deliberately hastened, it was whispered, by inattentive doctors in the pay of his political enemies—chiefly Ivan and Alexander Shuvalov. Alexander Shuvalov, "the terror of the court, the city and the entire empire," in Catherine's phrase, replaced Choglokov as head of Peter's establishment. Catherine went in dread of Shuvalov, not only because of the fear he inspired as head of the Secret Chancery but because of the grotesque tic that convulsed the right side of his face whenever he was gripped by strong emotion. The sight of Shuvalov's hideous grimace made Catherine shudder, and in an age when it was widely believed that whatever affected the mother affected her unborn child, the empress's choice of Shuvalov as the presiding spirit in the ducal household makes one question the sincerity of her concern for her niece.

Soon afterwards Catherine received another blow. Maria Choglokov was removed from court and it was said her place would soon be taken by Countess Rumyantsev, a troublemaker and gossip whose spiteful talk had injured Johanna many years earlier. The countess was a "sworn enemy" of Sergei Saltykov and no friend to Princess Gagarin, Catherine's closest companion. The meaning of her appointment was clear to Catherine, who "lost all patience" and cried bitterly at this "great misfortune." She felt certain that the countess would blacken her name, and do her great injury, and she begged Alexander Shuvalov to forestall the appointment.

The empress relented, and no more was heard of Countess Rumyantsev. Yet Catherine still had to endure the constant unwanted companionship of the gruesome Shuvalov, and a midwife was now assigned to watch her every move. In May the court traveled to Petersburg by slow stages, spending twenty-nine days on the road. On this journey Catherine was spared the rough jostling that had led to her first miscarriage, but she suffered nonetheless, confined for endless weeks with Shuvalov and his aggressive, impertinent wife and prevented from seeking even a brief passing conversation with Sergei, who was among the mounted escorts.

At last they arrived in the capital and for the next two months Catherine was wretched with apprehension, certain that Sergei would soon be sent away and fearing, in her most melancholy hours, that he might actually welcome the separation. She felt abandoned, ill-used, and utterly lovesick. "I was never without a tear in my eye and a thousand fears took possession of me," she wrote. She tried to throw off her dark mood by taking long walks, but could find no consolation.

When she entered her ninth month she learned that a birth chamber was being prepared for her within the empress's own suite. It was a severe shock. Clearly the empress intended closely to supervise every aspect of Catherine's labor and delivery. Catherine would be completely at her mercy. She was not to be allowed to give birth in her own bedchamber, in the presence of those dearest to her; she was to be deprived of friends, familiar possessions, familiar surroundings.

Alexander Shuvalov took her to see the birth chamber—a bare, bleak room furnished with a few plain pieces covered in crimson damask. Cold air off the Neva swept in through two large ill-fitting windows that didn't close properly. A tiny anteroom, also sparely furnished, opened off the main chamber. There were no comforts, nothing was being arranged for the new mother's ease or to help see her through the ordeal she would soon have to face.

"I saw that I would be isolated there," Catherine wrote, remembering her reaction, "without any sort of company, as wretched as a stone." Even Peter, whose companionship she normally loathed, would not be nearby, and this dismayed her. She blamed the disfigured Shuvalov, and complained to Princess Gagarin and Sergei. Both seemed concerned, but could do nothing.

After all, the baby she carried was a great treasure, the heir to the throne of the Romanovs. The child's birth would be something akin to a hallowed event, eagerly awaited and prayed for, a sign of divine favor upon Russia and her people. Catherine was to be the mere vessel through which the blessed gift would be bestowed. Her comfort or discomfort was of no significance in the light of the higher purpose she served. To suggest otherwise might be to call down the wrath of the empress.

Full of dread and misgivings, her heavy body unwieldy, Catherine was put to bed in the drafty birth chamber on the night of Tuesday, September 19. After several hours she awoke in pain, and the midwife was summoned. Her labor had begun.

Peter was awakened, along with Alexander Shuvalov—who sent word to the empress that Catherine's time had come. Elizabeth threw a cloak over her nightdress and came into the birth chamber, where Catherine lay on a hard pallet beside her bed, struggling and writhing in intense pain. On throughout the night the empress kept vigil, praying to her icons for a safe delivery, while the midwife prodded Catherine's belly and noted the frequency of the spasms that convulsed her.

All morning Catherine's agony continued, until at about midday the child was born at last. The midwife held him up: a boy, well formed and apparently healthy. As soon as he was washed and wrapped tightly in long strips of linen and flannel, following the Russian custom, the empress called in her confessor and told him to give the baby the name Paul. Catherine had not been consulted about the name; her wishes would not in any case have been considered significant. Paul had been the name of Elizabeth's brother, the first child born to Peter the Great and his second wife Catherine. He had not survived childhood.

As soon as the confessor finished his prayers the empress took the baby and, beckoning to the midwife to follow her, swept out of the room. Peter and the Shuvalovs also followed, leaving Catherine alone except for a single attendant, Madame Wladislava, who was so afraid of acting without the express orders of the empress that she neglected Catherine completely.

"I remained on my bed of misery," Catherine recalled in her memoirs. "I had sweated a great deal. I begged Madame Wladislava to change my linen, to put me to bed. She told me that she didn't dare." When Catherine asked for a drink of water she received the same response. For three hours Catherine lay where she was, cold, thirsty, and miserable, while the chill draft played across her sweat-stained coverlet. Madame Wladislava sent for the midwife, but the empress would not let her leave the newborn baby. Finally Alexander Shuvalov's wife looked in on Catherine, and was shocked to see her still lying on the hard pallet, in the same condition she had been in hours earlier. "It's enough to kill her!" she cried, and immediately went for the midwife. Half an hour later the midwife returned and ministered to her patient, putting her in her bed.

Even then, however, no one came to see her, and the neglect wounded Catherine deeply. Tears of anger and self-pity flowed freely as more hours passed and she remained in isolation. Rejoicing was going on all around her, in the empress's apartments, in the streets outside the palace, in Peter's room, where he devoted himself to carousing in celebration. But the mother of the heir to the throne had no part in the revelry. Stiff and sore, her breasts swollen with milk, full of longing to see the child that had been taken from her, she developed a high fever and a throbbing pain in her left leg.

The following day was much the same. Catherine "did nothing but cry and groan" in her bed, complaining to Madame Wladislava about her aching leg, watching the door and hoping that someone would at least send a servant to see how she was. But her only visitor was Peter, who came in for a moment and then left, saying that he was pressed for time.

"I didn't want to complain, or to give cause for complaint," she wrote. "I had too much pride. Even the idea of being in a wretched state was insupportable to me." She tried—through her tears—to maintain her dignity, but her suffering was acute. Hours passed. She heard artillery booming out across the river, all the bells in the city's hundreds of churches split the air with their ceaseless ringing. But the one sound she must have craved, the sound of her baby son's cries, was denied her.

On the third day following the birth one of the empress's ladies came in, not to inquire about Catherine's health, but to ask Madame Wladislava the whereabouts of the satin cape the empress had been wearing during her childbed vigil. The cape was found in the antechamber, and the attendant disappeared with it.

As Catherine was to discover later, there was an uproar in the empress's apartments. During the search for the cape, a packet of roots entwined with human hair had been found underneath the bolster of Elizabeth's bed. It was a charm, a thing of witchcraft. The empress erupted in hysteria. Next to assassination, she feared most becoming the target of sorcery. She recoiled from the packet as if from a snake, and ordered the hateful thing destroyed.

All the bedchamber women came under harsh scrutiny. Which of them had been doing black magic? Which of them had dared to place this wicked work of enchantment so close to the imperial head?

Suspicion fell on one of the empress's favorite waiting women, Anna Dmitrievna Dumachev, whose long friendship with her mistress made the Shuvalovs fear her. Anna was arrested, along with her husband and two young sons. She admitted, perhaps under torture, that she had concealed charms near the empress's person in order to bind the two of them together in friendship, and had also dosed the empress with adulterated Hungarian wine.

These admissions spread panic in the imperial bedchamber. For a time, even baby Paul was forgotten in the scramble to eradicate every evidence of witchcraft and purge the household of suspect servants. (Anna and her children were sent into exile; her husband, mad with terror, slit his throat with a razor.) By the time order was restored, several more days had passed and Catherine was beginning to heal.

All her concern was now focused on her son. She was desperate to hear whether or not he was thriving, and found a way to get word about him by secret means. For her to inquire directly about his welfare was all but forbidden, as it was taken to imply a criticism of the empress. She learned, to her dismay, that soon after birth he had developed ulcerated sores around his mouth, making it hard for him to suckle and thus imperiling his life. The sores eventually healed, but he was not out of danger. The nurses and old women who surrounded him all but smothered him with their unhealthy attentions. The empress herself ran to him—limping on her weak legs—whenever he cried, and he was kept in an overheated room, swaddled in flannel, under piles of coverlets of velvet and black fox fur.

Catherine was not allowed to attend the baptismal ceremony for Paul, but the empress did visit her afterward in order to present her with a draft on the imperial treasury, to be redeemed for a hundred thousand rubles, and a small cask of jewels. The jewels were scanty and of relatively little value—a necklace, a pair of earrings and two rings, all set with inferior stones and of undistinguished workmanship—but the treasury draft was very welcome, as Catherine had exhausted her allowance and was heavily in debt. She looked forward to receiving the actual coins. But when in due course the cabinet secretary, Baron Czercassov, appeared to honor the treasury draft he was empty-handed. The hundred thousand rubles intended for Catherine had in fact been paid to Peter, he explained; hearing that Catherine was to receive a large gift, Peter demanded one of equal size, and as there was not enough ready money in the treasury to cover both gifts, Catherine would have to wait for hers.

The days dragged by, autumn was ending and winter was closing in. Catherine returned to her own apartments, but, following tradition, remained in seclusion, with only her maids of honor to attend her. From time to time Peter paid her a visit, not because he was eager to see his wife but because he had become captivated with the least attractive of her women, the vulgar, pockmarked Elizabeth Vorontzov. Peter's flirtation aroused Catherine's pique, yet the impact of his waywardness was dwarfed by weightier sorrows. She learned that Princess Gagarin, her closest companion in recent years, was to be married and sent away from court. And she was informed that Sergei Saltykov was soon to depart on a mission to Sweden to announce the birth of the heir to the throne. His return could not be expected for many months.

That which she had dreaded most had come upon her. Sergei, having served his purpose in fathering her child, was to be kept away from her—perhaps indefinitely.

"I burrowed down further into my bed and curled up with my afflictions. I pled illness, I said that the pain in my leg had gotten worse, and I couldn't get up. But the truth was that I was unable to get up. I was so heartsore that I did not want to see anyone."

Catherine saw no one—but little Paul received visitors by the score. Everyone wanted to look at the long-awaited baby, lying in his fur-lined cradle. The empress mothered him, prayed over him, worried and fussed around him endlessly.

"How brown he is!" the courtiers exclaimed slyly, knowing that his father was the dark Sergei Saltykov and not the grand duke, who was as pale as a mushroom. But Elizabeth didn't care. She dismissed all references to Paul's doubtful paternity by muttering that he would not be the first bastard to be born into her family, and made no attempt to silence the stories about Catherine and Sergei. All that mattered was that a male heir had been born to the grand duchess. A child for the empress to love and foster, an assurance of continuity for the dynasty.

So maternal did the empress appear that a rumor arose at court that Paul was in fact her own child and not Catherine's. Despite her advanced age and multiple infirmities, Elizabeth did not seem utterly incapable of motherhood. Besides, she was known to consort with young and virile lovers. Why couldn't she have given birth to a child late in life?

The empress did nothing to silence the rumor, and she waited nearly six weeks before allowing Catherine even the most fleeting glimpse of her child. "I thought he was very beautiful," Catherine wrote, "and seeing him made me a bit happier." Yet he was snatched away almost immediately, and she felt more bereft than ever.

On November 1, the day set aside for Catherine to receive the official congratulations of the courtiers, servants decorated the grand duchess's bedchamber in unaccustomed splendor. Finely wrought couches and tables, rich hangings, elegant paintings and objets d'art were brought in to replace her own furniture, making the room nearly as grand as the empress's own bedchamber. The centerpiece was a magnificent bed, upholstered in rose-colored velvet embroidered in silver.

On this royal bed Catherine reclined in state, and waited patiently as one by one the members of the imperial government and household, the ambassadors from foreign courts, dignitaries from the city and members of the nobility passed before her, each of them kissing her hand. She was the picture of modest, radiant motherhood, an arrestingly pretty young woman whose delicately tinted white skin had only the faintest of blemishes, whose chestnut brown hair was thick and curly, her figure slim and her hands and arms as finely shaped as those of a classical statue. She spoke to each of her visitors in pleasant tones, and gave each an amiable smile. Only her eyes, large and blue and troubled, revealed what she had endured and was enduring, though she did her best to keep them bright.

After several exhausting hours the reception finally ended, and Catherine sank back gratefully into the rose velvet cushions. She was not allowed to rest, however. As soon as the last guest left, the empress's servants appeared and whisked away all the splendid furnishings. Every table and chair, every vase and candlestick was carried out, until the room was stripped of its elegance and left in its former condition. Even the great rose-velvet bed, a bed fit for the mother of a future emperor, was dismantled and taken away, its occupant left to stand unsteadily on her sore leg and ponder her fate.

Chapter Twelve

NEGLECTED AND ABANDONED, DENIED NOT ONLY THE comfort but the very sight of her baby son, Catherine turned inward, to the resources of her keen and ever-hungry mind. Where another woman might have gone mad or succumbed to illness or depression, Catherine retired to a small, ill-lit chamber—the only refuge she could find from the freezing wind off the river—and began to read.

She devoured Voltaire's *Universal History* (Voltaire was becoming her favorite writer) and a history of Germany, a thick pile of books in Russian, including two immense volumes of church history translated into Russian from the Latin of the erudite sixteenth-century historian Cardinal Baronius, Montesquieu's *Spirit of the Laws* with its acute and eloquent analysis of the origins and forms of governmental power, and Tacitus's *Annals*.

Voltaire amused her, Baronius filled her head with information, Montesquieu intrigued her, but it was Tacitus who fired her imagination and broadened her understanding. The *Annals* told the history of Rome during the unsettled years of the early Empire, a time of decadence and cynicism when the heirs of Augustus battled for preeminence. Republican ideals had crumbled, moral niceties were forgotten; palace intrigues and the brute force of the Praetorian Guard made and unmade emperors with bewildering frequency. Bewildering, that is, to the uninitiated, the naive outsiders who inevitably became the victims of all the perfidy and treachery. The insiders, those who had learned not only to watch their backs and protect themselves but to go on the offensive and hobble their enemies before they could be destroyed by them, succeeded in steering events to their own advantage.

Catherine, smarting from the effects of years of ill-use and insults, brimming with resentment and, despite her recent misfortunes, bursting with ambition, read Tacitus and envisioned her revenge. She would no longer be a victim. She would adopt the tactics of the victors of Tacitus's Rome, and so protect her interests in Elizabeth's Russia. Her eyes had been opened, she would never again be the eager young girl, desiring above all to please others. From henceforth others would be made to please her.

Reading Tacitus, Catherine wrote afterward in her memoirs, "made a singular revolution in my head, to which, perhaps, the sad disposition of my spirit at that time contributed more than a little. I began to see things in a black hue, and to search for deeper causes."

Winter closed in. The river was frozen, the pale, watery sun rose late and swam along the horizon, a yellow-gray blur, for only a few twilit hours. Catherine remained closeted in her pocket-sized room, napping on a chaise longue, reading at a small desk, her injured leg propped on cushions. Though she did her best to shield herself from frigid draughts, she caught cold again and again, and with the colds came fever. After two months of isolation she left her room to attend the long Christmas services, but was assailed by chills and pains and a very high fever, which sent her back to bed for days.

All winter long she nursed her revenge, ruminating on the play of faction and petty conspiracy at court in the light of her new-found understanding of the ways of the world—and the world of the court in particular. She was determined to remake herself. "I gathered my forces," she later wrote. "I made a firm resolution not to leave my room until I had regained enough strength to overcome my hypochondria." While the courtiers spent themselves in celebrating the birth of Paul at balls and masquerades, with illuminations and fireworks, while Peter and his entourage of guardsmen and hangers-on drank and reveled noisily amid clouds of reeking tobacco smoke, Catherine stayed in her ascetic retreat, growing stronger and more sure of herself. By the time Carnival season was over, she had forged a new persona.

The first test of her newfound resolve was painful. Sergei Saltykov returned to Russia from his long sojourn at the Swedish court, and was in no hurry to see Catherine. She knew, for Bestuzhev had kept her informed, that while in Sweden Sergei had resumed his flirtatious habits. This combined with his reluctance to resume their affair was telling; in her heart of hearts Catherine knew that he would be glad not to have to go on with their torturous liaison. Yet she had her pride—and her desire—to contend with. A clandestine meeting was arranged, but though Catherine waited in some anxiety until three in the morning for Sergei to arrive, he never came. She felt the snub keenly, and saw clearly that she had suffered a great deal over a man who was unworthy of her sacrifice. She had given birth to his child, she had been deprived of his presence for many months—months spent in much agony of spirit. Yet he cared nothing for her suffering, and could not even be bothered to keep a rendezvous with her.

She wrote Sergei an angry letter, condemning him for his treatment of her, and this brought him immediately to her apartments. Once in his presence she softened momentarily, and let her old infatuation rule her, but she soon steeled herself against him and all the others who had misused her. She resolved to let no one hurt her again with impunity, and when Sergei persuaded her to end her long isolation and make an appearance in public she made a formidable impression on all who saw her.

Peter's birthday was approaching, and the court gathered to commemorate the occasion. Catherine had her dressmakers make her a superb gown of blue velvet embroidered in gold, and in this she swept into the assemblage, tall, slim, and pink-cheeked, looking every inch the wife of the heir to the throne, and the mother of a future emperor. She drew stares. Worried glances and whispers followed her as she moved adroitly around the room, turning her back on the Shuvalovs and their confederates and showering their enemies with special attention and favor.

There was no mistaking the change in Catherine. Her assurance, her bold and entirely unexpected assault on the empress's favorite Ivan Shuvalov and his cousins Alexander and Peter startled all observers. Her bright laughter and pleasant voice carried throughout the room, making wicked fun of the Shuvalovs, ridiculing their stupidity and foolishness, exposing their malice. Her sarcasm was her best weapon; she was skilled at inventing quips and jibes and retailing stories that caught the imagination of the courtiers and were endlessly repeated.

"I stiffened my backbone, I walked with my head held high," Catherine wrote afterwards. "The Shuvalovs didn't know which foot to dance on." They huddled together in alarm, aware that Catherine posed an unforeseen threat to their dominance.

Catherine had thrown down the gauntlet to the most powerful faction at court. Alexander Shuvalov was not only head of the Secret Chancery and a preeminent voice in the royal council but head of the Grand Duke Peter's household. Alexander's brother Peter held the reins of finance and had enriched the country through his encouragement of commerce and factory-building, besides playing the key role in expanding Russia's army and holding the post of Master General of the Artillery. And the handsome, cultivated Ivan Shuvalov, nominally a chamberlain in the royal household, was the most influential of all, the empress's lover and intimate, a lover too of all things French who encouraged Elizabeth to adopt French styles in dress, manners and culture and to speak only French among her courtiers.

In opposing the Shuvalovs Catherine was aligning herself not only with those, such as Chancellor Bestuzhev, who were their personal enemies but with a political policy of opposition to

France and affinity with the German states and with England. This was a natural orientation for the Young Court, given Catherine's origins, Peter's fixation with Holstein and his idealization of Frederick II of Prussia, but there was a danger in it. Russians remembered with bitterness the reign of the German Empress Anna, Elizabeth's predecessor but one, who during her ten years in power had abused her subjects and burdened them with such heavy taxation that they all but starved. Nature itself seemed to rise up against Russia under the rule of the cruel Anne and her German minions, afflicting the people with huge storms and widespread famines, plagues and voracious fires that destroyed what little the empress left them with.

Beyond this, Empress Elizabeth had an abiding hatred of Frederick of Prussia, and Prussia's commanding military might and continual aggression were an ongoing threat not only to Russian sovereignty but to the political stability of Europe.

Catherine began to take a more aggressive role in court politics and foreign policy just at the time when Europe's precarious stability was threatening to collapse. Once again the expansionist ambitions of Frederick II were making war seem unavoidable, and Russia's treaties with her western European allies made it impossible for her to avoid becoming involved—though the empress was loath to go to war.

In June 1755 a new British ambassador arrived at Petersburg. He was Sir Charles Hanbury-Williams, a veteran diplomat albeit a less than distinguished one, a stout, ruddy Englishman in his forties with literary tastes and a quick wit. His mission was delicate: to persuade the empress and her ministers to commit Russian troops to the defense of Hanover in the event of a Prussian attack. (The English King, George II, was also Elector of Hanover; he was passionately devoted to the smaller of his two domains and, as he had no army of his own to speak of, he had to rely on foreign arms to defend his German territory.)

That Russia was predisposed to oppose the armies of Frederick II was not in doubt. What was in dispute was the price

Britain would have to pay to gain the Russian assistance. It was over this point that negotiations had broken down during the ambassadorial tenure of Hanbury-Williams's immediate predecessor, with the British convinced that the Russians were venal and the Russians skeptical of Britain's good faith.

Hanbury-Williams was a seasoned diplomat, but not an altogether tactful one; he had quarreled with Kaunitz, Maria Theresa's chief minister, had embroiled himself with Frederick of Prussia and his officials and showed a perverse talent for offending the great and the near-great with his outspokenness and lack of finesse. His wit was often cutting, and he lacked the discipline to hold his tongue. But he was a perceptive observer, and his government—which was not being entirely candid with him—relied on him to be Britain's eyes and ears in Russia at a crucial time.

In this they were not disappointed, for Hanbury-Williams's letters and dispatches during his mission to Russia offer a discerning glimpse of Elizabeth's court and its personalities.

He took up residence in a grand house on the Neva, which he rented and furnished at his own expense (heretofore the court had undertaken to provide the British ambassador with a furnished house), even sending to Britain for live goldfish to swim in the mansion's chilly ponds. He brought several dozen servants with him, and hired dozens more Russians to keep the stoves stoked and the kitchen provisioned. He was expected to hire Russian bodyguards, at a considerable expense, and complained of having to pay £60 a year to be guarded "against nobody," as he put it, by sixteen men and a sergeant who moved into his house and made a nuisance of themselves.

Hanbury-Williams was accustomed to foreign courts, having been in the diplomatic service for many years, but the Russian court amazed him. He had never seen anything like its extravagant luxury, the thick encrustings of gold and showers of gems with which the empress surrounded herself. Elizabeth's magnificent palaces, with their enormous salons and banks of sparkling crystal chandeliers, light glinting from a thousand facets, their intricately inlaid floors and tall mirrors reflecting every gleaming gem and spangle, their rich woven hangings and furnishings of polished wood and porcelain and marble were far costlier and more ostentatious than any royal dwellings the Englishman had ever seen. Even the renowned splendor of Versailles was not to be compared to the grandeur of the Russian palaces, where the smallest and humblest rooms were ornamented in solid gold and guests were served fine champagne in golden goblets and slices of pineapple on golden plates.

"The accidental expenses of this court are very high," the diplomat wrote to his superiors, hoping for an additional subsidy. He lacked the finery to make a decent appearance among the empress's opulent courtiers, and had to order new clothes at great personal expense. Even so, his velvets and brocades and flowing lace were shabby compared to the dazzling costumes of the great nobles.

Alexei Razumovsky, the village shepherd from Tchemer, launched a fashion for wearing diamond shoe buckles and diamond belts; on his broad shoulders blazed diamond epaulets from which hung the twinkling Orders his sovereign had granted him. The other prominent men around the empress were equally prodigal with their wealth. If Razumovsky ordered a carriage from Paris worth three thousand rubles, his rivals had to have carriages worth four thousand and more. Alexander Shuvalov dressed his footmen and even the meanest of his pages in liveries of cloth of gold, and was said to order his own superb costumes from his tailor not singly but in tens. General Apraxin, another of the gilded elite, never traveled without his collection of jeweled snuff boxes (he had one for each day of the year) and liked to round out his dinner parties by standing on the balcony of his Moscow mansion and tossing handfuls of gold coins and valuable trinkets to the beggars in the courtyard below.

The women of the court were no less gorgeously arrayed. Their wide silken gowns whispered across the parquet, their throats and wrists were thickly encircled with gems, from their hair gleamed diamond aigrettes and diamond-studded ribbons. Every woman wanted to be judged handsome enough to have her portrait hung in the empress's Cabinet of Modes and Graces at Peterhof, where some three hundred beauties smiled down from the walls. The empress could no longer pretend that she was the reigning belle of her court; age and illness had stolen her preeminence. So the women competed more openly than in the past for admiration, and Hanbury-Williams was astounded by the quantities of silver lace and gold embroidery, waving plumes and flashing jewels with which they adorned their gowns.

Among the women the Grand Duchess Catherine would have stood out even if her rank had not distinguished her. "Her person is very advantageous, and her manner very captivating," the Englishman wrote. He watched her walking with head held high, magnificently gowned, carressing her friends and hurling carefully worded barbs at her enemies. She was becoming a master politician, and he was impressed with her.

Seated next to Catherine at imperial banquets, Hanbury-Williams had ample opportunity to take the measure of her mind and judgments as well as her personal attractions, and he found her conversation "worthy of the good sense of Richelieu and the genius of Molière." Each sparked the other's wit. They discovered that they had read many of the same books, that they shared an admiration for Voltaire and an aversion to pretention in all its forms. ("I know of no dish so agreeable as good sense seasoned by ridicule," the diplomat remarked to Catherine, "when a conceited ignoramus or false confidence produce such fare." She heartily agreed.)

With the empress in failing health, and her successor rapidly descending into drunken impotence (Hanbury-Williams judged Peter to be "weak and violent"), Catherine appeared to be the natural heir to power. He wrote to his superiors in London that should Elizabeth die suddenly, Catherine would rule. For despite his petty cruelties, his clumsy posturing and unbounded ego, Peter deferred to his wife when it came to matters of substance.

He bowed to her breadth of knowledge; according to the ambassador, Peter told people that "though he did not understand things himself, yet his wife understands everything." He called her "Madame la Ressource."

Hanbury-Williams was struck by how intelligently Catherine had adapted herself to her circumstances. "Since her coming into the country," he told his superiors, "she has by every method in her power endeavored to gain the affection of the nation." She had applied herself to learning Russian, spoke it fluently (if imperfectly) and understood it very well. She had made herself "esteemed and beloved" to a high degree, the ambassador thought, adding that Catherine "has a great knowledge of this empire and makes it her only study." "She has parts and sense," he concluded, "and the Great Chancellor tells me nobody has more steadiness and resolution."

Certainly steadiness and resolution, not to mention common sense, were in short supply at the imperial court. "The court is governed by passion and events, and not by reason," the Englishman concluded after he had been in Russia six months. The empress, with her persistent coughing and breathlessness, her weakened limbs and swollen body, still ruled, though with a palsied hand. The Shuvalovs lacked the boldness to seize power, yet they made mischief; should a forceful French ambassador be sent to the Russian court, Hanbury-Williams thought, he could work through the Shuvalovs to undermine and gravely damage British interests.

The ambassador cultivated the friendship of the grand duchess, and she responded with all the warmth of a cultured woman starved for urbane company. They conversed at supper parties, he visited her at Oranienbaum where Catherine and Peter spent more and more of their time, and where she oversaw the planting of extensive gardens. She introduced him to her gardener Lamberti, who dabbled in prophecy and who predicted that Catherine would not only become sovereign Empress of Russia, but that she would live to see her great-grandchildren and would not die until she was well over eighty years old.

Together the ambassador and the grand duchess watched with a mixture of embarrassment and horror as the scandal of the summer unfolded.

Peter, already viewed with contempt for his love of Germany and Germans, now brought on himself the deep and abiding resentment of the Oranienbaum household troops. Most of these soldiers were Finns, from a region called Ingermanland. They were loyal to the Russian throne, but their loyalty was severely tested when the grand duke, their nominal commander and a lieutenant colonel in the honored Preobrazhensky regiment, began wearing the uniform of a Holstein officer and brought to Oranienbaum in the summer of 1755 a large contingent of Holstein soldiers.

The Holsteiners set up camp on the grounds of the grand ducal estate, at some distance from the mansion and outbuildings. There they raised their tents, established their arsenal and stabled their horses. They were a ragtag little army, not regular soldiers but vagabonds and drifters, runaway apprentices and deserters from the armies of a dozen German princelings. Many were not from Holstein, not a few were runty boys who could barely hold their muskets. Still, they were Peter's men, his very own, his toy regiments come to life. He drilled them as he had once drilled Catherine and his servants, waving the long military whip he carried, shouting commands, teaching them to march and countermarch with something like precision.

So enamored was the grand duke of his lifesize toys that he set up a tent alongside them and lived in their camp, carousing with his men, sharing their cheap brandy and their tobacco, drinking in the gratifying noise of their rough German speech and imagining himself back in Holstein.

By his side was his newest adviser Colonel Brockdorff, a tall, swaggering Holsteiner with limited intelligence and a large capacity for liquor. In his scarlet colonel's coat and tricorn hat, Brockdorff was a highly visible presence, and to the Russian troops a highly irritating one, especially when he ordered the Russians to serve the Holsteiners as menials.

The Holsteiners had to be fed; having no provisions of their own they were dependent on the Oranienbaum kitchens. So it fell to the household guard, who murmured among themselves that the Holsteiners were traitors and spies for the Prussian king, to carry out trays of food and drink to the despised foreign visitors and scrape up their leavings once they had dined. No extra pay was offered them for this service, and this, added to the insult itself, made them mutinous.

"Now we've become valets to those damned Germans!" they shouted, cursing Brockdorff, the Holsteiners, and the strutting grand duke.

As for Catherine, she held her peace in the face of this grand fiasco, though she let it be known that she did not approve of what her husband was doing. She taunted Brockdorff openly, calling him "a good-for-nothing and an idiot" and referring to him as "the pelican." He in turn called her "the viper" and used his influence with Peter to widen the gap between the spouses.

Catherine confided to Hanbury-Williams, as the summer wore on and the presence of the Holsteiners continued to offend not only the palace troops but the public in general, that her husband's behavior was becoming more and more disturbed. With Peter's enthusiastic approval, Brockdorff was serving as master of ceremonies for a perpetual round of drunken revels and dissolute supper parties that ended in "real orgies." The reek of sour wine, strong tobacco and unwashed linen clung to the grand duke and drove others away. His breath, never sweet, had become nauseatingly foul and his tantrums had become frenzies of sadism.

Catherine discovered him, when he thought he was unobserved, beating his dogs, or having his servants hold the helpless creatures by their tails while he whipped them without mercy. In his twisted mind he was convinced that the animals had committed some offense; they required correction and punishment. The sight of her husband's cruelty made the tender-hearted Catherine weep, but when she protested, he only lashed the poor beasts harder with his whip and she was forced to leave the room. Peter despised pity, Catherine thought. It made him angry, and drove him to worse atrocities. She knew that this was only one of many signs that his mind was unhinged—though she did not dare say so in so many words.

She thought she knew what had unbalanced him. As she wrote in her memoirs later, Peter had developed, in his early twenties, "a thirst to reign." Knowing that he was heir to the Swedish as well as the Russian throne, he nourished a secret wish to be rescued from Russia by a call to become King of Sweden. In 1750 he thought that opportunity had come, but in the end events proved that he had been mistaken.

"He died of envy," Catherine wrote. His disappointment gnawed at him, and made him bitter. Now he was trapped, forced to live in a place he hated, under the thumb of an aunt who despised him and whom he had come to abhor, yoked to a wife whom he could not love and who was in every way more capable than he was. His thirst to reign was certain to be thwarted, for the kingdom that would one day be his was galling to him. Hence his uncontrollable drinking, his spasms of sadism, the caustic inner rage that ate away at him and caused him to take leave of his senses.

As ever, Catherine fell victim to his dark moods. A few months before Hanbury-Williams's arrival in Russia Peter had come staggering into Catherine's room, shouting and waving a sword, "reduced to brute animalism," as she put it, by drink and furious anger. He told her that she was becoming insupportably proud, backing her up against the wall and threatening her with his sword.

She played along with him, fending him off, as she often did, with good humor. "I asked him what this meant," she wrote later in her memoirs, recalling the distasteful scene, "whether he was going to fight with me. In that case I'd need a sword too."

He sheathed the sword and told her scathingly that she was unbearably malicious. His speech was slurred but Catherine understood; he was complaining of her newfound boldness and assurance, her open attacks on the Shuvalovs.

She faced him, she did not back down. "I saw clearly," she wrote, "that the wine had separated him from reason." She told him firmly to go and lie down, and Peter, his head swimming and his brief burst of hostility past, staggered off to do as he was told.

She had won. She had nothing more to fear from Peter, for the moment. She had no illusions about him, she knew that he needed her and would continue to need her more and more in the future. Yet he was and would remain her enemy, and an enemy of the most dangerous kind, unpredictable, irrational, full of festering resentment.

Catherine had kept all this to herself. But now that Hanbury-Williams was on the scene, offering her his amusing company, delighting in her friendship, showing himself in every way her ally, she at last had someone to confide in. She knew full well that in cultivating her friendship the ambassador was furthering his own interests, and she was not above using him in turn to advance her own security and achieve her private ends. She gave him a great deal of information useful to his government; in return she asked him to loan her large sums of money, and used some of it to pay her informants who served in the empress's household.

But self-interest apart, the friendship between the middle-aged diplomat and the steadfast, resolute and embattled grand duchess flourished, and both were benefited. Catherine, who had heretofore had no political mentor but Bestuzhev, looked on Charles Hanbury-Williams as nothing short of a gift from heaven.

"What do I not owe to the providence which sent you here, like a guardian angel, to unite me with you in ties of friendship?" Catherine wrote to her English friend in April of 1756. "You will see, if one day I wear the crown, that I shall partially owe it to your counsels."

Chapter Thirteen

LATE IN OCTOBER OF 1756, THE EMPRESS SANK DOWN ON HER swollen legs and collapsed in a dead faint. Immediately her waiting women crowded around her, shrieking and calling for her surgeon, who came at once and put his ear to the old woman's chest.

She was breathing, but just barely. Low rasping sounds came from her lungs, and each breath moved through her throat with a strangulated cough. Her eyes were shut tight, and even though the women tried again and again to revive her, rubbing her feet and shouting into her ears, holding stinking bunches of herbs under her nose and applying hot and cold cloths to her temples, she remained in a corpselike stupor, the muscles of her face and jaw slack and her skin the dead white of marble.

Her confessor was summoned, she was lifted into bed and covered with fur blankets. The little knot of old women who had been keeping watch over her in recent months, peasant healers from the countryside, shook their heads and crossed themselves repeatedly. Their prognostications had erred. They had been certain that, though weak, the empress was gaining strength; each night they had watched the waning moon, confident that when the new moon rose in the sky, she would begin to throw off the ills that had assailed her. Now, however, they were sure of nothing, save that the imperial physician, the Greek Condoidi, had given up hope and that most of the courtiers expected the empress to die.

"A little patience, I implore you," the Greek was overheard to say to one of the old women after she had been keeping vigil at Elizabeth's bedside for two nights. "You have not much longer to wait. She cannot live."

Elizabeth had been dangerously ill for months. A stroke had laid her low at the beginning of the summer. Severe pains in her stomach, her legs, her head all tormented her, and she could hardly speak a word without bringing on fits of coughing. So tender was her tormented flesh that her women could no longer lace up her gowns without giving her unbearable pain. So she had the gowns cut from her body, and draped herself in long shapeless robes. In these she dragged herself from room to room, determined to appear in public despite the agony it cost her. She could not afford to have it known that she was dying, not with her country at war and the succession uncertain.

Peter and Catherine were kept out of the way at Oranienbaum, and little Paul, now two years old, was kept near his great-aunt in the imperial nursery. The empress's young relative Ivan, the former boy-emperor whom she had deposed many years earlier, had been brought from his exile in Siberia to the fortress of Schlüsselberg nearer to the capital, and from there, in great secrecy, he was smuggled in to the Winter Palace so that she could observe him.

Hidden behind a screen, through which she squinted at the pale, undersize creature she had kept in prison nearly all his sixteen years, Elizabeth listened while others interviewed Ivan. Once or twice she put on a man's boots, loose trousers and tunic, and talked to the boy briefly herself, without letting him suspect who she really was.

Ivan was a sorry specimen. His long years of isolation, his almost complete lack of education and normal companionship had made him feeble, a near-idiot. He was not a realistic alternative to either the infant Paul or the besotted Peter as heir to the Russian throne.

The succession weighed on the declining empress almost as heavily as the war in which her country had recently become embroiled. The armies of Frederick II were advancing, and the empress, when she was able to rouse herself, raved on about how she was going to lead her soldiers into the field herself against the hated Prussians.

"How can you?" one of her attendants asked her. "You are a woman."

"My father went," the empress replied. "Do you believe that I am stupider than he?"

"He was a man," the other insisted, "and you are not."

It was an unwise encounter. The attendant, who should have known better, succeeded only in making the cantankerous old woman even more irascible. She had been more irritable and peevish than ever since her stroke, frequently reverting to childish petulance. Now she swore angrily that she would go and join the soldiers, no matter what anyone said, and made a pathetic effort to get up and do so. Of course her frailty quickly defeated her, and the effort tired her and brought on terrible pains in her abdomen. Still, she would not be quietened, and Condoidi had to be brought in—he was always available, having moved into a room next to the imperial apartments—to give her drugs to put her to sleep.

On throughout the summer and early fall the death watch continued. Courtiers tiptoed through the corridors of the palace, vigilant for news from the sickroom, waiting for bulletins from the doctors and conferring about the latest information they had. Some said the empress had "water in the belly," which was known to be fatal. Others expected an imminent attack of apoplexy to be the agency of death. Hanbury-Williams's informants brought him word that the empress's "trouble" was "in her womb," a cancerous growth that would soon kill her.

All but breathless, half-drugged, suspicious of everyone around her, even her doctor (she clutched Condoidi's sleeve in her claw-like grip and forced him to swear that he was really treating her for illness and not being bribed to poison her), Elizabeth fought for life. When on October 2 a comet was visible in the sky, even at midday, she snatched her icons and held them to her chest in terror. Comets were known to be harbingers of death, and within hours of the visitation in the heavens one of the courtiers, Baron Stroganov, fell dead. The empress dreaded that she might be next, and her symptoms grew worse. She felt faint, and went into convulsions. "The fingers of her hands were bent back, her feet and arms were cold as ice, her eyes sightless," Catherine wrote to Hanbury-Williams. "They drew much blood from her, and sight and feeling returned."

Finally, after three weeks of increasingly severe attacks, in the last week of October the empress fell into a deathlike faint and entered what everyone at court believed would be her last relapse. The scramble for power began, and all those with political aspirations positioned themselves to fulfill them.

Peter Shuvalov set about raising a private army of thirty thousand men, and there were rumors that the Shuvalovs were plotting to capture Ivan, set him on the throne and make him their puppet. Catherine, who had been making plans with the aid and advice of Hanbury-Williams and Bestuzhev for over a year, braced herself to act as soon as she received word of the empress's death, and called in those pledged to aid her.

Peter, informed of the Shuvalov army, rushed to his wife, "full of alarm," as she wrote, "for in moments of great crisis he looked to me alone to suggest remedies." His Holsteiners had been sent back home, he no longer had them to rely on, and though he still had his Russian commands he would have been justified in doubting whether or not the Russian soldiers would obey him. He was in panic. The threat from the Shuvalovs "seemed to him terrible," and he did not know where else to turn.

Catherine managed, with difficulty, to quiet her husband and to make him feel some degree of confidence in the plans and preparations she had made. Their safety depended on the speed with which they acted, she explained, once the empress died. And she would know almost as soon as it happened, thanks to the three paid informants she had secured among the women who served the empress in her bedchamber.

Once word reached her that the empress had breathed her last, Catherine told Peter, she would send a trusted envoy to make absolutely certain that there had been no mistake. Then she would go immediately to Paul's nursery and fetch her son, whom she would entrust to a man whose loyalty to her was beyond doubt, Count Kiril Razumovsky—brother of the empress's husband and prior favorite Alexei Razumovsky—and Razumovsky's band of guardsmen. If through some mischance the count was not to be found, she would take Paul to her own room, meanwhile sending off swift messengers to alert five guards officers in her pay who would each bring fifty men to protect her, along with Paul and Peter. Each of these men had been heavily rewarded (with money Catherine received from the British government via Hanbury-Williams), and had sworn to take orders from no one but Catherine herself or Peter.

This done, Catherine said, she would enter the death chamber herself, summon the captain of the guard, and demand that he take an oath of loyalty to her and to Peter. Members of the imperial council and General Apraxin, the highest-ranking general, would also be summoned. Presented with a fait accompli, they could be counted on to agree to support Peter as emperor. If they balked, or if the Shuvalov faction attempted to order in their own forces or to interfere with Catherine's arrangements, her own sworn lieutenants would arrest them.

She had thought through this plan carefully—bearing in mind the lessons she learned from her reading of Tacitus—and had bought the loyalty of large numbers of guardsmen. Some, particularly the lower grade officers of the imperial bodyguard, were ready enough to follow her even without bribes. She had won their devotion over many years. They saw her—and not her husband—as Empress Elizabeth's natural successor. Most of the officers, Catherine told Hanbury-Williams a few months before the crisis of October 1756, were "in the secret." She relied on them to support her, though she was well aware that the Shuvalov faction would attempt "every dirty trick" in the first few hours after the empress's death.

The key to success or failure lay in the loyalty of Count Razumovsky, a few key guards officers, and the household troops. She believed that they would be reliable, that they would not desert her when the moment of truth came. But even if they did, she was determined to go down fighting. "I am resolved," she told Hanbury-Williams, "to perish or to reign."

Yet Catherine would not reign alone. The foundation of all her plans, her bribes, her carefully nurtured alliances was that her husband would wear the crown, while she would be, as she had always been, his principal adviser and supporter. Many said that Catherine ought to be, if not empress in her own right, at least co-ruler with Peter. Hanbury-Williams, who was Catherine's principal sounding board and mentor at this time, was confident that, whoever wore the crown, Catherine alone would in fact rule. ("You are born to command and reign," he told her. "You do not realize your real power. You have a great deal.")

Bestuzhev, whose own political position had become very tenuous as a result of the Shuvalovs' rise to preeminence, believed that Catherine ought to rule entirely on her own, or as regent for her infant son, and drew up elaborate written plans to that effect. (He did not say what was to become of the unfit Peter.) But Catherine, realizing the extreme danger she would be in in the event that the empress did not die and these documents came into her possession, prudently told the chancellor that his plan could not be put into effect.

She did not dare to admit that she, too, foresaw herself ruling alone, yet her correspondence with Hanbury-Williams assumed a future in which, having come to the throne, she did not share power. She knew perfectly well that no one at Elizabeth's court believed Peter capable of governing; if he reigned, it would be as a puppet ruler, with Catherine pulling the strings.

She already envisioned herself as empress, and referred to herself as such in her letters to the British ambassador. She told him how grateful she was for his support and advice, and assured him that when the time came she would repay him with imperial lavishness. "The empress will repay Catherine's obligations and her own," she wrote, giving herself a dual persona, adding "I shall try, as far as my natural weakness will allow me, to imitate the great men of this country." She had been reading about Russia's "great men," including Peter the Great and the fearsome tyrant Ivan the Terrible. She dreamed that one day her name, like those of Ivan and Peter, would "adorn the archives" of the European states.

Dread, apprehension, and an exhilarating excitement filled the short October days. Catherine knew that much was expected of her, that many people looked to her to lead them. She was not at all certain of her ability to lead wisely—though she felt more certain of her courage. ("There is no woman bolder than I," she told one courtier. "I have the most reckless daring.")

"I tell you in confidence," she wrote to Hanbury-Williams, "that I am afraid of not being able to live up to a name which has too soon become famous." She did not trust herself to maintain her independence of judgment. She knew that she had weaknesses, and that her vanity and ambition made her vulnerable. "I have within myself great enemies to my success," she confessed. She could not even be sure that she would not lose her "reckless daring" should she come face-to-face with Shuvalov's men, muskets at the ready, or traitorous soldiers of the household guard.

No one could foretell what would happen once the empress expired, for with her last breath all order would vanish. What if the Shuvalovs were better prepared than Catherine herself was for the transition of power? What if they had anticipated her carefully laid plans, and had already arranged to checkmate her whichever way she turned?

"The nearer I see the time approaching, the more I am afraid that my spirit will play me false, and that it will prove nothing but tinsel or counterfeit coin," she told her confidant Hanbury-Williams. "Pray heaven to give me a clear head."

When her apprehension grew, she drew on a unique source of hope. She had come to believe that a force greater than herself was guiding her toward a predetermined destiny. How else could she account for her survival? She had been through so much—severe illness, excruciating tension, prolonged over years, privations and dangers. "The invisible hand which has led me for thirteen years along a very rough road will never allow me to give way, of that I am firmly and perhaps foolishly convinced," Catherine told the ambassador. "If you knew all the precipices and misfortunes which have threatened me, and which I have overcome, you would place more confidence in conclusions which are too hollow for those who think as deeply as you."

There was one complication that even the invisible hand had not been able to prevent, however. Nearly every day Catherine's head throbbed and her stomach heaved. She was fairly certain that she was pregnant again.

The father of her child was a sweetly handsome, softspoken young nobleman who was Sir Charles Hanbury-Williams's secretary. Stanislaus Poniatowski was fair, with widely spaced hazel eyes and a bow-shaped mouth as pretty as a woman's. He was younger than Catherine, twenty-three to her twenty-six when they met, and his face combined choirboy innocence with a feline grace.

In the sordid world of the court, Poniatowski stood out as a model of innocent love and guileless affection. Before leaving Poland he had promised his mother that he would not drink or gamble, and that he would not propose to any woman until he was at least thirty. He did not promise chastity, yet the easy, complaisant amours of court life held no charms for him. He was intimidated by dalliance and intrigue, and when he fell in love with Catherine—his first love—he had every intention of loving her until the day he died.

Poniatowski was as different from the practiced seducer Sergei Saltykov as it was possible to be: fair where Saltykov had been dark, reserved where Saltykov had been aggressive, thoughtful and cultivated where Saltykov had been reckless and shallow. And most important, where Sergei Saltykov had seen in Catherine a dangerously exciting challenge to his powers of conquest, Poniatowski saw in her a radiantly beautiful, highly intelligent woman who was at the peak of her attraction. He admired and loved her, as only a soulful, reflective young man can love.

And Catherine, basking in Poniatowski's admiration, her boldness coming to the fore, embarked on a rash and exciting romantic adventure.

Poniatowski suited her very well—far better, in fact, than the tall, pale Count Lehndorff whom Bestuzhev had brought to court in hopes that he would help Catherine forget Saltykov. Lehndorff had good looks, but Poniatowski had a melting tenderness and trusting affection that was balm to her wounded spirit. He was in the entourage of her dear friend the British ambassador. He shared her love of French books and English government. Of the quality of their passion no evidence remains, but to judge from his letters, Poniatowski was an unusually sensitive, even poetic man who was morbidly afraid of giving offense. (Once when he thought he had displeased Charles Hanbury-Williams he threatened to throw himself off a high wall. The ambassador, horrified, forgave whatever minor infraction the young man was guilty of and begged him not to think of destroying himself over such a trifling matter.)

Though Peter was largely indifferent—and even, eventually, jokingly encouraging—to Catherine and Poniatowski's affair, discretion was still necessary and to Catherine, the need for secrecy was itself seductive. She liked arranging hurried, private trysts. She liked knowing that, at any moment, a guardsman or servant might come upon them by accident, and report their intimacy to the empress. They met as often as they could, at least once a week and sometimes two or three times. Leon Naryshkin gave them a refuge away from the palace, and Catherine, unable to trust her ladies, stole out of her apartments and put on the breeches, ruffled shirt and jacket she borrowed from her Kalmuk hairdresser for the walk to the Naryshkin mansion. Several times, having spent a long evening there, she had to walk back alone, braving the dangers of the dark streets.

"We took a singular degree of pleasure in these furtive meetings," she wrote in her memoirs, recalling her affair with Poniatowski. Certainly she enjoyed them; Poniatowski, aware of what had happened to Saltykov as a result of his liaison with Catherine and having read that Russian princesses treated their lovers harshly once they tired of them, may not have been so sanguine.

Escaping in secret from the palace, wearing disguises, dodging the empress's spies and then, her heart beating fast with excitement, falling into her lover's arms: it all brought a glow to Catherine's cheek and a shine to her eyes. The Chevalier d'Eon, a French spy who saw her at this time, wrote a memorable description of her.

"The grand duchess is romantic, passionate, ardent; her eyes gleam, fascinate, they are glassy, with the look of a wild beast. She has a lofty brow and, if I mistake not, there is a long and terrifying future written upon that brow. She is affable and obliging, but when she comes near me, I instinctively recoil. She frightens me."

The chevalier bore witness to Catherine's feral side. There had always been a wildness in her, even in childhood. Now, like a caged animal that has found a way to escape, she roamed free— although her freedom had distinct bounds, and she never forgot them. It was, in fact, only the illusion of freedom, for it was not long before her involvement with the cherub-faced Polish count was common knowledge at the court. The affair was tolerated primarily because Poniatowski's politics were acceptable to Bestuzhev and his imperial mistress.

Catherine and Poniatowski had been lovers for half a year and more, and then, in August of 1756, he had been sent back to Poland. Catherine's nausea and headaches began not long afterwards, and she thought Poniatowski had left her with a child. She did all she could to have him recalled to the imperial court, though her need for him had none of the desperation or anguish of her previous need for Saltykov. And with the empress's worsening health, other concerns were far more pressing.

Her stomach churning with nausea, her head throbbing, Catherine worked at her desk, alert throughout the day and much of the night for bulletins from the empress's sickroom. She was her own secretary, reading papers and writing responses, communicating with those loyal to her, copying out sheet after sheet of large thick writing paper in her own hand. "Since seven in the morning until this moment," she wrote to Hanbury-Williams, "omitting the hours for dinner, I have done nothing but write and read documents. Might it not be said of me that I am a Minister of State?"

Already, as the old reign waned, Catherine was feeling the weight of responsibilities she would soon bear. Several years earlier she had taken over management of her husband's Holstein domain—an arrangement that relieved Peter and gave Catherine a taste for governing. Now she was confronting the much greater task of imperial rule. It was all-consuming, fatiguing—all the more so given Catherine's daily sick headaches—but at the same time exhilarating. When she ran out of documents to read and respond to, Catherine put her hand to another task, that of writing her memoirs.

She was only twenty-seven, yet her life had been more eventful than that of most sixty-year-olds. She had spent nearly half of it in Russia, contending with the fierce climate and the treacherous hostilities of the court. At the suggestion of Hanbury-Williams, she made an effort to set down her recollections of her childhood, her education, the development of her mind and temperament, the course of her marriage. It was the sort of task to which she was well-suited. Her strong self-regard, her intellect, all those faculties of mind and spirit that had shored her up throughout her long ordeal, were now given voice.

The days were growing shorter, the air wintry. Cold drafts

swirled through the old empress's bedchamber, where she lay, pale and still, beneath a mound of fur blankets. A week passed. Still the wasted lungs pumped air, the ravaged throat gurgled with life. The old women who had been keeping their death watch around her bed began to mutter to one another.

Another week went by, and the court officials, their nerves in tatters from long anxious days and tense nights, took to their beds, leaving orders with their servants to awaken them the instant anything important happened. The Shuvalovs, sensing a change in the wind, paid off their soldiers and sent them away—with instructions to return on short notice. Peter, still fearful but easily distracted even in the midst of his fears, flirted with a niece of the Razumovskys, Madame Teplof, and invited a German singer called Leonora to dine with him in private in his rooms. Catherine's sick headaches got better, and then—much to her relief—her body gave her evidence that she was not, after all, pregnant with Poniatowski's child.

Condoidi, the imperial surgeon, was weary and exasperated. His patient refused to die. Fits of coughing still tore through the empress's chest but a hint of color had returned to her face, and she opened her eyes. The pallor of imminent death gave way to the faint bloom of reviving health. Condoidi had to admit the probability that she would recover.

The peasant healers nodded sagely to each other and pointed to the sky. They had been right after all, the doctor was wrong. Each night they stood at the windows of the imperial bedchamber, looking out into the blackness, watching for the rising of the moon.

Chapter Fourteen

PETER HAD FOUND THE LOVE OF HIS LIFE. TIRED OF SEDUCING worldly singers, promiscuous court ladies and innocent young serving girls, he found a soul mate in Elizabeth Vorontzov, the foulest and ugliest of Catherine's waiting women, and gave her his heart.

Even as a child Elizabeth had been singularly unattractive. When brought to court at the age of eleven as a maid of honor to Catherine, she had offended the eyes of the other women. Lame, squint-eyed and graceless, she developed into a blowsy, buxom girl who belonged on a farm and not amid the fine stuffs and marble halls of the palace. Fair skin was prized, but Elizabeth's was swarthy and coarse, and when after a few years in Catherine's service she contracted smallpox, her complexion was splattered with the marks of the pox and with lingering clumps of angry red scars that quite disfigured her. Only her high birth—she was the niece of Michael Vorontzov, ally of the Shuvalovs and Bestuzhev's rival in the imperial cabinet—protected her from being sent away from court. Elizabeth Vorontzov was not only ugly, she was gauche and ill-mannered. Her insolence and loudmouthed ranting drove everyone away and disrupted dinners and parties. She learned to swagger and swear like a soldier, and attacked anyone who tried to correct or restrain her. By the time she reached young womanhood she had become a brash, vulgar hoyden who rarely bathed and who punctuated her bursts of verbal abuse with generous sprays of spittle.

Peter saw in Elizabeth a kindred spirit. Like him, she was spoiled, undisciplined and ill-tempered—and physically unattractive. Like him, she enjoyed drinking and had the manners of a raucous barmaid. She invariably disturbed and upset people, just as he did. Peter had always preferred low company to the decorous, often brittle courtiers with their polished manners. It amused him to watch Elizabeth's rudeness collide with the finely honed civility of Catherine and her ladies. Indeed he found in the brassy, provocative eighteen-year-old Elizabeth the perfect foil for all that he disliked about the imperial court—and the perfect mistress with which to insult his wife.

Peter was in need of distractions. His worst nightmare had come true: Russia had gone to war against his idol Frederick the Great, and had actually won a major victory against the Prussians at Gross Jägerndorf. He wept, not only for the humiliation of the Prussians but because he was convinced that, had he not come to Russia, he would be a general in Frederick's army, a military hero and a leader of men. He tried in vain to ignore the disturbing probability that Russia would win the war, taking out his frustration and anger on the elite Russian guards units, whose members he snubbed and insulted, praising Frederick within their hearing and wearing a conspicuously large ring with Frederick's picture on it.

Privately, Peter compensated for his inability to take part in the war on the Prussian side by bolstering his military persona. His rooms, which had been cluttered with toy soldiers defending miniature fortresses, now became arsenals stocked with muskets, swords and pistols. Every summer his Holstein troops overran Oranienbaum in growing numbers, attracting hordes of camp-followers from Petersburg and turning the palace grounds into an open-air military camp complete with taverns and whorehouses. Hosting feasts for these boisterous guests was among Peter's chief pleasures; he and Elizabeth Vorontzov presided over long trestle tables where the wine flowed freely and entertainment was offered by singers and dancers from Peter's own opera company.

When the Holsteiners returned home in the fall, Peter continued to surround himself with military men, having none but common soldiers serve him in his chamber, and going nowhere without his coterie of two dozen Holstein officers, headed by the offensive Brockdorff. Brockdorff and Catherine were more than ever at odds. According to Catherine, who gave her husband and all his low-life companions a wide berth and retired to her apartments when their coarseness was at its loudest and most unruly, Brockdorff was a magnet for adventurers and tavern scum from all over, Germans and Petersburgers both, men who "had no faith, obeyed no law, did nothing but drink, eat, smoke and talk crude nonsense."

Without Catherine's influence to restrain him, Peter let his imagination fly, and began telling stories about how, as a boy in Kiel, hardly out of childhood, he had been sent by his father to fight bands of murderous gypsies and had vanquished them in mighty combats. In his darker moods, he went to Ivan Shuvalov and begged him to persuade Elizabeth to let him go abroad for a while, until the painful conflict with Prussia was over. When she refused, he began drinking more heavily than ever, and stumbled about the palace shouting wild threats in slurred German.

Poniatowski, who returned to the Russian court in January of 1757, looked on Peter as a farcical bumpkin too far gone in his cups to be taken very seriously. The Shuvalovs too laughed at the grand duke behind his back, dismissing him as a hopeless inebriate who could not live long. But Catherine, who was only too aware of the atmosphere of "extreme dissipation" in which her husband lived, was wary of him nonetheless. The empress hovered between life and death; every few months she had a relapse, which sent the entire court into a panic and unleashed a fresh scramble for influence with the Young Court. Peter could become emperor at any time. And Catherine knew, through her spies, that Peter had confided to the new British ambassador Lord Keith that he intended to divorce her and marry his mistress.

Peter had a plan, of that she was certain. He no longer looked to her for information, advice, consolation in times of crisis. His visits to her rooms were far less frequent than they had been, and although he appeared to be affable toward Poniatowski, liking the multilingual Pole because he could converse with him and confide his troubles to him in German, Catherine was suspicious of this surface congeniality. She was convinced that Peter was only biding his time, waiting until the empress was out of the way before he rid himself of her. The strident Elizabeth Vorontzov and her ambitious uncle were now giving the grand duke all the advice he craved, telling him to send his meddling wife away and make Elizabeth his consort.

On one point at least Peter needed no advice. He knew well, as Catherine did, that the church not only permitted divorce, it provided another convenient option to husbands desiring to disentangle themselves from unwanted marital unions. An irksome wife could be sent to a convent, where, with or without her consent, she would be immured with other rejected women—and wives who had run away from their husbands to the safe haven of the church. There she would be stripped of all that had bound her to the world, her possessions taken away, her head shaved, her body swathed in somber black. Never again to see her children or her other relatives, she would spend her life among those dead to the world like herself, without hope of rejoining the living.

Every time Catherine encountered the foul Elizabeth Vorontzov, or heard Peter carrying on with his low-life intimates, she shuddered. Peter was nearly always irritable with her, and though she knew that at least some of his irritability was the result of his being heartsick over the Prussian losses on the battlefield, she could not help but be aware that his attitude toward her had changed, probably permanently. In all likelihood, while Peter lived she could never again count on being safe from humiliation and the enduring threat of harm.

The triumphant Catherine leading her troops against Peter III in June 1762.
Engraving by Cockerell, from a portrait by Vigilius Ericksen.
Photograph courtesy of Hulton Deutsch.

Medal struck to commemorate the accession of Catherine II. Photograph courtesy of Hulton Deutsch.

Sergei Saltykov, Catherine's first lover and father of Paul I. Photograph courtesy of Hulton Deutsch.

Peter III. Engraving from a painting by G. C. Grooth.
Photograph courtesy of Hulton Deutsch.

*German Glass commemorating a
Russian victory over the Turks.*
Photograph by Ivor J. Mazure, Dealer
in Russian Antiques, London.

*Medal struck to commemo-
rate Alexis Orlov's
victory over the Turkish fleet
at Chesme.*
Photograph courtesy of
Hulton Deutsch.

Gregory Potemkin, the great love of Catherine's life and her trusted partner in the work of governing.
Photograph courtesy of Hulton Deutsch.

Catherine in middle age, dressed with "English simplicity" and accompanied by one of her greyhounds as she walks in the park at Tsarskoe Selo. Engraving by Borowikowsky.
Photograph courtesy of Hulton Deutsch.

Alexander Lanskoy, Catherine's beloved favorite who but for his tragically early death would have been "the comfort of her old age."
Photograph courtesy of Hulton Deutsch.

Catherine's portfolio or briefcase, with the monogram "E" for Ekaterina. For Catherine, work always came first.
Photograph courtesy of Hulton Deutsch.

Catherine at 57, a popular engraving after a painting by Schibanoff.
Photograph courtesy of Hulton Deutsch.

The elderly Catherine.
Photograph courtesy of
Hulton Deutsch.

Emperor Paul I.
Photograph by Ivor J. Mazure, Dealer
in Russian Antiques, London.

Partly to placate her choleric husband, and partly to impress her rivals and observers watchful for signs that the Young Court might be in eclipse, Catherine gave a grand ball in July of 1757. Entertainments of this sort were always looked on favorably by the empress, who had herself wheeled in, coughing and clutching her side, to watch the festivities from behind a screen.

Catherine outdid herself in planning her fete, and nature cooperated. It was the season of the long "white nights," and on the appointed evening the air was balmy. Long supper tables were laid in the sweetly scented garden, and the hundreds of guests arrived to find the Great Walk lit by thousands of lanterns, brightening the twilit night with such a blaze of illumination that objects appeared with the clarity of day. At the end of the first course a wide curtain was drawn back to reveal, in the distance, an immense wheeled vehicle pulled by twenty garlanded oxen. Seated on the huge cart were sixty musicians and singers, performing music and poetry specially commissioned for the occasion from the court poet and the singing master of the imperial chapel. Hundreds of dancers capered along beside the musicians as the cart rolled majestically toward the gathered company. Just as it reached the vicinity of the supper tables, the huge yellow moon rose behind it, as if orchestrated to match the unfolding spectacle.

Later in the evening, a fanfare sounded and the diners were invited to help themselves from little shops giving away fans, gloves, sword-knots, ribbons and china—fripperies each worth less than a hundred rubles, Catherine wrote in her memoirs, but which gave the recipients great delight. Still later, when vast quantities of wine had been served and the risen moon flooded the grounds of the mansion with silvery light, the dancing began. Forgetting for the moment all but their pleasure, intoxicated by the wine, the warmth and the moonlight, the guests whirled and stomped and gyrated until long after cockcrow the following morning.

The fete was a huge success, untarnished by spiteful carping or petty intrigues. In its immediate aftermath everyone, from the empress to the lowest servitor, lavished praise on the grand duchess and professed to be ecstatically happy with the fine wines, the excellent food, the entertainment and generous gifts. Even Peter, his rowdy Holsteiners and Catherine's bitterest enemies were temporarily won over by the great banquet and ball, and displayed their souvenirs proudly.

"This was given to me by Her Imperial Highness the Grand Duchess," people told one another, holding up their trophies. "She is goodness itself, she gave everyone presents." "How charming she is; she smiled at me quite pleasantly." "It pleased her to see us dance and eat and enjoy ourselves."

The talk went on for days, reported to Catherine by her informants and recorded by her later in her memoirs. Her good cheer and good humor were remarked on. It was noted that she went out of her way to make a place at her ball for everyone, even those with little or no social standing. A thousand new virtues were discovered in her.

"I disarmed my enemies," Catherine wrote. "That was my goal. But it was not to be for long." She spent a sum equal to nearly half her annual income on the entertainment—relying on money given her by England, through the good offices of Charles Hanbury-Williams, to make up the deficit. Yet her political cause was all but lost. Her great friend and mentor Sir Charles was recalled to England a month after Catherine's extravagant ball, his mission a failure, and was replaced by the mediocre diplomat Lord Keith who from Catherine's point of view could not even begin to take his place. Catherine wrote Sir Charles a tender letter, thanking him for all that he had taught her and for his invaluable support. "Farewell," she wrote, "my best, my dear Friend."

English influence was at its nadir; instead, the French had moved into preeminence at the Russian court. A new French ambassador, the Marquis de L'Hôpital, arrived at Petersburg in the summer of 1757, bringing with him not only a large staff and household but a host of spies. Now that Russia was allied with

France against the Prussians, and with Russian arms proving to be victorious in the field, the political interests of the Young Court were in decline. Catherine, Peter and the Chancellor Bestuzhev continued to look to England as Russia's staunchest and most advantageously placed friend, but the Shuvalovs and their ally Michael Vorontzov sided with the French, and they had the empress's ear. Elizabeth had always hated Prussia and the Prussians, and she had never really liked Bestuzhev; she despised Peter, and while she had from time to time shown affection for Catherine, it was nearly always barbed and at best intermittent. Clearly the political shift toward France was a threat to Catherine's security, no matter how many balls she gave.

And she had another grave concern. She was nearly five months pregnant with Poniatowski's child, and on the afternoon of the day she gave her ball, while riding in a carriage to inspect the preparations, she suffered a jarring fall. All that evening, while entertaining her guests and impressing them with her affability, she was afraid that she might miscarry. Fortunately she escaped danger, yet her hidden worries must have been great as she moved among her guests, choosing carefully which ones to caress and which to snub, the image of regal serenity.

Her pregnancy advanced smoothly, though the court plunged from rejoicing at the summer's military victories to anxiety when the empress had another stroke—a more severe one—in September. Since Catherine had already borne a son, her second pregnancy was not looked on as crucial to the succession. Yet precisely because of this, the issue of the child's paternity was an uncomfortable one. Peter, perhaps out of pride, refused to swear that the child was not his, but everyone at court knew that Poniatowski was the father.

Beyond this, Catherine had another worry. What if the empress died while she was in labor, or in the first few weeks after her delivery, when she would be too weak to defend her interests and put into effect the contingency plan she had been polishing for several years? Her enemies might then take advantage of her—or

Peter might choose that time, when she was at her weakest, to declare her an adulteress and order her removed to a convent.

It was in the fall of 1757, Catherine wrote in her memoirs, when the empress was bedridden in the aftermath of her stroke, that she began clearly to perceive her choices for the future. Peter was angry at her during October and November, for her increasing heaviness made it difficult for her to preside at public functions—which meant that he was pestered by the court officials to do the honors. He disliked having his desires thwarted; when he was preoccupied with arranging his private arsenal or drinking with his mistress he hated having to be interrupted to do something else. Catherine saw him, and her own situation, through new eyes in those tense months.

"Three routes, all of them equally dangerous, lay open to me," she wrote. "First, I could share His Imperial Majesty's fortunes, whatever they might prove to be. Second, I could make myself vulnerable to whatever fate it pleased him to accord to me. Third, I could chart my own course, no matter what happened. Put more clearly, I could perish with him, or at his command, or else save myself, my children and perhaps the state from the shipwreck which threatened."

Only the third course made sense, though it took all of Catherine's vaunted daring to adhere to it. She resolved, in the final months of her pregnancy, to continue to advise Peter on those increasingly rare occasions when he came to her, but not to offer any views which might offend him, and for the most part to wrap herself in what she called "a doleful silence" and look out for her own interests and those of her children as best she could.

During the night of December 8 Catherine's labor pains began. She sent Madame Wladislava to announce the fact to Peter and, through Alexander Shuvalov, to the empress. The midwives assembled and the "bed of misery" was prepared. After several hours, with Catherine suffering intense but infrequent contractions, Peter entered the birth chamber.

He was in full battle dress, wearing his Holstein uniform,

booted and spurred and with a sash across his thin chest holding his gleaming medals. An immense sword hung at his waist.

Astonished at his appearance, Catherine forgot her pains and asked her husband why he had gone to such trouble with his toilette at two-thirty in the morning.

"Only in times of need do we know our true friends," he answered in a dull monotone. "In this uniform I am ready to do my duty, and the duty of a Holstein officer is to obey his oath and defend the ducal house against all its enemies. As you are ill, I have come to offer you my aid."

Catherine had to look twice to make certain Peter was not speaking in jest. He was a pathetically comic figure, standing there in his polished boots, his long sword at the ready, amid the heaped towels and steaming bowls of the birth chamber. Then Catherine saw his glazed eyes, and realized that he was so drunk he could barely stand. She urged him to go away and lie down, lest the empress see him and be offended both by his uniform— Elizabeth detested the sight of the Holstein uniform—and by his drunkenness. He was reluctant to go, but with the help of Madame Wladislava and the midwife, who assured Peter that his wife would not give birth for several hours at least, Catherine finally persuaded him to leave.

Soon afterwards the empress arrived, and demanded to know why her nephew was not present at his wife's bedside. She was placated with lies and, after satisfying herself that the birth was not imminent, she too left.

Exhausted, her pains subsiding, Catherine managed to sleep until the following morning, when she got up and dressed as usual. Apart from an occasional twinge, she felt well, and decided that the previous night's episode had been false labor. She ate a hearty dinner, and the midwife, sitting beside her as she ate, urged her to eat still more, saying it would do her good. Then, just as she rose from the table, a new and terrible pain gripped her and she screamed. At once the midwife and Madame Wladislava seized her arms and took her back to the birth chamber, and Peter and the empress were summoned once more. Within a very short time Catherine was delivered of a daughter, and the empress, who barely managed to arrive in time to witness the birth, was informed that the baby was a girl.

Catherine asked to be allowed to give the baby the empress's name, but Elizabeth refused. She had already decided on a name: Anna Petrovna, after her own late sister, Peter's mother. So Anna Petrovna it was. Catherine barely had time to glimpse her daughter before she was snatched up and installed in the empress's apartments, along with little Paul.

Once again, in the aftermath of her delivery, Catherine was ignored and neglected. The empress gave orders that no one was to go near her. Madame Wladislava waited on her, but no one else came to inquire after her welfare or to congratulate her. "I was abandoned, left all alone like some poor wretch," Catherine wrote. "As before, I suffered a great deal from that abandonment." This time, however, she had taken precautions to remove herself from drafts and had arranged her bedchamber so that she had a great deal of privacy.

After a few weeks she discovered a way to circumvent the empress's ban on visitors and entertain her preferred companions—Poniatowski and several of her ladies—by concealing them behind a screen. When Peter Shuvalov, whom Catherine called "the court oracle," came in to spy on the grand duchess, he found her alone. (Her friends, holding their breaths and smothering their giggles, stayed hidden and afterwards laughed uproariously at how they had fooled the wisest man at the court.) With her pronounced taste for intrigue and adventure, Catherine loved these clandestine parties, yet at the same time she felt left out, knowing that, night after night, balls and feasts were being held to celebrate tiny Anna Petrovna's birth and she was not able to attend them. Peter and his mistress were prominent among the revelers, however, and Peter had an additional cause to celebrate; the empress sent him a gift of sixty thousand rubles—the same amount she sent to the new mother.

Now Catherine was the mother of two children whom she never saw. She seems to have accepted this unnatural and no doubt saddening situation as part of the high cost of her lofty position. One day, if the succession went as she hoped it would, her son would rule Russia; her daughter would enjoy a destiny nearly as exalted. Safe under the empress's care, the children were protected; should Catherine herself suffer disgrace, they would not be tarnished by it. That knowledge must have given her some comfort as the winter days wore on and she began once more to feel the noose of conspiracy tightening around her.

In February of 1758 a tremor shook the court. Chancellor Bestuzhev was placed under arrest, along with three others closely connected to him and to Catherine—the jeweler Bernardi, who had carried secret messages for Catherine and was privy to her political dealings, Ivan Elagin, a friend of Poniatowski's and a staunch supporter of Catherine's who believed that she and not her husband should succeed Elizabeth, and Vasily Adadurov, Catherine's former Russian tutor and for several years a close confidant of the chancellor. Bestuzhev's arrest was secret, but Poniatowski learned of it and managed to warn Catherine.

She knew at once that she was in great danger. Not only had she carried on a secret correspondence with Bestuzhev, but they had discussed at length the question of the succession—perfectly understandable in the circumstances yet treasonable nonetheless. Bestuzhev had sketched out an ambitious plan under which, when the empress died, Catherine would rule with the chancellor himself as her chief mainstay, holding most of the principal government offices. Catherine had not given her approval of this plan— in fact she had disapproved of it, showing more circumspection and caution than the aging chancellor. Still, the very existence of a secret correspondence between the grand duchess and Bestuzhev gave grounds for her arrest.

Fortunately for Catherine, the chancellor had burned his papers before Alexander Shuvalov and his army of agents and informants had time to find them. Catherine too burned her correspondence, but she knew that simply destroying all evidence of secret dealings with Bestuzhev would not be sufficient to save her. Bernardi, Elagin and Adadurov were banished from court, Bestuzhev was divested of his offices and honors and handed over to a special commission of inquiry.

In April Catherine was summoned to the empress's apartments. She had been expecting, and no doubt dreading, this moment for weeks. She had already begun to feel the empress's cold hand reaching out toward her. Alexander Shuvalov appeared one morning at the door of Catherine's apartments and took away with him Madame Wladislava, Catherine's servant of long standing. She wept so bitterly at the loss of this trusted intimate that she melted the ferocious Shuvalov's heart, and he, in tears, assured her that the empress would speak to her about the matter herself. Catherine felt compelled to warn her other servants that they too might find themselves in peril, and became so agitated that she could do nothing but pace back and forth, unable to eat or sleep.

Catherine's interview with the empress took place after midnight. Alexander Shuvalov came to escort her through the torchlit corridors to the antechambers of the imperial apartments. Just as they reached the door of the gallery, Catherine saw Peter entering the empress's suite by another door. She had not seen him for a long time; like most of the other courtiers, he had been avoiding any contact with her—a sure indication, she thought, that she was under suspicion and at risk of arrest. She could only imagine what role he might play in determining her future fate. He wanted her out of the way, so that he could marry Elizabeth Vorontzov. Of that she had no doubt. He was full of long-held grievances and resentments. He would say anything to be rid of her.

Desperate to circumvent him, and in anguish, as soon as Catherine saw the aged empress she threw herself at her feet and begged her with tearful urgency to send her home to her relatives.

Elizabeth, disarmed by Catherine's capitulation, urged her to get up but she remained where she was, abasing herself before the empress like a repentant child.

"How can I send you back?" Elizabeth asked her, tears now standing in her own eyes. "Remember, you have children."

"My children are in your hands and could not be better cared for," Catherine replied. "I hope you will not abandon them."

"But how could I explain sending you away?"

"Your Imperial Majesty will simply explain, if you think it appropriate, that I have disgraced myself in your eyes and brought upon myself the hatred of the grand duke."

So far Peter had said nothing. Both he and Alexander Shuvalov continued to be silent as the conversation between the two women continued. There was no one else in the large room, though Catherine thought other witnesses might be hidden behind some screens that shielded the tall windows.

The empress insisted that Catherine get up and face her.

"God alone knows," Elizabeth said, "how I cried when you first arrived here and fell deathly ill. If I hadn't loved you, I never would have kept you here."

Catherine thanked her for all she had done for her. She would never forget her goodness, she said, and would always consider it her greatest tragedy that she had incurred the empress's disgrace.

But Elizabeth was no longer to be placated. Her eyes were dry as she accused Catherine of overweening pride, of imagining herself cleverer than everyone else.

"If I believed myself clever," Catherine retorted, "nothing could more strongly convince me otherwise than the state in which I find myself at present—this very conversation, in fact."

Peter began whispering to Shuvalov. Presently the empress joined their private conversation, adding her whispers to theirs. Catherine couldn't hear much of what they were saying, as they were a long way from her and the room was very large. She did, however, distinctly hear Peter say "She is dreadfully ill-natured, and terribly obstinate."

"If you are referring to me," Catherine replied, addressing Peter, "I am quite comfortable stating in Her Imperial Majesty's presence that in fact I am ill-natured toward those who advise you to act unjustly, and that I have become obstinate since I observed that my being agreeable brought me nothing but your hostility."

"There," Peter cried, "you see for yourself how ill-natured she is. She admits it."

The verbal sparring continued, but gradually Catherine came to be aware that Elizabeth's attitude was softening. Peter, however, was more alienated than ever when he discovered that, in an earlier conversation with the empress, Catherine had blackened his beloved Brockdorff. Other accusations were made.

"You have meddled in many things which have nothing to do with you," the empress said, coming close to Catherine. "I wouldn't have dared to do such things in the Empress Anna's time." She pointed to several letters in a large gold basin, and accused Catherine of having written to Marshal Apraxin—who had become one of Catherine's supporters—while he was leading the army the previous year. The grand duchess denied having done anything disloyal. She wrote to Apraxin solely because she was fond of him and took an interest in his well being. Besides, she added, one of the letters wished him a happy New Year and the other congratulated him on the birth of his son.

"Bestuzhev says that there were many others," Elizabeth said menacingly.

"If Bestuzhev says that, then he lies."

"Well then, since he lies about you, I'll have to have him tortured."

Catherine knew that Elizabeth was hoping to shock her, but she remained impassive. For an hour and a half the accusations flew, and Catherine parried them. The empress, wide awake, her physical symptoms in abeyance, hammered away at Catherine. She entered and left the room several times, now addressing Catherine, now Peter, and even more often conferring with Alexander Shuvalov. Peter and Shuvalov kept up a running conversation, most of which Catherine could not hear.

Peter, growing more and more rancorous, was quite carried away. In frequent angry outbursts he did his best to rouse the empress's ire against Catherine. Yet she could tell that the empress was far more impressed by her well-reasoned answers than by Peter's impassioned spoutings. "She listened," Catherine later wrote in her memoirs, recalling the scene in detail, "with particular attention and a sort of involuntary approval to my firm, even-toned answers." Elizabeth knew perfectly well that Peter wanted to dethrone his wife and replace her with his mistress, and she was not about to indulge his whim. Still, there were serious issues to be discussed.

Finally, at about three in the morning, the empress spoke in low tones to Catherine. "I have much to tell you, but I can't speak, because I don't want you to become more embroiled than you already are." Catherine took heart, and whispered back that she wanted nothing more than "to open her heart and soul" to Elizabeth.

Catherine had won, for the moment. Once again she saw tears of sympathy glistening in the empress's eyes before she abruptly took her leave. Without so much as a glance at Catherine, Peter marched out and retured to his rooms. Catherine herself, her mind still whirling with all that had happened, made her way back to her apartments. Once there, while her women were preparing her for bed, she heard a knock at the door. It was Alexander Shuvalov, who had stayed behind to confer with Elizabeth.

"The empress sends her compliments," he said gravely, "and begs you not to be distressed. She will confer with you alone."

Enormously relieved, Catherine bowed deeply to Count Shuvalov and sent her compliments in return. In the following days Catherine's spies repeated to her what Elizabeth was saying to everyone: "She's brilliant, my niece," she insisted. "She loves truth and justice. But my nephew is an idiot."

Chapter Fifteen

THE WAR AGAINST PRUSSIA WAS IN ITS THIRD YEAR, AND THE Russian troops, once thought to be ill equipped and in disarray, were proving to be more than a match for the soldiers of Frederick II.

The business of soldiering consumed the capital. The roads were full of troops, soldiers spilled out of the taverns, singing and brawling and taunting one another while at court, little was talked of save the army and its fortunes.

Though her frequent attacks of illness made her involvement intermittent, the empress followed the course of the war with great vigor. No expense was too great, no sacrifice too extreme when it came to the well-being of Russia's fighting men, she declared. To finance the war she would, if necessary, sell all her clothes and jewelry. (She had vast stores of both, having replenished her wardrobe in the years since the burning of the palace.) When the Russians won a battle, Elizabeth ordered medals struck to commemorate it and issued decorations to the victorious officers. They strode about proudly, gold and silver flashing on their chests, talking of their exploits—and avoiding, if possible, any contact with the pro-German grand duke, with his Holstein guard and his ring-portrait of the Prussian ruler.

After each battle, the courtiers came together to discuss which

officers had shown the greatest bravery, which had been promoted, which had suffered wounds or had died in combat. At
times the losses ran high. In the grisly Battle of Zorndorf, a scene
of horrifying slaughter, tens of thousands of Russians and Prussians were killed. When news of the outcome reached Petersburg there was great consternation, and for weeks afterward the
courtiers met in anguished little circles to mourn their dead and
dying; nearly everyone in the imperial household lost at least one
relative or friend. It was difficult to believe, as the empress
claimed, that the Russians had won the battle and that celebrations
were in order.

Amid the lamentations there was one bright episode. People
repeated to one another the remarkable story of a certain Gregory
Orlov, an artillery officer in the elite Ismailovsky regiment.

A giant of a man whose broad shoulders, long muscular legs
and rocklike torso made him the most formidable soldier in his
regiment, Orlov had shown not only daring but phenomenal
stamina at Zorndorf. With men dying all around him, he hurled
himself into the thick of the melee, into the very teeth of the
murderous Prussian fire. His comrades, seeing him fall, called out
to him to save himself. To their amazement he rose again and,
instead of seeking safety, returned to the fray. Three times he was
wounded, and three times he overcame his pain to dare death once
again.

Orlov's praises were sung wherever soldiers gathered—in the
taverns of the capital, in the guards barracks, even in the drawing
rooms of the royal palace. His exploits were not limited to the
field of battle, it was said; he took huge risks at the gaming tables,
was an audacious hunter, and had survived many a bloody tavern
brawl. Women fell at his feet, charmed by the lure of his strong
body and handsome face. It was whispered that he was indefatigable in bed.

One woman in particular had not been able to resist him. She
was Helen Kurakin, the beautiful mistress of the colonel of
Orlov's regiment, Peter Shuvalov. With consummate audacity

Orlov had abducted Helen, risking—at the very least—execution at his powerful colonel's hands. Yet as always, by defying death Orlov defeated it. Before he could take vengeance on Orlov, Shuvalov died, leaving Orlov free to enjoy his lovemaking and greatly enhancing his reputation for fearlessness and invincibility.

Gregory Orlov came to Petersburg in the spring of 1759, in the retinue of an eminent Prussian prisoner of war, Count Schwerin, former adjutant to Emperor Frederick. The count was housed in splendid comfort, and became a frequent guest at the palace, where he spent his time with the grand duke. There Catherine saw Orlov—no doubt having heard of his remarkable war record, as everyone in the capital had, in advance of his arrival.

She was overawed by what she saw. Not only was the magnificent Orlov the bravest man in the war, he was obviously the best looking. So tall he towered over his brother officers, and so strong he could wrestle most of them to the ground, Orlov was an antique hero come to life. No ancient Roman could be more admirable, Catherine thought, than this intrepid guardsman with his dogged courage and bold warlike spirit—not to mention his reputed virility. She was enthralled, and she singled the tall Orlov out for special favor.

Catherine had reached an impasse. Her former political allies, chief among them ex-chancellor Bestuzhev, had been disgraced and exiled. She herself had narrowly escaped arrest, and held on to her status at court only at the empress's whim. Her lover Poniatowski had been sent away, and she knew that it would be unrealistic of her to hope for his return. She was in great need of supporters, yet to recruit or encourage them exposed her to more political danger. And though still attractive, she was no longer young; in the same month that Gregory Orlov arrived in Petersburg, the grand duchess turned thirty, and was, by the standards of the time, well past the prime of her beauty.

Jean Louis Favier, a French informant who saw Catherine often at this time, wrote his impressions of her—impressions based on close observation and shrewd assessment. Favier was no partisan of Catherine's, indeed he was resolutely opposed to the Young Court and inclined to debunk the rather exaggerated praise heaped on the grand duchess by her admirers.

As to her personal attractions, Favier wrote, Catherine was, "to say the least, dazzling." Her waist was slender, but not supple; she walked with a noble carriage yet lacked grace, affecting the grand manner and rather overdoing it. Her breasts were lacking in fullness, and her long, thin face with its faint blemishes, its prominent chin, flat mouth and nose "with a tiny little hump," was also too narrow for real beauty. Her eyes, "alert and pleasant," were not particularly lovely. On the whole Favier concluded that Catherine was "pretty rather than ugly," but without exceptional beauty.

As for her abilities and character, Favier dismissed the "unfounded praise" of others but noted that, because of the enforced isolation imposed on her throughout her time in Russia, she had become exceptionally well read; her mind, though not brilliant, was well furnished. She had educated herself in the expectation that she would one day need to serve as her husband's chief adviser. "Reading and reflection were for her the sole means to that end," it seemed to Favier. And she had done a creditable job not only of informing herself about many things but of teaching herself to think.

Catherine was nothing if not a speculative thinker; abstract questions and philosophical issues were meat and drink to her curious, lively mind. However, it seemed to the Frenchman that in indulging this pronounced intellectual taste she was making a fundamental error. "Instead of acquiring theoretical and practical knowledge of state administration," he wrote, "she devoted herself to the metaphysics and moral systems of current thinkers." (Apparently Favier was not aware that for some years Catherine had in fact been serving a useful apprenticeship in practical administration, governing Peter's Holstein estates.) From her reading of Montesquieu, Voltaire, and Diderot's *Encyclopédie* she had acquired lofty ideas about reforming the uneducated, edifying them and teaching them to reason and to think judiciously; she envisioned being able to govern them, not as Russians had traditionally been governed, through fear, brute force and superior strength, but through persuasion and the rigor of impartially administered law.

Catherine had evolved, Favier believed, "a code of political convictions, quite elevated, but unworkable in practice." It would be not only impossible but quite dangerous to try to apply such high-minded concepts to the harsh realities her husband would face—with her help—when he became emperor. The Russians were, after all, a barbarous people, according to Favier, "a rude people devoid of ideas and rich in superstition, lacking cultivation and accustomed only to dumb and fearful enslavement." The barbarity of Russia was immemorial, it would be the height of folly to attempt to teach the Russian people new traditions.

Yet if Favier looked unfavorably on Catherine's intellectual attitudes, he was quick to defend her character against the charge that because of her love affairs, she was a woman governed by her passions, and without moral integrity.

"Her inclination to coquetry has also been exaggerated," Favier wrote. She was "a woman of feeling," with a yearning for love; she "yielded only to the inclination of the heart and, perhaps, the quite natural desire to have children."

For a brief time in her early thirties Catherine's inclination toward motherhood was indulged. The empress allowed her to see her children once a week, and she made the journey from Oranienbaum to Petersburg regularly. Her baby daughter Anna Petrovna was still a gurgling, crowing infant, just beginning to crawl, when Catherine began her visits, and as the weeks passed she watched the baby learn to stand and then to take her first steps. Paul, a blond, brown-eyed child of four, was sickly when his mother first visited him, and notably undersized. No doubt Catherine could not look at him without being reminded of Saltykov, while baby Anna, daughter of the kinder and more devoted Poniatowski, aroused in her more pleasant, if sadly nostalgic, memories.

Little Anna was never to grow up. Late in the winter she sickened, quite possibly a victim of freezing palace drafts, and in March of 1759 she died. No one recorded the nature of the illness, or whether her death was a quiet fading away or the result of prolonged suffering. Was Catherine permitted to stay with her little daughter in her last days or hours? We will never know. Catherine left no record of her feelings about losing her daughter; perhaps her silence is eloquent testimony to her grief. Infant death was an all-too-common tragedy in the mid-eighteenth century, and daughters were valued far less highly than sons. Still, it is hard to imagine that the tenderhearted Catherine was not saddened by her loss, and she must have felt bereft as she stood beside the small coffin and listened to the funeral prayers and the chanting of the monks.

In those melancholy hours she must have felt keenly her son's precarious mortality as well. He was far from robust. Would he too die, depriving her of the all-important contribution she had made to the Romanov succession? If Paul were to die, Peter would have a plausible excuse for putting Catherine in a convent and marrying the younger, arguably more fertile Elizabeth Vorontzov.

The Vorontzov fortunes were rising. Michael Vorontzov had replaced the exiled Bestuzhev as chancellor, and his niece Elizabeth had installed herself in Peter's apartments, giving herself airs and doing the honors as if she were already his wife. Catherine was aware that nothing pleased Peter and his mistress more than her own current state of disgrace, and that Peter felt confident that he could count on remarrying before long. Catherine referred to Elizabeth as "Madame Pompadour," a joking reference to the younger woman's quite serious and quite dangerous campaign to supplant her, as Pompadour had supplanted Louis XV's Queen.

Once again the court was caught up in following the war. In the summer of 1759, the Russian army engaged the Prussians at Künersdorf, only sixty miles east of Berlin. For twelve hours the massed ranks formed, stood and fired, receiving fire in their turn, hundreds of men falling with each volley. The sun beat down mercilessly on the smoke-filled battlefield, and the Prussians, outnumbered, numb with hunger and fatigue, began to abandon their ranks. Emperor Frederick himself took the field to rally them, knowing that the fate of his capital hung in the balance yet willing to risk all for the sake of victory. His heroism turned the tide for a time, but eventually the Prussians were routed.

Stories of this victory made the rounds in Petersburg, and all the Russian regiments began to recruit more men. Winter closed in, the coldest winter in years. The Prussians, encamped in the snow and inadequately equipped, began to die of disease and hunger. Russia and her allies took heart. The final victory seemed close now. One more campaign and the Prussian menace would be quashed forever.

When spring came a huge army of Russians, Austrians and French, nearly four hundred thousand in all, marched against the Prussian strongholds. All summer the grand assault was pressed. In October of 1760 Berlin fell to a dogged Russian attack, and although the Russians soon abandoned their prize, they held it long enough to ravage its defenses and plunder its arsenal, enriching themselves with a huge ransom from the terrified Berliners. Still Frederick refused to surrender, though his losses were monumental and the loyalty of his men was being tested almost beyond endurance. Another Prussian victory at Torgau in November was sobering to the allies, and both sides settled in for the long winter respite.

Catherine, deeply engaged in her own fight for political survival, was preparing her defenses as best she could. While hoping against hope that the empress might cut Peter out of the succession and declare Paul her heir—with Catherine as regent—she built a new group of allies.

To replace Bestuzhev as her political adviser she chose one of the ex-chancellor's protégés. Count Nikita Panin was a diplomat and a confirmed Anglophile like Catherine herself. Panin had broken with the pro-French policies of the Vorontzovs and Shuvalovs and was serving as tutor to young Paul. He was astute and capable, and Catherine came to believe that she could trust him. For several years she had had her eye on Panin as a candidate to join the new government when the empress died. Now she confided in him, and was gratified to discover in what contempt he held Peter and how eager he was to see a regency replace Elizabeth.

Secret diplomatic approaches that would previously have been made through Bestuzhev now came to Catherine directly. Several European governments let the grand duchess know that they were prepared to lend financial backing to any plan to remove Peter from the succession. Russia's military allies, chiefly Austria and France, were alarmed at the possibility that the pro-Prussian Peter might come to the throne and immediately take Russia out of the war. They opened their treasuries to Catherine, and she gladly accepted what was offered, knowing she might need it quite soon.

One unlikely ally joined Catherine, as it were, from the enemy camp. Peter's mistress Elizabeth Vorontzov had a younger sister, Catherine, married to a guards officer, Prince Dashkov. Catherine Dashkov had little in common with her brash, slatternly older sister save that she was rather plain. Like the grand duchess, whom she greatly admired, Princess Dashkov had a roving, curious mind and a thirst for new ideas. At the age of seventeen, when she began her friendship with Catherine, Princess Dashkov was the proud owner of one of the largest libraries in the capital and had read widely from the works of the French philosophes. It was no wonder Catherine enjoyed conversing with the precocious princess. Before long, she discovered that the idealistic Catherine Dashkov yearned to see her on the Russian throne and was working behind the scenes to gather support for her.

Little by little, one by one, the roster of Catherine's supporters grew. A number of officers in the prestigious and strategically crucial guards regiments got word to her that they would support her should their loyalty be put to the test. Kiril Razumovsky, colonel of the Ismailovsky regiment, had told Catherine several years earlier that he would defend her "at the cost of his life" and that she had many other secret partisans who would do the same.

That the guards regiments were the key military prop to the imperial court, Catherine well knew. No government could stand for long should these regiments revolt, nor could any attempted coup succeed if the Preobrazhensky, Semenovsky, and Ismailovsky regiments remained loyal to the emperor or empress.

Everyone in the government knew the story of how Elizabeth's claims to her father's throne had been made good by the Petersburg guards regiments eighteen years earlier. On a bitterly cold December night in 1741 she had gone to the barracks of the Preobrazhensky Grenadiers. Beautiful in her courageous vulnerability, a leather cuirass around her slight shoulders and a Russian cross in her hand, Elizabeth had asked the men for their support against the regent Anna and her German ministers. With shouts and cries the soldiers had pledged her their undying loyalty, swearing that she deserved to reign as the wholly Russian daughter of Peter the Great. Elizabeth led the men on to the Winter Palace, riding in a sledge over the crusted snow, and there she woke the regent and sent her and the baby Emperor Ivan to prison.

The men of the Preobrazhensky regiment had created Elizabeth Empress. With their brother officers in the guards, they could do the same again—for Catherine.

Gregory Orlov, the handsome hero of Zorndorf, was a lieutenant in the Ismailovsky guards. And he had four magnificent brothers: Ivan, Alexis, Feodor and Vladimir. All guardsmen. All outsize and fiercely strong. All respected leaders in their regiments, looked up to by the men and able to sway them politically.

Nothing is known for certain about how Catherine and Gregory Orlov became lovers. She was an experienced woman of thirty, romantic and passionate, with pretensions to power yet handicapped by her gender and by the precarious state of her relations with her husband. She needed a man who would love her loyally and champion her cause. Orlov was a worldly, celebrated warrior of twenty-five whose rampant ardor expended itself in fighting, carousing and lovemaking. He was eager to advance himself, yet he lacked high birth, education, important connections at court. He needed an opportunity to make himself useful. Perhaps her passion ignited his ambition, or perhaps he loved Catherine as he had never loved before.

All that is certain is that by the summer of 1761, with Prussia still undefeated and war losses mounting on both sides, with the empress locked in a macabre cycle of sinking into deathlike swoons and rallying to life mouthing curses at the hated Frederick, with Elizabeth Vorontzov counting the days until she became Peter's wife and Peter secretly passing on military information to the Prussians, Catherine became pregnant with Gregory Orlov's child.

Their liaison was not common knowledge, and Catherine managed to conceal her pregnancy and to stay in the background as events unfolded in the fall.

No one knew what the capricious empress would do next. Desperate to ensure a Russian victory over her arch-enemy of Prussia, she issued order after order to the army, changing generals, heaping abuse on anyone who got in her way.

She could no longer stand; often she held her hand to her heart as if to still its erratic pounding. When she became excited, blood ran from her nose; her attendants kept lengths of linen ready to stanch the flow. A terrible sore that would not heal disfigured her left foot. The sore preoccupied her. She stared at it as if in a trance, muttering that it was a punishment from God, sent because her father, the Great Peter, had kissed her foot when she was a girl. Her mind at times seemed dormant, or lost in bizarre musings, yet time and again she roused herself from her mental lethargy and croaked out demands, orders, punishments.

New fears grew in all those whose fortunes depended on the succession. What if the empress were to go mad? For a number of years she had been intrigued by madness, setting aside rooms in the palace where lunatics were kept and increasing her stock of demented men and women at frequent intervals. On one occasion, Catherine noted in her memoirs, twelve mad women were brought to court at once, perhaps because the empress felt compassion for them, more likely because their freakish behavior entertained her.

Now there was a risk that Elizabeth herself might become as deranged as her pet lunatics. If she did, would Michael Vorontzov and his faction control her? Or could Peter manage to maneuver himself into power, as regent for his incapacitated aunt?

October came, the cold weather set in and despite it, the newly appointed Russian general Buturlin sent thousands of Russian troops into battle against the Prussians. Buturlin had reason to hope that this campaign would be the final one. Large armies of Austrians and Swedes were joining with his Russians in this grand assault against an exhausted and disheartened Prussian foe.

Prussia had been laid low by six years of warfare. Nearly half a million soldiers and civilians had died, out of a total population of less than five million. For every man who had died in battle or as a result of wounds, two more had succumbed in the suffering that followed the battles, with crops ruined, towns burned, trade destroyed. Every Prussian family was in mourning. There were no men left alive, apart from old men; boys of fourteen were being forced into the army to replace the fallen. The end could not be far off. Emperor Frederick, in great secrecy, had sent a message to the grand duke several months earlier; could he, in return for a bribe of two hundred thousand rubles, prevail upon his aunt the empress to make a separate peace with Prussia, and withdraw the Russian troops?

Before Peter could send his answer a fresh wave of panic rippled outward from the imperial apartments. The empress had gone into convulsions. She was hemorrhaging. Doctors and priests surrounded her bed, the former shaking their heads funereally, the latter intoning the prayers for the dying. The last rites were administered by the empress's confessor who, though he had often before seen her *in extremis,* now felt certain that he was truly preparing his mistress for eternity.

By an odd quirk of fate Peter Shuvalov too lapsed into the twilit world of the dying. His heart had failed, he lay pallid and unmoving on his silken coverlet, apparently senseless, his eyelids fluttering uselessly.

It was mid-December. Thick snow fell from a dark sky, the Winter Palace was ablaze with candlelight even at midday. In the imperial apartments, servants came and went quietly, while prayers were offered for the salvation of Elizabeth's immortal soul. Catherine was among those who kept vigil, watching by the empress's bedside, aware of the old woman's labored breathing and of the gradual weakening of her useless body. No doubt she rehearsed in her mind the essential acts she must carry out when the empress died: to secure her children, to gather around her Gregory Orlov and his brothers and all those guardsmen sworn to keep her safe, and to protect herself, should the need arise, from Peter's vengeance. She had decided, given her pregnancy, not to go beyond this, not to heed the voices that urged her to take advantage of the empress's death to seize the throne for herself.

Five days before Christmas Princess Dashkov came to Catherine in private and entreated her to lead her supporters in a coup. Catherine demurred.

"Whatever happens," she told the princess, "I shall face it with courage."

The princess was impatient. "Then your friends must act on your behalf," she said.

"I beg you not to risk yourself for me," Catherine insisted. "Besides, what can anyone do?"

With difficulty Catherine persuaded her supporters to restrain themselves. Even as she kept her deathbed vigil, she was interrupted by messages from those who wanted to see her proclaimed empress. She responded to all such messages with anxious negatives. "Don't lead us into anarchy!" was her urgent answer. Her best course, as she saw it, was to let Peter accede to power. Perhaps, after her child was born, when she was stronger and no longer vulnerable to the obvious charge that she was an adulteress and a traitor to the dynasty, she could make other plans.

Elizabeth removed any remaining uncertainty about the succession when she summoned Peter and Catherine to her side and gave Peter a series of final instructions. As Catherine stood silently by, she heard the empress counsel her husband to let go of old resentments and start the new reign in a spirit of forgiveness. With tears in her eyes Elizabeth begged Peter to look after his little son Paul, and to show kindness to the servants she would soon be leaving behind in his care. It must have grieved her to hand on all that she had valued in life—her throne, her power, all those she loved—to the peculiar man who knelt beside her bed, stiff and without visible emotion, seemingly oblivious to the solemnity of the occasion. It must have grieved Catherine too to see them thus, aunt and nephew, the one still majestic even in her dying, the other stunted, half-formed, wooden. Hardly fit to become an emperor.

Elizabeth had no final words for Catherine. She had always been envious of her niece, and this envy may have reared itself even in her final hours of life. She must have known, or sensed, that in handing her realm over to Peter she was in truth giving it to Catherine to govern, either in person or from behind the throne; it is possible that she deliberately snubbed Catherine in order to discourage plotters. Did her weak old eyes detect the growing bulk under Catherine's full gown? If so, she said nothing. The light was fading. She had done all she could.

Christmas morning dawned cold and clear. All over Petersburg, bells rang in celebration of the great church feast, and there was a further cause for rejoicing: word had arrived the evening before that the Russian army under Buturlin had captured the important Prussian fortresses of Schweidnitz and Kolberg. The war was all but won.

Yet at the Winter Palace the rejoicings were muted. A crowd of courtiers had gathered outside the empress's bedroom, waiting for word of her condition. Elated as they were about the war news, they were apprehensive about the new regime that would soon begin. Would there be an attempt on the throne? Would Peter be able to assume power, and if he did, how would he govern? Would he put aside his wife?

Hours passed, and no word came forth from the sickroom. The courtiers, weary of their vigil, watched the high carved double doors that led into the inner apartments. Finally, at four in the afternoon, the doors were opened and the dread announcement was made.

"Her Imperial Majesty Elizaveta Petrovna has fallen asleep in the Lord. God preserve our gracious sovereign, Emperor Peter the Third."

All in the assembled company fell to their knees, many weeping openly. Crossing themselves three times, they said their prayers, for the empress, and for her successor, and for the long-awaited return of peace.

Chapter Sixteen

CATHERINE KNELT AT THE FOOT OF THE EMPRESS'S BIER IN Kazan Cathedral, her body swathed in the heavy black of mourning, her face veiled. The hard, cold stones of the cathedral floor hurt her knees and her muscles were cramped and weary. Yet she stayed where she was hour after hour, keeping her head bowed, crossing herself, now and then lying prostrate in an apparent paroxysm of grief. These, she had been told, were the prescribed formalities of mourning to be observed by the wife of the new emperor, and she intended to carry them out to the letter.

The empress had been dead for nearly six weeks. Her body, embalmed and gowned in gleaming silver lace, a golden crown on her shrunken brow, stank so badly that the odor made Catherine gag, yet she did not dare to move away from the marble cata-falque lest she be thought disrespectful. Fortunately the acrid scent of incense masked the stink of death; the smoke from swinging censors filled the cathedral as dozens of priests in gold-embroidered vestments circled the bier, repeating the prayers for the dead.

Mourners filed past in their hundreds, officials, ambassadors of foreign courts, priests and monks, the people of Petersburg. All took note of the black-clad kneeling figure, and many commented on her piety. Catherine had been faithful in her attendance on the empress's body, despite the freezing weather and heedless of her own extreme discomfort. The same could not be said of her husband, now Peter III, who rarely made an appearance in the cathedral and never stayed long when he did. Peter, it was noted, did not kneel or pray or pay his respects to his late aunt, the woman who had made him emperor, but behaved like a school-boy, insulting the priests and making everyone uncomfortable with his loud laughter and jokes, his constant flirtation with the ladies of his entourage.

Peter was indeed giddy with joy. Elizabeth's death left him exultant, and he made no effort to conceal his delight. At last, after twenty years of coercion, humiliation, indeed virtual in-carceration, he was his own master, with no one to answer to, no rules to obey but those he made himself. For the first time in his adult life he was free of the looming shadow of the empress, no longer fearful of her whims or of her retribution, safe at last from the worry that she might designate someone other than himself heir to her throne. His long nightmare of submission was over. He could do anything he liked.

After six weeks of solemnities and prayers, Peter was im-patient. He cared nothing for the decaying body lying on the marble catafalque and would gladly have ordered it taken away and dumped in a ditch. He refused to wear black, and disliked seeing other people wear it, especially his wife, whose presence beside his late aunt's bier was galling to him. Instead of observing the prescribed rites of mourning, Peter ordered his chamberlain to arrange huge feasts at the palace to celebrate his predecessor's demise. Hundreds of guests were invited, all of them ordered to leave off their mourning clothes and wear light colored gowns and coats and all their jewels. He presided at his feasts in his favorite uniform, that of a Prussian lieutenant general, giving offense to all the Russian officers in the room and to the many families who had lost sons and brothers, husbands and fathers in the war.

Yet, as Peter reminded his guests, the war was over. Emperor

Frederick was no longer the enemy, therefore toasts could and should be drunk to him. The new emperor's first official act, performed on the evening of his accession, had been to send swift couriers to the Russian generals in the field ordering them not to advance any farther into Prussian territory and to cease all hostilities. Prussian peace overtures were to be welcomed, and Prussian prisoners treated to banquets, loaded with gifts and sent home.

And there was more. The new emperor announced that the entire Russian army would be reformed. A new commander-in-chief was appointed—none other than Peter and Catherine's Uncle Georg (Catherine's former suitor), who lacked military experience but could be expected to enforce Germanic discipline. The Russian Life Guards were to be replaced by troops from Holstein. The green uniforms of the Russian footsoldiers would be exchanged for short tunics in Prussian blue. New drills would have to be learned, new formations, new commands—all of them borrowed from the Prussian army. Even the officers would have to put aside their pride and be instructed anew—and instructed in the ways of their late enemies.

The soldiers, particularly the Petersburg guardsmen who had surrounded the palace in the empress's last days to ensure Emperor Peter's unchallenged succession, began to regret their role in safeguarding him. They had heard how in private he referred to them as "janissaries" and impugned their valor. They sensed that he meant to break their spirit and make them into puppets, and German puppets at that. All their years of suffering, all their bravery and endurance, every foot of Prussian territory that they had won at huge cost, was to be sacrificed at the whim of the new emperor. They looked at him, a slight, ugly man in a tight blue coat with gold buttons, a ceremonial sword strapped to his thin waist, and they despised him. He was not one of them, and never would be. They followed his orders, but with secret loathing, and longed for the day when they could serve a Russian master once again.

To some, it appeared that Peter took on newfound stature with
his assumption of power. The British ambassador Keith wrote to
his superiors of the greater expediency he observed in the workings of the Russian government under Peter's command, and
approved of how the emperor himself took charge, not leaving it
to others, as his predecessor had, to make decisions regarding
foreign affairs. Nor did Peter appear to be vindictive toward his
former political enemies. He exiled no one, sent no one to the
Fortress of Peter and Paul. He retained Michael Vorontzov as
chancellor, despite Vorontzov's pro-French sympathies, and
appeared to have an enlightened regard for the need for continuity
in political affairs, except, of course, when it came to prosecuting
the war.

Peter took actions of which even Catherine approved. He abol-
ished the Secret Chancery, that dread machine of terror which had
blighted or cut short so many lives. He opened the state prisons
and released the late empress's enemies. He recalled those Elizabeth had exiled—all but Bestuzhev, who had been too closely
allied with Catherine for comfort. He won over the nobility by
issuing a law freeing them from obligations to serve as state
officials, a burden they had borne since Peter the Great's reign.
Overall, in his first months as emperor Peter surprised many
people with his grasp of affairs and his sense of responsibility.
Instead of looking to his wife to be his guide, he had become his
own resource, and even displayed a modicum of maturity.

Yet Peter's old demons—drunkenness, waywardness, excitabil-
ity and sudden, rabid anger—lurked in the corners of his life. He
could not rein in his tendency toward dissipation. "The life the
emperor leads," wrote the French ambassador Breteuil, who had
replaced L'Hôpital, "is the most shameful imaginable. He spends
his evenings smoking, drinking beer, and doesn't stop until five
or six in the morning, nearly always falling-down drunk." Peter's
long nights of indulgence left him to face the next day's work
with a fuddled, aching head and, quite often, a savage temper.
Catherine stayed out of his way as much as she could, but Eliza-

beth Vorontzov, who had in many respects taken over Catherine's former role, felt the full brunt of his merciless rancor.

Tumultuous quarrels erupted between the emperor and his mistress, sometimes in public. Breteuil, who was no friend to the new regime and was only too happy to record in detail the violent scenes he or his informants witnessed, described a dinner party at the home of the chancellor where Peter, Elizabeth Vorontzov and Catherine were all present.

Elizabeth was annoyed and on edge that evening because Peter, ever the philanderer, had found a new favorite, a seventeen-year-old courtesan named Mademoiselle Schaglikov. The hunchbacked Mademoiselle Schaglikov was no great prize—to the French ambassador she appeared "fairly pretty," but hardly a beauty—but she had the advantage of being fresher and younger than the reigning mistress, and certainly less irascible. By two in the morning Elizabeth could not contain her jealousy. She began making scathing remarks, and Peter, who had drunk a great deal, became abusive in response. Oaths, epithets, accusations flew down the length of the thick oak dining table. Everyone present, except perhaps Catherine, who was inured to her husband's outbursts, squirmed in discomfort, bracing themselves for an imperial tantrum.

Finally Peter stood, balancing unsteadily on swaying legs, and ordered Elizabeth to go home to her father's house. She wept, scolded, and dug in her heels. She knew just how to disconcert him; he faltered, still angry but irresolute. The battle of wills continued, but in the end Elizabeth won. By five in the morning, with the guests bleary-eyed and aggravated, the emperor and his mistress had made up their quarrel and were on the best of terms.

Four days later, however, a far more prolonged and furious dispute broke out between them. This time the abuse was so corrosive that even the hardened courtiers held their ears, and there was no reconciliation. For days a black cloud hung over the palace; everyone knew that Peter and his mistress were estranged, no one knew what retribution he might seek, or whether the bitterness of this altercation might unhinge him. He redoubled his attentions to Mademoiselle Schaglikov, and sought consolation in his cups.

This was no ordinary quarrel. Elizabeth Vorontzov had raised a particularly galling issue, one that had rankled in Peter's mind for years. She had accused him of being impotent.

The succession was very much on Peter's mind as he began his reign. His predecessor had urged him to take an oath to protect his son, Paul, and he had complied. Yet Peter knew that Paul was not his son, but Catherine's. Catherine and Saltykov's. Peter wanted nothing to do with him. He refused even to see the boy, and his refusal caused comment. People whispered that if Elizabeth Vorontzov—or the hunchbacked Mademoiselle Schaglikov, or any of the other women Peter might favor with his attentions—were to have a child, the emperor would be justified in setting aside his wife and marrying the mother of his son or daughter. But if he was in fact impotent, such speculations were idle.

Peter wanted very much to put Catherine aside, yet he needed an heir, and if he could not father a child himself, he would either have to designate Paul as his successor (which was clearly distasteful to him) or find another suitable heir.

With these issues on his mind he went to visit the unfortunate Ivan, once Ivan VI, in his prison at Schlüsselburg. That Ivan was a simpleton Peter already knew; now he discovered that the poor man was completely deranged. His disordered mind wandered in strange directions. He confided to Peter that he was not really Ivan, the man who had once, as an infant, been Emperor of Russia, but another man, an imposter. The real Ivan had been in heaven for many years. It must have been a peculiar scene, with the disturbed Peter confronting the demented Ivan, each of them a ruler, neither of them truly capable of rule. When their interview was over, Peter ordered Ivan brought to Petersburg, whether to keep him under stricter guard or because he contemplated naming him as his successor. Either way, the sad "imposter" might become important once again.

In a move that made Catherine understandably apprehensive, Peter also brought Sergei Saltykov to court. Saltykov had been in Paris, serving in a minor diplomatic post, and the urgent summons from Petersburg must have terrified him. He could easily imagine what Peter wanted from him: a formal admission that he had been Catherine's lover and that he was Paul's father.

As soon as Saltykov arrived in the Russian capital, in April of 1762, Peter took him into his personal cabinet and spent hours talking with him. Their conversation was private, and no doubt intense. Saltykov was well aware of the danger he was in. If he admitted the truth, and the emperor chose to be vindictive, he could have Saltykov executed—or imprisoned for life. Knowing the consequences of a full confession, Saltykov refused to say what Peter wanted to hear. A second discussion took place, and a third. Still the frightened but glib Saltykov protested that he and Catherine had not been lovers. Her child was not his. In the end Peter gave up. Saltykov would not provide the grounds he sought for declaring Paul illegitimate and divorcing Catherine.

Catherine was under great strain that spring. Her pregnancy was nearing its end. Her husband hated her and sought to rid himself of her, his mistress was halfway to replacing her. Although she had won a good deal of sympathy by her punctilious and self-effacing observance of the intricate religious rites following the late empress's death, and many among the clergy and people of Petersburg were favorably disposed toward her, Catherine stood essentially alone. Her political supporters, who were ready to mount a coup on her behalf, remained in the shadows, waiting for a signal from her—a signal she dared not give until she had delivered her child and recovered from the birth. In the meantime, she endured daily proofs of Peter's scorn and contempt and Elizabeth Vorontzov's haughty slights, becoming accustomed to being ignored and dishonored.

Ambassador Breteuil, who became a confidant to Catherine as the new reign began, wrote in his dispatches that she was suffering the greatest humiliation, and that she seemed perpetually downcast. Yet beneath her abject pose he detected a growing resentment.

"The empress is in the cruelest condition, and treated with the most marked scorn," he wrote. "She puts up with the emperor's conduct toward her with great impatience and also the haughty airs of Mademoiselle Vorontzov. I do not doubt but that the will of this princess, whose courage and force I know well, will drive her sooner or later to take extreme measures."

He added that Catherine was only too aware of her husband's power to shut her away, as Peter the Great had shut away his first wife. The story was well known at court. Emperor Peter, tiring of the wife whom he had been forced to marry for reasons of state—just as Peter III had been forced to marry Catherine—had taken a mistress to whom he was devoted. He demanded that the unwanted wife, Eudoxia, voluntarily enter a convent and thus dissolve the marriage. When she refused, he ordered his servants to abduct her. They came to her apartments by stealth, stifled her protests and bundled her into a cart. No one came to her aid. A few months later Eudoxia became a nun, and the emperor married his mistress.

Peter's power to banish her was very much on Catherine's mind as she went into labor on April 18. She had recently moved into a suite of rooms far from her husband's in a newly completed wing of the Winter Palace. It was to her advantage to be far removed from the royal apartments, given her condition, yet in keeping her at a physical distance Peter was slighting his wife, and she knew it. (Significantly, Elizabeth Vorontzov was given rooms adjoining the emperor's.)

Preparations for Catherine's delivery had been kept to a minimum. The court did not officially acknowledge the pregnancy; Catherine's servants put out the story that their mistress had a "slow fever," and was indisposed. Those few people who saw her in the last days before she gave birth remarked that she was dangerously depressed and ill. They hardly recognized her and worried that she might not live.

It is not clear how many people actually knew that Catherine was carrying Orlov's child. She certainly did nothing to advertise it, and made every effort to disguise it. There can be no doubt that Peter knew, as did his closest advisers. But to him the child was merely one more proof that Catherine was disloyal and immoral. And if things went as he hoped, it would soon cease to matter what Catherine did or how many bastards she produced. She would be banished from court, she would never trouble Peter again.

The tiny boy that came into the world on April 18, just three days before his mother's thirty-third birthday, was given the name Alexis Gregorevich, Alexis son of Gregory. No bells rang, no guns were fired. There were no celebrations, official or otherwise. For the first time in Catherine's experience, her child remained with her, a healthy son whom she could gaze on and take pleasure in. He belonged to her—to her and to Gregory Orlov. No jealous empress could stride in and take him away.

On Catherine's birthday, when by custom the courtiers came to pay their respects, the new mother made herself presentable and received the congratulations of her friends. But she retired early, as she often did, too exhausted to sit through the long hours of dinner and the night of dissipation that was sure to follow it. She knew she would not be missed.

Only a week after the birth of her son Catherine had what must have been a tense and awkward interview. Etiquette demanded that she receive Sergei Saltykov, and she dared not refuse to receive him lest her refusal arouse suspicion. She knew why he had been brought to court, and she may have known—or surmised—that he had so far been silent when questioned by Peter about what had gone on between them so many years earlier.

In the years since they had seen one another, Catherine had matured into a shrewd, careful political survivor, visibly wearied by her role yet handsome in her maturity, while Saltykov, his good looks marred by sagging skin and age lines, his black hair

thinning and receding from his creased forehead, was an unctu-
ous, aging roué. That Saltykov had continued his career of casual
seduction Catherine knew from reports reaching her from the
foreign courts where he had been in residence. No doubt she had
long since ceased to care what he did, but given her romantic
sensibility, she must have felt an echo of her old pain when she
saw him. He had taken advantage of her, exploited her and left
her disillusioned. Now he was in a position to do her substantial
harm, but only at greater cost to himself. "People are always
driven by self-interest," she liked to say, quoting Machiavelli. If
ever there was a time when she hoped self-interest would prevail,
it was now.

No record remains of the meeting between Catherine and
Saltykov. Catherine wrote in her memoirs that when she first
knew him, Saltykov was "a very proud and suspicious man."
One wonders whether his pride continued to sustain him, for by
1762 he was both disgraced and disappointed. His indiscretion
with Catherine had sealed his fate; he would never be anything
but a low-ranking diplomat, kept in exile from his homeland, a
peripatetic cosmopolite wandering from court to court and
bedroom to bedroom. Even if he escaped the full force of
Peter's wrath, he could expect to suffer. Knowing all this, and
seeing what time had done to the man to whom she once yielded
in joyful abandon, the man who had taken her virginity, Catherine must have had to steel herself to get through her hour with
Saltykov, an hour of mutual politeness and surface pleasantries,
with, one assumes, no mention of the blond, brown-eyed boy
who would always remain a bond between them.

Events were overtaking the new regime. In the soldiers' barracks, murmurs of discontent had grown into clamorous shouts
of protest. Fed by the constant harangues of the Orlovs, who
stirred up the men by praising Catherine and defaming Peter at
every opportunity, and who passed out money and drink in
Catherine's name, dissatisfaction was ripening into rebellion.

Peter's military reforms were seen as punitive, his peace treaty with Prussia—a treaty, it was said, that had been drafted by an envoy of Frederick—an affront too grave to be borne. The men hated their new German commander, and hated having to wear the blue uniforms of Prussia even more. Their pay was slow in reaching them, and there was talk of a new campaign against Denmark, not to uphold Russian sovereignty but to preserve the integrity of the emperor's Holstein lands.

Preparations for the new campaign were intensifying as the cold weather retreated and the river ice, which had been a thick solid sheet, began to grind and tear itself into huge chunks that floated toward the sea. Quantities of arms and provisions, equipment and supplies were carted into the Petersburg barracks and stored in warehouses. Rumor had it that Peter intended to lead the Russian army himself, as soon as the warm season arrived and all the needed equipment had been delivered. It was to be his moment of glory, the chance the late empress had so long denied him, to prove himself on the field of battle. And he would be fighting on the Prussian side, just as he had always wanted to do. Some Russian units, it was said, were already being transferred to Prussian command.

As they made ready to follow a leader they detested into a military adventure they abhorred, the men began to talk openly of how much better things would be if the emperor's wife, a woman who knew and understood her adopted country instead of despising it, were on the throne. Some remained faithful to the man they viewed as their legitimate sovereign, however contemptible he seemed to them. But many hoped for change, and pledged themselves, in secret, to help to bring it about.

To the extreme disquiet among the soldiers was added the condemnation of the clergy when the emperor decided to augment his depleted treasury by seizing church lands.

Plans had been made in the previous reign to secularize vast amounts of property held by religious houses, but Elizabeth had not taken any steps to implement them. Now Peter revived the scheme, and with a vengeance. He had never bothered to disguise his contempt for the Russian church, with its lengthy and intricate liturgy, its rich, sonorous vocal music and its panoply of saints enshrined in jewel-studded icons. In truth, all religion was distasteful to Peter; Catherine had once said of him that she had "never known a more perfect atheist in practice than he, though he often feared the devil and God too, and more often despised them both." Throughout his years in Russia Peter had continued to prefer the relative simplicity and aesthetic severity of Lutheranism to the coruscations and labyrinthine rituals of Russian Orthodoxy, and he had often insulted priests and pious worshippers when he deliberately interrupted services with loud laughter and impudent remarks.

Troops of soldiers were sent out into the countryside to take possession of farmlands that had belonged to the church for hundreds of years. Where they encountered resistance, they seized the properties by force. Though many of the soldiers found this work odious, they obeyed when commanded to break into the houses of priests and higher clergy and ransack their contents. No chapel, hermitage or monastery was spared; even the bare cells of the monks were raided and rifled.

Official protests on behalf of the clergy were ignored and in fact Peter seemed to be carrying out a personal vendetta against the priests, commanding them to cut their long hair and waist-length beards and to exchange their long black robes for the sober dark coats and breeches, linen shirts and tricorn hats of Lutheran ministers. Insult was added to injury when the emperor announced that the sons of all married clergy were no longer to be exempt from conscription, as traditionally they had been.

But the worst was still to come. Not content to attack the wealth of the church and longstanding clerical traditions, Peter began to make what many believers saw as an assault on faith itself. He summoned Archbishop Dmitri of Novgorod, the man who only a few months earlier had saluted him as autocrat and led the senior court dignitaries in taking their solemn oath

of allegiance to him, and ordered him to remove from the
churches all icons except those representing Christ and the
Virgin Mary.

No greater blow to traditional Russian piety could be imagined.
The icons of the saints were at the heart of Orthodox belief. Every
day the faithful knelt to worship them, soldiers marched into
battle behind them, every Russian home displayed them in the
"beautiful corner," where a lamp was kept burning every hour of
the day and night to illuminate the elongated, thin-lipped faces
and glowing eyes of the holy images. In the marketplace, huge
piles of icons were for sale and merchants in sacred art carried on a
thriving business. Every Russian owned at least one icon; venerated icons were handed down through the generations and were
among a family's most valued possessions. Especially revered
images were believed to manifest miraculous powers to heal and
bless. In churches large and small, holy pictures overwhelmed the
worshiper, looking down from every pillar and wall, arranged in
glittering rows on the tall iconostasis that represented the gateway
to the holy of holies.

A cry went up from the faithful: their precious icons must not
be taken down. The saintly images must not be desecrated. The
emperor had finally gone too far. He must be replaced. And his
obvious replacement was Catherine. In the streets of Petersburg
and Moscow there was talk of the change that had to come.
Seditious speeches were made, rebellious murmurs disquieted
those with a stake in maintaining the present government.

"Everyone hates the emperor," Breteuil noted. "The empress
has courage in her soul and in her mind; she is as loved and
respected as the emperor is hated and despised." The hatred was
spreading, but it was as yet impotent. "To tell the truth, everyone
is cowardly and a slave," the ambassador added, not knowing to
what extent the people he saw as cowards and slaves were already
preparing to carry out a grand upheaval.

Baron Korff, chief of police, was well aware of the extent of the
dissatisfaction in the capital. Throughout April and May his spies

brought him word of disturbances in every quarter of the city, of disloyal talk in the guards barracks, of grievances held by the police themselves. He knew that unless the police took immediate and forceful action, there might well be an insurrection. Yet he decided to do nothing.

For months the baron had been among the emperor's intimates, enjoying the benefits of Peter's special favor. He had been a frequent guest at the lengthy banquets at the Winter Palace, both a witness to and a participant in the debauchery that went on there. But then, suddenly, at the end of May, the emperor's favor evaporated. Capriciously, and most unwisely, Peter picked a quarrel with Korff, with the result that the baron ceased to be a welcome guest in the imperial quarters. Within days the baron was making himself a familiar presence in Catherine's apartments. He had chosen sides; he was betting that, when the emperor went off to war, as he was about to do, Petersburg would rise for Catherine. And he meant to throw his weight behind the winning side.

Early in June Peter gave a great banquet to celebrate the peace he had made with Prussia. Hundreds of guests made their way to the grand salon where long tables had been laid with fine white linen, shining golden plates and huge silver epergnes. Long white tapers set in gilt candelabra illuminated the vast room, though the evening, glimpsed through the long windows, was softly bright. The sun would not set until close to midnight, and above its blue depths the Neva reflected the warm orange and gold tints of the sky.

The salon filled with guests, the first courses were served. The emperor sat on a raised dais, with Elizabeth Vorontzov, her ugliness adorned with the late empress's rubies and sapphires, seated beside him. Nearby was the evening's guest of honor, the Prussian envoy. Far down the table, separated from the dais by hundreds of guests, sat Catherine, self-composed and sociable, conspicuously dressed in black for she was still in mourning for Elizabeth.

Peter surveyed the room with satisfaction. He was master here, the officers and courtiers did his bidding now, just as they had once done the bidding of his hated predecessor. To be sure, there was some unrest in the city, and word had recently come to him of uprisings among the peasants of Astrakhan. But Astrakhan was far away, and besides a regiment had been dispatched to arrest the leaders and crush the rebellion. Slightly more irritating were the reports he was receiving from his generals, telling him that large numbers of soldiers claimed to be ill, and were unable to embark for the Danish campaign. But he knew how to deal with that. He had issued a ukase, a legislative order, commanding them to recover their health. They dared not go against an imperial command.

More courses were brought, and flagons of wine. The emperor drained his goblet again and again, until he began to have trouble holding it steady as he lifted it to salute the Prussian envoy. There were those, he knew, who cautioned him against leaving the country to command the Danish campaign. Even his mentor Frederick, whom he respected more than anyone, had written to advise him not to leave Russia until he had undergone the rite of coronation. The people were not to be trusted, Frederick had written. They might prove rebellious against a sovereign who had not received the divine sanction of coronation. But he meant to leave anyway, he was eager to be about the work of soldiering. He could not be bothered to go to Moscow—that hateful, priest-ridden city with its hundreds of churches and thousands of noisy clanging bells—merely to submit himself to some archaic ritual.

Peter ordered his goblet refilled and stood to propose a toast. "Let us drink," he called out, his words slurred, "to the health of the king our master." There was a rustling of silk and a scraping of chairs as the guests stood to share the toast.

"To King Frederick," Peter said loudly. "He did me the honor of giving me a regiment; I hope he won't take it back from me." He turned to the Prussian envoy. "You can assure him that, if he asks it of me, I'll go and make war in hell with all my empire."

With that the emperor drained his glass, and his guests joined him. More toasts followed, including one to the imperial family. Everyone stood to raise his or her glass, even the French and Austrian ambassadors, the resentful Russian officers, the servants and officials who had felt the lash of the emperor's tongue and the punishing impact of his wrath.

Everyone, that is, but Catherine. She sat where she was, provocative in her self-possession, alone in her mute defiance of her husband's salutes. He saw what she was doing, tried to ignore her, but finally lost his temper. Why, he demanded to know, had she not stood like the others?

The diners held their breaths, the servants stopped where they were. Not a glass clinked, not a knife scraped. Catherine turned toward Peter.

"We toasted the imperial family. I am a member of that family, along with the emperor and our son. How could I stand up to drink a toast to myself?"

As enraged by Catherine's calm as he was by her sophistry, Peter shouted at her.

"Fool! Fool!" His voice echoed in the huge chamber. The diners, frightened by the ugliness and bitterness in the emperor's tone, sat as if paralyzed, hardly daring to blink.

But Catherine, though fully aware of the danger she was in, retained her outward poise. Earlier that evening she had come to a quiet resolve. She would no longer sit by and watch her husband's pathetic charade of rule. She would not wait until he took his vengeance on her. She would let those who were eager to act on her behalf do what they planned to do. With their help, and trusting in the invisible hand that guided all things, she would seize the throne.

Chapter Seventeen

THE AIR OFF THE BALTIC WAS THICK AND HUMID, AND WARM even for June. On the horizon a pale gold, watery sun hung suspended as the murky twilit night gave way to a blurry dawn. The rickety carriage that sped toward Peterhof from the capital careened over the bumpy, pitted road but did not slacken speed, even when the horses stumbled and the fragile wooden frame shivered as if it would break. Inside were Alexis Orlov and his lieutenant Vasily Bibikov, the latter disguised as a valet. They were on their way to Catherine, bringing her a message of the greatest urgency. One of the men she was relying on most to help her take the throne had been arrested, and the others, fearing that under torture he might reveal the entire plan, had decided that the time had come to act.

It was June 28, two days before Peter was due to lead his army on campaign into Denmark. For weeks Catherine and her allies had been quietly making preparations to take power, meeting at the house of Princess Dashkov, drawing more and more guards officers into the conspiracy, along with thousands of the private soldiers who pledged themselves to come to Catherine's defense whenever she called on them. Gregory Orlov took the lead, throwing his immense energy and his immense prestige into a one-man campaign of persuasion. He and his brothers worked to circumvent the strictly military hazards—securing the roads, assuring the loyalty of the artillery corps, defusing potential pockets of resistance—while Panin, Catherine's principal adviser, addressed the political questions and took responsibility for safeguarding the heir to the throne, Paul, who, rumor had it, was about to be discarded by his putative father along with Catherine.

Panin and Catherine had drawn up a manifesto to be issued on the day she took power. It was even now being printed, in the greatest secrecy, by an officer at the risk of his life.

The carriage clattered to a halt outside the small villa called Mon Plaisir where Catherine was living, and the servants, already awake, admitted the tall Alexis Orlov to her bedroom.

Gently he woke the drowsing Catherine.

"It is time to get up," Catherine later remembered hearing him say, in a voice that conveyed a remarkable serenity. "All is ready to proclaim you."

It had been agreed by all the conspirators that, if their plan was betrayed, the guards would immediately be assembled and Catherine would be declared empress—no matter where Peter was or what he was doing. At the moment, Peter was at Oranienbaum, only a few miles away, with his fifteen hundred Holsteiners. But Peter was no doubt still in bed, sleeping the sleep of the inebriated, and if Catherine hurried to the capital, and her luck held, she had a good chance of securing the city before her husband could give orders for her arrest.

While Catherine's women rapidly dressed her in the simplest of black gowns—she was still in mourning for the late empress—Orlov told her of the arrest of Lieutenant Passek, who had been overheard giving encouragement to seditious talk by one of the emperor's spies. She understood at once the need for haste, and stepped into the waiting carriage, which sped off toward Petersburg.

During the tense hour and a half that followed, as the carriage lurched and jolted over the uneven road, with the driver whipping the horses to breakneck speed, Catherine came fully awake

and did her best to gather her thoughts. The hour had come at last
to test her resolve. She who had told the French ambassador
"There is no woman bolder than I," and who had confessed to
Charles Hanbury-Williams that her ambition was "as great as is
humanly possible," was about to prove to the world that her
boasts were not in vain.

Her thoughts may for a brief time have lingered on Hanbury-
Williams, who had believed in her and encouraged her and who,
sadly, had not long outlived his stay in Russia. She had often
talked to her English friend about her sustaining belief that her life
was guided by a supernal force that had preserved her and would
continue to do so until she fulfilled her destiny. She may well have
said a silent prayer or two as the suburbs of Petersburg came into
view and she turned her attention to more immediate concerns.

The original plan had been to choose a propitious time and
arrest Peter in his chamber at the palace, with the guardsmen
locking him up and then relying on their overwhelming numbers
to intimidate the palace bodyguard. Now the conspirators would
have to improvise. With the guards' backing, they would need to
secure the city, isolating Peter at Oranienbaum and laying siege to
the estate if necessary. At all costs, the emperor—and those with a
stake in keeping him in power—had to be prevented from communicating with foreign governments, and from fleeing abroad
to seek safety.

A hundred doubts must have raced through Catherine's restless
mind as the carriage hurtled over the rough stones and along the
scarred, unpaved track that led into the city. Would the guardsmen all acclaim her, or would some hold back? How many lives
would her bid for power cost? Would there be time to do all that
needed to be done before a counterattack came? Would the people
of the capital support her? Peter was known to be nearly as
popular among the ordinary citizens as he was hated by the
nobles, the soldiers and the clergy—though Catherine too was
popular, probably more so. Could she succeed? Had she the
stomach for the contest?

All doubts aside, there was no longer any choice. Only a few weeks earlier, on the night of the peace celebration, Catherine had sensed that a turning point had been reached, and that she dared not hesitate. She had known Peter too long and too well not to recognize a change in him, a new recklessness in his dealings with all those whom he perceived as his enemies. He was bent on a campaign of destruction, lashing out at the guards regiments, the church, the governing nobles, herself. Seeking protection from his wrath she had taken refuge at Peterhof, drawing as little attention to herself as possible while secretly sending and receiving messages from those who had promised to enthrone her. Now, suddenly, she and her fellow conspirators were out in the open. There was no longer any zone of protection. There were only two choices: the path of daring or the path of cowardice. And Catherine had never been a coward.

The carriage lurched to a halt at the side of the road, the lathered horses drooping and spent. Another carriage was waiting, and beside it stood the tall, strapping figure of Gregory Orlov, massive and imposing in his green and red uniform.

Seeing Orlov must have raised Catherine's excited spirits, for from the start he had been the heart and soul of the plot to depose the emperor. He had undertaken to ensure the support of the soldiers; his force of personality had been the catalyst that hardened the men's dissatisfaction with Peter into rebellion. With bribes, promises of drink, well-timed displays of bonhomie he had brought the wavering to heel while distracting the emperor's spies and keeping vital information from reaching them. "Everything was done by him in this enterprise," Catherine would later write of Gregory Orlov. He was her harbinger, her lover, her champion. She got into the coach beside him and the coachman cracked his whip.

Orlov had planned Catherine's entrance into the city with care. They drove first to the wooden barracks of the Ismailovsky regiment, where many of the men and ten of the officers had previously pledged themselves to support Catherine. His rousing speeches, supplemented by generous gifts of money and barrels of free vodka ensured that few of the men would resist the bold move to enthrone Catherine. Telling Catherine to wait, Orlov jumped down from the carriage and strode into the guardroom where a few yawning men were gathered. He found a drummer and ordered him to beat a tattoo. Immediately the men began to rush out, in disarray, many only half dressed, to answer the call to arms.

At a signal from Orlov Catherine descended from the carriage to stand before the scrambling guardsmen, whose eyes widened at the sight of her, a lovely, regal figure in an unadorned black dress, her rich brown hair unpowdered and coiled simply off her face. The men had heard the story of the emperor's threat to arrest his wife, they knew before she spoke to them that she was in danger.

"Matushka, Little Mother!" they cried out, sweeping toward her en masse to kiss her hands and feet. Some wept, others bowed or knelt in reverence, content to kiss the dusty skirt of her plain gown.

As more and more men poured from the barracks a few of the officers shouted for Paul and a regency, and a few more may have hesitated, thinking of the oath they had sworn to uphold their emperor and remembering that Peter, not Catherine, had been the choice of their late beloved Empress Elizabeth. But in the end all hesitation melted in the onrush of chivalrous emotion that greeted Catherine's appearance. The surge of feeling was redoubled when the regimental commander, Kiril Razumovsky, gave his endorsement to Catherine's claim to the throne and when the barracks priest, Father Alexei, administered an oath of fidelity to the assembled men.

Shouting, chanting, exhorting the onlookers who had begun to gather in the vicinity of the barracks, the guardsmen formed a procession behind Catherine's carriage as she rode on to the quarters of the Semenovsky regiment. Word of her coming preceded her; the men of the Semenovsky, elated at the prospect of ridding themselves of the emperor they detested and of rescuing their heroine Catherine from her peril, and with the enthusiastic backing of at least a dozen of their officers, ran forward along the road to meet her carriage and proclaim their allegiance to her.

By this time it was nearly nine o'clock and the capital was not only awake but alive with excitement. Soldiers from other barracks hurried to join the lengthening procession of supporters marching behind the imperial carriage, discarding the Prussian-style uniforms Peter had forced them to wear and putting on their Russian uniforms. Priests, troubled by recent reports that Peter had adopted the Lutheran rite in his palace chapel and greatly agitated by the emperor's order to remove the icons of the saints, gladly received the news that they were no longer to be ruled by an emperor but by the Empress Catherine. Rumors flew. Some said that Peter had died, and that Catherine was succeeding him. Others whispered that Peter had sold the Russian army to the king of Prussia, and that the soldiers had decided to dethrone him in consequence.

Meanwhile, men from the recently disbanded imperial bodyguard, many of whom had helped to put Elizabeth on the throne twenty-one years earlier, joined the growing crowd, as did the Horse Guards, riding in full order, with their officers at their head, and shouting in a fury of joy that Russia had been delivered. The surging crowd grew in numbers, cries of "Vivat!" filling the moist morning air. Now thousands of soldiers, riding and on foot, followed the vehicle in which Catherine and Orlov rode, with Father Alexei leading the long procession carrying his tall silver cross.

It soon became apparent that neither the police nor Peter's loyal Holsteiners—who were still at Oranienbaum, several hours' distance from the capital—nor any members of the emperor's government were going to contest the toppling of the regime. Catherine had been assured that the Grand Master of the Ordnance, General de Villebois, was on her side; he would guarantee that none of the artillery corps would fire on the rebels. As for the members of the Senate, in nominal control of the capital in the emperor's absence, they had long been opposed to Peter's radical

changes and bumptious bullying; during his few months in power
he had arrogated to himself many of their cherished prerogatives
and had only recently affronted the senators by prohibiting them
from issuing any decrees whatsoever without his prior approval.
They were only too glad to see the end of him. The entire
government capitulated without a whimper of resistance.

Only in the proud Preobrazhensky regiment, oldest and most
respected of the guards regiments, were there pockets of defiance.
As the men of the Preobrazhensky, heedless of their orders,
rushed out of their barracks to join Catherine's partisan horde a
few of their officers tried to stop them. There was the beginning
of a skirmish between the men loyal to Catherine and those
attempting in vain to defend Peter's cause, but before any blood
could be shed the emperor's defenders surrendered and swore
allegiance to Catherine, turning on their officers. One young
musketeer recalled later having watched a mounted officer in the
grenadiers charge his own men, flailing at them with his sword,
before he was overwhelmed and forced to flee for his life. But the
few contrarians, stubbornly faithful to their emperor, were soon
subdued and arrested by what had swiftly become the legitimate
power—made legitimate, in the judgment of those who took part
in the maelstrom of events, by the tumultuous acclamation of the
soldiers, the citizenry and the will of heaven.

With amazed speed the regiments secured the palace, where the
senators had incarcerated themselves, waiting to see the outcome
of Catherine's bid for power, and prepared to defend the city
against a possible assault from outside forces still loyal to the
emperor. Meanwhile Catherine hastened to legitimize her takeover by receiving the sanction of the church. She entered the
cathedral of Our Lady of Kazan, flanked by a phalanx of officers,
and there, in the presence of a large congregation of witnesses,
and under the eyes of the holy icons, she was proclaimed "auto-
cratrix," empress, and blessed by the Metropolitan of Petersburg.
Panin had brought Paul to the cathedral to stand beside his
mother. As incense wafted and bells pealed, the seven-year-old
boy was blessed as Catherine's designated heir.

The popular delirium that greeted the new empress as she emerged from the perfumed darkness of the cathedral exceeded anything seen in the capital in decades. The bad dream of Peter's capricious rule was ended. A new and benign mistress reigned. Bells pealed ceaselessly. Word spread throughout the city that momentous events were taking place. Breathless servants rushed in to tell their masters that, in less time than it took to eat breakfast, the emperor had been overthrown. His wife now ruled in his stead.

In the neighborhoods farthest from the palace—which remained the scene of wild rejoicing—the news was accepted gladly and on the whole calmly. No tumult or agitation swept along the broad avenues; indeed the only sign of change was that pickets appeared on every bridge and street corner, and cavalry patrols trotted efficiently along at regular intervals, to ensure that tranquility continued to prevail.

The only damage was done at the mansion of Catherine's Uncle Georg, commander of the Horse Guards and detested by his men. Georg had tried to leave Petersburg, no doubt on his way to join the emperor at Oranienbaum, and had been arrested. His captors mistreated him; vengeful elements in the crowd, eager to vent their resentments, ransacked the fine house Peter had given him and destroyed its expensive contents. Knowing that her uncle might be in danger, Catherine sent out a rescue party to save him, but it arrived too late to prevent harm.

Without pausing to savor her triumph, Catherine went to the Winter Palace where the Senate and the leading churchmen were, along with Panin. There her official manifesto was issued, and its stirring words were read out to the waiting crowd.

"We, by the Grace of God, Catherine the Second, Empress and Autocrat of all the Russias," it began—the first time the sonorous title had been applied to the German princess who had been christened Sophia of Anhalt-Zerbst.

"All loyal-hearted sons of the Russian Fatherland have clearly perceived the danger that threatened the Empire of Russia. The security of our Orthodox Greek Church has been put in danger through disrespect for our venerable forms of worship, and even threatened with being forced to conform to another creed. Our sublime Russia has been betrayed, her dearly bought prizes of war taken from her and her neck brought under the yoke of her ancient enemy—and for what? In order to agree to inglorious peace terms." The document went on to denounce the ruined state of Russia's governing institutions, which threatened the country's unity and well-being.

"For these reasons, because of the danger imperiling all our loyal subjects," the manifesto concluded, "we believed ourselves under obligation, with God's help and guided by His justice, and prompted by the evident and sincere desire of our faithful subjects, to ascend the sovereign throne of all the Russias, upon which all our loyal subjects have sworn their allegiance to us."

Catherine was the defender of Russia and the Russians, her declaration announced. What Peter had been destroying, she would restore. It was as a deliverer that she claimed the crown, not as the bearer of any hereditary rights, or legal prerogatives. In truth, Catherine was defying blood rights and ignoring the law in taking her action; all that she did rested on her publicly stated pledge to fulfill the role of savior of the realm.

No one realized this more clearly than the new empress herself. After reviewing her troops, more than forty thousand men in all, including guardsmen and soldiers of country regiments who were hastening to align themselves with the rest of the capital's soldiery, Catherine shut herself in the Winter Palace with her councillors to decide on her next course of action. She sent messengers to every provincial district with copies of her manifesto, and sent Admiral Taliesin to the naval base at Kronstadt to secure the loyalty of the navy. At the same time, she ordered the metropolitan to deliver to the palace the sacred symbols of monarchy—the crown, scepter and holy books—knowing their iconic value to her subjects and in acknowledgment of the fact that she would need to consolidate her accession by being crowned in the near future.

Couriers rode in and out of the palace courtyard all afternoon, bringing news from Peterhof and from every quarter of the capital, carrying directives destined for provincial governors and garrison commanders, relaying messages to and from diplomats and other officials. At the hub of the activity, Catherine and her advisers gave orders, wrote instructions, sorted through the messages, and formulated a strategy. She would go herself to Peterhof, supported by her army, and subdue whatever resistance Peter offered. If all went as they hoped, he would be taken prisoner, and confined in the fortress of Schlüsselburg, where Ivan languished. Only when Peter was locked away and under guard would Catherine begin to feel safe.

Late in the afternoon Chancellor Vorontzov arrived from Peterhof, the first member of Peter's inner circle to approach Catherine in her newly claimed role as empress. The soldiers allowed him to enter the city unimpeded, and escorted him to the palace. Once inside, confronting the woman who had been his political enemy for years, the woman who now held the capital under her authority, he showed no fear; disregarding Catherine as anything other than the emperor's rebellious wife, he chastised her. Without responding Catherine ordered Vorontzov to be led away to the cathedral, where under duress he swore his allegiance to her.

A more sinister pair of envoys arrived shortly afterward. Prince Trubetskoy and Alexander Shuvalov, Peter's trusted deputies, had been sent to investigate a troubling rumor reaching Peterhof that the Preobrazhensky regiment had mutinied in support of Catherine. Catherine herself believed that the two men had been given secret orders to kill her. Before they had a chance to make any mischief both men were led away to the cathedral and forced to swear the oath of allegiance to the empress.

Evening came, the bright midsummer twilight settled over Petersburg. Soldiers stationed throughout the city since midmorning yawned at their posts, still vigilant yet weary. The townspeople, more jubilant than ever over Catherine's triumph, had invaded the taverns and quickly sated themselves on beer and vodka. Most of the resulting unruliness was good humored, though as the night wore on fights broke out among the drunken revelers and there were outbreaks of vandalism. No police were to be seen; the police chief, Baron Korff, had been arrested despite his being a partisan of Catherine's, and though he was soon released he stayed aloof from the goings-on in the streets.

Catherine, no doubt yawning and weary herself, yet nerved by excitement and an occasional frisson of fear, prepared herself to face the next phase of her great undertaking. Borrowing a uniform, she put on the bright green and red coat of a colonel in the Preobrazhensky regiment, and received a deafening acclamation from the men as she rode out to meet them on her white horse, high black boots covering her legs and a gold-braided, fur-trimmed black tricorn on her head. She rode well, and held herself majestically. She was a splendid sight, youthful and erect in the saddle, the trappings of her horse glinting dully in the eerie half-light, her face pale yet resolute. For the second time that day the soldiers wept and cheered themselves hoarse at the sight of her, moved almost beyond speech by the poignant contrast between her womanly body and her stalwart, warlike dress and pose.

Catherine led the rearguard. With her rode Princess Dashkov, also in a guardsman's uniform, and an escort of officers. Included in Catherine's escort were the two men who had come to kill her, Count Shuvalov and Prince Trubetskoy. In a matter of hours both men had turned definitively against their old master, convinced, from all that they had seen and heard in the capital, that his cause was lost.

The army filed slowly out of the city along the road that led northwestward toward Peterhof. Late as it was, people came out of their houses to cheer the soldiers along, and to shout "Vivat!" for Catherine. Once they left the outskirts behind, however, there was no sound but the clopping of hooves and the rasp of metal on metal. Deeply weary, for four hours the host rode on through the

crepuscular light, until, drooping with fatigue, they came to an
inn and made bivouac until dawn.

Peter, meanwhile, had spent much of the long day of June 28
reacting to ever more troubling news.

The day had begun well. After a lazy morning he had ridden
from Peterhof to Oranienbaum with a party of courtiers, including Elizabeth Vorontzov, the Prussian ambassador Baron Goltz,
and several dozen women. He was in a buoyant mood; the party
was carefree, and he looked forward to leaving in two days for
Denmark, where he expected to show his mettle as a commander
and win military glory.

The carriage had not yet reached the grounds of Oranienbaum
when one of Peter's military aides, who had been sent on ahead,
rode up with a disquieting report. Catherine had mysteriously
disappeared. None of the servants knew where she was. Peter's
irritation flared. Angrily he turned the women out of the coach
and drove on in haste to Mon Plaisir, striding in through the same
door Alexis Orlov had entered a scant eight hours earlier and
demanding to know where the servants had hidden Catherine.
With a fine display of indignation he stormed through the house,
throwing open every cupboard and looking behind every hanging, sending the servants flying in fear. In vain he shouted his
wife's name over and over, as if in conjuring her he could evoke
her elusive ghost. But she was nowhere to be found, and by the
time his companions reached the house he had all but given up.

"What did I tell you!" he said to Elizabeth Vorontzov. "The
woman is capable of anything!"

For the next several hours Peter contemplated with mounting
apprehension just what Catherine was capable of. A Holsteiner
who by chance had been in the city when Catherine was proclaimed and who managed to leave before the roads were cor-
doned off brought word of the tumult in Petersburg. Stunned,
then angered by his wife's betrayal, Peter at first assumed that
what was facing his government was nothing worse than a brief
commotion, with brawling in the streets and scuffling in the

taverns. As for Catherine's absurd self-aggrandizement in naming herself empress, he could not believe that his subjects would give it more than passing attention.

Ignoring the alarm of his courtiers, who were clearly much more distressed about the situation than he was, Peter called for his secretaries and set them to work writing out scathing accusations against Catherine and condemning everything she had done. He authorized his chancellor, along with Alexander Shuvalov and Prince Trubetskoy, to go to the capital and to use either persuasion or force to remove Catherine from the scene. He sent messengers to Petersburg to find out what was happening there, and to deliver orders to the guards regiments to march at once to Oranienbaum to join him and defend his court. He ignored the advice of the Prussian ambassador, who suggested that he drop everything and ride as fast as he could toward Finland.

He dispatched a rider to Peterhof to summon the Holsteiners to Oranienbaum in his name, ordering them to bring their artillery. If Catherine should be foolish enough to try to beseige him in the palace, then so be it. She would find out what his troops were made of.

While he waited for his messengers to return from Petersburg and for the guards regiments to arrive in response to his summons, Peter busied himself planning how he would array his defenses. Earlier in the day he had brushed aside the advice of the aged General Münnich, a seasoned and shrewd judge of palace revolutions, who strongly urged him to ride to the capital with a military escort and confront the rebels in person. Now he dallied in following another of Münnich's sensible suggestions: that he take refuge in the strongly fortified island of Kronstadt, just across the water from Oranienbaum, where he would have the protection not only of several thousands of troops but of the entire Russian fleet.

Peter did send two officers to Kronstadt—unaware that the commandant had already received orders from the new empress to seal the fortress off—but did not immediately make plans to go

there. While waiting for his Holsteiners, he supped in the garden
with his mistress and the other women, toasting his future suc-
cesses, letting himself be lulled into inactivity by wine and false
hopes. He put aside the nagging realization that none of his
messengers had come back from Petersburg, and that Vorontzov,
Trubetskoy and Shuvalov were also overdue in returning.

When the Holstein guards arrived he ordered them here and
there, moving them around on the chessboard of Oranienbaum
as he had once moved his toy soldiers in his palace chamber.
The task absorbed him, crowding out the doubts that tugged
at the corners of his mind. He had never actually commanded
troops in a battle, despite his boastful claims to the contrary. If
Catherine led a force against him, would he have the courage to
face them? And what if the guardsmen from Petersburg defied
his summons?

Sometime after ten o'clock, bleary-eyed and too tired to resist
any longer, Peter allowed himself to be persuaded to go to Kronstadt. Something in him must have known, by this time, that
reinforcements from Petersburg were never going to arrive, and
that his power had been snatched from his hands by his clever
wife. But he could not admit it to himself. Instead he drank, and
bullied the courtiers, insisting that he would not board the galley
for Kronstadt until a large supply of liquor had been put on board,
along with all his kitchen equipment. It took at least an hour for
the servants to load the emperor's bottles and casks, pots and
pans, and entire entourage of fifty people into the galley, with the
excess baggage crammed onto a small yacht. Finally, just before
midnight, the boats set sail.

The chilly voyage was unpleasant, and Peter relieved it by
continuing to sip his brandy, his brain a muddled tangle of puzzle-
ment, apprehension and dread. He had no one to turn to for
comfort but his mistress, who was no doubt ashen-faced with
worry and fatigue. When at one in the morning the lights of the
fortress came into view, and the pilot of the galley reported that
the harbor chains were closed, preventing their entry, Peter must

have felt his dread increase. Still, the shreds of his vainglory remained.

He got into a rowboat and had himself rowed toward the fortress.

"Loose these chains at once! It is I, the emperor!" Peter commanded when he came within hailing distance of the watchman. Ordering a lantern held close, he opened his coat to display a decoration blazing on his chest, proof that he was who he said he was.

The response made his blood turn to ice.

"There is no emperor—only an empress."

As the rowboat retreated, trumpets and drums sounded in the fortress, summoning the men to arms. Their shouts reached Peter's ears: "Vivat Catherine! Vivat Catherine! Vivat!"

All was not lost. Once aboard the galley, Peter still had a chance. He could attempt to evade the fleet and sail to safety in a western port, even though armed vessels stood in his way. Should he reach a provincial fortress, he might find that some troops were still loyal to him. With their backing, he might yet regain the throne.

Peter heard the clamoring voices around him, yet did not hear them. He could no longer think, let alone act. He was numbed by wine, by the cold, by the shock of having been dispossessed. Ordering the pilot to sail back to Oranienbaum, he retreated into the depths of his cabin and went to sleep in his mistress's plump lap.

Chapter Eighteen

On the following morning, June 29, Peter surrendered to Alexis Orlov and his hussars at Oranienbaum. Shortly afterward he signed a hastily composed document of abdication, gave up his sword and, utterly forlorn, took off his beloved uniform and handed it to his captors.

He was no longer Emperor of All the Russias. He was merely Peter, consort of Empress Catherine, a helpless prisoner at the mercy of his longsuffering wife, who had every imaginable reason to wreak a terrible vengeance on him.

Peter wrote Catherine a pathetic letter, admitting that he had treated her badly and begging her to forgive him; all he asked, he said, was to be allowed to leave Russia and take refuge in Holstein along with his mistress and a military escort. Panin, who watched the sad spectacle of the ex-emperor's disgrace, was utterly mortified when Peter grasped his hand and tried to kiss it, begging for mercy. Elizabeth Vorontzov, in terror of the new empress, fell to her knees and implored Panin not to separate her from her dishonored lord. But the empress's orders were explicit: Elizabeth Vorontzov was to be sent home to her father, while Peter was to be escorted, under heavy guard, to his estate at Ropsha, and kept there under the close supervision of Alexis Orlov while more permanent quarters were made ready for him at Schlüsselburg—where the hapless Ivan VI still languished.

Though no opposition to the transfer of power had yet man-
ifested itself neither Catherine nor her advisers could be certain
that Peter would not become the object of a countercoup; spineless as he was, he remained a dangerous liability, a potential focus
for discontent. And given the unsettled state of Petersburg, it was
as well to have the former emperor far away and kept out of sight.

For days following the thrilling events of June 28 the capital was
in a state of excited confusion. Work and commerce were interrupted, drunkenness and brawling increased to such an extent
that all the taverns had to be closed by imperial order. Noisy
parades of soldiers, pealing bells, shouting throngs of wine-
soaked revelers made such a constant din that ordinary life was
impossible. Yet the joy was mingled with apprehension. Though
armed troops were posted on every street and in every square,
neither the populace nor the soldiers felt safe. There were periodic
rumors of Prussian perfidy, and anyone seen wearing a Prussian
uniform had to run for his life. The Ismailovsky barracks ex-
ploded into bedlam late one night, the men agitated to a frenzy by
a wild story that a Prussian army, thirty thousand strong, was on
its way to dethrone Catherine. Only after the empress herself
appeared at the barracks to calm the men's fears did the fracas die
down.

Then on July 6 came word from Ropsha that Peter was dead,
the victim of a sudden violent quarrel with one of his guards,
Prince Feodor Baryatinsky. It was a chilling beginning to Catherine's reign, and one that would haunt her for the rest of her life.

According to Alexis Orlov, who sent Catherine a letter from
Ropsha, the "misfortune" was sudden and unavoidable. A quarrel
erupted, blows were exchanged, "we could not separate them,
and already he was no more." More likely the truth is much
darker; Orlov or his subordinates strangled Peter, secure in the
knowledge that they were doing the empress a favor.

When or by whom the suggestion was made to murder the
former emperor will never be known with certainty. Catherine
certainly benefited from the crime, which was carried out in the

presence of her key ally Alexis Orlov and a number of others. To impute Peter's death to Orlov's overzealousness would be to ignore both the toughness of Catherine's resolve and her political astuteness, as well as her capacity for encompassing the unthinkable. She had just taken over a kingdom; she was neither too tenderhearted nor too ethical to shrink from doing what had to be done, however distasteful, in order to safeguard her precarious authority. Yet she may not have given a direct order to kill her husband, or even hinted that his demise would be welcome to her. Still, her critics took note that she punished no one for the crime.

When word of the villainy reached her Catherine took it in stride, though on the following day she gave way to tears and sobbed on Princess Dashkov's shoulder. Two things concerned her above all: the popular reaction to Peter's death, and the reaction of her trusted adviser Panin, who, she feared, might be so appalled at the wickedness of the crime that he might want to disassociate himself from her government. Panin had after all preferred to see Peter replaced by a regency, not by Catherine as empress. He might see in Peter's death not only a crime but a colossal miscalculation—proof that Catherine was not fit to govern.

For a tense few hours Catherine, Panin and one or two others met to discuss the crisis. No record of what was said at that meeting has ever come to light, but it must have been a crucial test of Catherine's leadership. According to the French ambassador Berenger, Catherine summoned all her persuasiveness to convince Panin that she had not been complicit in her husband's murder. In the end he proved cooperative, and helped to draft the official announcement of Peter's death.

According to this announcement, the former emperor had died of colic—from which he had, in fact, been suffering during his captivity—following a severe attack of hemorrhoids. The Russian people were instructed to regard the tragedy as "evidence of God's divine intent," a sign from heaven that Catherine was meant to reign. They were also summoned to view the body, which was to lie in state at the Nevsky monastery.

Thousands of people made the journey to witness the lifeless remains of Emperor Peter III—and many among them drew back in horror at the sight. For the face of the corpse, imperfectly disguised by a large military hat, was a ghastly purplish-black and a voluminous cravat covered the entire throat—carefully arranged, people murmured, to conceal the bruises made by the murderer's hands. It was rumored that Peter had been poisoned and then strangled.

A disturbing wave of feeling against the new regime gathered force and swept outward from the capital. In the provinces, where Peter had never been the hated ogre that he was to the citizens of Petersburg, the late emperor was sincerely mourned. Some provincial soldiers denounced the Petersburg guards regiments for taking power into their own hands and using it to create a new empress. Many denounced Catherine—sometimes openly, more often in whispers—for compounding the iniquity of usurpation with the evil of regicide.

The manner of the late emperor's burial also led to mutters of dissatisfaction. Catherine had denied her husband burial in the honored resting place of the Russian rulers, the Cathedral of Peter and Paul. Instead he was immured in the Nevsky monastery, isolated from his ancestors, as if in a sort of eternal disgrace. To be sure, Peter was unlike his predecessors in that he had never been crowned, and so lacked the spark of divinity lent by the sacrament. Still, the unconventional burial seemed to confirm the general suspicion that the manner of his death had been both ignoble and deplorable. And Catherine, who did not even attend the funeral, ostensibly dissuaded from doing so by the Senate for reasons of health, was clearly to blame.

The reaction of Catherine's subjects in Russia was disturbing enough, but that of the journalists and newsmongers in Western Europe was upsetting in the extreme. Almost without exception they denounced the empress as the barbarous ruler of a barbarous realm, where cruelty and murder were the hallmarks of power and where the light of reason and humane government had yet to penetrate. To Catherine, who saw herself as a beacon of enlightenment in a swamp of vulgarity, ignorance and dissipation, such aspersions were distasteful in the extreme. To be compared to Ivan the Terrible, or to the English Queen Isabella, who had ordered the murder of her husband Edward II, was deeply vexing, particularly when she saw herself in the mold of Peter the Great, and the English Queen Elizabeth, sovereigns who were masters of their own and their realm's destinies.

Few observers, in Russia or outside it, believed that Catherine's government would last long. A young woman ruling alone, lacking the protection and authority of a husband and largely without experience in rulership, would surely be devoured by a palace revolution, or a governmental crisis, or a revolt of the guards. The English ambassador Lord Buckingham referred to Russia as "one great mass of combustibles with incendiaries placed in every corner," and the other representatives of foreign courts agreed with him, all the more so when the Semenovsky guards revolted in August.

The volatile guardsmen, always combustible, were ignited by some ember of discontent—a rumor, a brawl, an insult, a challenge—which set off a small conflagration. At midnight their drummers beat the call to arms, all the men scrambled for their weapons and rushed out into the barracks courtyard, shouting and calling out to one another. Weapons were discharged, blows flew. Entire neighborhoods were aroused to panic, and people thought that another revolt was under way. With great difficulty the officers managed to corral their men and quell their turbulence, but not before the police, the authorities and Catherine herself had become alarmed.

On the following night the same thing happened again: the midnight summons to arms, the pell-mell rush into the courtyard, the noise, the panic. This time some officers joined the men in unleashing chaos, and the remaining officers were all but helpless in extinguishing the tumult.

Catherine moved swiftly to respond. Many officers and soldiers were arrested and whisked off to unknown destinations where they were detained indefinitely. But the threat of a guards' revolt did not dissipate; everyone knew that, having put Catherine where she was, the guardsmen could supplant or overthrow her with equal ease.

Even if Catherine's fledgling government succeeded in controlling the explosive guardsmen, it could hardly hope to surmount the huge obstacles of debt, disorganization and administrative chaos that were the legacy of Elizabeth's reign. These alone, observers believed, would combine to overwhelm the new ruler and her advisers, who would then be vulnerable to another palace revolution.

Catherine's government faced disaster. The fiscal crisis was of enormous proportions, and demanded an immediate and drastic solution. The treasury was utterly depleted, debts were running into many millions of rubles and mounting fast, and, because Russia's credit had become worthless in foreign markets, no further loans could be raised. The severe shortage of money produced another predicament: army pay was in arrears, and the government relied on the army, not only to protect itself and the realm against attack, but to keep order, collect taxes, and suppress revolts.

Calamities of many sorts were descending on the new regime. Crops failed, bringing famine and leaving many peasants unable to pay their taxes; some fled from their masters, or rebeled, and as local government had all but broken down, the rebellions flared unchecked. On the Ukrainian borderlands, Turks and Tatars made frequent forays into Russian territory, carrying off peasants and enslaving them. Bandits terrorized the roads, pirates raided traffic on the Volga. Added to these were natural disasters and the vagaries of a harsh climate, which left some regions devastated by floods and others prey to fierce storms or prolonged droughts.

To deal with this array of catastrophes the empress relied on the Senate, a handful of underpaid, unreliable provincial governors, and an antiquated bureaucracy far too small in numbers to control the huge expanse of Russia. No one knew better than she did how difficult was the task that faced her. As she herself wrote, recalling the early weeks of her reign, "The Senate remained lethargic, deaf to the affairs of state. The seats of legislation had reached a degree of corruption and disintegration that made them scarcely recognizable."

And there was another obstacle to surmount. Well aware that her hold on power was precarious, Catherine had to constantly woo the senators and senior civil servants, to earn their loyalty. She knew that while no one wanted to undertake the hard labor of governing, everyone in the government wanted to feel important. So she spent long hours with elderly officials who offered her uninformed advice, made longwinded requests and proposed impractical plans. Every court day brought a fresh group of importunate petitioners and would-be counselors, who tried her patience and took up her time with their demands and their rambling conversation. She did her best to convince each one that she took his needs or proposals seriously, she acknowledged each suggestion as best she could, and when she could not follow a particular piece of advice, she made an effort to explain why.

All this effort left her drained. She confided to the French ambassador that she felt like a hare being hounded by hunters, forced to dart this way and that, running in a dozen directions, ever alert to danger.

Still, she rose to the challenge. Within days of Catherine's accession it was clear to every secretary, clerk and minister that a new pair of hands held the reins of power. Where Elizabeth had been indolent and averse to business, and Peter had been an empty martinet, Catherine was industrious, pragmatic, attentive to detail and full of common sense. She and Panin had clear ideas about the direction in which they wished to guide the empire and how to guide it there.

Early each morning the empress was at her desk, reading reports and dispatches, answering petitions, deciding on appointments. She wrote to each provincial governor and regional military commander ordering him to send her regular written summaries of conditions within his jurisdiction, and she addressed herself to drafting orders, or ukases, on everything from the conditions of road transport to disputed fishing rights to the consecration of religious shrines.

To protect her subjects against exploitation by grain speculators she ordered that an imperial granary be established in each town, so that she could regulate the price herself. Perhaps remembering the wretched lunatics whom Elizabeth had kept at court for her amusement, Catherine instructed the College of Foreign Affairs to gather information from European countries on how the insane were treated there, so that the best available western models could be instituted in Russia.

Determined to reinvigorate the premier governing body, the lethargic Senate, Catherine restored to it powers removed by her husband, principally the right to legislate and to review petitions. She divided it into departments, with each department responsible for a different facet of governance, and added more clerks and secretaries to improve efficiency. Instead of emasculating the Senate, as Peter had done, Catherine intended to rely on it to oversee routine tasks, so that she and Panin would not be overburdened with time-consuming mundane labors and could concentrate on the more difficult and longer range issues facing the empire. At the same time, however, Catherine made it clear that she meant to stay firmly in charge; instead of the brief summary reports the senators usually sent to the sovereign, she demanded detailed reports, leaving nothing out. She might delegate, but she would remain watchful.

For years Catherine had been turning over in her mind the

riddle of how Russia ought to be governed. She had defined her political principles, with the help of Montesquieu. "I want the laws obeyed," she wrote in one of her notebooks several years before she became empress, "but I want no slaves. My general aim is to create happiness without all the whimsicality, eccentricity, and tyranny which destroy it." She wanted to set in place just laws, to enforce them fairly and humanely, to raise the state above faction and above the fallibility of the rulers. Rulers come and go, generations of subjects are born and die, she wrote, but a wisely constituted governing system goes on forever.

To a large extent, that governing system, as Catherine envisioned it, must enshrine morality and counteract the primitive ferocity, greed and self-seeking inherent in mankind. Institutions exist to promote the primacy of reasonable relations among men, to foster moderation and toleration, above all to create a bastion against the excesses to which humanity's lower nature makes it prone.

Such were the empress's lofty aims, formed to a large extent by her thoughtful reading but also by her observation of her predecessors' incapable rule. She was determined not to be capricious, as Elizabeth had been, or narcissistic, as Peter had been, or lazy and inconsistent, as both had been. Where they had vaunted themselves, she meant to vaunt the state itself, and to make it an instrument of progress. She would be the midwife of that progress, bringing to birth a reformed, enlightened Russia.

Panin and his assistant Teplov drew up a document stating the aims of the new government. In it they made clear that henceforth there would be no favoritism, no individuals advanced to high office merely because the sovereign found them pleasing. The era of arbitrary rule was at an end, and a new era was beginning, in which established legal procedures would govern the exercise of power and the monarch would surround herself with professional advisers who would be her conscience, helping her to rein in her impulses so that she would never slip into tyranny.

These high-minded aims would have been empty had Catherine not possessed the energy, thirst for goodness and fervor for betterment to carry them out. Without being a zealot, she was profoundly and intensely committed to her goals, and she had the patience, sanity and even-tempered steadiness of purpose needed to implement them. Her personal symbol was the bee, tirelessly flying from flower to flower, gathering whatever it could use; the bee appeared on her crest, with the inscription *L'Utile,* "The Useful."

Her constant inspiration throughout these early days was Peter the Great, whose larger-than-life energy, visionary ambition and administrative ability she emulated. The great Peter's successors had been unworthy of him, but Catherine would not be. Among the things she carried with her everywhere was a snuffbox decorated with his portrait. It reminded her, she told her advisers, "to ask each moment, what would he have ordained, what would he have forbidden, what would he have done, if he were in my place?"

Catherine felt the ghost of Peter the Great looking over her shoulder, weighing her actions, calling her to account. He had brought Russia into the sphere of European influence, reinvigorating her with his own dynamism and introducing fresh habits of mind, aggressive, active policies and forcefulness in effectuating change. He had challenged all that was static, passive and timeless in Russian culture, churning the old ways with the force of his own vitality and forward-looking plans. She hoped to continue his work—work that had virtually come to a halt during the reigns of his three far less capable successors.

And Catherine meant to do more. Where Peter the Great had been preoccupied with importing the military skills and technological expertise of Western Europe, she would bring to Russia the invigorating breezes of European thought.

She would import a valued freight of new ideas, bold assertions of human freedom, of emancipation from the deadweight of tradition. She would introduce to Russian intellectuals—admittedly a very small group, to be enlarged through widened education—the concepts of limited government, free-ranging religious thought, unhampered by centuries-old dogmas, rational challenges to superstitious folkways, fresh and creative approaches to learning. She would teach Russians to play with ideas, setting them against one another, weighing them not according to age or the dictates of accepted authority but according to their real merits, as determined by the collective judgments of discerning, educated minds. She would make the members of the Russian intelligentsia, insofar as she could, into copies of herself. And she would continue to model herself, as far as possible, in the likeness of Voltaire.

Voltaire, the archpriest of European letters, was sixty-eight in the year that Catherine became empress. His works filled dozens of volumes, and included histories, plays, essays and criticism. Every well-read citizen of Christendom knew of his unrivaled reputation for combating ignorance, prejudice, inequality and oppression; for decades he had waged a one-man campaign against intolerance and clerical tyranny, and for free expression, his only weapon his pen, and the witty, trenchant, unsparing and devastating critiques he wrote with it.

From his estate at Ferney on the Swiss border Voltaire reigned over literary Europe. Hundreds of admirers made the pilgrimage to visit him in person (some of them coming away disappointed, dismayed to find that their hero was a shabbily dressed, uncombed, cantankerous and eccentric old nobleman), thousands more wrote to him, and became part of his vast network of correspondents. Voltaire's letters in reply were much more than personal messages; they were treasured relics, passed eagerly from hand to hand, read out loud to those who could not read themselves. Some were published. Voltaire disseminated information and opinions on every significant issue of the day, and his opinions had influence in high places and low. What Voltaire thought and wrote mattered.

Thus when Catherine began a correspondence with the patriarch of Ferney she had several goals in mind besides the obvious one of opening a dialogue with the man she called her "teacher." She knew that if she could gain his good opinion, the resulting positive notoriety might counteract the bad press she had received following her husband's death. She hoped that by interesting him in her efforts to bring about positive changes in Russia, she could give those changes wider publicity, and draw esteem to herself.

Her initial letters to Voltaire (to which she signed the name of her secretary Pictet, though the letters' true authorship was an open secret) elicited no more than a lukewarm response, but Catherine was persistent, and soon she and her "teacher" were on good epistolary terms. She begged him to send her his most recent writings, and let him know that several of his plays were being presented at her court. She lauded him as having "combated the massed enemies of mankind: superstition, fanaticism, ignorance, intrigue, evil judges, and the abuse of power." She saluted him for having conquered the obstacles standing in the way of progress, and for showing the way to others.

Voltaire, who had an abiding interest in Russia as a "new civilization," created by Peter the Great out of the murk and marshes of barbaric Slavdom, responded well to Catherine's sincere if opportunistic flattery. His response grew warmer when he learned that Catherine had invited his friend Diderot, author of the *Encyclopédie,* to come to Russia to resume publication of his great work. (The French government had banned the work, and Diderot's efforts to continue publication in secret had become increasingly fraught.) She also invited Diderot's erstwhile colleague D'Alembert to become her son's tutor.

Convinced that the empress's dedication to progressive ideas was genuine, Voltaire became lavish in his praise of her, calling her "the brightest star of the north," and comparing her favorably to her illustrious predecessor Peter the Great. He was also inclined to overlook her lapse of morals in tolerating the elimination of her husband. ("I know that she is reproached with some trifles about her husband," he wrote to one of his correspondents, "but these are family affairs with which I do not meddle.") So much for regicide.

Catherine had made a good beginning, building a foundation of political loyalties, making what use she could of existing institutions and planning to establish stronger ones, working to counteract the firestorm of condemnation that greeted her at the outset of her reign. She had set forth an ambitious and idealistic program for her government to follow. Above all she had demonstrated her capacity for strenuous, ceaseless labor.

Empress Catherine II stood on the brink of an abyss, threatened by potential rebellion, provincial anarchy, soldierly hostility, and the constant menace of a palace revolution. Yet, calmly and surely, she forestalled disaster by carrying out her duties and acting as if all were well. She showered her supporters with tens of thousands of rubles as if her treasury were overflowing. She presided over her officials as if in charge of the best-run empire the world had ever seen. She planned confidently for the future as if no threat to the throne existed. And to set the seal of divine favor on the long and prosperous reign she envisioned, she made immediate plans for her coronation in the very heart of old Russia, the holy city of Moscow.

Chapter Nineteen

WHITE-STONED MOSCOW, THE GLOWING CITY THAT ROSE on its hilly eminence and loomed frostily over the surrounding forested countryside. Moscow, city of five hundred churches and five thousand gleaming golden domes, steeples, cupolas and crosses, each more rich with color than the next, the crosses linked one to another with bright chains of gilded metal. Moscow of the brilliant rooftops, scaled with red and green tiles, enameled in blue and silver, painted with gold stars, or a checkerboard of black and white squares. Crenelated Moscow, ringed by its six fortresslike monasteries and dominated by the towering splendor and magnificence of the Kremlin on its high hill.

Moscow of the bells. From each of the sixteen hundred bell towers sounded the incessant clangor of dozens of huge and sonorous metal bells, their great throats pealing forth until the earth shook, drowning all conversation and driving newcomers to the city to cover their ears and pray for deliverance. They rang on Sundays and festival days without ceasing, all day and all night, and at other times to call worshipers to services, to warn of fires or other danger, to signal the beginning and end of the workday, and to mark the occasion of funerals or saints' days or simply in token of rejoicing. Whenever the population felt the menace of sickness or bad weather, or the hovering presence of evil, all the bells were rung together, their cacophonous stridor at once a plea to heaven and a ritual meant to affright the demons of bad fortune. Bells were magical, and Moscow had more of their magic than any other city in Christendom.

Every visitor to the great city was deafened by its bells, and awed by its magnificence. Peasants bringing goods to the market-places crossed themselves whcn the outskirts of the city came into view, and saluted "Mother Moscow." European travelers approaching the city for the first time had their coachmen pause on the summit of the Sparrow Hills so that they could admire the sprawling timbered sweep of the huge metropolis, its white churches forming a luminous halo around its vast circumference.

Moscow was God's holy city, according to its citizens, the holiest city in Christendom. Moscow would stand forever, the saying went, because it was the Third Rome, and an ancient prophecy had said that the Third Rome was destined to be eternal. The first Rome had been corrupted by heresy and had been conquered by barbarians in late antiquity. Her mantle had fallen on Byzantium, and Constantinople had become the Second Rome. But in 1453 Constantinople had fallen to the Turks, whereupon the burden and glory of bearing Christian truth had been brought to Moscow.

For three hundred years the Third Rome had stood as a beacon of faith, ruled by the successor of the Caesars, the divine emperor. Now Catherine II would come to the holy city to be anointed by God as his representative on earth.

But Catherine hated Moscow. Her contempt and loathing for Russia's second most important city had grown throughout Elizabeth's reign until it became a monumental abhorrence. "Moscow is the seat of sloth," Catherine wrote in her memoirs, "partly due to its immensity. One wastes a whole day trying to visit someone or delivering a message to them. The nobles who live there are excessively fond of the place and no wonder—they live in idleness and luxury, and become effeminate. It is not houses they own there, but regular estates."

The very grandeur of scale dwarfed all purpose and promoted languor and inactivity; a kind of sleepy torpor overlaid Moscow life. To the ever-diligent, hard-working Catherine, who could hardly bear to let a day go by without accomplishing as much as possible, this attitude toward existence was inexcusable. What was worse, the Muscovites seemed to Catherine to busy themselves with gossip and triviality, insulting their intelligence by indulging their appetites, whims and fancies.

Law was ignored in Moscow, in Catherine's view; the result was that the upper classes turned into petty tyrants, lording it over their inferiors and treating their servants cruelly.

"The inclination to tyrannize is cultivated here more than in any other inhabited part of the world," Catherine wrote. "It is inculcated from the tenderest age by the cruelty which children observe in their parents' behavior toward servants." Every home had its chamber of horrors where chains, whips and other instruments of torture were kept for use in punishing servants—and the punishments were severe for even the smallest infractions. To protest, as Catherine forthrightly did, that servants were no less human than their masters was to risk loud censure from the "vulgar gentry" whose brutality was exceeded only by their stupidity.

All the worst tendencies in Moscow life were exacerbated by the religiosity that flourished there—not an honest piety, of the kind Catherine favored, but the darker sort of religion that led to intolerance, irrationality and mental aberrations. "The town is full of symbols of fanaticism, churches, miraculous icons, priests and convents," she wrote. Endless processions, day-long rituals, the mad ringing of the thousands of bells created an atmosphere, not so much of otherworldliness as of murky illogic, inhospitable to the concrete and the commonsensical; in Moscow, reason withered under the icy blast of the supernatural.

As intractable, elusive and labyrinthine as Petersburg was regular, ordered and rectilinear, Moscow outraged Catherine's admiration for harmony and organization. Its magnificence offended her taste for simplicity, its extravagant luxury was an affront to her sense of proportion, its brazen inertia was an annoying challenge to her vision of a revitalized Russia bestirring itself in vigorous pursuit of reform. It was no wonder she hated the superstitious, reprobate old city, and gritted her teeth as she prepared to enter it for her coronation.

For all its luminous splendor when viewed from a distance, Moscow proved to be a dirty, ramshackle, unpaved shambles when seen near at hand. Because fire swept through the city frequently, wiping out hundreds or even thousands of dwellings and outbuildings in a matter of hours, rebuilding was always going on. Blackened timbers lay in charred heaps in every quarter of the city, freshly cut logs and green timbers were piled randomly along the winding streets, as were untidy mounds of bricks and the remnants of falling-down dwellings. Moscow had suffered from neglect over the two generations since Petersburg became the seat of government; many dwellings had been allowed to fall into ruin, and others, though occupied for part of the year, showed signs of severe decay.

And there was dirt everywhere. Refuse heaps higher than the housetops spread their stench over every neighborhood. Undrained cesspits mired every street. The mean, dark little houses of the poor reeked of ordure and rancid oil and human and animal waste. Even in the mansions of the great, filth was piled in anterooms and corridors and staircases were hidden under accumulations of excrement and the dust of ages. Visitors deplored the Russian custom of spitting unceremoniously on the floor, "in all directions and at all times," and held their noses whenever they crossed the streets—not paved lanes but quagmires full of stinking sludge.

The large animal population of Moscow contributed to the barnyard odors. The spacious grounds in which the houses of the nobles and gentry were set accommodated cows and pigs and chickens and ducks, along with stables and kennels, and the reek of pigsties and cattle byres, stables and dog runs was an inescapable part of Moscow life.

Urban splendor often clashed with rural squalor. With her sharp eye for all that was absurd, Catherine described how "in Moscow one quite often sees a lady covered with jewels and elegantly dressed, emerging from an immense yard, filled with all possible refuse and mud, adjoining a decrepit hut, in a magnificent carriage, drawn by eight horrible hacks, shabbily harnessed, with unkempt grooms wearing handsome liveries which they disgrace by their uncouth appearance."

Such a sight was common in the noble quarter, where the commodious houses of the titled families sprawled amid stands of forest, lakes and streams. Nearer the heart of the city were the dozens of craftsmen's districts, where weavers, hatters, brewers, icon painters, armorers, tilers, and coppersmiths created and sold their wares. The districts were highly specialized. Breadmakers occupied one area, bakers of fancy loaves another. Pancake makers did not mix with biscuit bakers. Bell founders were distinct from blacksmiths, and painters of holy images kept themselves apart from painters of other sorts.

In the German suburb—where Catherine was no doubt most at home—foreign merchants had built over the centuries a small replica of a northern European town, with a grid of wide streets, houses with gardens, public squares and neoclassical architecture. But this oasis of relative tidiness and patterned order seemed out of place, hemmed in as it was on all sides by warrens of patternless, unplanned dwellings, shops and shrines, Tatar temples and Chinese pagodas and pavilions, with here and there a Turkish mosque.

The bustling heart of Moscow was the Kitaigorod, or market district, with its rows of stalls running along the bank of the Moskva River under the high walls of the Kremlin. The Kitaigorod was a hive of commerce, where twisting alleys seemed to go on forever under a dense vaulted roof, and goods from half the world were displayed in the dimness: metalwork from Yaroslavl and Kholmogory, hides from Kazan, velvet and brocade from France and Italy, swords from Damascus, enamels from Kiev and Solvychegodsk, even bone carvings from far away Archangel. Siberian furs were heaped next to pottery from Samarkand, fruit and vegetables from Astrakhan and stale fish (the Muscovites were said to prefer it stale) from Moscow's twenty rivers and streams and the lower Volga.

Tradesmen and artisans set up shop in low stalls lined with tree bark, with icons nailed to the beams and lamps hanging below them. While waiting for trade they drank tea and said their prayers, gossiped with friends, played ball and fed the huge flocks of pigeons that roosted under the vaulted ceiling. Pigeons, like bells, were holy objects; Muscovites revered them as symbols of the holy spirit, and protected them from harm.

Rich merchants visiting Moscow stayed in the inns of Kitaigorod, and even princes and important noblemen maintained farms along its outskirts. Horse-drawn sleds brought goods to replenish its ancient stalls every day, and traders scoured the city and outlying villages for rags, broken dishes, discarded furniture and curiosities to sell in the flea market. What could not be bought in the vast bazaar was not worth buying. One could even have a tooth drawn there, or buy charms and medicines, or visit a barber, or have one's fortune told.

The Moscow poor crowded the Kitaigorod on market days, picking their way along, haggling for bargains, crossing themselves at the sight of holy pictures, priests and funeral processions, clutching their purses and watching out for thieves, closing their ears to the hubbub and holding their noses when the mingled scents of sour beer, cooked cabbage, leather, boot grease and musky cologne became unbearable. Disease came from the market, and crime and mayhem were rampant there; still, it was worth the risk, for the best prices were to be had in the worst areas, where the stalls were built over a muddy swamp and rain and snow fell through gaps in the roof canopy.

In the wood market, coffins were laid out by the hundreds, in sizes small enough for infants or large enough for the tallest and most bearlike Russian man. They were little more than hollowed tree trunks, cut in half and fitted with crudely shaped lids; coarse and unfinished though they were, they sold briskly in the long freezing winters and nearly as well in the short, plague-ridden summers. In addition to coffins, timber merchants also sold entire houses, each board numbered so that they could be disassembled and easily rebuilt at the buyer's preferred location. With every devastating fire there came an immediate and voracious demand for new houses, and the wood merchants, carpenters and cabinetmakers thrived.

In Red Square, in front of one of the principal gates leading into the Kremlin, was the official city center, where imperial orders were read and where patriarchs stood to bless the faithful. Here the many-domed church of St. Basil rose in all its fantastic splendor, each of its domed structures more fancifully decorated than the next. Here blind beggars sang for coins and trainers of dancing bears set their beasts to performing. Actors and acrobats vied for the coins of the ever-present crowd, while peddlers sold live fish from tanks and pushcart vendors offered meat pies, hot mead and kvass, a drink made from fermented rye bread.

Priests without churches sold their services in Red Square, offering to perform masses for hire. Nearby, scribes sold carefully copied lives of the saints, accounts of miracles and chronicles. For a price, they also offered earthy stories and vulgar verses, though they kept these manuscripts well hidden. Equally well hidden were the prostitutes who frequented Red Square, staying away from the ancient round platform called the Place of the Brow where holy relics were buried and executions were carried out.

Grisly judicial murders drew onlookers to the Place of the Brow. Here murderers and thieves were beheaded by axe-wielding executioners. Rebels were beaten with knouts and broken on the wheel, suffering a slow, tormenting death. Renegade priests, accused of inciting discontent, were hanged under the domes of the cathedral, their bodies left to rot where they hung from one season to the next as a warning to the populace. Notorious criminals were slowly dismembered, each limb hacked off with a hatchet before the writhing, bleeding torso was severed from the head.

When Catherine entered Red Square on September 13, 1762, huge crowds greeted her carriage. The weather had been dull and gray and cold and the cobblestones in the square were encrusted with ice. Still, the warmly wrapped Muscovites cheered her and called out blessings as she passed along her route, which was marked out with arches wrapped in green boughs. Prince Trubetskoy, who had been charged with making all arrangements for the coronation, had done his best to prepare the city to receive the empress. He cautioned her that the people were disgruntled; between the drenching autumn rains, which left the streets all but impassable and interrupted the supply of food from the countryside, and the high prices that invariably set in with the early frosts, there was much grumbling and disquiet.

Catherine nodded graciously to the thronging Muscovites, most of whom were seeing her for the first time. She had her son with her, and encouraged him to show his small pale face at the window. Paul had been ill, and was not yet fully recovered, but Catherine needed him at her side when she confronted her subjects, to increase her appeal. She wanted them to think of her, not as the ambitious German woman who had ordered her husband's murder, but as a madonna figure, a compassionate mother protective of her son.

In truth her mind was not on her son—though his fragile health was a concern, for if he should die she would lose an important pillar of her legitimacy—but on the need to keep good order in Moscow over the following ten days, when the coronation festivities were to begin. There must be no food riots, or disturbances caused by troublemakers or opportunists who denounced her as morally unfit to reign. She was aware of disloyalty and potential disloyalty all around her, even among the women who served her and were in and out of her private apartments dozens of times a day.

These women were in a position to know all that mattered most to her, like it or not she was vulnerable to them. They knew, just now, that she was carrying another child. Once again, it was Gregory Orlov's child, only this time it would be born, not to the grand duke's wife, but to a reigning empress. If the baby were to be a boy, the succession could be altered, with the sickly Paul set aside in favor of Orlov's more robust son. (Catherine's other child by Orlov, the infant Alexis, was being cared for by her chamberlain Shkurin, kept out of sight of the court; his future fate was uncertain.) But for the time being the only sign of Catherine's pregnancy was her sour stomach—a symptom that she had learned over the years how to disguise.

During the ten days that Catherine spent in the Kremlin Palace, ostensibly fasting and cleansing her soul in preparation for the holy ritual of coronation, she met with her councillors, learned the words she must pronounce during the ceremony, and went over every detail with Prince Trubetskoy. The treasury was bare, yet the coronation had to dazzle. There had to be gorgeous carriages, richly caparisoned horses, everything must be gilded and encrusted with gems. Catherine's own gown of shining golden silk thickly embroidered with gold and silver threads had to draw all eyes to her, as the radiant focus of the spectacle.

The late Empress Elizabeth's wardrobe was plundered for finery for the coming coronation. Jewels were gouged from buckles and buttons, pearls stripped from skirts and headdresses. Old velvet was turned into new liveries. Old silk was cut and stitched and re-hemmed. Master goldsmiths crafted a crown for Catherine, set with five thousand small diamonds and seventy-six large and lustrous pearls. A gigantic ruby shone from the top, surmounted by a cross. The rest of the regalia were burnished and made ready to be presented to the empress. In her scepter, symbol of her ruling authority, shone the hugely magnificent Orlov diamond, which gleamed like a beacon and reminded her of the man who had helped to put her on the throne.

All the cannon of the Kremlin thundered forth early on the morning of Sunday, September 22, to salute Catherine's coronation day. Bells clanged and tolled, regiments formed up and marched to their appointed positions in Cathedral Square, musicians took their places and the first of a long train of carriages rolled in through the Kremlin gates.

For four hours the nobility, foreign dignitaries, court officials and finally the golden-robed priests assembled in the Cathedral of the Assumption, where thousands of candles and tapers illuminated a wealth of gold and silver crosses, shrines and lamps and a profusion of gem-encrusted icons. A huge tentlike baldaquin had been erected over a raised dais. Here Catherine was to sit during the ceremony, in full view of the spectators.

Finally at ten o'clock Catherine emerged from her apartments in the palace, resplendent in her golden gown, its sweeping train held up by six attendants, and with a mantle made of four thousand ermine skins over her slender shoulders. Her confessor walked before her, sprinkling holy water on the carpet, the staircase, the stone steps that led into Cathedral Square. A loud fanfare greeted Catherine's appearance in the square, and the crowds waiting outside the walls of the Kremlin echoed the huzzas and shouted blessings.

While massed choirs sang Catherine entered the cathedral, her head held high, her pace majestically slow, and mounted the dais beneath the ornate baldaquin. She listened to the archimandrite read a long sermon in Church Slavonic, the archaic tongue reserved for religious ritual, then took up her book and recited the creed. This done, she took the imperial purple mantle and draped it over her gown, and received from the hands of the venerable priest the replica of the twelfth-century Cap of Monomakh, the golden crown with which all the rulers of Russia had been crowned for six centuries. When she had placed the cap on her head more prayers were said, and she was invested with the orb and scepter.

Crowned, bearing the symbols of her high office, arrayed in majesty, Catherine stood before her people for the first time as their sacred sovereign. "In his mortal form, the emperor resembles all men," went the words of the coronation ritual, "but in his power he is like unto Almighty God."

Once again cannon were fired, triggering renewed shouting and cheering. By this time Catherine, who had eaten nothing for many hours, must have felt faint. Cinched into her tight gown, her mantle heavy and the regalia heavier still, her stomach unsettled and her mind led into fantasies by the mosaics of dark angels and saints looming over her from every pillar and wall, she must have longed for the ceremony to end.

But there was more to come. Catherine prayed at the tombs of her predecessors, the grand dukes, emperors and empresses of Russia, and invested herself with the silver star of the Order of St. Andrew on its blue ribbon, with the accompanying gold cross and gold chain. The archimandrite then celebrated mass, and throughout the very long service the empress knelt and stood and knelt again, listening to an interminable sermon and a succession of prayers and sung psalms. Nearly four hours went by before the entire exhausting ritual was over, and the new empress, anointed with the chrism and having received the consecrated bread and wine, was ready to rejoin her people.

When she came into view in the square she was greeted with tumultuous acclaim. Moved beyond measure, the onlookers wept and sang and knelt on the frigid cobblestones, while Catherine went into the cathedrals of the Annunciation and of the Archangel Michael to pray before the ancient icons. Later she ordered her servants to break open a hundred and twenty barrels of small coins and fling them into the crowd. This traditional display of imperial generosity brought forth fresh roars of delight, as Catherine knew it would. But her gift to the people was insignificant compared to the gifts she presented to her courtiers:

lucrative appointments, titles, decorations and jewels in abundance. Gregory and Alexis Orlov were conspicuously rewarded, but there were abundant presents and favors for everyone. Not even the least of the palace servants was forgotten.

By the time night fell the courtiers could scarcely stand. They leaned against the walls, their eyes glazed over with fatigue. Catherine may have napped, or, buoyed by the excitement of the day's grand events, she may have found her second wind. In any event she made one final appearance at midnight, standing atop the Red Staircase next to the Granovitaia Palace to witness the glorious illumination of the Kremlin towers and gateways with yellow lamps. The lights, which brought every turret and crenellation into sharp focus, turned the heavy, brooding fortress into a delicate fairyland. People still milled about in the hundreds in the square below, enjoying the carnival-like aftermath of the day's solemnity. They broke into cries of joy when they saw Catherine, wishing her long life and health and cheering themselves hoarse.

Catherine's coronation day was only the beginning of months of official and unofficial festivities. Every day there were banquets, receptions, formal gatherings in honor of the sovereign— more than enough activity to disturb the customary Muscovite sloth and to provide luxury-loving idlers with occasions to exchange gossip and drive about in their showy carriages drawn by thin, spavined horses.

Catherine appeared at many of these gatherings, her smiling charm and affability always in evidence, the discomforts of her early pregnancy no apparent hindrance to her blithe facade. Gregory Orlov was often at her side, invariably the tallest, most broad-shouldered, best-looking man in the room, resplendent in gold-embroidered coat and breeches, jeweled rings and other prominent tokens of his sovereign's particular favor, his chest a glitter of orders and medals. A consort in all but name, Orlov was more than superbly decorative. He played his role expertly, never upstaging the empress yet enhancing her presence, treating her with broadly affectionate familiarity yet never appearing to exalt himself or overreach his actual standing.

Orlov's towering, rocklike support was vital to Catherine, for behind her composed exterior she was anxious and apprehensive.

Ten days after the coronation, Catherine heard from her trusted chamberlain, Vasily Shkurin, that some among the young officers who had supported her coup were conspiring to dethrone her and replace her with the imprisoned Ivan VI. She acted immediately, ordering the arrest and torture of the men involved, and bringing back into existence a secret agency (little different from Elizabeth's Secret Chancery) to investigate, apprehend and punish all those suspected of political conspiracy and treason.

The affair was sobering to the fundamentally humane and just Catherine. Now that she had joined the long line of absolute rulers of Russia, stretching back over centuries, she was beginning to see why they had become tyrannical. She had always deplored what she had perceived as the abuse of power, yet now that she had been touched by the chill breath of perfidy, she understood its wellsprings. Her authority had its own imperatives, she discovered. Absolute power demanded ironclad obduracy toward traitors. Unwavering sternness alone could protect her. And she might never again be able to trust anyone completely.

During October, as a thick carpet of snow blanketed Moscow and a new round of feasts and amusements preoccupied the citizenry, the empress devoted herself to ferreting out disloyalty. She bought information, she paid some officers for denouncing others. She discovered who was prone to criticizing her, who was discontented, who became indiscreet when drunk. She had known that not all the men supported her completely, and that her every initiative, indeed her every move was being watched and judged by those who had made her accession possible. Some of the men felt slighted, others were jealous of the Orlovs' prominence. Still others, correctly sensing the vulnerability of the new government, were greedy for power themselves. But she had not realized how vigilant she would have to be to ensure that discontent did not turn into outright conspiracy. And she had not anticipated how combating the climate of disloyalty would drain her and tax her physically.

In the last week of October she announced to her subjects that a treasonous challenge to her authority had been discovered and circumvented. She had intended to have the principal instigators of the plot executed, but in the end she ordered them exiled to Siberia, with loss of their military rank, their noble status and of all privileges.

Once again crowds gathered in Red Square to hear the sentences read out and to watch while the prisoners, now reduced to the status of ordinary laborers or peasants, had their military swords broken over their heads. Catherine received a thorough report on the events in Red Square, but she could not watch them herself. She was confined to her bed, pale and sad-eyed, with midwives in attendance and her physicians waiting just out of sight in the next room. She had lost her baby.

Chapter Twenty

CATHERINE'S FIRST WINTER IN MOSCOW AS EMPRESS PASSED in a blur of balls, suppers, and receptions and formal gatherings. She rose early and worked late, interrupting her labors to put on her silks and her diamonds and preside graciously at court fetes and private soirees, to attend weddings and sit through long church services.

Thick snow blanketed Moscow, the shroud of soft white ennobling the city's shabbiness. During the chill afternoons, in the intervals between snowfalls, people raced sledges on the frozen Moscow River, the horses flying along the ice, the bells on their harnesses jingling. Bands played at the river's edge, where spectators gathered to watch skaters glide past and to place wagers on the sledge races. The empress too watched, and wagered, and observers commented on her carefree cheerfulness and good humor.

She was determined to give the appearance of feeling completely secure, of not being afraid, though she had good reason to be fearful. She did not want to give anyone an excuse to say that she was becoming like the late Empress Elizabeth, consumed with apprehension for her safety, so alarmed that she dreaded falling asleep, her life a nightmare of clandestine maneuvers and precautions. Catherine often ordered an open carriage and rode out in it at night with only a small escort to protect her. When she rode to the Senate, she took only two lackeys with her in her carriage— hardly the entourage of a frightened woman. She gave every evidence of being at ease.

Yet she knew the risk she was taking. Incipient conspiracies were uncovered at least once a month, sometimes every week. Agents of the reinstated Secret Branch brought the empress word of treasonous utterances, secret plotting, small but significant betrayals that undermined Catherine's authority. Two of the maids of Catherine's bedchamber were arrested for gossiping about her, sneering that she was more man than woman. They were sent away from court. Guards officers threatened to raise another rebellion, or boasted of their ability to do so. They were banished to Siberia. Nobles and others, chagrined at the favoritism Catherine showed toward Gregory Orlov—having granted him the title of count, she made him chamberlain, gentleman of the bedchamber, and general adjutant, adding other lucrative positions and giving him generous gifts of money and jewelry— plotted to remove him or even kill him. They were ferreted out, interrogated, and sent away.

Still, no matter how active the Secret Branch was, the climate of insecurity could not be dispelled. The British ambassador Lord Buckingham wrote to his superiors in London in February of 1763 that "great confusion" reigned within Catherine's government. "One does not see the same air of general satisfaction and contentment which appeared two months ago," he added, "and many people dare to let show their disapprobation with the measures taken by the court." Muscovites paused in their winter amusements to grumble about the empress and her paramour Orlov. Peasants bringing goods into the city to sell complained that ever since Catherine became empress the weather had been poor; her accession had brought bad luck, they said, crossing themselves and redoubling their prayers.

Catherine did her best to keep her balance amid the unsettled atmosphere, dividing her time between work and pleasure. "The life of the empress," Lord Buckingham reported, "is a mélange of frivolous amusements and an intense application to business—which application has not produced anything yet, due to the obstacles which people throw deliberately in Catherine's path, and also due to the diversity of her projects." "Her plans are numerous and vast," he noted, "but very disproportionate to the means at her disposal."

Day after day she took council with her six secretaries, the men who brought her official documents and with whom she consulted on decisions to be made, edicts and other pronouncements to be issued. She talked with Panin and the elderly Bestuzhev—she had recalled the latter from his exile, and listened to his advice with the greatest interest—and read, studied, and thought through a wide range of issues. And day after day, having put in hours of effort, she was forced to admit that her efforts were largely wasted. Inertia, hostility, the petty self-interest of those she was forced to rely on to forward her plans thwarted her and drove her projects backward.

Ruling was not proving to be what she had imagined it would be, and in her inmost heart she was disappointed.

Catherine opened her heart to the French ambassador Breteuil early in 1763. She admitted to him that "she was not at all happy, and that she had to govern people who were impossible to please." She expected that it would take her subjects several years to become accustomed to her, and this left her ill at ease, she told Breteuil.

The ambassador was struck not only by the empress's candor, but by her vanity. "She has a high opinion of her grandeur and her power," he wrote. In talking to him she referred again and again to her "great and powerful empire," using the phrase almost as a talisman. She alluded more than once to her sustaining ambition, which had propelled her toward power from the day she first set foot in Russia.

Clearly her exalted position had turned her head—yet it was as clearly causing her anxiety, and no wonder, Breteuil noted, given all the chicanery surrounding her. Everyone at her court, even those she trusted most, was maneuvering for influence, wealth and high status, the Frenchman thought. "The intrigues, the manipulations, could not help but make her uneasy." Factionalism was growing, and in the midst of all the countercurrents, it seemed to the ambassador that the formerly rock-steady Catherine was wavering and at times losing her sense of command.

"The empress," he wrote, "is feeble and indecisive, defects which never before appeared in her character. . . . The fear of losing what she had the audacity to seize is easily read in her conduct. Everyone takes advantage of her, sensing this."

If Catherine was indecisive, many people said, it was because she needed a husband. Bestuzhev in particular urged her to marry, and, with her knowledge and agreement, began sounding out opinion on the subject.

He soon discovered that, not surprisingly, the question of whether or not the empress ought to marry, and whom she ought to marry, was embroiled in politics. Two factions had emerged among the royal advisers, one coalescing around Panin, the other around Gregory Orlov and his brothers and Bestuzhev himself. As the senior statesman well knew, the Orlovs and their allies wanted Catherine to do the logical, natural thing and marry the man she loved, the man whose personal magnetism, vigor, and influence had been the driving force behind her coup. With Gregory Orlov as her husband Catherine could strengthen the dynasty by having more children. After all, Orlov had already given her one son, and she would have had a second child by him had her recent pregnancy not ended in a miscarriage. Should the weak Paul die, there would be no succession crisis. The empress and her virile, attentive husband would be certain to provide another heir to the throne.

Gregory Orlov himself had been urging Catherine to marry him every since the conspiracy among the guardsmen was brought to light in October of 1762. What form his inducements took can only be imagined, but in addition to his emotional and no doubt sexual hold on the empress he had precedent on his side: Empress Elizabeth had married a man who was a commoner by birth, Alexei Razumovsky. Catherine could do the same.

Panin and those who supported him took an opposing view, contending that if Catherine married at all, it should be a prince of royal blood, perhaps a brother of the deposed Emperor Ivan VI, or another, more distant Romanov relation. If she married a commoner such as Orlov she would inevitably weaken her own position, while she ought to be strengthening it. Then there was the scandal of Peter's death, in which the Orlov brothers had been instrumental. How would it look, Panin argued, if the empress married a man who was generally believed to have been her accomplice in killing her husband?

Catherine's own musings in the winter and spring of 1763 on the question whether or not she should marry are difficult to surmise. She admired women who had ruled unmarried, such as Elizabeth I of England, yet she saw the political advantages to be derived from taking the right husband. Her own experience of marriage had been as bad as possible, a nightmarish ordeal of suffering, cruelty and neglect. Yet for that very reason she may have dreamed of healing her wounds and finding redemption in a happier union with a benign and pleasing husband of her own choosing.

Clearly Orlov pleased her, though she was neither blind to his flaws nor overly impressed with his talents. She knew that he was, in her phrase, "nature's spoiled child," and that he relied on his handsome face and brawny body, his courage and charisma to carry him through life without his having to put forth much effort. He was intelligent, but indolent and self-indulgent. He was excessive in his appetites and extravagant with the money she lavished on him. He gambled, he put pleasure before business, he did as little business as possible.

Yet Orlov pleased Catherine because, as she confided some years later to her friend Melchior Grimm, she always liked to be propelled forward by men more purposeful and active than she was. She had never known a man who suited her better in this way; Orlov, she told Grimm, "instinctively leads, and I follow him." He had lead her to the throne, she could trust him to lead her on through life, as her husband.

But Catherine was cautious, and took her time making up her mind. In May she made a pilgrimage to the monastery of the Resurrection in Rostov. Muscovites, critical of Orlov and convinced that the empress meant to marry him before long, assumed that while at the monastery, and temporarily free of the influence of Panin, she would secretly be wedded to her favorite.

The circumstances gave rise to imaginative stories. The stories built on one another, growing more and more threatening with the retelling. Orlov was forcing Catherine to do his will, people said; Catherine had never wanted to be empress, indeed she would have been content to be regent for her son had Orlov not insisted that she take power for herself. Orlov was behind it all, using Catherine to carve out a powerful niche for himself at her side. Now the final part of his devious plan was coming into being.

Jealousy and suspicion of Orlov fed the gossip, and inevitably, conspiracies blossomed. A group of guards officers were discovered plotting to overthrow Catherine and murder Orlov if a marriage between them were to be made public. The conspirators knew, and the knowledge encouraged them, that Panin was opposed to an Orlov marriage. "Mrs. Orlov," Panin was quoted as saying, "would never be Empress of All the Russias."

The scathing pronouncement attributed to Panin was repeated throughout the city, and lead to a popular outcry. Unruly Muscovites gave vent to noisy protest, and within days the city seemed to be on the brink of rebellion. Loyal guardsmen took up positions in Red Square, in the suburbs, along every major thoroughfare. Taverns were closed, unruly assemblies dispersed. The Secret Branch moved furtively to detain and interrogate sus-

picious protesters, while the empress issued a "manifesto of silence" forbidding "improper discussion and gossip on matters
concerning the government."

The brief, hot summer descended. Huge black flies buzzed in
the dusty streets, the pounding of carpenters' hammers rang
through the suburbs damaged by fires during the cold months.
The Moscow nobles left for their country estates, having had their
fill of the empress and the servile creatures who surrounded her.
The nobility of Moscow prided itself on its antiquity and independence; many families had held their titles for a dozen generations, some even longer, while Catherine's pet noblemen were
of very recent creation. Some, like the Orlovs, had risen to their
high status with dizzying swiftness. That Catherine should consider marrying one of these upstarts only revealed her own inherent vulgarity, the Muscovite nobles told one another. After all,
she was only the daughter of a German soldier, even if he had
called himself a prince.

Quite aware of the hauteur of the Moscow nobles, and un-
nerved by the plots and uprisings that seemed as endemic in the
old city as the flies and the stenches, the churches and the echoing
bells, Catherine gave up all thought of marrying Orlov and
slowly resigned herself to the realization that she might never be
free to act as she chose. For as long as she sat on the throne, there
would be opposition. She had enemies, she would make more
enemies. Ingratitude, not admiration and appreciation, would be
her lot; she had to learn to lower her expectations.

Somehow, she came to terms with Orlov. It may be that he too
saw the wisdom in her decision not to marry him, though he
cannot have relished the political defeat the decision represented.
Henceforth Panin was in the ascendant, and by the fall of 1763,
having lost the battle over the marriage, Bestuzhev had left court
and gone into involuntary retirement. Catherine had made her
choice. Panin, the careful pragmatist, had won.

Once they returned to Petersburg, both Catherine and Orlov
were more at ease. But there was an ugly postscript to their

Moscow sojourn. Orlov received a carefully wrapped package from Moscow. No letter accompanied it, there was no way to identify the sender. Inside the package was a large cheese, hollowed out and filled with horse dung. A huge truncheon had been stabbed through the center of the cheese.

No doubt the dauntless Orlov shrugged off the incident, but it must have worried Catherine. It was not enough that she had given up the idea of marrying him. For as long as he remained at her side, as her lover, there were Muscovites who continued to meditate his death.

Years were to pass before Catherine returned to Moscow for an extended stay. She settled into her Petersburg routine, devoting her working days to practical matters which concerned the entire empire.

One thing that absorbed her attention was that Russia, though enormous in land area, was thinly populated. Montesquieu and other writers associated the relative strength of a realm with the size of its population. "We need people," the young Catherine had once written, long before she became empress. "If possible, make the wilderness swarm like a bee hive." She brought foreign settlers into Russia by the thousands and set up a government agency, the Chancellery for the Guardianship of Foreigners, to recruit colonists and establish new settlements for them. Gregory Orlov was nominally in charge of the chancellery. Under his increasingly fitful leadership colonies were set up on the lower Volga, on fertile steppe lands. In addition, the area around Petersburg, a barren landscape of deep swamps and groves of pine trees, was tamed and made habitable. Catherine ordered the swamps drained and the forests removed; by the fall of 1766 there were three prospering villages where only a few years before there had been nothing but reeds and sedge and stagnant water.

A more delicate and controversial area of the empress's concern was the church—not as a religious but as an economic institution. The Russian church owned very extensive lands worked by over a million serfs. The government was desperately in need of money and resources. Why should the church be so rich when the imperial treasury was insolvent?

Both Empress Elizabeth and her successor had eyed the lands of the church with envy. Both had been on the brink of secularizing the lands, yet had held back from actually doing so. Catherine did not hesitate. In February of 1764 she ordered that the ecclesiastical estates, which in the words of her decree had been acquired illegally, be turned over to an agency of the crown, the College of Economy. At one stroke the imperial government became, for the time being, solvent once again—though what it gained in solvency it lost in popularity.

Once again a spate of disturbing reports crossed Catherine's desk, reports of seditious talk, subterranean plots, pockets of dissatisfied guardsmen seething with discontent and on the verge of taking overt action against the government. Riots broke out in Pskov, Orel, Voronezh—areas distant from the principal seats of bureaucratic control. Bandits terrorized villages and laid siege to noble estates. To put an end to the chaos, Catherine gave added authority to the nobles. Yet she soon found that they often abused their power, extorting more in taxes from the peasants than the legal amount, taking bribes, stealing the government's money. Not infrequently the enraged peasants rose up en masse and murdered their landlords. The dilemma weighed on the empress; how could she create peace and order without advancing tyranny?

And something even more distressing was happening. Here and there, always in areas remote from Moscow and Petersburg, strange men were emerging in peasant communities, claiming to be the lost Emperor Peter III.

It happened every few months, this spectral resurrection of the dead emperor, a phenomenon as threatening to Catherine as it was unnerving. The impostors were welcomed eagerly by the rural populace. They received gifts, honors, pledges of support. They began to gather bands of followers, partisans eager to fight on their behalf to reclaim the throne. One by one, the false Peters were hunted down by soldiers and captured. But as soon as one was removed, another came forward to take his place. And as the months passed, the idea took deep root among the peasants that the true emperor was alive and well. Now it was said that he was away in the Crimea, raising an army; at another time he was said to be in the east, resting, awaiting the advent of good weather before he began his grand campaign to regain his rights.

Impostors could be captured, punished and shut away, but, as Catherine knew very well, ideas were too powerful to be eradicated by force or threats. It was as if the idea of Peter III had declared war on her. For nearly twenty years her husband had tormented her in life. Now he continued to torment her from the grave.

When Catherine had been empress for two years, a grand masked ball was held in Petersburg. The entertainment went on for two days and three nights, with the guests, disguised in expensive costumes, dancing, eating and drinking themselves into near exhaustion. A visitor from Venice, the celebrated Giovanni Casanova, was present and described the exuberant scene.

While the revelry advanced, a modestly dressed guest slipped in, her short figure entirely encased in black. Fully masked, she mingled with the laughing, animated crowd, sometimes losing her balance when someone jostled her unintentionally. Casanova's acquaintances told him, in whispers, that the mysterious black-clad guest was the empress. However, most of the guests did not know who she was, and she preferred it that way.

Now and then she joined a group of diners and listened unobtrusively to their conversation. Very likely, Casanova thought, she overheard opinions about herself, some of which no doubt were wounding to her. But she did not let on. Not once, throughout her stay at the ball, did she reveal her true identity. Casanova was impressed, not only by her self-possession but by her astuteness in acting as a spy at her own court.

Now that she had ruled for several years Catherine had learned a great deal about power, its sources and satisfactions—and its limitations.

She was in charge; no one had managed to wrest authority from her hands. She made the important decisions, and scrutinized the work she delegated to others. She dominated. Her "majestic air," Buckingham thought, and her "happy mixture of dignity and ease" won her respect, while her devotion to the improvement of Russia and her hard-working efforts to achieve it impressed all observers.

Catherine was the glittering center of a dazzling court. She liked to shower herself with diamonds, they were a symbol of her wealth—or rather her appearance of wealth, for despite the seizure of the church lands, the treasury was not solvent for long. Gleaming from head to hem, richly gowned, carefully coiffed and heavily rouged—visitors to the Russian court remarked on the brightly rouged cheeks of the women, including the empress—she made the rounds of her guests at the Sunday court concerts. She appeared to be imperturbable, and was invariably in a good humor, or so the ambassadors thought; though her glance was always shrewd (one visitor to court called her expression "fierce and tyrannical") there was an evident gentleness and softness in her features, and she treated people with exceptional kindness. She seemed to know everyone, even the lowest ranking servants, and spoke to each with the same easy familiarity.

Yet though she was never haughty or formal, she retained her dignity. She tried not to let herself be perceived as vulnerable. That, she had learned, was essential to retaining power.

In subtle ways she kept people at a distance, careful to preserve a perceptible distinction between the monarch and those who were under her control, however lightly exercised or benevolent. Her bearing was commanding. Except in the privacy of her apartments or with those she trusted, she acted as if she expected to be obeyed. She rarely allowed herself to form a close bond with any of the court women, and when she did, it lasted only a short time.

Princess Dashkov, with whom she had once seemed on sisterly terms, soon lost her favor and was ordered to leave the court. The princess worked off her disappointed vanity and ongoing ambition by visiting the guardsmen's barracks and dressing in uniform, as she had on the day of the coup. Princess Dashkov was succeeded in the empress's favor by Countess Matushkin, who lasted less than a year before being turned aside. Catherine complained that the countess was meddlesome and unsettled. Countess Bruce (the former Praskovia Rumyantsev, Catherine's girlhood companion), a talented, soignée and worldly beauty, quickly took Countess Matuschkin's place, but she remained the empress's malleable, amenable follower, not her confidante; she was adroit at catching Catherine's moods and preferences and imitating them, even to the point of becoming the mistress of Gregory Orlov's brother Alexis.

Though she surrounded herself with a circle of lively, active young people, and liked nothing better than to be among them, playing silly games, doing her animal imitations, romping and singing and telling stories, Catherine was always conscious of wanting to remain the puppet-master, with the court her stage.

All the courtiers, even the elderly ones, were expected to take part in frequent performances. Gala concerts, ballets, and plays were staged, and for weeks the talented (and not so talented) amateurs rehearsed their parts, under the critical eye of the empress. Gentlemen were expected to play in the orchestra, ladies to learn elaborate dances. Preference in stage roles was given to Catherine's favorites.

One of the empress's pet projects was the production of a Russian tragedy, performed in a magnificent hall on a specially built stage. Gregory Orlov took a principal part, and "made a striking figure," as one who saw the performance wrote. Countess Bruce took the lead, acting with a degree of spirit and skill a professional actress might envy. No doubt professional musicians were sprinkled in among the dilettantes in the orchestra, and at least a dozen of the dancing ladies went lame. Still, the overall effect was dramatic, and the court troupe went on to further triumphs.

The most recalcitrant of Catherine's performing courtiers was Orlov, who by the time she had ruled for several years had begun to sulk and imagine himself ill-used. When Catherine, for sound political reasons, made her former lover Stanislaus Poniatowski King of Poland, Orlov was aggrieved. Why should Poniatowski receive a kingdom when he, who had made Catherine empress, remained only a count? She would not marry him, she was always attempting to instruct him on some issue or other. He found her love of learning tiresome. In fact Orlov confided to Buckingham that he was suspicious of learning and the arts. He thought that creative and intellectual pursuits tended to enervate the body and weaken the mind.

Catherine continued to enrich Orlov and to offer him important posts and opportunities to exercise his gifts, but he chafed under her efforts to mold him into something he was not and never could be. The English ambassador noted a change in him, an air of "stiffness and surliness" that replaced his natural affability, a peevish and rebellious side to him that showed itself in sloppiness of dress and inattentiveness to Catherine. He was often away at the hunt, and when he was present at court he neglected his appearance and flirted shamelessly.

Buckingham recorded a telling incident. A young woman of the court, much younger than Catherine, confided to the ambassador that Orlov had been pursuing her for some time but that she resisted his pursuit, not only because he was the empress's lover but because she was in love with someone else. One day when a group of the courtiers, including the young woman, Orlov and Catherine, were visiting a country estate Orlov renewed his advances. All of a sudden Catherine entered the room where Orlov and his beloved were having a tête-à-tête.

The young woman "was a little confused," Buckingham recalled her saying, "upon which the empress came behind her and leaning upon her shoulder whispered 'Don't be embarrassed; I am convinced of your discretion and your regard for me. You need not fear making me uneasy; on the contrary, I think myself obliged to you for your conduct.' "

Catherine, always busy, frequently too preoccupied with her own concerns to gratify her lover's whims and demands, was relieved that someone else was keeping Orlov amused. Besides, they had begun to quarrel; observers noticed "little differences" between the empress and Orlov, and remarked that even in public, Orlov was "wanting in due respect and even in common attention to her." Some of the courtiers took this want of respect and attention to mean that Catherine and Orlov were secretly married; everyone knew married men tended to neglect their wives. Others interpreted it more astutely, as "the folly of a vain young upstart and the weakness of a woman in love."

Catherine was still in love with the churlish Orlov. She wanted and needed him. She was unwilling to face the increasingly difficult challenges of reigning Russia without an emotional partner beside her, though she knew better than to marry that partner.

Hemmed in by criticism, menaced at every turn by traps laid to ensnare her, Catherine needed to be able to lean on Orlov—now more than ever.

In July of 1764 a young officer at Schlüsselburg, Lieutenant Vasily Mirovich, attempted to rescue the ex-emperor Ivan from his imprisonment in the fortress with the intention of making him emperor. Catherine had left Petersburg for a three-week tour of the Baltic provinces. Unfortunately for Ivan, and unknown to Mirovich, the ex-emperor's guards had orders to murder their prisoner should any attempt be made to liberate him. The guards did their duty, foiling the coup attempt, but Ivan's death gave rise to a fresh wave of accusations against the empress.

Now, it was said, Catherine had murdered two emperors, Peter and Ivan. It was widely assumed that she had been in collusion with Mirovich, and that the alleged conspiracy was nothing more than a ruse to justify Ivan's murder. That Mirovich was tried, condemned and ultimately executed did not stanch the flood of abusive letters reaching the palace and satirical publications circulated in the capital. All said the same thing, that Catherine, an adulteress, was also a murderer twice over. For good measure, debauchery was now added to the list of her sins.

The pleasures of the Baltic journey, though gratifying and diverting, did not compensate for the fear that the incident at Schlüsselburg aroused in Catherine. To be sure, she enjoyed the naval parades and the pageantry each city mounted to honor her, the shouting crowds and speeches of praise, the rash young men who impulsively unhitched the horses of her carriage and drew it themselves. Catherine had launched immense building projects along the Baltic littoral, dockyards, shipyards, improved roads. To view these undertakings at first hand was satisfying, even if the experts cautioned her that the Russian ships were greatly in need of work and the dockyards were behind schedule. Still, when she received word that Ivan was dead and Mirovich arrested, Catherine was much alarmed.

She made an effort to appear calm. She did not suddenly cancel her trip and hurry back to Petersburg at once, to avoid giving the impression that the events at Schlüsselburg were grave. But in truth she felt shaken, and the most perceptive of those around her saw clear evidence of her careworn state.

"Her face and figure are greatly altered for the worse since her accession," Buckingham wrote of Catherine. "It is easy to discover the remains of a fine woman, but she is now no longer an object of desire." His words were blunt, even brutal, but their meaning was unmistakable. The skin around the empress's eyes was becoming thin and lined, her cheeks had begun to sag, her waist, once tiny, was thickening. Though she tried her best to hide her anxieties she had a wary look, and when startled or caught off guard by some unfamiliar sound or action, she showed naked fear.

"The least sinister appearance causes cruel alarms to the empress," wrote one ambassador. "But she often mistakes shadows for substance. It takes long and precise investigation to calm her fear and disperse her illusions." Twice Buckingham saw Catherine "very much afraid without reason." Once she was stepping from a small rocking boat onto a ship; her foot slipped, she gasped and went into a panic. Another time a slight noise coming from an antechamber frightened her, and she started nervously, clearly terrified.

That a woman bold and daring by nature should be reduced, however infrequently, to sheer terror was a measure of the heavy burden of rule. Time would tell whether Catherine had the fortitude to shoulder the burden, or whether, as many predicted, she would falter, stumble, and eventually fall prey to the many snares and dangers that threatened to bring her down.

Chapter Twenty-One

I N THE SPRING OF 1767, EMPRESS CATHERINE II MADE A GREAT journey through the heartland of western Russia. She traveled down the Volga River in great splendor, with a fleet of a dozen galleys, taking with her hundreds of court officials, government staff and servants who made up the gigantic imperial household. Though a number of people had urged her not to undertake the vast expedition, reminding her that the last time she left Petersburg there was an attempt to overthrow her and that she ought not to risk her safety on the flood-swollen river during the chill, uncertain weather of April, Catherine dismissed the warnings and went anyway.

She had been planning the journey for months. She wanted to show herself to her subjects and to see for herself the life along the mighty river. And how better to do it than with an imposing fleet, decorated with her insignia and manned by sailors from the imperial navy. It was to be a waterborne caravan, a spectacle never before seen in Russia, in keeping with Catherine's idea of her own grandeur and the exceptional significance of her reign.

The galleys set forth, and almost at once frigid winds whipped up the water and freezing rain beat down on the decks of the vessels, sending the passengers into shelter. To amuse themselves they played cards—no small feat in the rolling and pitching ships—joined the empress in game-playing and conversation, ate, smoked, flirted, and read. Catherine had brought along a number of books, including a French novel set in the reign of the Byzantine Emperor Justinian. To pass the time, she translated part of it into Russian.

By the time the imperial fleet had been on the river a week, the empress and her companions, including Gregory Orlov and his handsome younger brother Vladimir, were bored and restless, chilled to the bone and tired of the stormy Volga. The carefully planned itinerary Catherine had drawn up was not being followed. Bad weather and mishaps slowed the pace of the journey, and it was proving to be difficult, if not impossible, for the empress to remain in daily contact with the government offices in Moscow via couriers. Still, Catherine could not admit that her project had been ill-advised. She drew up a new schedule, wrote letters, read, chatted with the sailors, and when all else failed, stood on deck watching the turbulent green river flow past, judging it to be more majestic and more pleasing to the eye than the Neva.

When the flotilla reached Yaroslavl Catherine's mood brightened. The townspeople celebrated her arrival with exuberance, and the town dignitaries and notables from the surrounding regions paid their respects to the empress and escorted her on a tour of the most important local factories and landmarks. It was the same at Kazan two months later, where Catherine encountered the exotic world of the Tatars (known to Europeans as Mongols) and felt as if she had entered Asia. Here mosques outnumbered churches, and some tribal groups were so far from the sphere of either Christian or Muslim influence that they worshipped the spirits of trees and rejected all orthodoxies.

Fascinated by the varied pageant of costumes, the wild dancing of the tribesmen and the babel of tongues in Kazan, Catherine was at the same time uneasy. How would it be possible, she wondered, to impose on so varied a people a single set of laws and governing principles?

For that was what she was about to do. Over the past three years the empress had been working at the mountainous task of compiling a set of instructions to be followed in drawing up a law code for her empire. Hundreds of hours of reading, study and thought had gone into the instructions; though the empress had incorporated much material from the writings of her favorite political author Montesquieu, and from the Italian jurist Beccaria, the instructions were a distillation of her own best thoughts and highest ideals. They encapsulated her hopes for Russia.

"The Christian law teaches us to do mutual good to one another, as much as possibly we can," the instructions began. "Laying this down as a fundamental rule, prescribed by that religion . . . we cannot but suppose that every honest man in the community is, or will be, desirous of seeing his native country at the very summit of happiness, glory, safety and tranquillity."

To see her realm and its population at the apex of happiness was Catherine's sincere aim. To achieve it, she envisioned a government headed by a European-style monarch, not a capricious despot but a benign, wise ruler whose principal goal was to guide her subjects toward their "supreme good." Believing that "it is moderation which rules a people, and not excess of severity," Catherine attempted not only to define sound legal principles but to look beyond them to the wellsprings of human behavior and social peace or unrest. Thus in her view the death penalty ought to be meted out to murderers, not merely as a just punishment for a grave crime but because "capital punishment is the remedy for a distempered society." The laws, in her view, and those who enforce them, ought to have as their primary goal the reform and re-education of the public, so that in time punishment of all kinds would no longer be necessary.

"The people ought not to be driven by violent methods," the empress wrote, "but we ought to make use of the means which nature has given us, with the utmost care and caution, in order to conduct them to the end we propose." Nature has provided every man and woman with a conscience, she believed, and makes each one feel accountable to the community; the primary disincentive to crime ought to be the desire to avoid being shamed in the eyes of others.

Catherine's instruction covered a wide range of themes, from the promotion of population increase to the recommended abolition of maiming and torture of prisoners. Humane treatment, lenience wherever possible, were her guiding principles. "Unhappy is that government which is compelled to induce severe laws," she wrote. "To prevent crime, reward virtue." On the subject of serfdom and slavery, Catherine wrote a great deal. Government, she wrote, should "shun all occasions of reducing people to a state of slavery." Serfs were not slaves, yet they often lived in conditions virtually indistinguishable from slavery. She was concerned about abusive landlords who looked on their serfs as property, treating them punitively and often cruelly. In her instructions she made clear her own views—which, she knew, differed from those of many serf owners—that serfs should be provided for in old age or if they became incapacitated; that they ought to be allowed to acquire possessions, and even to buy their freedom; that their bondage should be only for a limited term, and that the amount of work they were required to perform should also have fixed limits.

Where serfdom was concerned Catherine reworked her instructions substantially after giving them to her advisers, members of the Senate and others whose views she respected. But on other matters she did not let herself be swayed. "No man ought to be looked upon as guilty before he has received his sentence," she wrote, in a startling departure from conventional practice. Judges should not take bribes. Defendants ought to be able to speak on their own behalf in court. No one ought to be taxed so heavily that he is reduced to bare subsistence.

Page after page, Catherine poured her best judgment and the wisdom of her mentors into over five hundred separate nuggets of political counsel, grouped under twenty headings. Guided by her "heart and reason," as she later wrote, she brought her best judgment to bear on what she saw as the central task of rule: to teach and educate her people to pursue their own betterment.

Catherine's view of human nature was emphatically optimistic. It was in full accord with the prevailing view among the French encyclopedists and philosophes, one that saw humanity as intrinsically good or at worst redeemable, and institutions such as the law, the state and the church as instruments of corruption and repression. As both philosophe and monarch, Catherine was in a unique position to try to put the tenets of Enlightenment thought into practice by enshrining them in law. It was with this noble endeavor very much on her mind that she undertook her journey down the Volga, knowing that soon after its completion she would convene a great assembly where delegates chosen from among her subjects would draft legislation based, she expected, on her voluminous instructions.

In her instructions she had stated confidently that "Russia is a European country." Now, in Kazan, feeling very much as if she were in Asia, not Europe, Catherine began to perceive the limitations of her own knowledge. Kazan was a little universe in itself, with a distinctive cultural profile and distinctive needs and problems. Each town she visited was unique. Beneath the very thin veneer of European-style government, ancient traditions lingered and ancient feuds simmered. There was an immemorial quality to Russian provincial life that defied change of any sort, a primordial resistance, like the resistance of a stubborn beast. Catherine felt it, and observed it, and found it humbling to her understanding.

Something else disturbed her as well. The region along the Volga was prey to violent unrest and attacks by outlaw bands, and the frequency of these incidents was increasing. More and more serfs were rising up against their masters, burning crops and mansions, maiming and killing. Some serfs joined army deserters and vagabonds to form large gangs of brigands, heavily armed and difficult to subdue. All the major Volga towns had suffered attacks from these brigands, who sometimes turned cannon on the townspeople and always left terrified victims in their murderous wake. The lawlessness, and the relative defenselessness of the towns, was worrisome to the empress; it challenged her vision of a peaceful society and a contented polity as nothing else ever had.

After six weeks on the river Catherine cut short her Volga journey, which was taking longer than she expected it would, and hurried to Moscow to await the convocation of the Legislative Commission, the assembly of delegates that would grapple with the huge task of overhauling Russia's laws.

Nearly six hundred deputies, including delegates from towns, from Cossack communities, from noble assemblies, and meetings of state peasants gathered in the Granovitaia Palace in the Kremlin to commence their work. Although the deputies did not constitute a representative body—Catherine was no democrat, and had no intention of becoming a constitutional monarch—they did bring with them statements of concern and grievances (the taxes were much too heavy, labor services too arduous, restrictions on merchants too binding) that spoke for the subjects at large. No one spoke for the serfs, of course; even though they made up more than half of the total population, they had no rights and hence they chose no delegates. In theory their masters spoke for them.

The empress opened the Legislative Commission in great state, wearing her crown and mantle, flanked by her son, court officials and an imposing retinue of priests and dignitaries. Her instructions, leather-bound and voluminous, were prominently displayed. The deputies sat on benches in the spacious hall, the nobles in front, then the Cossacks, the delegates from the towns and finally the state peasants. All listened in respectful silence as the vice chancellor addressed them, reminding them of the solemnity and importance of the task they faced. They were to rewrite the laws in such a way as to bring about that perfect commonwealth Catherine envisioned, in which each person would put aside his selfish desires for the sake of the common good, in which humane values would replace vice and crime, bringing lasting happiness and creating a model for other societies to follow. They were to "glorify themselves and their times" by looking beyond the old order toward a felicitous, if not quite utopian, future.

Visionary sentiments soon gave way to practicalities. The hundreds of deputies were divided into dozens of committees and subcommittees, each of which began burrowing through piles of recommendations. Elaborate protocols were followed, with secretaries making notes, editing drafts, recording the contents of debates. Progress was difficult, as the delegates were mired in paperwork and procedures. Views were freely aired by the delegates, some of which horrified the empress when they were reported to her. But it soon became evident that the magnitude of the undertaking was too great for swift progress to be made. The deputies were better at talking than they were at arriving at a consensus, written or oral; they attacked one another (verbally only, as they were prohibited from carrying swords during sessions); they came and went at will, reluctant to commit themselves to staying in Moscow for as long as it took to complete the commission's work.

By the winter of 1767, the empress, who was always impatient with anyone who could not work at her own lightning pace, was frustrated and irritable. She was uncomfortable in her apartments, she resented having to spend months among the arrogant, gossipmongering Moscow nobility, and she was eager to get on with other projects.

Abruptly in December Catherine ordered the deputies to cease work and to reassemble in Petersburg in mid-February. Many failed to make the journey to the capital, including officials whose work kept them in Moscow. The remnant seemed to lose energy and momentum, though the debates remained long and lively. Months went by, until after a year of labor only one document, a draft law on the rights of the nobility, had been completed, and even this could not be adopted because of interminable amendments, reconsiderations and differences of opinion. Meanwhile Catherine was reeling from another blow. More conspirators had been uncovered, one group intending to kill Gregory Orlov, another sworn to assassinate the empress.

Amid these alarms, and the looming threat of conflict with Turkey, the empress lost her last ounce of patience with the Legislative Commission. Disillusioned not only by the evident failure of the grand legislative effort but by the ignorance and boorishness of the noble deputies in particular, she adjourned the commission at the end of 1768. A few sub-committees continued to meet on and off for three more years, but no significant work was accomplished. The experiment with populism was over. The great event that was, Catherine hoped, to represent "the cast of mind of this century," ended in nothing.

But if the commission created nothing substantive it did add an important dimension to Catherine's international repute. Copies of her instructions were translated into French and German, and made their way to the West as well as being publicized in journals and newssheets. European journalists wrote of the Russian empress's efforts to reach out to her people, Voltaire praised the great northern lawgiver, and even King Frederick, still recovering from his virtual defeat at the hands of the Russian armies, had to admit that the lawgiving work of the clever Catherine was worthy of admiration. The deputies themselves fawningly offered Catherine the title of "the Great, Most Wise, and Mother of the Fatherland," but she declined to accept it—and her modesty resulted in even more praise.

Outside the salons where the commission met, there was less eagerness for Catherine's reexamination of the laws, and some unrest. Stones were thrown at the palace, guardsmen complained that the empress and her commissioners were bent on freeing the serfs and undermining the time-honored social structure. Clearly the population at large was not yet ready for the kind of overhaul of the laws the empress envisioned.

In October of 1768, while the commission was in its last weeks, hostilities broke out at the southern town of Balta, an area under Turkish protection just across the Polish border. For several years

Catherine, with Panin's enthusiastic support, had been aggressively advancing Russian interests in Poland, placing her client Poniatowski on the Polish throne and intervening militarily to try to force the Polish Diet to protect the rights of Orthodox Poles, who were being harassed by the Catholic majority. Now her policy led Russia into unforeseen conflict.

A Russian military presence in Poland was bound to be provocative to the Turks, and to create a tense and volatile situation. Beyond this, the French government, well aware of Catherine's gallophobia and convinced that her hold on her empire was fragile, poured three million livres into the treasury of the Porte in hopes of financing a quick and decisive Turkish victory.

Certainly the advantage lay with the Turks, for their army of more than half a million men outnumbered the Russian forces by three to one, and their control of the Crimea gave them logistical superiority. It was not clear whether the Russian soldiers would fight willingly for Catherine; she was unproven as a war leader and her generals had not taken the field in a decade.

By January of 1769, however, the empress and her advisers had begun to gear up for war, and Catherine was displaying a fine zeal for battle. With an overconfidence that was coming to typify her, she made plans for a bold assault on the Turkish forces by sea and by land. Orlov was a member of her war council, and as in the past, she led where he followed, though she also listened to the more cautious Panin. Orlov proposed meeting the Turkish fleet in the Mediterranean while at the same time moving against key enemy fortresses in Moldavia and at the head of the Sea of Azov. Armies under Field Marshal Golitsyn, General Rumyantsev, and later Nikita Panin's brother Peter Panin were swelled by some thirty thousand new recruits, and by late summer Khotin, Jassy, Azov and Taganrog were all in Russian hands.

"My soldiers go to war against the Turks as if they were on their way to a wedding," was Catherine's boast. To Voltaire she wrote, "We are at war, to be sure, but Russia has long been used to warfare; she ends each war in a more flourishing state than

when she entered it!" Catherine reminded her admirer at Ferney
that in capturing Azov and Taganrog she was completing a work
begun long before by Peter the Great. In war, as in so many other
spheres of Russian life, she was following the lead of her great
predecessor and indeed surpassing him. She referred to the two
strongholds as "two jewels which I am having mounted" and
crowed that the Turkish sultan Mustafa III was so unmanned by
the ferocity of Russian arms that "all the poor man can do is cry."
"So much for the terrible phantom that I was supposed to be so
afraid of!" she went on. The empire of the Turks might be large,
their armies as numerous as the grains of sand on the sea shore.
But were not her own armies even stronger? Had not the Russians
sent the Turks fleeing for their lives, not once but twice, each time
routing a Turkish force twice its size?

The second year of the war saw the most resounding victory of
all. The Russian fleet, refitted, manned by Russian and Livonian
seamen and with many officers recruited from Britain, made its
way from the Baltic to the Mediterranean. The European states
were taken aback. Russian armies had proven themselves formidable, but a Russian navy, never.

On June 24, 1770, twelve Russian ships engaged twenty-two
Turkish vessels in the Aegean off Khíos near Chesme on the
Anatolian coast. Neither fleet was well manned; both the Russians
and Turks were poor sailors and blind courage was no substitute
for seamanship. Still the Russians, though outgunned, made the
most of their opportunities and, having driven the Turkish fleet
into Chesme harbor, sent in fireships and destroyed it completely.
By one reckoning, eleven thousand Turkish sailors drowned.

The Battle of Chesme demoralized the Turks, sent the Russians
into transports of nationalistic ecstasy and made Catherine an
international heroine. The Russian David had slain the Turkish
Goliath, for centuries the quintessential enemy of Christendom.

Fireworks, grand celebrations, and church services of
thanksgiving went on in Petersburg for weeks. All the Russian
sailors were given special rewards, and Alexis Orlov, architect of

the Mediterranean naval venture, was granted the title "Chesmensky."

The public mood was higher than it had ever been since the thrilling, tumultuous early days of Catherine's reign. Ever since the start of the war people had been talking excitedly of the transit of Venus, convinced that such a significant event in the heavens inevitably meant that human affairs had come to a critical juncture; a momentous change was under way. The victory at Chesme was taken to be the turning point in that momentous change. With it Russia moved into the forefront of European affairs as a great power, a power to be reckoned with, bargained with, and feared.

Catherine promoted her famous victory enthusiastically, setting aside a room in the Peterhof Palace as the Chesme Room and ordering medals, paintings, and commemorative memorabilia in abundance.

"What an ugly thing war is!" the empress wrote to Voltaire in mock horror. "Count Orlov tells me that on the day following the burning of the fleet, he was aghast to see that the waters of the bay of Chesme—a fairly small area—were tinted red with blood, so many Turks had perished there."

Catherine's lament was a thinly disguised boast. She gloated over her victory, not only for the renown it gave Russia and the prestige conferred on her but because it gave the lie to those who had dismissed her as a weak woman whose reign was sure to be a nine days' wonder. Though she privately credited luck as much as skill in causing Russia to win the day, publicly she swaggered.

She, Catherine, unmarried and in sole command of her own beloved Russia, had done what even the great Peter could not do. Like the unmarried, commanding Elizabeth of England two centuries earlier, she had won a stupendous naval victory, and had become a heroine. Just as Elizabeth had repulsed the dread Spanish Armada, so Catherine had crushed the fleet of the hated Turk.

Though she wrote to Voltaire that she truly wanted peace—and indeed she did want to end the costly drain of the war on her finances—in actuality she was elated by all the adulation, the sense of power the war had brought her. In 1770 she was forty-one, and "not exactly improving in intelligence or looks," as she confided to her mentor. Her long affair with Orlov still brought her the comfort of familiarity (along with the pangs caused by his casual affairs) but held little or no passion. Her son Paul brought her no joy, only obligation tinged with uneasiness. But her fame, her newfound sense of triumph, made her pulse race and filled her heart with maternal love for her adoptive realm and its people.

As long as Russia was triumphant, Catherine was happy. And she felt sure that there were more triumphs to come.

"See, the sleeping cat has been awakened!" she wrote to Ivan Chernyshev, her ambassador in London. Russia, long in slumber, was rousing herself to full vigor. "People are going to talk about us!" she promised Chernyshev. "You won't believe all the noise we're going to make!"

Chapter Twenty-Two

GRAND DUKE PAUL WAS GROWING UP. HE WAS TURNING
out to be a small man, short and compact, with a slight yet
well-proportioned body—the body of a dancer or an actor suited
for juvenile roles. In 1773 he was nineteen, yet he looked much
younger, like an unformed boy. His round face and tightly com-
pressed, unattractive features had none of the depth or character
of his mother's open, inquisitive, engaging face; his blue eyes
were intelligent, but full of distrust, and he moved with a nervous
quickness that betrayed his deep-seated unease.

To observers, Paul seemed driven by fear—fear of his mother,
who was cold to him and, as he grew toward his majority,
apprehensive about his popularity, fear of his immature body and
fragile health, fear of falling prey to court intrigues. His fear drove
him to lie, to hide, to deceive those around him in petty ways.

He had no special talents on which to pride himself. Though
quick to learn he was no scholar, and in any case his indifferent
education had been conducted in a rather lackadaisical fashion by
the indolent Nikita Panin, the lessons interrupted far too often by
the boisterous Gregory Orlov, who distrusted learning and
wanted to toughen Paul by taking him hunting. Nor was Paul an
athlete—he was agile but not muscular—nor was he gifted in
music or drawing or any other polite accomplishment.

He was, in short, nothing but his remarkable mother's son. Of his paternity he now, at nineteen, knew the worst, as did everyone else at Catherine's court: that Sergei Saltykov, and not Peter III, was his father; that his mother despised him for his illegitimacy, and for reminding her of the circumstances that led to it; that, according to court gossip, his putative father Peter had wanted him put to death, along with Catherine; and that his mother had almost certainly been complicit in Peter's own death.

Fatherless (for Saltykov was away in Dresden, kept abroad by Catherine in one minor diplomatic post after another) Paul looked to Panin, who tutored him and hovered over him, even sleeping in his bedroom, as his guide to life. Orlov he had liked as a young child, but once Paul discovered the role the Orlov brothers played in his mother's coup and the late emperor's death, he could no longer trust the jovial, bearlike companion of his childhood.

In his teens Paul began to understand and appreciate his importance as grand duke, heir to the Romanov throne, though he remained so fearful of his mother that he could hardly imagine taking any kind of independent action. He aped the showy superficiality of the younger nobles, "speaking ravishingly of the French and of France," as one observer noted, and insisting that all his possessions come from Paris. He paraded in front of his mother dressed in extravagantly costly coats and breeches gleaming with jewels and trimmings of silver and gold. Waterfalls of fine lace adorned his throat and wrists, his shoe buckles were sparkling diamonds, his buttons glittering rubies.

Catherine, who often spoke to her son about her preference for what she called "English simplicity" in all things, pretended indifference but privately gritted her teeth, as he knew she would. Mother and son were nettlesome to each other, and though Catherine took great pains to guard Paul's health, having him inoculated against smallpox and whisking him away from any place where infection threatened, he knew that she did it more for her own political safety than for his well-being. Paul inherited his mother's gift for verbal sparring, though not her wit; his tongue

was his sharpest weapon, and as he grew older he was occasionally able to overcome his terror and lash out at her to some effect.

In the summer that Paul was sixteen he succumbed to a very
grave attack of influenza, and for over a month he hovered
between life and death. He had often been ill before, but never at
so critical a time, with Russia still at war with the Turks in the
Crimea, poor harvests creating discontent in the countryside and
high prices in the towns, turmoil in Poland and fears of pestilence
in the army and in the southern provinces.

At such a time Catherine could not afford to have her official
heir die. As Paul sank deeper into what many feared would be his
final illness, there were troubling rumors that Catherine would
declare her other son her heir. This boy, Catherine's son by
Gregory Orlov, was nearly nine years old, and was in every way
healthier, more robust, good-looking and presentable than the
unfortunate Paul. He was called Alexis Grigorevich Bobrinsky,
and though he was kept away from court he was not forgotten.
Should Catherine decide to declare young Bobrinsky heir to
the throne, Gregory Orlov's power would reach new heights;
he might even be able to persuade Catherine to marry him at
last.

There was universal surprise when Paul rallied, and after five
weeks he was able to get up from his sickbed, apparently fully
restored to health. Still, the episode had left Catherine and the
members of her government shaken, and in the immediate aftermath of the crisis Catherine became fearful. Paul was popular, and
he was male—officially, if not biologically, he was the last surviving male of the line of Peter the Great. His claim to the throne of
Russia was unimpeachable, while she herself had no claim at all,
she held the throne solely through conquest—and capability.
When Paul and Panin were in Moscow, huge crowds poured into
the streets to shout greetings. Many Muscovites, resenting
Catherine, cried out to her son that he was their "only true
sovereign," and pledged to support him to the death.

When he celebrated his eighteenth birthday, in September of
1772, Paul came of age and left childhood and tutelage behind.

But his mother, reluctant to acknowledge any advancement in his status, put off officially recognizing that he had reached adulthood. Paul was a thorn in her side. He was beginning to assert opinions of his own, critical of Catherine's enduring war with the Turkish empire and of the costly conflict with Poland. He was gathering a following of sorts, not yet an influential following, but an irritating one nonetheless. Troublemakers were beginning to rally to him as the natural focus of opposition.

Early in 1773 one such troublemaker, Caspar von Saldern, a shady Holsteiner who held a petty diplomatic post, attempted to organize a conspiracy to force Catherine to let her son rule along with her. Von Saldern, who supplemented his meager earnings by bribery and theft—he stole a diamond-studded gold snuffbox from the empress—was too inept a conspirator not to be discovered, and the indignant Catherine banished him from the kingdom. But the episode deepened her resolve to keep Paul under tight control, and to guard against any further plotting on his behalf.

At eighteen Paul was old enough to marry, and Catherine was eager for him to start a family in order to assure the continuity of the succession. There was no doubt of his ability to father a child. When he was sixteen he had been initiated sexually by a suitable older woman, probably provided by Panin, with Catherine's knowledge and approval; his mistress had given birth to a son, who was given the name Simon Veliky. Catherine kept the infant with her, just as Elizabeth had kept the infant Paul in her apartments.

To choose a bride for Paul from among the Russian noble families would have invited factionalism of the most dangerous kind, so Catherine looked to the German principalities for eligible young women. As always, there were princesses without number, but finding a presentable, intelligent girl of good character who would not overshadow the bland grand duke or tower over him physically was a challenge.

In the summer of 1773 Countess Caroline of Hesse-Darmstadt was invited to come to Petersburg with her three unmarried daughters, all under the age of twenty. The middle daughter, seventeen-year-old Wilhelmina, pleased Paul—and Catherine. She was outgoing and obliging, and if her complexion was rather blotchy at least she had been spared the marks of the pox. More important, Wilhelmina was healthy and presumably fertile.

Catherine may have assumed that, because Wilhelmina's mother was an exceptionally cultivated woman, the daughter would also have intellectual tastes. In any event, she made up her mind to accept Wilhelmina, and the girl began her instruction in the Orthodox church and was rechristened Natalia. On September 29 the wedding took place.

Having taken pains with the choice of a bride for her son, Catherine was equally painstaking in her preparations for their life together. She designated a new suite of rooms in the Winter Palace for the bridal couple and had them redecorated according to her own designs. "English simplicity" was forgotten as the empress wrote out her instructions: the formal bedchamber was paneled in gold brocade with a blue velvet border, while the inner, private bedchamber had columns faceted with blue glass and white damask wall coverings. The empress specified all the details of ornaments and upholstery for the various rooms and even supplied some of the gold fabric to be used from her own store of finery. All was intended to make Natalia happy, and to elicit from her a willingness to work hard at fulfilling her role as grand duchess.

Remembering her own arrival in Petersburg nearly twenty years earlier, her painful isolation, and the severe emotional burdens of her grotesque marriage, Catherine wrote a special letter of advice to her daughter-in-law. She cautioned her to avoid political entanglements and ill-advised friendships with foreign ministers (something Catherine herself had not been able to do), and to stay out of debt and live as simply as possible. She should learn Russian right away, Catherine told Natalia, and make an effort to embrace the customs and manners of her adopted country, while devoting herself with singleness of heart to being the best wife she could be. To help Natalia in her adjustment Catherine granted her a generous allowance of fifty thousand rubles a year. Catherine could be certain that Natalia would enjoy one advantage she herself had not had: the good will and steady support of her mother-in-law.

A conspicuous figure in her gown studded with jewels and pearls, Catherine dominated Paul's wedding ceremony. Guests noticed that the empress's chestnut hair had grown quite gray, and that she wore it pulled severely back off her face in an unflattering, no-nonsense style. Her once small waist was now thick and matronly, and she no longer moved with the grace and lightness that once had distinguished her. Still, onlookers thought, her fair complexion was soft and smooth, albeit heavily rouged, and her expressive blue eyes were open and friendly, full of benevolence and intelligence. Everyone commented on the empress's strong teeth. (Women tended to lose their teeth in Petersburg by the time they reached middle age; it was a universally acknowledged hazard of the climate and diet.) When Catherine smiled her kindly, good-humored smile, her teeth winked out in all their pristine whiteness, leading many of her ladies to hide their own less than intact smiles behind their fans.

Only when Catherine stood near her friend Countess Bruce, the lovely, exceedingly well-preserved companion she had known since girlhood, did she look her age. Another member of Catherine's entourage, Countess Bruce's mother, Maria Rumyantsev—once Catherine's nemesis but now, in old age, a trusted companion—put all the women of the court to shame, for though she was elderly she was still miraculously beautiful.

Catherine found birthdays galling. "I hate this day like the plague," she announced when another year came to a close. Birthdays wounded her vanity—though she made fewer concessions now to vanity than she had a decade earlier—and besides that they were a reminder that time was passing and the problems of the empire were only marginally nearer being solved.

Advancing years brought minor infirmities. Catherine's back

hurt from time to time, and she got severe headaches from long hours of reading by dim candlelight. Stronger light and spectacles helped the headaches, but for her aching back the only cure the doctors could suggest was a medicinal powder intended to make the patient sweat profusely. The powder failed, and the backaches went on.

By and large, Catherine distrusted doctors and apothecaries and preferred unorthodox therapies. She was a strong believer in the health benefits of alternating exposure to heat and cold. She had her own preferred routine, in which she and her female attendants shrouded their bodies in long petticoats and wound scarves around their necks, then jumped into a pond, shivering in the freezing water; they subsequently scalded themselves sitting in front of hot stoves. Between the shock of the cold and the enervating, sweat-inducing heat, disease was kept at bay.

Catherine had been under great strain in recent years. The Turkish war, whatever fame and glory it brought, was proving to be a hugely expensive drain on Russia's human and financial resources. (The treasury, enriched by newly discovered silver deposits in Mongolia, was still solvent, but was diminishing rapidly.) Plague had devastated Moscow, killing tens of thousands of people and unleashing riotous chaos and mayhem. Would-be assassins, some half mad, some with the intention of avenging the death of the late Emperor Peter, broke into the palace and terrified the empress; Gregory Orlov discovered one murderous officer lying in wait for Catherine, a long pointed dagger in his hand.

It was no wonder the empress began to see conspiracy everywhere, and to fear the consequences of her growing unpopularity. Only a year earlier a major plot had been discovered in the Preobrazhensky regiment, and Catherine was deeply shaken by it. Some thirty officers and men (some said as many as a hundred) were involved in a conspiracy to proclaim Paul emperor. Fortunately for Catherine, imperial agents learned of the plot and the Secret Branch went to work ferreting out the disloyal men, interrogating and punishing them. Soon all that was left of the conspiracy was seething resentment—and, on Catherine's part, wariness and apprehension.

In response to the alarming conspiracy, which she knew to be as much a rebellion against the perceived political dominance of Gregory Orlov and his brothers as against herself, Catherine took a number of her trusted advisers and left the capital. The danger to her regime from the metropolitan regiments had to be faced. That danger was likely to grow rather than diminish now that Paul was of age of claim the throne, and the empress meant to confront it proactively. She wanted to remove all the regiments from the capital and scatter them, so that they could not quickly join forces to overwhelm the household guard. After long discussion her advisers persuaded her against this plan, as too politically explosive. But Catherine, ever resourceful, had by this time decided on a different tactic.

Suddenly, to the amazement of the entire imperial household, Catherine sent Gregory Orlov away and replaced him with a dark, handsome, rather retiring lieutenant in the Horse Guards, Alexander Vassilchikov.

Swiftly the young Vassilchikov was promoted to adjutant general, gentleman-in-waiting, and then to chamberlain. He was presented with the Order of St. Alexander and was installed in the suite that had previously belonged to Orlov. Catherine's political enemies sniggered. Vassilchikov was twenty-eight, the empress forty-three. She risked making herself ridiculous, or worse. Yet even her enemies had to admit that what she had done was politically astute.

There could be no clearer signal to the guardsmen that the power of the Orlovs was broken once and for all. For a time, the plottings and murmurings ceased. Catherine breathed more easily. Besides, the change was personally beneficial to Catherine—or so she hoped.

"After eleven years of suffering," she told a friend, she intended to live "according to her pleasure, and in entire independence."

Orlov's hold over her was broken. There would be no more scenes, she would no longer have to tolerate his infidelity, humor his whims, or salve his ego. The shy Vassilchikov would be her escort, confidant and lover. But he was only a good-looking overgrown boy. He headed no faction, he had no formidable brothers. He would never try to control her. And if he did, she would be able to dismiss him at a moment's notice.

Orlov did not accept his demotion meekly. True, he knew that for some time his preeminence had been at risk. He had disappointed the empress in the last assignment she gave him, when she sent him to attend peace negotiations with the Turks at Focsani and he had failed to achieve any results—indeed, his haughty behavior had actually worsened relations and dimmed peace prospects. True, Catherine had discovered him with his newest love, his delicate young cousin, a girl barely out of childhood, and had been deeply hurt by his betrayal. Yet Catherine still owed him a great deal. He was determined not to yield his place at her side without standing up for his rights.

In the end, as was characteristic of her, the empress gave her former lover a generous settlement. Besides endowing him with large grants of money, property and serfs, she obtained for him a princely title abroad and, after he completed a relatively brief period of self-imposed exile, she readmitted him to her circle of advisers. Now he was once again a prominent courtier, and at Paul's wedding he looked as toweringly handsome, wealthy, and intimidating as ever. Certainly he made a stronger impression than the diffident Vassilchikov, who looked uncomfortable and was in fact troubled by pains in his chest.

The wedding of the grand duke and grand duchess was followed by weeks of parties, masquerade balls, theatrical entertainments and imperial receptions. Night after night the feasting and celebrating went on, now in the white-and-gold salons of the palace, now amid the cut crystal and silver and gold plate of nobles' dining rooms. Catherine lent her gracious presence to most of these gatherings, beaming at her new daughter-in-law and doing her best to seem less icy toward Paul. She relied on Vassilchikov to attend her, but otherwise ignored him. She could not quite ignore Gregory Orlov, however. He irked her a great deal by paying court to one of Natalia's sisters, unleashing a new flood of gossip. What if he married the new grand duchess's sister? That would make him Paul's brother-in-law, and, by extension, part of the imperial family. Was there no end to Orlov's brazen ambition?

The court was still preoccupied with festivities when Catherine's regular bi-weekly imperial council met on October 15, 1773. A message was read to the councillors and the empress: the Yaik Cossacks were in revolt, led by an army deserter who claimed to be Peter III.

The empress and her advisers heard the news with equanimity. Cossack revolts were common. Over the past century the Russian government had had to confront the Cossack bands, or hordes, dozens of times but in the end authority had been restored and resistance broken.

Catherine was aware, as her predecessors had been, that the threat of rebellion was inherent in the always-tense alliance between the Cossacks and the throne. For the Cossacks were frontiersmen, fiercely independent, democratic, bitterly hostile to any attempt to restrict their largely self-directed way of life. They occupied the relatively empty southern steppe lands, along the Volga, eastward to the shores of the Caspian Sea and into western Siberia. They were the descendants of runaway serfs, criminal fugitives, army deserters, marginal men and wanderers who instinctively avoided the authorities and remained on the fringes of settled society. Yet they served the emperor by forming themselves into fierce mounted fighting units and forming a living cordon between Russia and the hostile tribespeople that menaced her ill-defined eastern borders.

The Cossacks were loyal to the ruling authority, and valuable fighting allies, but their loyalty was in conflict with their need to be, and to remain, their own masters. Whenever they felt that their independence was threatened, they rose in rebellion, and each time they rebelled, they invoked the near-mythic figure of Stenka Razin, the great Cossack folk hero, who had once kindled the spirit of revolt until it blazed across the steppes like wildfire, threatening to engulf all Russia.

A century earlier, in the reign of Peter the Great's father, Emperor Alexis, Stenka Razin had posed as the deliverer of the Russian people and had drawn thousands to follow his banner by promising freedom from noble oppression and the establishment of a vast Cossack republic to encompass the entire Volga littoral. Time after time the armies of the emperor had been turned back by Razin and his peasant hosts, and Razin's Cossacks had carried out fearsome massacres, crop burnings, and general devastation throughout northeastern Russia. Muscovites had feared that the mighty rebel would sweep down and destroy their city, and for a time it appeared that no force could stop him, so fierce and forceful was his army and so powerful his message of liberation. In the end his own people had betrayed Razin, but not before he had become a strong prince in his own right, with a fleet of two hundred galleys and an extensive territory where his commands held sway.

Stenka Razin had terrorized the government and the ruling elite. Like a force of nature, a whirlwind or a terrifying storm, he and his hordes had seemed to rise up out of the black earth itself, threatening to overturn every obstacle in their path. Razin and his followers were a fearsome reminder to those in command that beyond their relatively limited circle of power lay the vast, uncharted, chaotic reaches of Russia—the real Russia, not the Russia of a Westernized few living in artificial splendor surrounded by the artifacts of a borrowed culture. The real Russia was peopled by rough, fur-clad peasants who lived in squalor, could neither read nor write and whose only true loyalty was to God. Razin had awakened these people, stirred their resentments, brought their age-old grievances to the boiling point. Under his leadership, they had spilled out across the steppes to imperil the precarious social order of the Russian state. And they had very nearly overbalanced it.

Now, it seemed, the old grievances had been stirred up afresh, by a leader claiming to be the lost Emperor Peter III.

The imposture was not in itself troublesome. Over the past decade, nearly every year had brought at least one impostor claiming to be Peter; in time this one, like the others, would be exposed as false. In the meanwhile, however, the empress and her councillors took prudent measures to put down the rising, for the Yaik Cossacks had mutinied only a few years earlier and the executions, fines and beatings imposed on the rebels had left the horde angry and full of hate.

Soldiers were dispatched to confront the defiant Yaiks, local leaders in the area were put on alert. Couriers were sent out along the slow, rutted provincial roads with instructions to return to court as swiftly as possible with news of the situation among the Yaiks. Then, having done what could be done, the council turned to other concerns.

In Moscow, chilly days and frost gave way to the first snow-falls. Sleigh rides and skating parties preoccupied the courtiers, and the empress, having launched her son and daughter-in-law on their new life, turned her attention to a distinguished visitor from France.

Denis Diderot, whose *Encyclopédie* had for years been Catherine's bible, and who some years earlier had been the object of her generous philanthropy, arrived in Russia after an arduous five-month journey and settled in to spend the winter in Petersburg.

Catherine was delighted to meet the man who, with Voltaire and Montesquieu, had been the intellectual idol of her youth. The *Encyclopédie* had greatly influenced her thinking, moving her along the path toward toleration, moderation and humanitarianism. Catherine associated Diderot with all that was progressive in social thought, and now she could hear from his own lips the ideas, old and new, that had enlightened Europe. She lost no time in sitting down with him and talking—and they continued to talk, sometimes daily, for hours at a time.

Diderot, for his part, had admired Catherine from a distance as a ruler who had her subjects' best interests at heart and whose breadth of knowledge and thoughtful approach to governing were bound to lead to beneficial changes in Russia. He was charmed by Catherine when he met her, impressed by her curiosity and intellectual rigor yet put at his ease by her informality. She combined, he wrote, "the soul of Brutus with the charms of Cleopatra," and he looked forward to his late afternoon visits with her.

Both the philosopher and the empress had strong personalities, neither was the least bit diffident or inclined to false flattery. They soon sized one another up, and approvingly. Diderot told his family and others in France that in Catherine's stimulating company he felt a wonderful freedom to vent his opinions, and that he found Russia to be quite liberating. "In the so-called land of free men I had the soul of a slave," he wrote, "and in the so-called land of barbarians, I have found in myself the soul of a free man."

"His is an extraordinary brain," Catherine wrote to Voltaire of Diderot. "One does not encounter such every day." Indeed the Frenchman was extraordinary in many ways. His manner was impassioned, at times almost frenzied. When carried away by a thought he talked louder and louder and faster and faster until, rising from his seat, he paced the room, waving his arms and shouting. He had a habit of snatching off his wig and flinging it away. Catherine recovered it and handed it to him, whereupon he thanked her and stuffed the unwanted wad of powdered horsehair into his pocket.

Catherine looked past Diderot's frenetic intensity and applauded his wide-ranging, searching genius. She found him incomparably more worthwhile than the only other philosophe she had so far encountered, Mercier de la Rivière, who had bored her on his visit to Petersburg six years earlier by "spouting nonsense" and babbling on egotistically until she was ready to throw him out. Even though Diderot had a disconcerting tendency to emphasize his points by grasping his imperial companion's arm or thumping her on the knee—Catherine took to sitting behind a table when the Frenchman came to visit, for protection—he continued to make himself welcome, week after week, and to delight his hostess with his inexhaustible imagination and his wealth of words. His curiosity more than matched her own. He wanted to know everything about Russia, and eagerly took in all that she told him. Indeed, he not only took it in, he wrote it down, making written notes from memory of all that he and Catherine said to one another and adding his own commentary.

One snowy afternoon in November a messenger rode up to the palace gates, dismounted and hurried inside. He carried vital news, from the region of the Cossack revolt.

The situation had grown radically worse. The government forces had been unable to stop the advance of the rebels. The impostor who called himself Emperor Peter Federovich now had an army of his own, a force of ten thousand men, and with it he had laid siege to the town of Orenburg. There were four garrison battalions defending the town, and seventy cannon, but the rebels too had guns, and the soldiers of the garrison were ill prepared to face a long siege.

And there was more. The imposter was said to have sent emissaries to the Bashkirs who lived in the vicinity of Orenburg, and to discontented laborers in the Urals. In village after village he was being proclaimed as the true emperor, come to save his people from the false Empress Catherine and her high taxes, her wars, her invasive laws. Soon, it was said, the imposter would have twenty thousand men in his army, or even thirty thousand, and then, with such a huge massed force at his command, nothing short of a miracle could stop him.

Chapter Twenty-Three

Emelian Pugachev was a short, heavily muscled ex-soldier, combative and untamed, a Don Cossack from the village of Zimoveisk who had fought in the imperial army before being discharged because of poor health. Dark-haired and dark-eyed, the skin of his face and chest mottled with white patches where he had suffered from scrofula, he was an unprepossessing figure on first glance, but he had the power to engage and hold the attention of his Cossack comrades, and he was always watchful for opportunities.

Abandoning his wife and children Pugachev drifted among the discontented Cossack hosts, and spent some time in a monastery of Old Believers. He observed, and perhaps participated in, the rising of 1772, and was imprisoned for a time but escaped. He also acquired a new wife, a Yaik woman, and began to formulate an audacious plan.

In September of 1773 Pugachev appeared near the town of Yaitsk in a new guise. He wore a long red caftan and a velvet cap, the cap of a nobleman, and he had an entourage of a hundred men—Cossacks, Kalmuks and Tatars—who paid reverence to him and called him Emperor Peter. His wife, who had with her a circle of reverential peasant girls, was addressed as empress.

The parade of self-proclaimed dignitaries passed through village after village, and in each Pugachev paused long enough to be presented to his subjects as the long lost emperor and to display his "tsar's marks"—the scrofula scars on his chest—for the benefit of the skeptical. Banners displaying the symbols of the Old Believers brought many followers to his side, for the "new" faith was still regarded with distaste (though it had been in force for a century) and there were many who associated it with the imposition of devilish European forms of thought and government from Petersburg.

With surprising rapidity the counterfeit Peter III gathered a horde of followers. Word spread from village to village that the emperor had returned, and that he was bringing back the old faith and the old ways. Pugachev enlarged his entourage. He now had a secretary of state—a local Russian landowner who, though he knew the dark, stocky Cossack to be a fraud, nonetheless saw in him great promise as a lightning rod of dissent and a galvanizer of rebellion. Pugachev's wife Yustina, who posed as his true empress (not as Empress Catherine, for Catherine was said to be the villain in the drama, having deposed her husband), had a group of maids of honor who followed her everywhere she went. A Cossack youth dressed like the son of a noble family played the role of Grand Duke Paul. There were secretaries, clerks, even courtiers to whom Pugachev gave the names Orlov, Vorontzov and Panin.

Wherever he appeared, Pugachev trailed clouds of majesty and mock authority. His entourage lent him dignity, and formed a backdrop for his imposture. He was a persuasive actor; he could cry at will, one who saw him remembered afterwards, and he had the gift of making his hearers believe whatever he said. When he stood before the people in his velvet caftan and cap and wept, assuring them that he was the true emperor and that he cared for them as Christ had cared for his own, he stirred their hearts and won their loyalty. He knew well what his own Cossacks and the non-Russian peoples among whom they lived wanted to hear. Surrounded by his sham court, with priests waving incense and embroidered banners bearing the symbols of the Old Belief gleaming in the autumn sunshine, he made extravagant promises and aroused extravagant hopes.

All those who joined his "great order," Pugachev said, would enjoy "the freedom of the rivers from their sources to their mouths, and the land and the growth thereon and payment in money, and lead and powder and supplies of corn." If only they would help him to regain the throne from which he had been unjustly driven by the power-mad usurper Catherine, he would not only reward them but put an end once and for all to the harmful sway of Petersburg over the free-ranging, untamed Cossack way of life.

Plenty, wealth, the restoration of the old customs and the old belief: these made up the false Peter's platform. He knew how to cloak his message, and his person, in semimystical rhetoric. "Those who are lost, worn out and in sadness," he proclaimed, "who long for me and who wish to be my subjects and under my orders, hearing my name, should come to me." He was the Christlike, all-forgiving, loving Russian father who offered his children not only absolution but victory over the faroff false empress and her rules and demands.

Pugachev presented himself as a martyred saint, the hallowed emperor chosen by God to lead his people but wronged and wounded by those who had snatched his powers from him. He told all who would listen that he had been away from Russia for many years, wandering in Egypt and the Holy Land, in mourning for his lost birthright. Now that he had returned, he tearfully asked for help in retaking what was his. Hundreds, then thousands, of peasants, laborers, soldiers, and townspeople knelt before him reverently and swore to do whatever he asked.

The first military effort of the rebels failed. When Pugachev led his army against the town of Yaitsk, they were beaten back, although many of the imperial troops defending the town abandoned their posts and joined the rebel army. But by the time the counterfeit emperor and his horde reached the key fortress town of Orenburg, and set siege to it in October of 1773, their numbers had reached ten thousand. Emissaries of the false Peter III were sent out to carry his message into the mining regions and factory towns of the southern Urals and beyond. And the imposter's success was emboldening him to employ coercion.

All the power of the imperial image was summoned to curse those who refused to join the growing army of Emperor Pugachev. Anyone who remained faithful to the government of Catherine in Petersburg was threatened; "they will soon feel," the rebel leader warned, "how many cruel tortures are prepared for traitors to me." Strewn along the trail of the rebels were the corpses of those who resisted joining the rebellion—dozens of hanged soldiers, officers and Cossacks, even executed priests. Now terror was added to Pugachev's tearful persuasion, and many joined the rebels out of fear alone. Month after month, as the siege of Orenburg continued and winter closed in, Pugachev's ragtag army grew.

The empress, with the concurrence of her advisers, sent three thousand troops against Pugachev, commanded by General Kar. Other provincial troops marched toward the rebel stronghold as well. But Pugachev, with his swelling horde, was too strong for them. Kar was defeated and forced to retreat, and all other attempts to assault the rebel camp at Berda just outside Orenburg were repulsed. Survivors of these assaults who made their way back to the capital toward the end of November painted a gruesome picture of violence and anarchy. The sham emperor had ignited class hatred in his followers, they said. Not only were all imperial officers being murdered but manor houses were being burned, landowners and their wives and children executed. Pugachev had declared war on the elite of the Russian Empire.

Catherine had her hands full. Russia was still at war with Turkey, thousands of soldiers and sailors were dying every month and thousands more being recruited to replace them at their deadly work from among the beleaguered serfs. And the Russian economy was once more in grave peril. The government

had begun printing paper money, secured against an ever-
dwindling treasury. Abundant assignats replaced scarce rubles,
and the resulting inflation, coupled with several years of poor
harvests, sent prices so high that Catherine and her councillors
feared riots in the cities. With resentment against the war and its
toll in lives reaching a peak, with the country once again facing
the threat of severe economic instability, if not outright bank-
ruptcy, and with Russia's rivals only too eager to exploit
Pugachev's rebellion to weaken Catherine's government, it
was imperative that the threat to internal order be controlled.
The rebels had to be crushed. The false emperor had to be destroyed.

The empress acted decisively. With characteristic thoroughness
she informed herself, through maps and the reports of provincial
authorities and informants, about the regions threatened by the
rebels and satisfied herself that the town of Orenburg could
withstand a winter siege. She prepared a new manifesto denouncing Pugachev and ordered it to be read publicly by every village
priest. She chose a capable commander, General Bibikov, to
replace the overly cautious Kar. Most important, she did not give
way to fears, and she remained consistently, firmly vigilant.
Having sent Bibikov to oppose Pugachev and his horde, she
awaited news of his success; day by day, hour by hour, she was
master of the situation, and her calm clear head and unwavering
vigilance lent ballast to the volatile discussions of her advisers.

Catherine remained steady as Moscow became infected with
the Pugachev heresy. Emissaries of the false Peter III brought his
message to the recalcitrant, disaffected city and soon the Cossack
rebel was the talk of every tavern. Some Muscovites believed that
Emperor Peter had indeed come back to claim the allegiance of his
people; many more, knowing or suspecting the rebellion to be
based in imposture, nonetheless expressed support for the
enigmatic figure who appealed to them for loyalty against the
European, warmongering Catherine.

The state police tried to suppress all dangerous talk about Emperor Peter, arresting and beating those guilty of seditious murmurings, reading all mail and forcing those suspected of sympathizing with Pugachev to swear allegiance to the empress—something only the most irreligious would do cynically. But the appeal of the false tsar was seductive; Moscow dreamed romantic dreams of subversion, nobles longed for a savior emperor who would oust Catherine, traditionalists hoped for the restoration of the old customs and the old belief, servants imagined that the man who called himself Peter III, once restored, would give them their freedom.

Outbreaks of hysteria, random gunshots, rumors of a rising on behalf of the "true emperor" became a predictable part of Moscow life in the winter of 1773–1774. One dark evening in early March, people rushed into the streets in every suburb of the city shouting "Long live Peter III and Pugachev!" So sudden was the onset of the tumult, and so widespread, that ordinary citizens panicked. Surely the shouts were a signal. Dreading riot, revolution, massacre, or worse, they armed themselves, gathered their valuables, and took refuge where they could, embattled against the mayhem to come. The police tried in vain to isolate the troublemakers and restore calm, but the pandemonium went on for hours, until at last the comforting presence of Prince Volkonsky, visiting each suburb and assuring the residents that the shouting had been nothing more than the work of mischief-makers, brought an uneasy peace.

Catherine heard of the uproar in Moscow, and of the many Muscovites who hoped for the success of the impostor, and it took all her fortitude to carry on as if General Bibikov's success was assured. "As far as possible," she wrote to Bibikov, "don't lose time, and try to end this ugly and degrading mess before spring." She knew that Pugachev had been joined by thousands of followers from among the non-Russian peoples of the area—Tatars, Bashkirs, Kirghiz, Mordvins and others—and that he had at his disposal heavy guns supplied by the foundries of the Urals. He was becoming bolder and more aggressive, conscripting men to fight under his banners, killing those who refused to swear loyalty to him.

Pugachev was undergoing a change. No longer a Christlike martyr, he now held court in a lace-trimmed red coat and displayed himself to his followers holding a scepter and a silver axe. He surrounded himself with tinsel and mock ceremony in a caricature of court life. He issued orders, and had his secretaries seal them with an official-looking seal bearing the imperial double eagle. He continued to assure his followers ("my children, my bright falcons," as he called them) that he would look after them, and promised the peasants their freedom, but he demanded that they play a bloody role in bringing the new order into being. Peasants were ordered to kill their landlords, in return for a fee. "He who kills a landowner and destroys his house will be given a wage of a hundred rubles," one of Pugachev's orders read. "He who kills ten landowners and destroys their houses will get a thousand rubles and the rank of general." From his camp at Berda Pugachev commanded thousands of would-be assassins, all loyal to the man they had begun to call Nadezha Gosudar, the "Tsar of our Hopes."

As if the specter of Pugachev and his wild-eyed assassins were not enough, Catherine was aggravated just at this time by a tart memorandum from her son—his first recorded attempt to influence his mother's governance. Paul drew up a long analytical document, which he called "Considerations about the State in General, Relative to the Number of Troops Needed for its Defense and Regarding the Defense of All Borders." Despite the cumbersomely military title, it was in fact less a document about the military than a persuasion to peace. The Turkish war, Paul argued, with its attendant costs and sacrifices, had led Russia into internal dissension and near ruin; only many years of peace, with lower taxes and a smaller, dispersed, less oppressive army could restore the empire to her natural condition of prosperity and harmony.

That her son should propose weakening the army at a time when the eastern part of the realm had burst into rebellion— a rebellion that was spreading virtually unchecked—must have galled Catherine and soured her opinion of her son's judgment. She was annoyed by her critics: it was not only Paul who took her to task but Diderot as well, who questioned her closely about her governmental methods and hinted broadly that she had crossed the line separating benign monarchy from tyranny. She needed friends and allies, not critics. Only Melchior Grimm, a visiting Parisian with whom Catherine felt immediately at ease and whose worldliness and sympathetic intelligence made him a delightful companion for her, gave her the diversion and friendly support she craved.

Catherine was in need of support just then, as she had embarked on uncertain waters in her emotional life. She had discarded her longtime partner Orlov in order to gain independence, yet Orlov's replacement, the boyish, correct, vapid Vassilchikov, bored her to tears and beyond. At forty-five, gray-haired and heavy-footed, disappointed in her son and greatly beleaguered by the cares of state, Catherine needed a helpmeet—a lover, yes, but also a friend and colleague who could ease her burdens by sharing them.

She had tried to accustom herself to Vassilchikov, but she soon became scornful of him, and she could not hide her scorn; he withdrew, she cried, he clutched his chest in pain, she cried still more. (She was later to remember her time with Vassilchikov as the most tearful of her life.) She had become habituated to the tedious young man, yet she feared that she had made a bad bargain. Would she become so emotionally bonded to him that she couldn't bear to send him away? Was she destined to be miserable with him for the rest of her life?

The sour Vassilchikov was not happy either. ("I'm just a little

whore," he was heard to say.) His chest hurt, he was unable to
please his powerful, aging mistress. The empress's entire household despised him, and let him know it. He must have longed to
return to the contented obscurity of his former life.

Catherine thought anxiously of sending Vassilchikov away, as
she had Orlov, but something held her back. Unsatisfying and
insipid as he was, Vassilchikov was nonetheless someone to love,
someone to cling to. Catherine needed love, or at least its sim-
ulacrum. Without someone to love she felt lost, bewildered, in
thrall to the bleakness of life. Yet the longer she tolerated the
inadequate Vassilchikov, the more depressed she became. Real
satisfaction, the deep contentment of love, eluded her.

Melchior Grimm, who became Catherine's close friend during
the winter of 1773–1774, and who was present at the palace every
day from midmorning until late at night, observed her closely in
this unhappy season. She often sent for him after supper and sat
with him, talking and doing needlework, until nearly midnight.
She preferred Grimm's conversation to the usual evening entertainments. Plays were tedious to her, the comedies bored her and
the tragedies were not to her taste. She had never been able to
appreciate concerts or opera. Gambling for high stakes never
piqued her interest for long. She had never lost her enthusiasm for
ideas, but after eleven years of rule, idealism in and of itself
irritated her. Diderot had grown irksome to her, with his endless
queries about serfdom in Russia and his naive assumptions about
human nature. She had discovered at first hand how government
must assert its primacy over chaos by force alone; all considerations of public good and individual liberty had to be secon-
dary. Diderot had made himself a prickly voice of conscience, and
she was not sorry when the Frenchman left Petersburg in March
of 1774, though it did distress her to learn of his many mishaps on
the return journey.

Grimm was in any case much more to Catherine's taste than the
searching, volatile, high-minded Diderot. The Swiss was down-
to-earth and gossipy, as Catherine herself was, a man of the world

who had few illusions when it came to human betterment. With Grimm Catherine could talk of the follies and foibles of her courtiers, and chatter on, as she liked to do, about what she called "this iron century" and its peculiarities. Grimm wrote that by the end of the winter he and the empress were on the most cordial of terms. He was enchanted with her company. "I entered her apartments with the same assurance as that of the most intimate friend," he confided, "certain of finding in her conversation an inexhaustible store of the greatest interest presented in the most piquant form."

Catherine turned to Grimm for companionship in part because of her boredom with Vassilchikov. But by February she was working on another sweeping change in her personal life. She brought to court a giant of a man, huge and ugly, disfigured by the loss of an eye and so slovenly in his dress and uncouth in his manners that he made the more fastidious courtiers shudder. He was Gregory Potemkin.

Potemkin burst in upon the court like a hot wind off the faraway southern desert, strange and exotic and with more than a hint of threat. He was outsize and ungainly, and his blinded eye—which he kept uncovered—was an affront to the prettified courtiers accustomed to veiling their defects behind patches and wigs and yards of frothy scented lace. Potemkin did not blend with Petersburg society, and he could not have cared less. He was utterly different, an alien being, and no one knew what to make of him. A hero of the Turkish war, decorated for bravery and gallantry, he had none of the dash or swagger of the soldier. His dress was unmilitary in the extreme; he favored flowing caftans in soft glowing silks, his large fleshy fingers sparkled with jeweled rings, his hair was long and unpowdered, and he carried himself with a world-weary slouch that made everyone around him vaguely squeamish.

He was extremely clever, and could be entertaining when he was in the mood to be (one could never tell, his moods varied widely and he was frequently morose or misanthropic). In short,

Potemkin brought little to court but his quick-thinking, well-stocked mind. He was not highborn, in fact his father was an army colonel who owned a mere four hundred serfs. (Wealthy nobles owned tens of thousands of serfs.) He was certainly not handsome, though a few women admitted to falling prey to his raw animal magnetism. He was no longer young, and had never held any important post. But he unsettled everyone, he caused a tremendous stir. And it soon became evident that he would be the empress's next lover.

The British ambassador Gunning was convinced that Potemkin's arrival and meteoric rise (Catherine conferred on him the rank of adjutant-general, installed him and a number of his relatives in the Winter Palace, and rewarded him with honors and orders) marked a major turning point in Catherine's reign.

"We have here a change of decoration which to my mind merits more attention than any other event which has happened since the beginning of the reign," he wrote in a dispatch to London. "Mr. Vassilchikov, who was too dull-witted to have any influence in affairs and to enjoy the confidence of his mistress, now has a successor who promises to have both to a supreme degree." The shaggy, odorous Potemkin caused "general astonishment, even consternation," the ambassador wrote. He was no Vassilchikov, callow and retiring; Potemkin was a force to be reckoned with, fearsomely clever, physically intimidating, with untapped capabilities and high aspirations. He was said to have unusual discernment and what the ambassador called "a deep knowledge of men."

"Given these qualities, and thanks to the indolence of his rivals, he ought naturally to hope that he can elevate himself to the heights envisioned by his boundless ambitions," Gunning concluded. In short, he might well take over the governing of Russia.

Catherine was obviously enraptured with the huge, erratic, cerebral Potemkin. Her mood, which had been sour and truculent, abruptly became sanguine, buoyant, elated in the extreme, and her new favorite was clearly the source of the change. "She is

mad about him," one of her senior officials, Senator Elagin, told
another. "They must really love each other, for they are exactly
alike." Alike or not, Catherine felt that at last she had found the
soul mate for whom she had been waiting all her life. She was
radiant, beside herself, quite giddy with joy.

"Oh, Monsieur Potemkin!" she wrote in one of her numerous
love notes, "what a confounded miracle you have wrought, to
have so deranged a head that heretofore in the world passed for
one of the best in Europe!. . . . What a shame! What a sin!
Catherine the Second a prey to this mad passion!"

At the age of forty-five, Catherine felt as if she were discovering love for the first time. "Everything I have laughed about all
my life has happened," she wrote to her beloved, "so much so
that my love for you dazzles me. Sentiments which I used to
consider as idiotic, exaggerated and unnatural, I feel them now. I
cannot tear away my stupid look from you. I forget everything
my reason tells me and I feel I become quite stupid when I am in
your presence."

Love sent Catherine's mind reeling, even as her spirits soared.
She lost her customary reasonableness and balance. Her zest for
intellectual conversation flagged. She was not herself, she was
"somebody with delirium." Yet that somebody wore a perpetual
smile. "I forget the whole world when I am with you," Catherine
wrote to her new favorite. "I have never been so happy as I am
now."

Potemkin knew how to touch Catherine's heart and make her
feel cherished. He sang to her, the songs sweet and melodious, his
voice soft and full of sincerity. He admired the ruins of beauty in
her, the fleeting traces of youthfulness in her bright eyes and
overpainted complexion. He awoke her passion—he called her "a
woman of fire"—and made her believe that for him, she was the
only woman in the world.

Potemkin was, it seems, genuinely in love with the sovereign
he greatly admired. As a very young officer he had played a minor
role in her coup, helping to bring her to the throne. No doubt he

remembered her as she had been then, a thrillingly daring figure on a great white horse, riding in triumph toward a unique destiny. He loved her daring, it matched his own. He loved her forthright, far-ranging mind, with its visions of betterment and change; he too had broad and soaring visions. He loved her strong, responsive, womanly body, that freely sought love and as freely gave it; his appetite matched hers, and in her he found satiety.

The senator was right: Catherine and Potemkin were very much alike, and if their volcanic romance had, on his side, overtones of adoration and self-serving ambition, it was no less an earthshaking, once-in-a-lifetime romance for all that.

"There is something extraordinary between us that cannot be expressed in words," Catherine wrote. "The alphabet is too short, the letters are not numerous enough." In the midst of calamities great and small, time-bound in that iron century, on the threshold of age with its bleakness and futility, Catherine stumbled upon the great love of her life.

Fortune smiled on Russia even as it blessed the empress. In March of 1774 the rebel Pugachev, strutting in his lace-trimmed red coat, was attacked and decisively beaten before Orenburg, his fierce but untrained army scattered to the four winds. The impact of his imposture was blunted. He slunk away, his forces in tatters, his tawdry court reduced to a ragtag masquerade. Everywhere the earth warmed, the ice melted, the rivers ran high and swift, and even the floods that drowned the land and swept away houses, cottages, whole villages, seemed no more than momentary misfortunes in a benign and benevolent grand design.

Chapter Twenty-Four

ACCORDING TO ONE ACCOUNT, TOWARD THE END OF THE year 1774 Empress Catherine went in great secrecy—perhaps in disguise—to the small church of St. Samson in an obscure suburb of Petersburg, taking with her only a single female attendant. There she met Potemkin, accompanied by one of his nephews and a chamberlain from the palace. A priest appeared, and for the next hour and more the church was closed to worshipers for the duration of a private ceremony. A wedding ceremony.

The bride, matronly, gray-haired and bright-eyed, her face flushed with delight, stood quietly while her attendant passed the gold crown over her head three times. The groom, towering and massive, his one good eye fixed on the glowing holy pictures in the iconostasis, had to stoop each time the crown was passed over his head. The choir sang, the couple was blessed and at length dismissed. For the second time in her life, Catherine acquired a husband.

It is impossible to say with certainty that Catherine underwent a marriage ceremony with her beloved Potemkin, but it seems likely that she did. In her notes to him she often called herself his wife, and called him "dear husband." Referring to herself in the third person, she asked coyly in one letter, written in 1776, "Was she attached to you two years ago by holy ties?"

Catherine knew that Empress Elizabeth had married her lover Alexei Razumovsky, and that Razumosvky possessed documents to prove it, though he gallantly burned them when the existence of a marriage contract threatened to dishonor the late empress's good name. There was thus a recent precedent for the private marriage of a Russian Empress.

Only a few years earlier Catherine had decided against marrying Gregory Orlov, leaving Orlov aggrieved. But Potemkin was not Orlov. He was that dazzling blend of ideal lover, stimulating intellectual companion, and potential collaborator in governing who she had always longed for. He was everything she needed, and more. If she married him there would be no inconvenient dynastic complications, for she was past childbearing age. Besides, no one need know; the marriage would be their whimsical, sentimental, romantic secret, a symbol of what Catherine vowed would be "an eternal love." The evidence, and Catherine and Potemkin's state of mind and heart, suggest that a wedding ceremony may well have taken place.

Catherine needed the fortifying reassurance of Potemkin's love and support more than ever, for her realm was still recovering from the violent upheaval of a widespread peasant war, a war that had challenged her own security to a greater degree than any earlier crisis.

During the previous summer the rebellion originally sparked by Pugachev's imposture became something larger and more terrifying than a localized revolt among marginal peoples. Tens of thousands of peasants throughout east and southeast Russia rose against their masters, proclaiming their freedom and condemning the time-honored laws and customs that bound them to cultivate the land for the benefit of privileged landowners. Inspired by word of Pugachev's revived leadership, bands of peasants armed with axes and knives, wooden clubs and crude pointed sticks descended on the houses of local gentry and began an orgy of maiming and massacre.

Noble victims were decapitated, their hands and feet cut off, their mangled torsos displayed as gory trophies. Women were raped and murdered, children cut down pitilessly to die beside their parents. No one was spared, not the aged, not infants, not monks or priests. Houses were burned, churches looted and destroyed, barns and outbuildings put to the torch. The traditional deep-going piety of the peasants was overwhelmed as bloodthirsty emotions were unleashed; rebels gouged out the eyes of holy icons, desecrated altars, defaced religious paintings and stole the precious vessels that held the host. Altogether thousands of innocents lost their lives at the rebels' hands, and many thousands more were left without food or shelter or the means to provide them.

As the summer advanced the terrifying wave of violence continued to spread. Townspeople, dreading attack by the murderous peasant gangs, tried to flee to safety yet found none. Word reached Moscow that the town of Kazan had been overrun, sacked and burned to the ground by Pugachev and twenty thousand vengeful followers, and there was widespread fear that Moscow would soon come under assault. Catherine's spies informed her that assassins had been sent to murder her and her son; for weeks thereafter it looked as though the forces she had sent to hunt down and destroy the insurgents would not be able to succeed.

Finally, late in August, the tide turned. Government troops harried and captured roaming gangs of lawless peasants and subjected all those suspected of taking part in the mayhem to horrible punishments. The reprisals were as savage as the crimes they were meant to avenge. Entire villages suffered; in some villages, every third man was hanged, while the remaining inhabitants suffered severe beatings and mutilation. Soldiers erected torture-wheels and gallows in each village and before they moved on, left the

ditches piled high with corpses. Coincident with the gory back-
lash, crops failed throughout the Volga region, adding famine to
the parade of atrocities. The imposter and arch-rebel Pugachev,
betrayed by his own men, was captured and brought to Moscow
in an iron cage, where he still languished on Catherine's wedding
day.

That after twelve years of benign government her empire could
be convulsed by peasant war must have disheartened Catherine,
bringing her long-range hopes for Russia into question and
challenging her belief in the possibility of human betterment. She
had long been sustained in her efforts by the expectation that she
could be a teacher and guide for her subjects, leading them toward
abundance, moral improvement, and harmony. In time, she
thought, with sufficient prosperity and under the suasion of improved administration and just laws, crime would diminish and
eventually disappear.

But the defiance, venom and bloodlust unloosed by Pugachev,
and the eagerness with which his imposture had been embraced,
forced her to acknowledge the shortsightedness of her expectations. The peasants who formed the overwhelming majority
of her subjects had shown themselves to be, not a docile and
devoted collection of willing learners, waiting to be led into the
light, but an ugly combustible mass of haters, seething with
murderous rage, ready to avenge themselves on their betters.
Pugachev's rebellion, and the peasant war it ignited, had laid bare
the dark side of humanity, and Catherine, chastened by the experience, saw that she had to incorporate those dark impulses into a
revised set of expectations for herself and her realm.

Her accomplishments thus far had not been few. She had given
her people a code of laws, the foundation stone of her program of
improvement. She had reformed and reorganized the government
agencies in Petersburg, and had begun to reform provincial government as well, though progress had been frustratingly slow.
She had begun the building of dozens of new towns, issued
dozens of new edicts, ordered the mapping of her realm (an

ambitious and unprecedented undertaking) and a census to accompany it, and had enjoyed some success in establishing orphan-
ages and making prisons more humane. She had encouraged the
growing of tobacco in the Ukraine, distributing seeds and providing pamphlets to growers to teach them the newest and most
efficient methods of cultivation. She had subsidized Russian
shipping, founded factories for tanning, candle-making, and the
manufacture of silk and linen. Under her auspices, skilled workers
were imported from France to show imperial craftsmen better
ways of weaving hangings, embroidering lace, and making fine
china.

In keeping with her belief that both boys and girls ought to be
educated from the age of five, the empress had given a good deal
of attention to projects to build schools, founding the Smolny
Institute, an academy designed for five hundred girls and young
women modeled on Madame de Maintenon's Saint-Cyr, and
visiting the school often. (Diderot saw her there in the year of the
peasant rebellion, smiling and opening her arms to the pupils,
who ran to hug her and clung to her; the sight "touched him to the
point of tears.") Though books were still a rarity in Russia, apart
from religious works, the empress had made great strides in
promoting the value of reading and learning and took pride in the
forty thousand volumes belonging to the Academy of Sciences.
She founded and endowed a medical college to educate Russian
physicians and apothecaries, and commissioned the first Russian
pharmacopeia. And she did her best to prop up the fledgling
Moscow University, not yet twenty years old, plagued by a
sparse and underqualified faculty, incompetent direction, and a
paucity of students, few of whom remained enrolled long enough
to complete degrees.

In foreign affairs the empress had most to boast of—not only
major military victories but triumphs of a more pervasive and
lasting kind. She had succeeded in transforming the image
Europeans held of her empire from that of a backward and
barbarous place, stigmatized by credulousness, culturally and in-

tellectually feeble and insignificant on the world stage to that of a major power with a fearsome army, led by an enlightened philosopher-empress of astounding gifts, a land of promise of which great things could be expected. In July of 1774, as the rebellion roared on unchecked, Catherine learned that at last her envoys had succeeded in concluding peace with the Turks, closing an immense chapter in her recent endeavors and allowing her to look to the future with a lighter spirit.

Important shifts were taking place in European politics, and thanks to the combined efforts of the empress and her advisers, chiefly Panin, Russia would play a large role in the new order. England was embroiled in North America, where her colonies were restive and rebellious; Spain was moribund; France was in transition, with the death of Louis XV and the accession of his shy, inept young grandson Louix XVI and the latter's beautiful young Austrian Queen Marie Antoinette; the aging Frederick II still ruled in Prussia, but could not last long. Now was the time for Russia to advance herself territorially, to move Europe-ward by absorbing western lands.

Catherine had begun this process by joining Frederick and the Austrian co-ruler Joseph II, son of Empress Maria Theresa, to divide roughly one-third of the Polish kingdom between them. With one stroke of the quill Russia gained vast lands and more than a million and a half new subjects. A second annexation of Polish land had swiftly followed, adding more valuable territory and more new subjects. Russia's role in the destruction of the chaotic kingdom of the Poles was lauded by European observers, adding to Catherine's prestige. Poland was widely regarded as an artificial entity, in a state of constant turmoil, where a Catholic tyranny stifled freedom. The relatively more benevolent rule of Austria, Prussia and Russia was seen as an improvement over the prevailing situation; Catherine was regarded as a savior of the Poles, not their oppressor.

She had done a great deal, but much more needed to be done,

and with Potemkin beside her, as husband, partner, perhaps in time even co-ruler, it would be accomplished. Together the empress and her cherished, greatly admired lover dreamed large and expansive dreams. They liked to meet in the steambath, lolling and sporting in the near-scalding water like two whales. Both were capable of being as playful as children, and both loved to play. Both were mimics, and Potemkin made Catherine laugh uncontrollably with his imitations of the courtiers; she may have brought out her old repertoire of animal noises to amuse him. When play turned erotic she reveled in his lovemaking, in his capacity to thrill and disarm her. For a powerful woman to surrender her power in the arms of a trusted and skillful lover must have given infinite pleasure and release. Potemkin offered the empress that release as night after night they met, loved, and talked beside the steaming waters, reclining and refreshing themselves from platters of meats and fruit and sweet confections, washed down by fine wines.

Potemkin was happiest wearing nothing but an embroidered caftan, the soft flowing silk billowing over his huge bulk. Possibly he taught Catherine to enjoy the ease of shapeless silk as well; certainly he helped her relax amid his preferred surroundings— yielding divans, thick cushions and pillows, scented air and myriad delights of touch and taste.

Lulled and warmed by his abundant sensuality, hers bloomed. Though she had always been an earthy woman with a hearty sexuality, Catherine had never been one to indulge her sexual side. Now, however, at the very time when the intense irritations of menopause made her sleepless with night sweats and caused her joints to ache and her cheeks to flush beet-red as heat rose in a sudden wall of flame from her chest to the top of her head, she allowed her muscles to unclench and gave in to the seductions of satiety. Ever the rigidly self-disciplined German daughter of a Prussian officer, Catherine began, with Potemkin, to savor doing nothing, to sink deep into contented emptiness for hours at a time. Ever her mother's ugly duckling at heart, with Potemkin Catherine became the loveliest swan of all, restored to youth and hope by the sweetness of his wooing.

And always, along with the wooing, there was, at some point, mutual cogitation. Catherine was planning to prepare another fundamental document, as important and far-reaching as her law code. It was to be a statute reforming provincial government, addressing the corruption and laxity of the present system and installing a more accountable system in which police would maintain order, local officials would keep the roads in good repair, oversee schools, prisons and the workings of commerce, and facilitate the collection of taxes while dispensing justice with an even hand. Catherine had been reading, in a French translation, the six thick volumes of the great English jurist Blackstone ("Oh, his commentaries and me, we are inseparable," she remarked) and taking detailed notes. She talked to Potemkin about Blackstone's concepts, and how they differed from those of Montesquieu and from the thoughts that had flowed so volubly from the fertile brain of Diderot during his six-month seminar with the empress.

Potemkin and Catherine conversed at length, he impressing her with his quickness of apprehension and his ability to perceive nuances and to cast aside irrelevancies to point up essentials. Their minds worked as well together as their bodies, and one way and another, they communed late into the night.

Early in 1775 the empress entered Moscow in triumph, to begin many months of official celebrations of the end of the Turkish war and Russia's deliverance from the peasant rebellion. Amid splendor recalling that of her coronation, Catherine rode into the city in state, a jeweled figure in a gilded coach, smiling amiably and waving to the crowds that lined her path. With an entourage of hundreds of guardsmen and liveried servants the imperial coach moved slowly through huge triumphal arches built specially for the occasion, rolling past gaudy pageants representing the conquest of the Turks, the destruction of Pugachev and the restoration of peace and right order in the realm.

Though the cold was severe thousands of people came to watch the spectacle, stamping their feet and flapping their arms and emitting thin halfhearted cheers in response to the glowers of the guardsmen. The crowds were much larger and their shouts more spirited, though, when Grand Duke Paul made his official entry into the city several weeks later. He rode at the head of his regiment, looking taller and more princely on his magnificent horse than he did when at court, and the Muscovites, seeing in Paul their hope for the future, cheered and clapped and shouted out blessings until long after the last of the soldiers had gone past.

Catherine was well aware of the contrast between her own reception by the people of Moscow and that of her son. It was galling to her—though hardly unexpected—that Paul should be received with such enthusiasm, particularly when she knew how openly contemptuous he had become of Russia and the Russian people. But then, the Muscovites had always been perverse in their preferences. She knew that many of them had been secret supporters of Pugachev. They were not only perverse, they were ungrateful, these indolent, decadent, pleasure-loving Muscovites; they did not appreciate Catherine's clemency toward them, her general pardon of all ex-rebels, her many benefits to the city, her recent lowering of the salt tax and her continual concern to keep bread prices low. They greeted each official announcement of her imperial benefactions not with shouts of gratitude but with mutters of suspicion.

An ambassador looked on one day as Catherine stood at a window of the palace when her edicts were read to the Muscovites outside. She watched their reactions, how they crossed themselves as if warding off evil, and then melted away into the city.

"What stupidity!" the ambassador heard the empress say.

She could not stand the Golovin Palace, and had ordered the vast wooden Kolomenskoe Palace torn down several years earlier. Intensely ill at ease amid the onion domes and tent roofs of the old city, she chose to move into a large estate some distance away, to which she gave the name Tsaritsyno. Here she entertained the Moscow nobles—she gave eight receptions and three balls during her first month of residence—and held court.

When her birthday came, toward the end of April, she ordered her servants to prepare a special ball and supper. At least five thousand guests were expected. Supper tables were set up and decorated, enormous quantities of food prepared. The appointed hour arrived. Catherine, splendidly dressed to greet the start of her forty-seventh year, awaited her well-wishers.

They trickled in, a dozen here, a dozen there, a sparse group of merrymakers alighting from a thin stream of carriages. Onlookers noticed that the empress "could not hide her surprise" at how few guests were in attendance. She was mortified. The perverse, cruel Muscovites were deliberately insulting her by staying away in droves. "She spoke of this emptiness in a way that revealed that it humiliated her," the British ambassador Gunning wrote. In Petersburg Catherine would have been mobbed on her birthday; in Moscow she was snubbed.

This intensely unpleasant incident, following on the heels of too much excitement and perhaps too many late nights in the steambath, made Catherine ill. "I have had fever and violent diarrhea," she wrote to her friend Madame Bielke, "of which I was cured by strong bleeding." The highlight of the peace celebration, the feast held for all the people of Moscow, had to be postponed for more than a week because of the empress's indisposition, but when the day came at last the ungrateful Muscovites were treated to a spectacular entertainment.

In a huge open field two miles from Red Square a vast pleasure-ground was built, covering four square miles. Enormous temporary kitchens produced enough spitted meat, roasted fowl, loaves of bread and barrels of pickled vegetables to feed a hundred thousand people for twelve hours. Fountains flowed with wine, beer and kvass were freely available. Musicians played, rope-dancers performed daredevil tricks, peddlers sold trinkets and plays were presented in a large theater. In the evening, fireworks lit up the sky and all the temporary buildings shone with candle-light. The entire festival ground was christened the Black Sea, and decorated with replicas of ships. Every building was given a name commemorating a town or region Russia had gained in the peace treaty: Azov and Taganrog, Kerch and Yenikale and Kinburn.

"Everything went off well," Catherine told Voltaire in a letter. "The weather was the finest in the world; there was no confusion, and the utmost gaiety; not the slightest little disaster spoilt this celebration." "I would love to have danced with you there," she added, a little wistfully, for Voltaire was now quite aged and she knew they would never meet.

Catherine remained in Moscow for the better part of a year, devoting herself primarily, in the intervals between council meetings, working with her six secretaries, and maintaining an ever larger correspondence, to her monumental labor of provincial reform. Looking to key regional governors for advice and ideas, and relying on Potemkin—who was rapidly gaining political experience in his various important court posts—for help and encouragement, she drafted and redrafted her long document, writing out changes in her own hand, revising some parts nearly a dozen times. It was a difficult task requiring constant acuity, sober judgment, and a sense of the pragmatic that the empress was honing with every passing year of her rule. She commented to one of her secretaries that she felt it essential to act with "prudence and circumspection" in writing new laws or reforms.

"I examine the circumstances, I take advice, I consult the enlightened part of the people," she told him, "and in this way I find out what sort of effect my laws will have. And when I am already convinced, in advance, of general approval, I issue my orders, and have the pleasure of observing what you call blind obedience. And that is the foundation of unlimited power."

When the reforms were complete, and given the support of the Senate, they inaugurated a process of slow but deep-going change. Local administrative units, which had been huge, sprawling, and understaffed, now became smaller and more manageable. Local officials were more accountable to the empress and her deputies in the capital and less captive to the whims and caprices of the nobles in their vicinity. Bureaus of public welfare, endowed by the central treasury in Petersburg, were set up to establish hospitals and schools, asylums and poorhouses. New towns were founded, laid out along grids in the European manner; they were a symbol of how planning, orderly execution and systematic, steady purpose could create a changed Russia. Overall, Catherine's reforms marked a profound turning point in local governance; tradition-bound inertia gave way to an atmosphere of innovation and slow improvement. Though many were suspicious of the alteration, there was no denying that it brought to the stagnant, troubled countryside a breath of fresh air.

Preoccupations of a more personal nature ate away at Catherine as her year in Moscow drew to a close. The "deep, frank and extraordinary love" she shared with Potemkin was turning sour. That astonishing rapport, compounded of physical chemistry, intense desire, playfulness and rare mental kinship was being shattered with increasing regularity by quarrels, coldness, recriminations. Catherine was on the whole even-tempered and kind, magnanimous in personal relations; she did not tend to provoke quarrels and when they arose, she tried to bring them to an end as quickly and as painlessly as possible.

Potemkin, on the other hand, was always either sunk in torpor or nervous, restless and dissatisfied. His elation was inevitably short-lived, and gave way to melancholy. He had taken to shutting himself away for days at a time, abandoning Catherine to her worries about their future together, and when he did emerge from his self-imposed isolation he tortured her with questions about her past relationships with other men. Catherine did her best to reassure him, but his incessant need for reassurance must itself have grated on her. And besides, he had a gift for discovering new occasions for disagreement and bad feeling.

"You simply like quarreling," Catherine wrote to her lover in exasperation. "Tranquillity is a condition unacceptable to your nature." There were still times when passion flared and quarrels were forgotten, but the complications, crises and conflicts were mounting. In vain Catherine recited the litany of her earlier liaisons: "I took the first [Saltykov] because I was compelled to, the fourth [Vassilchikov] because I was in despair. . . . As for the three others [Peter III, Poniatowski, and Orlov], God knows it was not from wantonness, for which I have never had any inclination."

She talked to Potemkin sensibly, calmly, soothingly—but he brooded and paced the room and bit his nails in anxiety, until at last she saw that there would be no end to the tension between them.

Larger issues loomed. Would Catherine ever make Potemkin a full co-ruler, if not in law then in fact? How much of her authority would she be willing to turn over to him? And if she held back, could she keep his love?

Potemkin knew full well that he owed his standing entirely to the empress's sponsorship. "I am the work of your hands," he told her candidly. Yet his pride must have rebeled. Was he not the male, the naturally dominant one in their partnership? And was not her exalted status an obstacle, both to his advancement and to their harmonious relations? A French diplomat, the Baron de Corberon, who was at Catherine's court in 1775 recalled how Potemkin was "puffed up with pride and egoism," his "lively, supple, facile spirit" veiled by less attractive qualities of voluptuousness and "Asiatic softness" and apparent passivity.

Issues of dominance and authority, both in their love affair and in the rulership of the empire, lay between them and widened the gap caused by his insecurity and her unwillingness to capitulate to it. "We always fight about power, never about love," Catherine wrote in a note. She longed for peace, for an end to uncertainty and torment. For one entire day "without disputes, without debates, without discussions."

It was proving to be impossible to go on as they were. Not only were their clashes and tensions interfering with her work of

governing, but more basic differences between them were surfac-
ing, differences that made a fundamental change in their relationship inevitable.

With Catherine, work always came first: the relentless, demanding work of ruling. It preoccupied her, it was what gave her
life and her days meaning. It was her craft, what she called "her
métier." In the service of that work, she arranged her life so that
she greeted each morning with a clear head and, if possible, a
serene mind. She liked to go to bed early, to read for a while, or
do a bit of needlework, then settle down for the night. She needed
and craved love, but she was unwilling to let love tyrannize her or
upset the balance and order of her life—at least, not for long.

Potemkin was an altogether different creature. Work never
ruled him, indeed casual observers believed him all but incapable
of it, fond as he was of napping on his soft divans in his preferred
state of undress. He seemed to find a hundred diversions and
pleasures, any one of which sufficed to let him postpone the
beginning of his labors.

In truth he accomplished a great deal, but in short bursts of
prodigious activity, preceded and followed by long naps or
meditative trances. Immoderation suited him, whether it meant
endless nights of drinking or lovemaking, extended religious
meditations or long periods of somnolence or erratic wakefulness. Ordered domesticity of the kind Catherine was nourished
by bored him, indeed routine of any sort was anathema to him.
And after nearly two years of sharing the empress's bed—or
bath—he was eyeing other women and more than likely having
affairs.

Yet Potemkin continued to share with Catherine a unique and
undiminished passion, and in the intervals between their quarrels
and periods of estrangement, their mental kinship continued to
give pleasure to them both and purpose to their joint endeavors.
Potemkin sought increased power and authority; Catherine, with
a shrewd perception of his abilities that was not clouded by her
infatuation (or exasperation) with him, wanted to delegate to

Potemkin as much power and authority as she felt she dared. And there remained a strong tie of sentiment between them. She was still his "little wife," he her "beloved husband."

Somehow, during the winter of 1775–1776, they came to an agreement. Potemkin would continue to have the empress's love, and would be her chief deputy in the work of governing. But another man—a young, good-looking one, someone Catherine could mold to suit her tastes—would deputize for Potemkin in the imperial bedroom. To make Potemkin feel more at ease with this arrangement, he could participate in the choice of the younger man.

It was a bizarre, perhaps an unprecedented arrangement, a highly idiosyncratic variation on the ménage à trois. Few people at Catherine's court or outside it ever understood it, or the empress who initiated it. In time it gave rise to an avalanche of dispraise.

On January 2, 1776, the empress's young, handsome Polish secretary, Peter Zavadovsky, moved into the suite of rooms assigned to the imperial favorite—the rooms Orlov had occupied, then Vassilchikov, then Potemkin.

At once a nearly palpable wave of apprehension swept through the court as servants, officials and others began to calculate how best to ingratiate themselves with Zavadovsky. Potemkin was out, Zavadovsky was in, they assumed. But closer observation revealed that Potemkin was still very much in favor. He did not entirely vacate the suite into which Zavadovsky had installed himself, and though Catherine presented her "husband" with the beautifully redecorated Anitchkov Palace as his own residence, he preferred to stay near her, either in the imperial palace itself or in a nearby house on the palace grounds.

In March of 1776, Catherine informed her court that Potemkin would henceforth enjoy the title His Serene Highness, or Prince Potemkin. Though Zavadovsky was her lover-in-residence, Potemkin was her lord and master, her consort, almost her co-ruler. A new order prevailed.

Just at the time Catherine was making these new arrangements, she learned that Grand Duchess Natalia was pregnant. Natalia, whom Catherine had initially welcomed as a "golden woman," vital and fresh and charming, had proven to be more dross than gold. She was flighty, superficial and much less intelligent than Catherine had hoped. She "loved extremes in all things," as Catherine wrote to Grimm, and in particular, fell extremely in love with Andrei Razumovsky, one of the grand duke's favorite companions. Paul did not suspect Natalia of being unfaithful to him, but the entire court knew of the liaison, and when Natalia's pregnancy was announced, there was much speculation as to the child's paternity.

Still, the child Natalia carried, especially if it was a son—as everyone fervently hoped it would be—would become the next in line to the throne, assuming Paul succeeded his mother. The continuity of the imperial line depended on the birth of a healthy heir.

Paul sent a servant to his mother very early on the morning of April 10, 1776, to announce that Natalia had gone into labor. The aged Countess Maria Rumyantsev, who in her six decades at court had helped hundreds of babies safely into the world, was acting as midwife to the grand duchess, and there were doctors on call to give their assistance should the traditional techniques of midwifery fail.

As the morning advanced, the courtiers gathered in clusters outside the birth chamber, waiting for word that the baby had been born. Noon came, then afternoon. There were sounds of movement in the room, but no servant came forth to announce the birth of a prince. All evening they kept up their vigil, but by midnight they retired to their quarters, fully expecting to be awakened before dawn with the good news of Natalia's delivery.

The empress visited her daughter-in-law from time to time during that long Sunday and conferred with Countess Rumyantsev. No doubt Catherine recalled her own excruciatingly uncomfortable first labor, the near-fatal neglect she had suffered and the long hours of agonizing pain. She saw to it that Natalia was as comfortable as possible.

On the following morning, Catherine visited the birth chamber again. Natalia, exhausted, was still not delivered of her burden, and the countess was worried. The empress ordered two German accoucheurs, doctors Kruse and Tode, to examine Natalia but their long consultation did not result in decisive action. Surgeons were available to cut open the grand duchess's belly, a drastic operation that might perhaps save the child but at the cost of the mother's life. It was decided not to attempt the operation.

This decision, however arrived at, proved to be fateful. With Catherine constantly in attendance, Natalia struggled bravely on, but could not muster the strength to expel her baby. Her piercing screams gave way to hoarse cries, then to whimpers. Her tear-stained face was white. By this time she had been in labor forty-eight hours, and more doctors were called in. Countess Rumyantsev, weary and defeated, in great distress, told the empress that she feared neither Natalia nor her child could now be saved. The doctors agreed; there was no longer any apparent movement in the womb. Most likely the baby was dead.

Still, this was an imperial infant, and every effort had to be made to save it, and the mother as well. The doctors could be wrong. Catherine, who had slept little since Natalia's labor began, and who was suffering strong spasms of pain in her back in sympathy with the wretched girl, became completely caught up in the tragic events.

"Never in my life have I found myself in a more difficult, more hideous, more painful position," she wrote to Grimm later. "I forgot to drink, to eat, and to sleep, and my strength sustained me I know not how." It was harrowing, standing by and watching in helpless sorrow as Natalia inched toward death in great pain. In all, fourteen doctors, surgeons, and midwives were in attendance, plus a large staff of assistants and servants. Yet they could do little or nothing.

Natalia took five long days to die. When she finally expired, something died inside the empress.

"I turned to stone," she wrote.

The body was opened and a very large, "perfectly formed" boy was found in the womb. He had been so large that the grand duchess, who suffered from a deformation of the spine, could not deliver him. The wretched business was traumatic for everyone. There was universal disappointment that the succession had not after all been assured. Paul indulged in a torrent of grief-stricken rage, breaking chairs and smashing mirrors and even threatening to destroy himself. Catherine, in a badly miscalculated effort to restore his sanity, arranged for him to discover the fact of his late wife's infidelity, which only increased his maddened frustration besides making him hate his mother all the more.

While she prepared for the grand duchess's funeral at the Nevsky monastery, with the whole court in deep mourning, Catherine passed a melancholy forty-seventh birthday, convinced that if this nervous ordeal had not destroyed her, nothing could.

Chapter Twenty-Five

As she reached the age of fifty Empress Catherine astounded the Western world. She had risen in rank as the insignificant daughter of an unheralded soldier to become ruler of an enormous realm stretching from the Baltic to eastern Siberia. Her achievements were legion: military conqueror, peacemaker, lawgiver, patron of the arts, beacon of enlightenment to a benighted people in an iron age. Her praises were sung throughout Europe, her name known wherever cultivated people gathered. And if a certain dark rumor still clung to her—that she had arranged her husband's murder in order to seize the throne—many years of exceptionally benevolent rule had gone a long way to dissipate it.

The Prince de Ligne, an Austrian envoy of exceptional sensitivity who came to Petersburg to aid in the close military cooperation Russia and Austria were to have, came to know the empress well. He described her as she reached her half-century mark. "Her face," he wrote, "disclosed genius, justice, courage, depth, equanimity, sweetness, calm, and decision." "Frankness and gaiety dwelt on her lips," he added. "One scarcely noticed that she was short."

If Catherine, who was in fact of moderate height, seemed short to de Ligne it was because of her increasing stoutness. ("People generally grow fat in Russia," Prince de Ligne remarked.) Gray-haired and heavy, her hair drawn efficiently and severely back into a knot, Catherine gave an impression of soberness and good sense. Her dress as a rule was elegant, yet simple; in the eyes of European visitors, it appeared almost stark at a time when, at the court of France, women spent many hours lacing themselves into impossibly fantasticated costumes and having their hair dressed into intricate mounds of curls a foot high.

The Baron de Corberon, attempting to take Catherine's measure, confessed that he was baffled. He recognized how remarkable she was, yet he could not reconcile what he viewed as Catherine's "unheard-of mixture of courage and weakness, knowledgeability and incapacity, firmness and irresolution. Ever darting from one extreme to the other," he wrote, "she presents a thousand different surfaces to the observant onlooker, who wishes in vain to grasp hold of her and find her essence and who, frustrated by his futile efforts, ends, in his uncertainty, by placing her among the ranks of the leading actresses, unable to place her among those of the great rulers."

Corberon was baffled, partly because of his own incapacity to reconcile Catherine's humanity with her majesty and immense capability, partly because the empress was in truth a mercurial figure, able to transform herself from regal commander to informal hostess to witty conversationalist at will. She had never been a poseur; her naturalism and authenticity set her apart in an artificial age. She did not trouble to hide her many selves from those at her court (except, of course, the self that wept and showed weakness; that she endeavored to conceal, with partial success). As her correspondent Frau Bielke wrote, Catherine "gave laws with one hand and did needlework with the other."

Catherine's reputation suffered as Zavadovsky was installed as official favorite—with Potemkin still being treated as the empress's consort and receiving more rewards than before—and moralists sneered and gossiped as never before. And not only moralists: people who did not condemn Catherine for her irregular personal life nonetheless were quick to see how politically damaging her behavior was likely to be. As a sovereign she was not free to follow her own inclinations where love and sex were concerned; she had the honor of her high office to think of. And she was putting that honor in peril.

The English ambassador Sir James Harris, embittered by his failure to hire Russian troops in England's struggle with the American colonists, sent a very unflattering portrait of Catherine to his superiors in London. According to Harris, Catherine had recently undergone a transformation, and was very much the worse for it. In the first seven or eight years of her reign, he believed, she had governed judiciously and with dignity. But she had allowed herself in latter years to be too much influenced by Frederick the Great. She had become cynical, she had lost her moral compass. What was worse, her "propensity for voluptuousness" was unleashed, leading her into "excesses that would debase a female character in any sphere of life."

Catherine's break with Gregory Orlov had been a grave mistake, in Harris's view, for Orlov, though far from brilliant, was "a man of integrity and completely honest." Orlov never flattered the empress. But after his departure she was surrounded by flatterers who corrupted her; she allowed their flattery to color her judgment. Her "unworthy tendencies" took over, and she gave herself up to them without restraint.

"Her court," Harris wrote, "which she had ruled with the greatest dignity and with the utmost decorum has gradually become an arena of depravity and immorality. This fall into decadence has been so rapid that in the brief time that I have been in this country a profound revolution has occurred in the mores and conventional habits of the courtiers."

Only a miracle could rescue the empress from her present unfortunate state, Harris informed his government, adding that in his view no such miracle was likely to occur at her age. Potemkin was behind it all, in Harris's judgment. He ruled Catherine completely. He was unscrupulous, using his intimate knowledge of the empress's weaknesses and her desires to maintain an unhealthy hold over her. He frightened her into thinking that her son intended to overthrow her, and that he, Potemkin, was the only one she could count on to prevent the takeover attempt when it came. Moreover, Potemkin had worked to undermine Catherine's reliance on the Orlovs, her staunchest allies for twenty years and more, by telling her that Alexis had cast his lot with Grand Duke Paul in expectation of a coup and by holding the ailing Gregory up to ridicule for marrying his child bride.

All in all the imperial court was in a sorry state—if the dispatches of foreign ambassadors are to be believed. In actuality the empress was weathering the censures and sneers of her critics with equanimity. De Ligne had a name for her: the Imperturbable. And imperturbable she was, on the whole, maintaining a remarkable degree of balance in her life between work, physical recreation— she liked to take long walks and went hunting when she could— and the pleasures of friends and of her favorites' company.

Throughout the late 1770s the favorites succeeded one another rapidly. Zavadovsky, a retiring character who fell in love with his imperial mistress and suffered very much when he was replaced by the dashing hussar Simon Zorich, complained of being kept under too close surveillance. Zorich, tall, handsome and moustachioed, had a weakness for gambling and generally lacked integrity where money was concerned. (Catherine confided to her intimates that she always expected him to "do something shady.") He made the mistake of quarreling with Potemkin, which guaranteed his departure from court after only eleven months. His successor Ivan Rimsky-Korsakov, a dandy who favored embroidered suits sewn with diamonds, was nicknamed by Catherine "Pyrrhus, King of Epirus" for his beautiful Greek profile. He betrayed the empress by dallying with Countess Bruce and left court after a little over a year.

None of these liaisons satisfied the empress's need for romance and undemanding sexual intimacy for long. Catherine found Zavadovsky to be jealous and demanding of her time. ("As often as possible," she wrote him, "I am only with you, but majesty, I confess, interferes a lot.") In the beginning he "fed her passion heart and soul," as she told him, yet later on his childishness, fits of weeping and periods of aggrieved isolation ended in a permanent breach—though the broken-hearted Zavadovsky continued to function in a variety of official positions. Neither Zorich nor Rimsky-Korsakov were any more satisfactory than Zavadovsky, and by the time Catherine and Potemkin's odd ménage à trois had been in operation for three years the empress must have felt robbed of her emotional peace.

She who had written with devastating self-awareness that her "heart would not willingly remain one hour without love" had not found a way to secure that love without sacrificing either power or constancy or real fulfillment. Short-term sexual consorts gave her as much pain as pleasure, it would seem, either by being unfaithful, as Rimsky-Korsakov was, or by their moodiness and immaturity, or simply because they were personally shallow. Good-looking they certainly were, yet they fell far short of offering all that Potemkin had been able to give her. It was not only that she was personally disappointed; in addition, she had to be constantly vigilant, concerned lest Potemkin, whose jealousy and possessiveness were never far below the surface, might muscle in and send away any man he perceived as a serious rival.

So she went on, loving Potemkin and relying on him, and at the same time hoping to find with another man the joys of infatuation, craving a soul mate and a helpmeet, someone she could both turn to for romantic consolation and at the same time train to share her arduous labors. In 1779 she believed she found such a man. He was Alexander Lanskoy, a twenty-three-year-old captain in the Cavalier Guard, the imperial personal bodyguard.

All the men of the Cavalier Guard were supremely good-looking, and Lanskoy was no exception. Tall and strapping in his magnificent court uniform with silver armor (one courtier described him as "a very strong man, though ill made below and without the appearance of muscularity"), the fair young man with

the poetically beautiful features captivated the empress, and renewed her hope for love and solace. In Lanskoy she believed she
had found the one man who, she told Grimm, "would be the
support of my old age."

Nothing was too good for her "Sashinka," as she called him.
She showered him with jeweled swords and gorgeous suits of
clothes embroidered in gold and silver thread, gave him estates
and houses, a library, paintings and tapestries and art objects
worth millions of rubles. In time, she hoped, she could begin to
delegate responsibilities to him. As she aged, he would grow in
maturity and competence. Theirs would be an ideal union, satisfying to them both and of benefit to Russia.

Catherine nurtured Lanskoy, tutoring him in poetry—which he
had a gift for writing—and in history, teaching him to appreciate
fine art and encouraging in him a love of good music and elevat-
ing reading. Their relationship was complex: she was more than
old enough to be his mother, and she mothered him; he looked on
her with a devotion that had much of the filial in it; she was his
teacher, and he her eager student, sincerely desirous of advancing
himself culturally; there was a winter-spring romance, though of
a unique kind, between a powerful empress and a poor young
man from the Polish provinces; presumably there was tenderness,
infatuation, intimacy. And there was, hovering in the background, the empress's true consort, Potemkin, at whose suffrance
the liaison continued, and whose disapprobation could end it at
any time.

By and large, these complexities escaped notice. In the eyes of
the courtiers, visiting dignitaries and ambassadors from the European courts, the Russian empress had become an unrestrained
nymphomaniac.

Gossips vied with one another over who could embroider or
invent the most outrageous story. It was said that in addition to
her official favorites Catherine entertained many other men, in
fleeting liaisons. It was whispered that Catherine's friend Countess Bruce took each of Catherine's potential lovers to her bed and

tested him before he was allowed to make love to the empress. Potemkin was seen as a procurer of young flesh for the insatiable empress, encouraging her in her descent into debauchery and then profiting from it since both his mistress and her lovers paid him well. Nearly as many stories swirled around Potemkin as around Catherine: that he had tried to poison Gregory Orlov, that when he began to feel threatened by Catherine's involvement with Zavadovsky he became enraged and violent and at one point threw a heavy metal candlestick at the empress's head, that his private sexual appetites were even more sordid than Catherine's.

The reputation the empress had cultivated in western Europe, that of a wise and benevolent ruler, a patron of intellectuals and philosophers, a beacon of humanitarian sentiment, was tainted by accusations of immorality and base excess. The more straitlaced rulers of the Western states were appalled and offended by the stories coming out of Russia. The English King George III, an ultra-respectable married man and father of a huge brood of children, refused to offer Potemkin the Order of the Garter when Catherine requested it—"and was shocked," his ambassador noted. The Austrian Empress Maria Theresa was as bourgeois as King George, and militantly moralistic. She had organized a Chastity Commission in her empire, and attempted to cleanse her court of adultery (a task equivalent to cleansing the Augean stables, an impossibility that only made her look ridiculous; Catherine called her "Saint Theresa"). She could hardly bring herself to utter the name of her vice-ridden counterpart in Russia, and referred to Catherine simply as "that woman." Other sovereigns made appropriately censorious noises, remarking that, at the very least, Catherine was engaging in behavior unbecoming to her high office, and particularly reprehensible in a woman.

The political climate at the imperial court seethed with intrigue, talebearing, titillating rumormongering. Believing the empress to be in the grip of her insatiable passions (and many of those at court, servants and officials alike, remembered well how irrational Empress Elizabeth had been in her last decade, and saw a similar fit of irrationality developing in her successor), they speculated constantly on when the present favorite would fall and who would be chosen next, and spread tales of shadowy figures seen going in and out of the imperial bedchamber. Families with handsome young men tried to thrust them in the empress's path, sometimes subtly, sometimes blatantly. Gregory Orlov suggested to Princess Dashkov—now a middle-aged widow, recently returned to favor in the circle around the empress—that she ought to prepare her attractive son for a career as imperial favorite. Though the princess did not view the suggestion kindly, many another mother hoped that her son would be the one to turn Catherine's head, if only for a night or two, believing that the reward of such a dalliance would be wealth and influence.

The whispers and laughter, the deriding of the empress, whose passion for younger men made her an object of ridicule, the scramble for power kept the court in a state of churning immobility. In such a climate, and given the empress's measurable loss of respect, a coup was not impossible. People nervously watched Grand Duke Paul, and even more Potemkin, whose military authority had increased and who by 1780 commanded thousands of soldiers, wondering when either or both might make a bid for power.

In actuality The Imperturbable was in firm command. Though fully and no doubt unhappily aware of what was being said about her, she continued to live as she chose, taking heart from her happy liaison with Alexander Lanskoy. As she entered her sixth decade, new challenges beckoned. The empress was gathering her forces for the most ambitious undertaking of her astounding career.

She had decided, as she confided to a visitor to her court, "to chase the Turks out of Europe and to enthrone herself in Byzantium."

Potemkin went to work with relish carrying out his mistress's grand scheme. With a large army and an abundant store of funds at his disposal, he extended Russian influence to the south, bringing in colonists and building new towns to serve as administrative centers and garrisons, spearheads of a future Russian takeover. In the Crimea, nominally independent of both Russia and the Ottoman Empire but in actuality ruled by a puppet khan whose tenure in power was dependent on Russian support, Potemkin was poised to invade the peninsula himself as soon as the empress ordered him to.

But first Catherine had to come to terms with the other power in the region: Austria. She approached Empress Maria Theresa's son and co-ruler Joseph and proposed that they meet in person to discuss issues of common concern. It was a bold suggestion, and one that revealed the extent to which the empress had taken foreign policy matters into her own hands. No longer looking to Panin for advice, she alone determined the nature of Russia's aims and the diplomatic strategies to be used to achieve them. She asked the opinions of Potemkin and her secretary Bezborodko, and weighed their views, but hers remained the primary will and the only authority. She read every ambassadorial dispatch, read and approved all correspondence, presided over every significant council meeting. The future direction of the Russian Empire was in the empress's confident hands.

Or rather, her right hand; her left one was becoming weakened and tender from repeated attacks of rheumatism. She wrapped it warmly against the late spring chill when she set off in May of 1780 on a month-long journey through the newly reformed western provinces of her empire. She was eager to discover at close range how the new regulations she had put in place were working, and to this end she sent investigators on ahead to each of the towns she intended to visit, ordering them to inquire about the functioning of the schools and hospitals, the courts and tax offices so that when she arrived she would know what to expect.

Rain spoiled the elaborate ceremonies prepared for the empress's arrival in the provincial towns. The roads were kneedeep in mud, and muddy streams ran along the cobbled streets and through the gaily decorated squares. Forlorn bands played on, dripping and sloshing water with each step; damp dignitaries stood under rain-soaked canopies to deliver speeches of welcome, while hundreds of people congregated wherever the empress went, following her coach, waiting outside banqueting houses or mansions where she went to dine, standing for hours under dark, weeping skies while she attended parties and balls.

Ignoring the rain and the flooded roads that delayed her progress from town to town, Catherine beamed appreciatively at those who came to gawk at her and received the speeches and rituals of homage with gracious words of thanks. She was gratified at her reception, and even more gratified to hear that great and far-reaching changes had taken place in the towns. Her investigators painted a glowing picture of improved commercial life and greater general prosperity, more efficient administration and a more law-abiding populace. The good news and thronging crowds more than compensated for the rain and chill winds that made the empress's swollen hand hurt; she looked forward to the climax of her tour, her meeting with the Austrian Archduke Joseph at the town of Mogilev.

Afterwards, Catherine recalled the day of her meeting with Archduke Joseph as "the best and most memorable day of my life." They spent the entire day and evening together, and Catherine wrote to Grimm that Joseph "didn't seem to be bored. I found him to be very knowledgeable," she added. "He loves to talk and talks very well." Joseph was in fact a man after Catherine's own heart—well informed, blunt, candid, utterly lacking in pretension and unafraid of facing unpleasant truths.

Empress and future emperor met as equals, each wielding great power (for Maria Theresa, elderly and ill, had conceded very substantial authority to her son and co-ruler), each able to survey Europe from a lofty eminence and make decisions as to its future. For Catherine this must have been a heady experience, being closeted with her fellow-sovereign, two crowned heads together, communing about the satisfactions and impediments of ruling large and tumultuous empires.

Catherine and Joseph had much in common: both were simple, even austere in their personal styles (Joseph liked to tour the European capitals incognito, as "Count Falkenstein," accompanied by only a single servant); both were well read, opinionated, and garrulous; both were liberal and inclined to follow the principles of Montesquieu and Voltaire; both were considered eccentric—Joseph could be sharp, tactless and curmudgeonly on occasion, and contemptuous of his high-born peers—and both took pride in their singularity and even, one suspects, in the gossip their eccentricity gave rise to.

They attended a comic opera together, and talked throughout the performance, Joseph making observations that Catherine thought "worthy of being printed." They went together to a Catholic mass sung by the bishop of Mogilev, and laughed and joked throughout the ceremony in the most irreligious way. "We talked about everything in the world," Catherine told Grimm with evident delight. "He knows everything." She preferred to let the man take the lead, and Joseph led easily, though he was eleven years her junior; with pleasure she listened, fascinated, as he trotted out his views and aired his prejudices—many of which she shared.

"If I tried to summarize his virtues I would never come to the end," she told Grimm. "He is the most solidly intelligent, profound, and learned man I know."

Joseph, for his part, was favorably impressed by the witty, commonsensical empress about whom he had heard so much. "Her spirit, her high-mindedness, her bravery, her pleasing conversation have to be experienced to be appreciated," he wrote in a letter to his mother. He approved of her, and his approval was not lightly given. Yet he saw through her. She was self-centered, and vain of her looks and feminine appeal. She had not the knack of diplomacy, she could not disguise her obsession with conquering the Ottomans. She brought up her "Greek Project" again and again, always, tacitly or overtly, soliciting Austrian participation. Even when she showed Joseph portraits of her small grandsons, two-and-a-half-year-old Alexander and year-old Constantine, products of Paul's second marriage, the Greek theme was brought forward. Constantine was named for Constantinople, the city she meant to conquer; she had had the infant's portrait painted against a classical Greek backdrop. Someday, she said, the tiny Constantine would rule over a revitalized Greece, liberated by Russia from centuries of Turkish oppression.

The meeting between the two sovereigns accomplished Catherine's goal. In 1781 Russia and Austria signed a secret alliance; henceforth they would stand together against the Turk. Now Catherine had the might of the Austrian Empire behind her in her grand endeavor. And now Joseph was no longer archduke, but emperor, his mother Maria Theresa having recently died.

Catherine's Austrian initiative led to changes at her court. Panin, who had always favored a northern orientation in Russian foreign policy and who advocated a close alliance with Prussia, not Austria, left for his estates in the spring of 1781 and did not return. Paul too was gone for a time, sent away to travel in Europe with his wife.

Paul was becoming more and more of a liability, and the hardheaded Catherine, who did not allow herself illusions where the security of her rule was at stake, recognized that she had to protect herself against him. He and his new wife, Maria, had done what she needed them to do: they had produced two healthy heirs to the throne. But Paul, described by King Frederick after the two men met in 1776 as "haughty, arrogant and violent," was acting at cross purposes to Catherine's political aims. Partly from angry frustration, partly because he had well-formed (if undistinguished) views of his own on what the aims of the Russian Empire should be abroad, partly because he was Panin's student, and shared many of the former chancellor's prejudices, Paul did not agree with his mother. He was critical of the increasing rapprochement with Austria. Frederick II had become Paul's hero, as he had once been Peter III's, and Paul's secret correspond-

ence with King Frederick—a secret he could not manage to keep
from the all-knowing Catherine—aroused the empress's suspicions. She decided it was best that her son leave Petersburg for a
time.

The first stages in the accomplishment of Catherine's sweeping
Greek Project took quite a different turn from what the empress
expected. Though she authorized Potemkin to launch what
amounted to a full-scale invasion of the Crimea, he hesitated for
many months, suffering from one of his periods of lassitude and
inertia. Joseph too dragged his heels, despite Catherine's ex-
hortations ("I think that there is little our two strong states could
not do, given our united efforts," she wrote to him). In the end
the Crimea fell into Russian hands. In 1784 the puppet khan gave
his territory to the Russian empress in return for an annual pen-
sion of a hundred thousand rubles, and Potemkin belatedly
marched his troops in and took possession of the newly christened
"Tauride Region." Potemkin himself, named governor-general,
took the title Prince of Tauris.

Catherine had made a start on gaining her vast objective. But
she had had to do it alone. Potemkin had let her down, losing his
courage just at the time she needed him most, while Emperor
Joseph was proving to be a fair-weather ally. In international
affairs, as in the more treacherous, more delicate matters of the
heart, Catherine was discovering that, in the end, she had no one
to rely on but herself.

That sobering truth announced itself cruelly in June of 1784.
One afternoon while the court was in residence at the summer
palace of Tsarskoe Selo Alexander Lanskoy began to complain of
a sore throat, and went to his quarters to lie down. By six o'clock
he was well enough to accompany Catherine on a walk around
the garden pond, and suffered through a social evening that had
been planned in advance, not wanting Catherine to cancel it on his
account. Such an accommodating attitude was like him; it was
among the things the empress valued most in him—his mild and

sweetly self-effacing nature. Lanskoy took himself off and went to lie down again, sending a messenger to fetch a surgeon who lived in the neighborhood of the palace.

The following day the surgeon informed Catherine that Lanskoy's pulse was intermittent and that he and a colleague he had consulted both thought that the young man had much more wrong with him than just a sore throat. Catherine summoned a German specialist from Petersburg, who told her, in blunt German, that Lanskoy had a virulent fever and would die of it.

Full of dread, yet continuing to get what medical advice she could and taking note of Lanskoy's worsening symptoms—severe fever, swelling, and changes in skin color—Catherine kept vigil by the bedside of her Sashinka. Since Natalia's death she had been having to come to terms with mortality all too often: her mentor Voltaire had succumbed, and a number of her courtiers; only months earlier Diderot had died, and the previous winter she had buried her beloved greyhound, Tom Anderson, after sixteen years of close companionship.

Lanskoy was a robust man with a strong constitution, but he could not seem to shake off the affliction that was weakening his heart. He refused to eat or drink and would not take any medicine until a friend of his, a Polish doctor, persuaded him to drink a little cold water and eat some ripe figs. After three days he was terribly pale and burning with fever, but the Petersburg specialist gave Catherine some hope. Taking her aside he said that if Lanskoy did not become delirious, he might recover.

By this time Catherine had a sore throat of her own, though she told no one, unwilling to let her advisers force her away from her beloved Sashinka's bedside in order to nurse her own illness. Another day passed, and Lanskoy was able, making a supreme effort, to get up and walk under his own power into a different bedroom. He confided to Catherine that the previous night, feeling terribly ill, he had made his will.

An hour later he began raving, and Catherine knew that the hope the specialist had held out was gone. Lanskoy still recognized her, and knew her name, but he no longer knew where he was. He kept on calling for his carriage and grew angry when the servants would not hitch his horses to the bed. In a final effort to stave off death Catherine ordered her physician Dr. Rogerson to administer to Lanskoy a cure she had heard of called "James's powders," but the medicine had no appreciable effect.

"I left his room at eleven at night," Catherine wrote later to Grimm. "I could do no more and I concealed my own illness." That night, or early the following morning, Lanskoy died.

"I am plunged into the most lively sorrow," she told her correspondent, "and my happiness is no more. I thought I would die myself from the loss of my best friend." Lanskoy had been the hope of her future, she told Grimm, referring to him as "the young man whom I was raising." He had sorrowed with her over her difficulties and rejoiced with her when things went well. He had been gentle and decent, and very grateful to her for her patronage. He had responded quickly and well to her training. Now she had lost him, and she felt as if she had lost everything. "My room, once so pleasant, has become an empty cave; I drag myself around in it like a shadow." She could not bring herself to face anyone, and though she did what work had to be done ("with order and intelligence," she assured Grimm), life had lost all its color and savor.

"I can't eat, I can't sleep," she told the Swiss. "Reading bores me, and I can't muster the strength to write. I don't know what will become of me, but I do know that I have never before in my life been so unhappy as I have since my best and most lovable friend abandoned me."

For nearly a year Catherine mourned Lanskoy. She shut herself in a tiny room and read ancient Russian chronicles and began work on a comparative study of words in two hundred languages. Servants brought her books—a Finnish dictionary, a multivolume study of early Slavonic peoples, atlases and grammars—but for months she felt too crushed by grief to face her court, and there were rumors that she had died. Her four grandchildren were a slight consolation, especially the youngest, a pretty infant girl who people said resembled her grandmother. ("I have a weakness for her," Catherine admitted.) Yet she continued to "suffer like one of the damned," inconsolable over her great loss. After six months Potemkin, who had arrived from his new kingdom of Tauris soon after Lanskoy's death to console her, forced Catherine to leave her cramped study and learn to live and breathe again. She rebeled, she fought him with every step, but in the end she was grateful to him. Finally she was able to put on court dress and appear in public. In private, however, she remained "a very sad being," she told Grimm, "who speaks only in monosyllables . . . Everything afflicts me."

The depth of the empress's mourning, and her unprecedented personal sorrow over the loss of Lanskoy did nothing to stop the tide of scurrilous tales about her. Atrocious stories circulated about the death of the gentle and poetic young man. Catherine had exhausted him with her sexual demands, it was said. He had died in her bed, while trying in vain to satiate her insatiable passion. She had forced him to swallow poisonous aphrodisiacs, potions so strong they had made his body swell up and burst. She had poisoned him, as surely as she poisoned her husband Peter, and the proof was that his corpse gave off an unbearably foul odor and his limbs separated from his torso.

The real Catherine grieved, while the Catherine of legend, unrepentant and ever more sexually voracious, called for more young men and got on with her unsavory career.

Chapter Twenty-Six

HUNDREDS OF BLAZING TORCHES LIT THE IMMENSE COURT-yard of Empress Catherine's palace of Tsarskoe Selo in the pre-dawn hours of January 7, 1787. Deep snow covered the ground, frost rimed the elaborate wrought iron gates and the four classical statues that presided over the entryway to the imposing palace were waist-deep in white drifts.

The torches sputtered in the cold, clear air, their hissing and crackling audible over the creaking of carriage wheels and the clatter of horses' hooves, the shouting of servants and the scraping of wooden crates. Fourteen huge traveling carriages, mounted on wooden runners, were being made ready to receive their distinguished occupants. Their wheels were newly gilded and their painted panels retouched. In the empress's carriage, largest and most splendid of all, were stored fuel for the stove, baskets of food and drink, warm rugs, extra clothing, toilet articles and—just in case—needed medicines.

Despite the bitter cold that stiffened the beards of the men and reddened the hands of the shivering serving girls, preparations for the great imperial journey proceeded. Nearly two hundred sledges were being loaded with trunks and coffers, barrels of beer and wine and honey, sacks of grain, chests full of cheeses, fruit, and other provisions, linens and napery, warm fur-lined blankets and braziers—all the supplies necessary for an extended journey.

Grooms and stable-boys attended to the thousand horses that
would pull the hundreds of vehicles, while pages and footmen,
maids and kitchen servants scrambled to find their own places in
the grand procession.

Empress Catherine was about to undertake the longest and
most ambitious tour of her reign, to visit the southern reaches of
her realm and display her magnificence and military power there
to afright the Turk. Planning for the long journey had begun
nearly a year earlier, and for many months household officials had
been preoccupied with arrangements, under the exacting supervision of their imperial mistress.

The journey was one of Catherine's principal enthusiasms. It
would further her aims of conquest while advertising what she,
and especially her sometime consort and deputy Potemkin,
had done so far. It would give her an opportunity to show off
her wealth and power. She could hardly wait to start on her
travels.

There were many at her court who had tried to dissuade her.
She was, after all, nearly fifty-eight years old, they told her,
reminding her that she suffered from the accumulating aches and
pains of advancing years and could no longer expect to summon
the stamina for travel that she had once enjoyed.

"I was assured on all sides that my progress would be bristling
with obstacles and unpleasantness," Catherine told Grimm in a
letter. "They wished to frighten me with stories of the fatigue of
the journey, the aridity of the deserts and the unhealthiness of the
climate. Those people had a very poor knowledge of me," she
added. "They do not know that to oppose me is to encourage me;
and that every difficulty that they put in my way is an additional
spur that they give me."

At fifty-eight, no less than at any earlier point in her life,
Catherine was stubborn and headstrong, determined to have her
way. It had become her outstanding quality, this obstinate de-
termination to follow through and bring to pass what she desired.
("God, grant us our desires, and grant them quickly," had be-

come her favorite toast.) Nearly all those who encountered her remarked on this characteristic: Ambassador Harris called her "a vain, arrant, spoiled woman" who would not be denied anything; Emperor Joseph thought that it was Catherine's misfortune that there was no one in her entourage who dared to restrain her. ("Be on guard against the force and impetuosity of her opinions," Joseph confided to the English ambassador in Vienna.)

All her secretaries felt the heavy weight of her insistent desires; though in the past they had always found her to be the kindest of mistresses, she could now on occasion be irascible, difficult and disagreeable. ("Swell-headed with her own power to a singular degree," the sour Harris wrote, "and obstinately attached to her own views, she is jealous or dissatisfied with nearly all those who approach her.") Even Potemkin told Harris that the empress "has become suspicious, timid and narrow-minded"—though the ever-shrewd Potemkin may have been echoing the ambassador's opinion merely for political reasons.

For every report of the empress's irascibility there were two praising her warmth and unaffected simplicity; though her temper may not have been as even as it once was, she could still show a degree of consideration and genuineness that visitors to her court found stunning, and it gave her particular pleasure to extend herself personally to help members of her household and others who came to her in need.

She was more egocentric than ever when it came to politics. "I am firmly decided," she told Potemkin, "to count on no one but to trust entirely to my own resources." So far, her resources, personal and material, had proven to be more than adequate.

At last all was in readiness and the huge, sprawling procession of carriages and sledges started off on the first phase of its long journey. By three in the afternoon the light was failing. Darkness enveloped the entourage by four. But the way ahead was lit by huge bonfires, on both sides of the road. For weeks gangs of imperial timber cutters had been at work cutting down trees and piling them in high mounds along the roadway. Now they were

set alight, turning night into day and making several more hours
of travel possible.

With the empress in the principal carriage were a trusted waiting maid and her new favorite, Alexander Dmitriev-Mamonov, a
tall, black-eyed, free-spirited officer, nearly thirty years her junior, who was a cheerful and amusing companion. She called him
"Red Coat" and relied on him to keep her from being bored as the
miles crawled by. Like Catherine herself, Mamonov was a "chat-
terer," as she liked to say; he had "an inexhaustible fund of gaiety"
and could match wits, as well as literary and historical references,
with his imperial mistress. He drew on his exceptionally good
Jesuit education and excellent memory to recite poetry—
Catherine was especially fond of Corneille ("he elevates my soul,"
she liked to say)—and could invent impromptu verses and draw
clever likenesses of people on demand.

Mamonov was no substitute for Lanskoy, whom Catherine
continued to mourn, but he was far superior to Lanskoy's immediate successor, Alexander Yermolov, a nonentity whose period of favor lasted less than a year and a half. Yermolov was sent
away after he managed to offend Potemkin—as usual Catherine
was reluctant to retain a lover who could not manage to stay on
good terms with the formidable, increasingly erratic Prince of
Tauris.

Along with her female attendant and Mamonov, the empress
had room in her carriage for three others; she made these seats
available on a rotating basis to the favored guests she had invited
to join her on her expedition. The most important guests were the
Prince de Ligne, Catherine's peer in age and her superior in
sophistication and creative intelligence, the younger Count Louis-
Philippe de Ségur, who kept a journal of the trip full of penetrat-
ing observations, and Alleyne Fitzherbert, British ambassador,
who had to make the best of an awkward diplomatic situation, as
Catherine was becoming colder toward Britain with each passing
year. The lively, portly Austrian Count Cobentzl rounded out the
diplomatic contingent. The Grand Equerry and unofficial court

jester Leon Naryshkin frequently sat in the imperial carriage, telling jokes, making faces, imitating other members of the traveling party and in general keeping Catherine laughing. There were no women guests; the empress had had few women friends in the course of her life, and liked male company.

No one was surprised that Grand Duke Paul was not invited on the empress's tour—it was rumored that she no longer intended leaving her throne to him, and that she had made up her mind to confer the honor of the succession on her grandson Alexander. Yet neither Alexander nor his younger brother Constantine was with Catherine as she left on her journey; both were recovering from illnesses and were not thought to be strong enough to travel, particularly in the dead of winter. Catherine was chagrined. ("I am quite angry that Alexander and Constantine didn't come with me on the voyage and they are quite disappointed too," the empress wrote to Grimm.) They were promising children, attractive and precocious, affectionate and full of charm. Alexander was nine, Constantine seven. Paul and Maria had had three more children, all girls; Catherine was fond of the lively, three-year-old Alexandra and her beautiful sister, whom her grandmother dubbed "la belle Hélène." Tiny Maria was still an infant in her cradle. Catherine hoped for more grandsons.

Day after day the sledges were dragged along the icy roads by tired horses whose breath froze as soon as it left their nostrils. Nearly six hundred horses had to be assembled at each posting station, and the work of hitching and unhitching was made more difficult by the fierce cold and the crowds of villagers who came to see the fairytale coaches and their highborn occupants. Each of Catherine's guests had been supplied with a thick black coat lined with warm fur; fur hats, fur-lined gloves and thick fur booties completed their attire. Though the cold was severe, the empress noted in one of her long letters to Grimm, none of her guests lost noses or ears to frostbite. She herself was in surprisingly good health, untroubled by digestive problems or headaches or leg pains. She spent the long hours of travel conversing with Mamonov—who was just then interested in reading Buffon and wanted his own copy of the complete works—and with her other guests.

On their best days the array of sledges managed to cover forty miles, over enormous undulating snowfields, through dense stands of fir and birch, the dark trunks of the trees stark against the intense whiteness of the high-piled snow, their branches sparkling with ice crystals. At midday they halted, sometimes at a village, sometimes at a nobleman's house, for a meal, then, as the afternoon light began to wane, they took to the road again, their way lit as ever by blazing bonfires.

After a month on the road the empress's train reached Kiev, where it halted for many weeks. Here delegations from all parts of the empire met to greet the empress and make petitions to her. They came, Tatars and Kalmuks, Georgians and Khirghiz, all the non-Russian peoples who had followed Pugachev and who had resisted the armies of Potemkin. There were Polish nobles as well, paying tribute to the powerful woman who had seized a large part of their homeland and, they feared, was poised to seize more.

When Potemkin joined the party, traveling to Kiev from his semi-kingdom of Tauris, all was changed, according to Ségur. He acted as host to the empress and her entourage, staging splendid balls and firework exhibitions, sponsoring concerts and banquets, entertaining guests at the venerable convent of Petchersky, where he took up residence. He cut a brilliant figure. On public occasions he appeared in a grand marshal's uniform, "smothered in decorations and diamonds," Ségur wrote, "covered with lace and embroidery, and with his hair all powdered and curled." At Petchersky, however, he appeared more in the guise of a Turkish vizier, his hair uncombed, his legs and feet bare, swathed in a silk dressing-gown, lying languorously on a huge sofa surrounded by his female relatives (several of whom were known to be his mistresses) and assorted officers and foreign envoys.

He appeared to be lost in an Asiatic dream, yet the shrewd Ségur perceived that behind the air of languor Potemkin was wide

awake and working. He conferred with officials, sent and received intricate messages, played chess while conducting unofficial negotiations with ambassadors and generally furthering
the aims he shared with his sovereign. According to Ségur,
Potemkin was able to work on dozen of projects at once without
seeming to be very busy at all, overseeing progress on buildings
and agricultural experiments and sending orders to civil and military officials about an endless array of separate undertakings.

Memoirs of the empress's stay in Kiev do not record that
Catherine spent private time with Potemkin, and perhaps she did
not. Yet their old bond cannot have withered away completely;
certainly they cared for each other, and it is possible that they still
slept together occasionally. Catherine professed to miss Potemkin
terribly when they were apart. Both the empress and her beloved
Potemkin had acquired reputations for dissolute living and un-
quenchable sexual desire; in his case there was some foundation
for the ill repute. Potemkin had a virtual harem of mistresses.
Besides his nieces, and the series of noblewomen with whom he
fell passionately—if briefly—in love, Potemkin was said to frequent brothels and to take advantage of the offers he received
from courtiers to share their wives with him in return for political
favors.

In April cannon boomed to announce that the ice on the river
had begun to break up. The empress and her party had been in
Kiev for three months, waiting for the long winter to loose its
grip on the waters. By May 1 the Dnieper was navigable, and
Catherine and her favored guests went aboard seven brand-new
galleys built under Potemkin's supervision and fitted out like
miniature mansions.

Each of the large, ornately painted vessels in what de Ligne,
christened "Cleopatra's fleet" had its own staff of uniformed
servants and its own small orchestra with twelve musicians. Each
had elegantly appointed bedrooms fitted out with comfortable
beds and taffeta bedcovers and mahogany writing desks. Dressing

rooms and sitting rooms had divans upholstered in rich Chinese fabric. Gold and silk gleamed everywhere. Meals were eaten in a special galley designed around a large dining room. With only a few guests to each galley, socializing became a feat of balance and daring, for the travelers were forced to go back and forth between each other's vessels in tiny rowboats and with the river in flood accidents were unavoidable. Every day people and goods were spilled out of the small boats into the river, and during one severe storm, several galleys went aground on sandbars.

Catherine noted in a letter to Grimm that navigation on the flooding river was difficult. In all there were some eighty boats in the imperial flotilla, and collisions could not be avoided. The current was swift and treacherous, there were many sharp bends and many tiny islands; conditions were so unpredictable that it was impossible to raise the sails on the galleys. Catherine, as always, worked at her desk and sent and received several large and heavy dispatch-bags each day sent by courier from Petersburg. In the intervals between work, however, the empress and her guests played word games, had lively conversations, and competed in contests of literary skill. "If you knew all that is said each day on my galley," the empress told her correspondent in Paris, "you would die laughing."

The Count de Ségur, who knew the empress well as he had been in attendance at her court in Petersburg for several years, thought that she was in exceptionally good spirits during the spring days on the river.

"I never saw the Empress in better humor than on the first day of our journey," he wrote. "The dinner was very cheerful, we were all delighted to leave the town of Kiev, where we had been shut in by ice for three months. Spring rejuvenated our thoughts; the beauty of the weather, the magnificence of our fleet, the majesty of the river, the movement, the joy of the crowds of onlookers who ran along the banks, wearing an odd mix of costumes from thirty nations, our certainty of awakening each day to fresh curiosities sharpened and stimulated our imaginations."

Mentally the guests were in superb form. De Ligne extemporized verses in classic alexandrine meter, with Ségur supplying him with end rhymes. Fitzherbert displayed his gifts as an entertaining and amiable raconteur. Naryshkin capered and contributed his usual inspired silliness. Cobentzl, who liked to act in his spare time, proposed that the company act out proverbs with him in Catherine's bedchamber. The empress too came up with verses and matched wits with the others, though the brilliant and mercurial de Ligne found her to be somewhat heavy-footed and literal. She had not his agile mind (though to be fair to her, she was preoccupied), in truth she had begun to slow down mentally. In the games of wits, she was outclassed, but by competitors of rare caliber.

Catherine's letters to Grimm reveal the distractions that beset her as the great golden galleys sped down the wide river toward Kherson. Persistent rumors reached her that another usurper, bent on succeeding where Pugachev had failed, had appeared near Orenburg. Other reports from the countryside told of stories kept alive among the peasants that Pugachev himself had not died (he had in fact been executed in January of 1775) but was in hiding, and would soon emerge to lead another revolt. Catherine had been hearing such things for years, yet she did not dismiss them; knowing that her subjects were as unpredictable as the spring floods and the strong currents in the swollen river, she took note of when and where each upwelling of rumor appeared, and remained alert.

During her working hours she sat on the deck of her golden galley, wearing a long, loose gown, enjoying the warmth of the sun, reading the papers her secretaries brought her and composing replies. She had found a young Greek dressmaker who was "adroit as a monkey," in her phrase, at dressing her, "always according to her fantasy." And her fantasy ran to youthfulness at times. While socializing aboard her galley one evening, the empress appeared in an orange taffeta gown with blue ribbons, her gray hair loose like that of a young girl. Knowing that she was among friends, she allowed herself a touch of girlish coquetry and charm. And despite her years, it still suited her.

Like Potemkin, Catherine had two wardrobes: European-style gowns (costly but never extreme in style) for public occasions and for work and relaxation, draping Muscovite robes that spilled out in comfortable folds over her expanding belly and jutting hips. Her non-Russian subjects applauded her Muscovite attire; from where she sat she could see them, clustered at the river's edge, calling out and waving. She smiled at them, then turned once again to her papers.

That there would be war with the Turks, and soon, seemed to her inevitable. Indeed, her journey was meant to goad the Turkish enemy into action, so that she could have an excuse to declare war. The outcome was not certain, yet she felt optimistic in her daring. The Austrians were with her, though she was uncertain whether Emperor Joseph would be able to meet her as originally planned along the southern route of her journey, as he was ill with erisypelas. The British and French would oppose her, but they were far away, and the French, at least, were not likely to interfere as they were coping badly with an increasingly severe political crisis.

During the course of her journey Catherine followed with interest the accounts reaching her of the French Assembly of Notables, called into being to solve the country's mounting financial crisis. She disapproved of the frivolity of Queen Marie Antoinette (Emperor Joseph's youngest and prettiest sister) and of the ineptitude of the stolid Louis XVI. The French government was all but bankrupt, and the country seemed, if not ungovernable, at least intractable. It pleased Catherine to think that the ideas of enlightened rulership born in France had taken root in Russia; she, Catherine, and not Louis XVI, was the true heir of Montesquieu, Diderot and Voltaire.

Letters reaching Catherine aboard her galley brought news of personal matters. Her grandson Alexander and his sister Helen had measles. Constantine had come out in a rash. Her son by Orlov, Alexei Bobrinsky, living in high style in Paris, had run through his generous allowance and needed more money to pay his creditors. (Catherine asked Grimm to take the young man in hand, to coerce him into vowing solemnly not to go further into debt. On receipt of this vow she authorized Grimm to give Bobrinsky more money.) Grand Duchess Maria's sister-in-law Zelmira, married to Maria's violent and dangerous brother, had come to Catherine for asylum with her three small children; knowing at first hand the agonies of an abusive marriage, Catherine gave Zelmira the peace she sought and, throughout her journey, wrote letters to Zelmira's in-laws in an effort to secure a safe future for her.

An amusing letter came informing Catherine that Lavater, father of the fashionable science of phrenology, had studied Catherine's features in order to read her character. Her face showed recklessness, Lavater said, not greatness or distinction. She was not to be compared with the late Queen Christina of Sweden, a truly sage monarch. No doubt Catherine dismissed Lavater's judgment and thought no more about it. Queen Christina, after all, had abdicated her throne and gone to live in Rome in the shadow of the Vatican. She had not succeeded, as Catherine had, in the work of government. Judged against Catherine's measure of a worthwhile life—usefulness—Queen Christina had failed. While she herself was succeeding, so far.

Emperor Joseph's illness passed quickly enough for him to join the Russian traveling party and together he and Catherine visited the Crimea. For five days they stayed in the former khan's palace at Baktshi-Serai, a fairyland of Turkish, Moorish and Chinese architecture where sparkling fountains played in lush courtyards and elaborate mosaics decorated every inch of the walls, ceilings and graceful pillared colonnades. In the grand audience hall, resplendent with gilding and tilework, colored marble and intricate stone traceries, Catherine took her place where once the khans had presided. A golden inscription on one wall informed "the whole world" that "there is nothing as rich as this in Ispahan, Damascus, or Istanbul."

Leaving the site of the khans' former glory, empress and emperor traveled across wide stretches of waste, once occupied by Tatar tribes but now, scoured of their inhabitants by Potemkin's pitiless troops, returned to their natural state. Sleeping in huge tents erected by servants of the Prince of Tauris, the imperial pair marveled at the extent of Russia's newly conquered lands, and were taken to see the results of Potemkin's efforts to transform the wastes into fertile ground. New villages had been built, new groves of trees planted, new crops introduced. A few foreign immigrants had been established, many more, Potemkin said, were on their way.

Catherine was astounded by Potemkin's ingenuity in planning spectacles to gladden her journey—and to show off Russian might to the Turks. Military reviews featured thousands of smartly dressed, smartly marching soldiers. Troops of Tatars on swift horses maneuvered their mounts in a dazzling display. One evening just at sunset the hills surrounding a town where Catherine was staying lit up with fireworks. The ring of fire covered several miles, and at its center, high on one hill, was her imperial monogram set off by an explosion of tens of thousands of rockets. The very ground shook. Never had so much might been concentrated in one place. The Russians appeared to be formidable, if not invincible.

Catherine and Joseph were now on the best of terms. They shared confidences about the burdens of power. They talked of the other European states, and their interests, and of the prospects for France, which Joseph had visited. Observers thought there was "no reserve" between the two sovereigns.

"Has anyone ever tried to kill you?" one asked. "As for me, I've been threatened."

"I've received anonymous letters," the other replied.

Yet despite their harmonious rapport, Catherine and Joseph were not able to reach a detailed agreement about the coming war. According to Ségur, who talked privately with Joseph on many occasions, the emperor had no plans to actively support Catherine in her grand schemes of conquest. He had learned of a revolt against Austria in the Netherlands, and knew that restoring order there would have to be his first priority. (Catherine too knew of the Netherlands uprising, and feared that it might dissuade the Austrians from sending troops to engage the Turks, though she did not say this to Joseph.)

The climax of the empress's tour was her visit to the Black Sea ports. Here Potemkin outdid himself. When the empress's party arrived at Sebastopol, and sat down to a sumptuous banquet, the Prince of Tauris presided. He spoke expansively of the might of Russian arms.

"A hundred thousand men await my signal," he announced, and no sooner had the words left his mouth than the closed shutters of the room opened to reveal a panorama of military splendor. Outside the windows, stretching toward the vast bay, rank on rank of soldiers stood at attention. Entire regiments, some outfitted in the traditional costumes of their regions, waited alertly for Potemkin's signal. One Greek battalion was made up of warrior women, powder horns and pouches slung over their skirts, glittering feather-trimmed turbans wrapped around their heads.

Beyond the massed soldiery, out in the tranquil bay, the stillness was shattered by an ear-splitting burst of cannonfire from the decks of several dozen ships. From ten thousand throats roared forth a shouted pledge, repeated again and again: "Long live the Empress of Pontus Euxinus! Long live the Empress of Pontus Euxinus!"

It must have been an overwhelming moment. Warmed by the excellent local wine, heartened by all that she had seen and heard over five months of travel, gratified by the applause of her guests and the thunderous approbation rising from her loyal fighting forces, Catherine must have been profoundly moved. The new Russian fleet, which Potemkin had built, stood ready to attack Constantinople, which was scarcely a two days' sail distant. The portals of Byzantium stood open. She had only to gird up her loins, give the signal to her army and navy, and make her determined way through them.

Chapter Twenty-Seven

As it turned out, events moved more swiftly than Catherine expected. Her Tauride tour and display of military might led the Ottoman officials immediately to arrest the Russian minister in Constantinople, effectively precipitating war.

Hardly had Catherine returned from her prolonged journey than she was faced with crisis. At the end of August 1787, she met with her council and ordered Potemkin to move rapidly against the Turkish foe, believing that no more than a few weeks were needed to launch a full-scale offensive. She asked Alexis Orlov, hero of the great battle of Chesme, to take over command of the Black Sea fleet, to be enlarged by the addition of ships from the Baltic fleet. To her annoyance, Orlov declined. He was jealous of Potemkin, and coveted supreme command of the army, which would make him Potemkin's superior. Unless he received higher rank than his rival, he told the empress, he would not serve.

Catherine needed Orlov, yet she could not afford to offend Potemkin. (She feared him, wrote one who observed her closely, "as a wife fears an angry husband.") She relied on Potemkin completely. Without him, as she once told him in a letter, she felt like a person without arms. So Orlov had to be disappointed.

In the first weeks of the war the Russians seemed to take two steps backward for each advance. General Suvorov defended

Russian-held Kinburn successfully against a Turkish assault, but Potemkin's Black Sea fleet, which was to make Russia invincible at sea, succumbed to a severe storm and was unable to engage the Turks.

The fleet had been built in great haste. Pressured to have it ready by the time the empress reached the Crimea, Potemkin had ordered the shipwrights to use available timber of inferior quality rather than waiting for sound materials to be sent from the northern forests. The vessels were weak and fragile, unable to stand up to harsh weather and untrustworthy in battle. In addition, there were shortages of powder and shot, crews were not at their full complement, and provisions were running short.

Worst of all, Potemkin himself, Catherine's "arms," had given in to depression. He delayed sending couriers to Petersburg with the bad news about the fleet, and when at last he did write to Catherine he asked her to allow him to give up his command. Tauris, he feared, was indefensible after all. Catherine should retreat from the peninsula and let the Turks reclaim it.

This was the last thing the indomitable Catherine wanted to hear. Her response to Potemkin was gentle, even motherly, in tone—she knew that a firm rejoinder would only deepen his depression—but encouraging in content. She urged him not to give in to despair but to launch an attack by land, meanwhile waiting for ships from the Baltic fleet to arrive to replace those that had been damaged or were unreliable. She did not tell him that, according to reports she was receiving from the Western capitals, the outbreak of war with Turkey might well be only one dimension of a larger, Europe-wide war.

The winter of 1787–1788 took a harsh toll on Catherine's nerves. Potemkin continued to be intractable, and uncommunicative. Poor harvests led to food shortages and high prices in the Russian towns, always a cause for unease, and in addition the empress worried that an outbreak of plague—an everpresent danger along the border with Turkey—might disrupt the war effort and carry off Potemkin. Catherine was besieged by

Potemkin's detractors, both at her court and abroad. Alexis Orlov continued his running critique of the Prince of Tauris's inertia and ineptitude. Accounts in the western European press, based on the inaccurate but vivid assertions of the Saxon ambassador, accused Potemkin of deceiving Catherine on a lavish scale, treating the Crimea like a colossal stage set where peasants dragged in from elsewhere paraded through sham villages (so-called Potemkin villages) built of cardboard and paste. Even Catherine's waiting women derided Potemkin, calling down their mistress's violent wrath; she ordered several of the women whipped for their insolence.

It must have been galling to Catherine to have to defend Potemkin to his critics while feeling such dissatisfaction with him herself. She wrote to him, pleading with him to send her news more frequently than once a month, telling him how much his silence made her suffer agonies of uncertainty and anguish. Her head ached, her stomach rebeled. She was worried about money, and had to borrow heavily as war expenses mounted. She was worried about Emperor Joseph, who was holding back from launching an attack because of Potemkin's inertia. She feared that the British King George III and his ministers, alarmed at Russia's growing might, were giving secret encouragement to the Turks. And she was worried over reports that her cousin, King Gustavus of Sweden, was amassing soldiers and fitting out his fleet. Should the Turkish war go badly, she might face a second enemy on her northern border.

Grand Duchess Maria was pregnant for the sixth time, and hoped to present her mother-in-law with another grandson. On a frigid afternoon in mid-May Maria went into labor, and Catherine, preoccupied with stories of a Turkish-Swedish alliance and pressed hard by some in her council to attack the Swedish fleet before the unpredictable King Gustavus unleashed his ships against Russia, interrupted her consultations to visit the birth chamber.

Maria was struggling bravely, but was losing the battle; she could not expel the child. No doubt recalling the terribly pro-longed, ultimately fatal labor of her first daughter-in-law, Nata-lia, and combating her own dread of illness and incapacity in others, Catherine forced herself to supervise the midwives as they tried in vain to bring Maria's child into the world. Catherine took command, refusing to permit the fatalistic midwives to give up on poor Maria and exhorting her time and again to make a supreme effort.

For nearly three hours the ordeal continued, with Maria shriek-ing and screaming, Catherine shouting impatient orders, the mid-wives pummeling and tugging at the young mother's swollen belly and frightened servants scrambling to fetch cloths and coals, burn herbs and prepare the swaddling blankets. A fire blazed in the small room but the cold was so deep that everyone, even the sweat-bathed Maria, shivered and could not get warm.

Convinced that Maria was dying, Catherine made a last effort to save her, and she believed that her intervention prevented tragedy. Against the odds, a tiny girl was born, and quickly wrapped up warmly against the deepening cold. She was apparently healthy and gave a lusty cry. Weakly, Maria cried too—because the baby was not a boy. To reassure the mother, as well as from vanity, Catherine gave the baby her own name before seeking the warmth of her own apartments, chilled to the bone.

By June it was evident that King Gustavus was indeed intent on war. Encouraged by promises of clandestine British assistance he attacked a border fortress and soon afterward sent the empress an ultimatum.

Catherine laughed at her cousin's extravagant demands for territory in Russian Finland and his rumored boast that he would soon be in Petersburg with his army, calling him "Don Quixote the Knight Errant." All the same she met personally with her entire council and pressed Bezborodko and the others hard to arrange in haste for the defense of the capital and the port of Kronstadt.

Orders went out for garrison troops to come to Petersburg posthaste. Arms and artillery were brought in from neighboring towns and peasants were commanded to relinquish their horses to the army. Horses from the imperial stables were hitched to carts and cannon and palace servants put aside their regular duties to form militias and go on watch. In addition to the elite regiments, citizen bands were organized to help defend the city. Merchants from the bazaars, street sweepers, police and even clergy prepared to fight the terrible Swedes under their bellicose king, who was rumored to be mad. Within days, all Petersburg was in a frenzy.

Catherine's declaration of war against Sweden was officially announced on July 2. Buoyed by recent minor naval victories against the Turks, the empress was ebullient and resolute. She put on a naval uniform and celebrated the triumphs, announcing that she intended to stay in Petersburg and face King Gustavus.

"God is with us!" Catherine told her councillors, and Zavadovsky, her former favorite and currently a high court official, was struck—not for the first time—by her courage. "The spirit of bravery never leaves Her Imperial Highness," Zavadovsky commented after one meeting. "She is our inspiration."

The Swedes were in Finland, on Russian soil. Grand Duke Paul took his regiment and marched to intercept them, while ships of the Russian Baltic fleet, delaying their scheduled departure for the Black Sea, patroled the coast. The scent of gunpowder filled the streets of Petersburg, men drilled and marched every hour of the day and much of the night. Catherine supervised all, assured her officials frequently of divine support for Russian arms, and, in the privacy of her rooms, suffered colic and insomnia.

August came and still the Knight Errant had not managed to enter the Russian capital. Catherine wrote to Potemkin, telling him about the "foolish Swedish war"—in reality a very dangerous situation—and urging him to send her more frequent bulletins from the south. King Gustavus had meanwhile discovered a mutiny among his Finnish troops. He pulled back, and did not muster the daring to attack a second time before the onset of winter weather.

Over the next few months Catherine found time, despite recurrent illness and endless hours of meetings and paperwork, to write a comic play about her enemy cousin. *The Knight Errant* was performed at the palace in January 1789, and the laughter of the courtiers temporarily broke the tension that had prevailed for so long.

On Catherine's sixtieth birthday, April 21, there was no public celebration. The empress spent the day alone, except for her servants. Her advancing age weighed heavily on her, all the more so as many of those she had known and worked with closely over the years were dying off. Her ally Emperor Joseph was fatally ill, she learned (though in fact he lingered on until the following winter). The spring thaw and warm, mild air could not lift Catherine's spirits. She was often in tears, her servant Khrapovitsky wrote in his diary. Her many cares absorbed her and made her despondent. A host of chronic complaints, from dizziness to nervous attacks to excruciating back pains, assailed her with more and more frequency. And her favorite, Mamonov, was rarely with her anymore. Their estrangement had been going on for months, and Catherine had fallen into the habit of keeping her own melancholy company. It may be that, at sixty, she was learning a new lesson: that despite what she had always believed, she could, in fact, live for long periods of time without love.

The ultimate break with Mamonov came in late spring, and when it came, it was deeply painful and humiliating for the failing, white-haired Empress.

Many contemporaries noted how the morals of Catherine's courtiers, always casual, had become much more lax in recent years. Illicit liaisons, sexual flirtations, betrayals of spouses and lovers were becoming commonplace. Mamonov succumbed to the epidemic of sexual intrigue and began a passionate affair with Daria Scherbatov, a rather plain, lumpish young woman with a disagreeable disposition who was one of the empress's maids of honor.

For several years Mamonov had complained petulantly to his friends of his "imprisonment" by the empress, and his complaints had led to bruising scenes with tears, quarrels, and, for Catherine, great nervous strain. She had confessed her anxieties and upsets to Potemkin, who on occasion had tried to mediate between the lovers during his visits to court. More often, however, Potemkin had told Catherine privately that Mamonov was not worth all the turmoil and grief he had caused her. ("Eh, Little Mother, spit on him!" was his earthy advice.)

Finally things came to a head when Daria became pregnant. Mamonov confronted Catherine, and though his hands trembled and his voice shook, he asked in a rather roundabout fashion to be dismissed as her official favorite. She was indignant; he lost his temper. She brought up all their old quarrels, and his neglect of her. He accused her of being his jailer. Neither got what they wanted.

Later, however, Catherine had a change of heart, and wrote Mamonov a letter. Knowing nothing of Mamonov's involvement with Daria, she proposed that he marry a wealthy young heiress, thus freeing him of his burden of service to herself while assuring his future prosperity. She would do all she could to further the match, she promised. "In that way," she added at the end of her letter, "you will be able to remain in attendance."

Mamonov was dismayed. He did not want a great fortune—in part because the empress had already enriched him and his family. He wanted the plain, sour, pregnant Daria Scherbatov. With enormous trepidation he wrote to Catherine and told her so.

"I kiss your little hands and feet, and I cannot see what I am writing," he concluded, still in the tone of a tender lover. Yet he confessed that he had promised to marry his beloved Daria six months earlier.

When she read Mamonov's letter with its shocking avowal, Catherine fainted. Later, when she came to her senses again, she felt by turns astonished, bewildered, angry and deeply wounded. She had sensed that something was terribly wrong, she had known that sooner or later the hidden toxin would work its way to the surface. She had quarreled with Mamonov often over his flirtations with other women; indeed her jealous scenes had been a factor in their estrangement. (An even more powerful factor, according to Mamonov, was the corrosive effect of political intrigue. "Being surrounded by courtiers," he confided to an acquaintance, was like "being surrounded by wolves in a forest.") But to discover that he had been, in effect, cuckolding her behind her back, and with a much younger woman, was a huge blow to her pride.

Khrapovitsky wrote in his diary that the empress wept a great deal after reading Mamonov's letter. She retreated to her private apartments and allowed no one but her old friend Anna Naryshkin to be with her. For several days, while she wrestled with her feelings, she did little but work at her desk and take her usual constitutional after supper. Then she came to a decision.

Summoning Mamonov and Daria Scherbatov, Catherine formally announced their engagement and granted them a hundred thousand rubles and several rich estates. The young people knelt before their sovereign, both of them overcome by her forgiveness and generosity. When she wished them happiness and prosperity, one observer noted, everyone in the room wept along with the future bride and groom.

Outwardly recovered from Mamonov's betrayal, Catherine nonetheless nursed her inner wounds.

"I have received a bitter lesson," she wrote, predicting unhappiness for Mamonov and Daria and writing to Grimm that Mamonov was about to be "punished for life by the most idiotic of passions, which has made him a laughing-stock and has shown up his ingratitude."

In truth, Catherine was the laughing-stock; jokes at her expense redoubled in the wake of her break with Mamonov, who was despised by the courtiers for his arrogance, spite and shrewd self-seeking. The empress who stood up so bravely to the armies of the Turks and the Swedes had been forced to concede defeat to a mere guardsman. She might triumph on the battlefield, but in Cupid's wars she was outmatched. But then, what could she expect, cruel onlookers sneered, a chronically ill old woman matched to a virile young man?

Mamonov's wedding was barely out of the way when a new favorite was installed—Platon Zubov, a beautiful, physically slight boy of twenty who was an officer in the horse guards. Zubov was more grandson and apprentice clerk than lover; indeed it is possible that he and Catherine had no sexual intimacy at all. (Catherine called Zubov "the child" when referring to him to others.) She chose him more for his innocence, mild manner and lack of guile than for any of his other qualities. She could not afford to be hurt again as Mamonov had hurt her. Zubov, Catherine told Grimm, had "a very determined desire to do good." She felt certain that he would be loyal and devoted to her, and that he would stand by her, affectionate and supportive, through her days of fever and long nights of insomnia, gastric upset and stabbing back pain.

"He takes such good care of me," she told Grimm, "that I don't know how to thank him." Gone were the days when the empress would succumb to the most idiotic of passions. From now on she would take a safer, saner course.

The news from Paris that summer, the summer of 1789, was exciting to some, but to most, unnerving. Catherine received daily reports of startling upheavals in the French political landscape. The disappointing King Louis, yielding to the terrible pressures of an economy in collapse, had summoned representatives of the nobles, the clergy, and the Third Estate—in theory all other French men—to deliberate in Paris. The Third Estate had declared itself to be a separate body, and had begun proclaiming freedoms and rights in the name of humanity.

Distempered Parisians, full of hatred for King Louis's Austrian Queen Marie Antoinette, and sensing that the monarchy had begun to totter, rampaged through the streets and tore down a despised symbol of royal absolutism, the old fortress of the Bastille. And in early August, in a single wild night of expansive republicanism, many aristocrats gave up their privileges and estates and aligned themselves with the popular delegates who had declared their intention to reform France.

Catherine, convinced that France was, in her phrase, "going to ruin" and that the spineless, irresolute King Louis was responsible for the calamity, was on guard for signs of rebellion in her own kingdom and urged all her commanders to redouble their efforts to bring the Swedish and Turkish conflicts to a swift conclusion. The "French infection" was spreading, she thought; no government in Europe could rest easy. As for King Louis and his queen, Catherine was certain that, unless they managed to flee in secret to England or America, they were doomed.

Despite both Russian and Austrian victories, the campaigning season ended without prospects of a swift peace. Catherine was anxious, gravely concerned about the future of Europe and dogged by the pains and inconveniences of her own declining health.

"All the powers are in turmoil," she remarked, denouncing the perfidy of Prussia under Frederick the Great's successor Frederick William II. She anticipated a Prussian attack, and was both alarmed and angered when she learned, in March of 1790, that the Prussian emperor had made a secret pact with the Turkish sultan. News of losses on both war fronts sent her into seclusion, where she spent hours reading Plutarch with Zubov. They attempted a translation together, and Zubov's boyish, unassertive presence was balm to the empress's troubled mind.

Once again the stink of gunpowder filled Petersburg streets in May and June. The thunder of cannon shook walls and broke hundreds of windows. King Gustavus's fleet menaced Kronstadt, and Catherine, ignoring the advice of those who implored her to escape to Moscow lest Petersburg be overrun, actually had herself driven to Kronstadt in the pouring rain in hopes of witnessing a great naval battle; of course she expected the Russian fleet to be victorious. She had grown very shortsighted, yet she held a spyglass to her best eye and watched the maneuverings of the ships as best she could, her nerves rattled by the continuous booming of cannon.

"God is with us!" she exclaimed at supper, raising her glass in tribute to the sailors who, she hoped, would soon secure a major victory and then a lasting peace.

Peace did come, and sooner than Catherine expected, but the treaty Russia signed with Sweden in August of 1790 did not end the empress's anxieties. The Baltic fleet had been diminished in numbers and weakened in effectiveness by Swedish fireships and incessant cannonades. Prussia continued to threaten, with British encouragement. The Turkish war dragged on, occasioning further loans and more conscription of peasants for the army—the last a worry to Catherine, for it led to unrest and, with the "French madness" in the air, could conceivably breed revolution.

Hemmed in by difficulties, and with the cold weather returning, the empress fell prey to yet another siege of debilitating illnesses. She may have had a stomach ulcer. Her entire digestive system was so erratic that she could only tolerate coffee, a few sips of wine, and hardened bread. After weeks of this austere diet she lost weight, her energy fell to a new low and she spent many unhappy days lying on her large Turkish sofa or in bed.

The endless, icy winter was very hard on Catherine. Her fits of weeping, depression, and nights of severe pain were more frequent than in the past, and she felt blocked and frustrated. Zubov, "the child," was some comfort but the only man she could truly rely on, Potemkin, was far away and in danger. Catherine admitted to feeling as if there were "a stone lying on her heart." She steeled herself against age, pain and loss, refusing to let her doctors dose her with their medicines and seeking relief in home remedies and the therapeutic effects of heat.

When at last she learned in February of 1791 that Potemkin was on his way to Petersburg, the empress roused herself and prepared to give him a hero's greeting. But Potemkin, as often in the past, took center stage on his own. He announced that he would give a grand ball at the Tauride Palace for three thousand guests, in honor of the empress, on the occasion of her sixty-second birthday.

On the evening of April 23 Potemkin's sumptuous neoclassical mansion was grandly decorated, lit by thousands of wax candles—it was said he had bought every candle in Petersburg, and had sent to Moscow for more—and ornamented with glowing tapestries, thick carpets and costly works of art. All the servants had new liveries. The kitchens had been stocked with choice foodstuffs and the wine cellars filled with excellent vintages. Every sign of damage from the recent cannonades—the broken glass, fragments of plaster and broken ornaments—had been cleared away, leaving the magnificent house in polished, pristine splendor.

A parade of carriages entered the courtyard and guests alighted, masked and in costume. The imperial coach, painted and gilded, its wheels gleaming with diamonds, swept up to the entrance and the small, portly empress was handed out. Simply dressed, her white hair bound on top of her head, her face deeply lined but her faded blue eyes amiable and alert, she waved off all attempts at ceremony and walked slowly into the marble entrance hall.

The men bowed, the women curtseyed deeply to the old woman. Potemkin, his ample girth enclosed in vivid red, with a cloak of black lace hanging from his shoulders, came forward to kiss the empress's hand and lead her into the ballroom. An orchestra of three hundred musicians began to play, and Catherine, with all the guests following her, walked the length of the huge, high-ceilinged salon to take her seat on a raised platform and watch the dancing.

Her handsome grandson Alexander, now fourteen years old, joined four dozen couples in dancing a quadrille. His tall, well-proportioned body was set off by the diamond-studded blue costume he wore. He was fair, with a face as beautiful as a girl's and a princely bearing. People had been saying for years that Alexander, and not Paul, would succeed the empress. On this night, as she watched the agile, graceful boy step and turn in time to the music, Catherine may have had the succession very much on her mind.

The dancing over, all the guests strolled through a long colonnade into another vast room, as huge as a domed temple, bare save for tall vases of Carrara marble. Beyond this was another immense room full of trees and flowering shrubs. The April chill was forgotten here; the warm, humid air was fragrant with the scents of exotic blossoms and marble fountains played in the blazing candlelight. At the heart of the lovely garden was an expanse of grass, from which rose a transparent obelisk whose prism-like shape refracted the light in a thousand glowing colors.

The guests marveled at the inventiveness of their host, and the ingenuity of his servants. For Potemkin had done what appeared to be the impossible: he had ordered an ice cave to be built right next to the tropical garden, so that the frigid walls of the cavern, sparkling with frost, would turn an aqueous pale green reflecting the green of the lush trees and the grass.

At supper the empress charmed all those she chatted with. "Her extreme affability does not diminish at all her dignity," wrote Count Esterhazy, who visited Russia in 1791 and spent many evenings in Catherine's company, "and those she admits to greatest familiarity with her do not dare talk to her about business, unless she broaches the subject. Her conversation is very interesting, and quite varied. When she speaks of herself, or of the events of her reign, it is with a noble modesty, which puts her above any compliments which one might be tempted to make to her."

Guests who had never before seen the empress, and who knew nothing of her beyond what they had read in European newspapers or in the growing body of satirical writings attacking her, were astonished to discover how gracious, natural and cultivated she was. Expecting a dissolute harridan, they found a voluble, intelligent old lady with an enchanting play of sweetness and shrewdness across her aging features. She was immensely impressive, all the more so for never being too impressed with herself.

It was late in the evening when Potemkin clapped his beringed hands and the curtain rose on his private theater. The guests trooped in to watch two new ballets—the dancers brought from France and Italy—and two comedies, followed by a choral concert and folk dancing with performers from all corners of Russia.

A never-ending banquet was spread on plates of silver and gold, wine and champagne ran freely, music played and the guests danced long into the night. Catherine became tired at around midnight, and began making her farewells. All at once a burst of choral music arrested all activity. It was a hymn of victory composed in the empress's honor.

She stood in the large entrance hall to listen, and as the rich voices blended, rising together to end in a triumphant crescendo, she must have felt deeply moved. For once she may have allowed herself to reflect on all that she had achieved in her sixty-two years, and on the will and unbreakable spirit that had sustained her through adversity, the sturdy body that resurged each time illness struck, the fine, discriminating mind that had guided her empire to greatness. On that night, Catherine must, for a moment at least, have put her customary modesty aside and let herself feel very proud.

Chapter Twenty-Eight

CATHERINE SAT AT HER WORKTABLE IN HER BEDROOM, wearing her dressing gown of heavy white silk, a white crepe cap covering her hair. She was absorbed in writing a letter to Grimm, dipping her quill again and again into the pot of thick ink. It was cold in the room; outside the window the streets were hidden under deep piled snow and ice crusted thickly on the windowpanes. The snow and oppressive cold reminded Catherine of another February day long before, and she put her thoughts about it into her letter.

"Fifty years ago today I arrived in Moscow," she told her correspondent. "I do not believe there are ten people here who remember that day." She listed those she recalled meeting as a girl of fifteen, newly arrived in Russia: Ivan Betsky, who had become her mother's lover, now worn out and nearly blind, his wits failing; Countess Matushkin, ten years older than Catherine, now a spry old woman who had recently remarried; the jokey Leon Naryshkin, master of silliness, who had been making Catherine laugh for half a century; one of the ancient, bent waiting-women. She ran out of names. "These, my friend, are the most convincing proof of old age."

She would soon be sixty-five. Over and over again the European newspapers had announced her death. She herself had prepared a memorandum—a sort of will—to guide those around her in the event of her demise. It instructed them to lay out her corpse in a white gown, with a golden crown on her cold brow bearing the name Ekaterina. They were to mourn for only six months, "the shorter the better," and the mourning was not to interfere with festivals or other traditional observances. Catherine had no wish to cast a pall on anyone's good times.

She continued her letter in a lighter vein. "In spite of everything," she told Grimm, "I am as eager as a five-year-old child to play blind man's buff, and the young people, my grandchildren and great-grandchildren, say that their games are never so merry as when I play with them. In a word, I am their merrymaker."

Catherine had seven grandchildren, the youngest barely two years old, and she managed, despite a painful rheumatic knee and the increasing unwieldiness of her body, to romp with them and keep them running and laughing with excitement. Something young, warm and lively was always with her, either a grandchild or two or a dog or a pet squirrel. People noticed that she did not like to be alone. When Zubov was with her, he was often accompanied by his pet monkey—though unkind observers told one another that Zubov himself was the real monkey, the silly pet of the empress's old age.

Catherine told Grimm about her current writing project, something she knew few people would ever care about but which kept her active mind stimulated during the long dark hours of winter. She was doing research on Russian medieval history, specifically on the later fourteenth century. She loved deciphering old documents, and in recent years her interests had become more and more antiquarian. And as she herself was now an antique, she had taken to writing and rewriting her memoirs. In all, she wrote the story of her early life seven times, always breaking off her account in the last years of the reign of Elizabeth. Telling and retelling the story of her early years was both satisfying and cathartic, though it entailed reliving, if only in memory, the horrors of her marriage to Peter and her years of fear and anguish under the capricious empress who had chosen her as Peter's wife and brought her to Russia.

Catherine's scholarly bent served her well and even brought her comfort, for in the process of rewriting her memoirs she came across documents that helped her to understand why things had happened as they did. Once, searching through the palace archives, she came across an old trunk full of papers, covered with dust and half eaten by rats. Methodically she went through the contents. The papers had been written in the 1740s, and they concerned her, albeit peripherally. She read on and on, and the more she read the better able she was to perceive, with hindsight, why the empress had been so suspicious, what factions she feared and why the succession so preoccupied her. Catherine's new-found insights were incorporated into the last versions of her memoirs.

Her letter to Grimm complete, the empress turned to another of her interests and read for a while. She wore spectacles and also used a large magnifying glass to read. ("Our sight has been blunted by long service to the state," she liked to tell people, using the imperial "we.") She enjoyed reading classic French plays, and was avid for anything to do with ancient languages, particularly languages spoken within the borders of her empire. She liked astronomy. She once idly asked Grimm whether, "when the material of which the planets are made was detached from the sun," the sun was diminished in size. To the end of her life she went on reading about law, and legal philosophy, though other preoccupations tended to push such reflective reading aside.

Her intense hatred for the Jacobins, the Paris radicals who had taken command of the political changes in France, became stronger every year. With their lust for egalitarianism the Jacobins had presided over the Terror, that orgy of carnage during which thousands of innocent people had been guillotined. The Jacobins had ordered the executions of Louis XVI and his wife, and were keeping their only son in a dank prison. The Jacobins, Catherine believed, were out to change the world, they wanted to kill all monarchs and all aristocrats everywhere. In her view they were rabid dogs who ought to be shot, poisoned, exterminated.

Pausing in her studies, Catherine got up from her desk and walked to the window, opening it long enough to toss handfuls of bread crumbs to the ravens perched on the icy ledge outside. The cold bit into her face and hands, and she quickly closed the window again. Then, sighing, she rang the little bell that sat on her desk to summon her chamberlain Zotov.

For the next several hours she talked with her secretaries and with the chief of police, who gave her the latest information about suspected Jacobin subversives in Moscow and Petersburg, suspected assassins, and other criminals. She was so anxious to prevent any radical French ideas from gaining a foothold in her domains that she forbade the sale of revolutionary calendars (which did away with the traditional names of the months and substituted poetic, naturalistic names) and of red hats such as the Jacobins wore.

Last of all Count Zubov was ushered in, the chamberlain bowing low to him and all others giving way before his authority. He wore a silk frock coat sewn with large sequins along all the seams, white satin trousers and green boots. His pet monkey trailed along behind him, now climbing on him, now jumping from bed to desk to cupboard.

No longer the gentle, grateful young guardsman, Zubov had become a major figure in Catherine's government, a lieutenant-general, with his own chancery and his own staff of clerks and officials. Zubov had learned a great deal since taking over Mamonov's post; he had assumed most of Potemkin's former powers, along with Potemkin's former apartments in the palace. Because of his influence, and his perceived hold over the empress, Zubov was widely condemned for his "uncommon hauteur."

The courtiers had hated Potemkin, but they had been forced to acknowledge his idiosyncratic genius. Zubov, by contrast, they regarded as contemptible without possessing any countervailing merit at all. He was dull, thick-witted and boorish. The empress, foolishly besotted with him, called him brilliant, and heaped on him responsibilities far beyond his capacity. ("I am doing a great service to the state by educating young men," she told one official, who passed along her comment to others later with a knowing laugh.)

In truth Zubov was a hardworking but plodding civil servant, who, according to one relatively clear-sighted overserver, "tortured himself with his struggles over documents, having neither the quickness of mind nor the capacity of understanding which alone could move such a terrific burden." He was a novice, encumbered with a master's tasks. Too often he failed to live up to Catherine's overly high expectations. Still, he had more than enough power to make others cringe, and he defended himself ably against all attacks.

At noon Catherine's elderly hairdresser entered the room. He swiftly combed out the empress's thinning white hair, twisting it into a simple knot with a few small curls behind the ears. The empress's four maids, all of them older than she was, prepared her toilette. One handed her a cup so that she could rinse out her mouth. Her teeth were gone, and her mouth and jaw had gone slack, coarsening her appearance somewhat. Yet the whiteness of her hair, and her relatively unlined face and pink complexion gave her a pleasing appearance.

The maids brought in her day-dress, a flowing white underskirt, a dark apron, and wide pleated sleeves. She preferred dark gray or mauve aprons, and wore them each day as a kind of uniform. Wearing the same thing every day made for efficiency—her entire toilette occupied about ten minutes—and Catherine had always believed in efficiency. Her time, she once told Zavadovsky, belonged "not to herself, but to the empire." She had no right to squander hours on her appearance when her subjects' needs came first.

After a light meal, sparing her delicate stomach, the empress drove out in her carriage. She greeted all those she passed with a nod and a friendly "Good day," and smiled benignly when people called out blessings on her. When the weather was severe she spent her afternoons indoors, reading or doing embroidery with the help of her spectacles and magnifying glass, or listening to Zubov read her the foreign newspapers.

She laughed at the frequent accounts in the foreign press of her "secret and obscene life." The Catherine depicted by hostile journalists was a man-hungry demon, insatiably sexual and avid for ever stronger thrills and outlandishly exotic sensations. Pornographic stories of her excesses abounded. Her needs were said to be so great that no man could satisfy them; only a stallion was big enough to fill her. Once Voltaire had called her "the Semiramis of the North." Now, in revolutionary, antimonarchist Paris, she was known as "the Messalina of the North," after the voraciously sexual wife of the Roman Emperor Claudius.

Once she had cared very much what the English and French journalists thought of her. She had coveted a reputation as a humane and enlightened monarch, the embodiment of all that was rational, tolerant and benign. Now, with France in the hands of petty regicides and all Europe in ferment, she gave up her hopes for a glorious name. She did not like her subjects to refer to her as "Catherine the Great" (an honorific meant to echo Peter the Great, her idol), though she had once seriously suggested to Voltaire many years earlier that he ought to write a book on "The Age of Catherine II." Still, the older she became, the more the title "Great" dogged her.

It worried her, this sweeping epithet with its solemn, heroic connotations. She had never aimed for exaltation; a baroque-style Apotheosis of Catherine was hardly her preferred self-image— indeed pretention and self-styled grandeur invariably made her laugh. When the Petersburg nobles tried to confer on their empress the title "the Great, Most Wise Mother of the Fatherland," she ordered them to desist. "This is absolutely my will," she insisted. To Grimm she noted, referring to herself, "not everyone likes flattery."

One of the worst things about personal exaltation, in Catherine's view, was that it led to false expectations. The Prince de Ligne confessed to her, after they had become friends, that when he first came to Russia he expected Catherine to be "a large woman, stiff as a poker, who spoke only in short sentences and who demanded perpetual admiration." He was very relieved to discover that she was nothing like that. Far from being large, stiff and aloof she was of modest height, warm and full of chatter.

Still, formal public occasions took their toll on her. "When I enter a room," she told de Ligne, "I produce the same effect as Medusa's head." Embarrassment and constraint were the inevitable harbingers of monarchy; Catherine was used to causing discomfort by her presence, then having to thaw the frozen faces and draw out the timorous, withdrawn guests who stood painfully in awe, not so much of her as of the majesty she represented.

To her intimates, Catherine remained all her life a voluble, pleasure-loving and entertaining companion who liked to do animal imitations and who occasionally, after announcing that she would perform "the music of the spheres," sang for her guests in a hilariously off-key contralto, adding to the effect by miming "all the solemn self-complacent airs and grimaces of musicians." Her pièce de résistance was a "cat concert," in which she purred and growled ludicrously, adding "half-comic, half-sentimental" words to the animal sounds, then suddenly "spitting like a cat in a passion, with her back up." The great Catherine disappeared, leaving only a hissing, clawing alley cat.

Once the ice broke the Neva rose rapidly that spring, and toward the end of April it overflowed its granite banks and spread out over the city. People said the flood was a portent of evil let loose upon the world; great and tragic events would soon befall Russia.

In fact dramatic events were occurring on Russia's doorstep. Polish rebels led by Thadeus Kosciuszko massacred the Russian garrison at Warsaw and, denouncing the tyranny of Catherine and the Prussian King Frederick William, drove thousands of Russians into panicked flight. Hundreds were killed.

Catherine immediately concluded that the Jacobin plague had infected Poland, a conclusion strengthened when she learned that the rebels were declaring all men equal and advocating the freeing of the Polish serfs. Fearing that France might move in to shore up the rebel army, Catherine began to contemplate the final incorporation of Polish territory into her own realm (she had seized the Polish Ukraine, Minsk and Vilnius the previous year, while Prussia gained Torun and Danzig as compensation for supporting Russia diplomatically).

Catherine's territorial aggrandizement at the expense of the Poles was an offense to the newly emerging consciousness of national identity in Poland. With hindsight, the eradication of Polish sovereignty has seemed to Catherine's modern critics an act of barbarism out of keeping with her vaunted enlightened values. Yet politically, Poland had been unstable for at least a generation. And in 1794, with the Terror in full spate in France and treacherous Jacobins assumed to be behind every uprising, the crushing of a dangerously radical state on Russia's border seemed to Catherine's contemporaries prudent, even laudatory.

Warsaw surrendered to the superior Russian army late in October of 1794, and over the following months Russia absorbed Courland and what had been Polish Lithuania into her empire. King Stanislaus Poniatowski abdicated, and entered private life. If he saw Catherine, or attempted to see her, no surviving document records their encounter, though he did take up residence in Petersburg.

Through the months of the Polish crisis Catherine tried to bring Zubov forward as a statesman, but despite her aggressive sponsorship he impressed no one. She spent hours writing out summaries of the European situation for him, condensing her years of experience into pages of advice and maxims, but though Zubov pored over the material, he emerged from reading it little wiser than before.

Privately Catherine was increasingly aware that she could not rely on Zubov as she had once relied on Potemkin, and the realization must have been wounding. The entire burden of decision-making, giving orders and delegating tasks large and small fell on her. In one day alone, she told Grimm, so much mail and so many dispatches arrived—including numerous packets of books—that it took nine large tables to contain their heaped excess. To spare her red-rimmed, tired eyes, now subject to recurrent infections, Catherine had various officials read the mail to her. It took three days, reading twelve hours a day, to get through the mountain of words. And still Catherine found time to do a bit of research on the history of Armenia, from a book lent to her by General Popov.

The tyranny of work bound the empress and robbed her of her time, her moods, her preferences and pleasures. She tried to save an hour or so each day for her grandchildren, especially Alexander, now seventeen and married to a German princess. Constantine, Alexandra, "la belle Hélène," Maria and six-year-old Catherine tagged after their grandmother on her promenades through the palace gardens, though often the walks came to a sudden halt when the empress felt severe pains in her legs. Early in 1795 another baby, Anne, was born to the grand duchess and in the same year the toddler Olga, only two and a half, succumbed to a rare malady that accelerated her growth until she became deformed and repulsive and then carried her off after weeks of acute suffering.

The succession was an ongoing concern. The empress knew that she could not go on ruling for too much longer, her infirmities were crowding in on her and before long she would have to hand over her power. Many people at her court believed that Paul would never reign, but whether Catherine made a will, or tried to take specific steps to exclude Paul from the succession, are unknown.

Certainly Paul felt slighted, and showed his extreme discontent in outbursts of violent rage and a constant expression of sour disgust. All he had contributed to the future of the Russian Empire was his fertility, he remarked dourly to an acquaintance. He may well have been envious of his handsome, favored eldest son, though he was careful not to display any hostility toward Alexander in the empress's presence. It became Paul's personal campaign to vindicate and avenge his putative father Peter III, and he vowed that, once Catherine was dead, Peter would no longer be a forgotten figure or a subject of scandal.

Paul had not involved himself directly in choosing a bride for Alexander, and when early in 1796 Constantine was married to Julia of Saxe-Coburg his father remained in the background, leaving the matchmaking to the empress. The same situation prevailed when Paul's oldest daughter, thirteen-year-old Alexandra, was courted via meetings of diplomats by the young King of Sweden, Gustavus IV. (The groom-to-be's father, Catherine's old enemy Gustavus III, had been assassinated several years earlier.) Alexandra, a very pretty, very clever girl in her grandmother's estimation, had not been Gustavus's first choice, but Catherine had made up her mind that Alexandra should be Queen of Sweden, and had threatened and cajoled until the Swedes capitulated. The seventeen-year-old king, accompanied by his uncle, who served as regent, and an entourage of several hundred servants, arrived in Petersburg in mid-August of 1796, ready to discuss the final arrangements for the wedding.

Catherine was eager for all to go well. Though she could barely walk now on her badly swollen legs, and could no longer climb stairs at all, she attended the ball held to welcome the Swedes and admired the blond, blue-eyed Gustavus, finding him to be quite satisfactory despite a certain shyness and awkwardness in society.

Gustavus and Alexandra appeared to get on well, and by September preparations for the wedding were under way. However, it appeared that the Lutheran Swedes expected the Orthodox Russian princess to convert. Catherine, who had abandoned her own Lutheran unbringing and embraced Orthodoxy when she married the Russian grand duke, would not permit Alexandra to do the opposite. Russia was a far greater, far more important power than Sweden, after all; Alexandra would be marrying down. Furthermore, Catherine would give Sweden a large subsidy when the marriage negotiations were complete. She ought not to have to compromise on the question of Alexandra's creed.

Weeks passed, and the discussions reached an impasse. Catherine became imperious. The Swedes remained intractable. There was one ray of hope. Gustavus seemed kind-hearted enough to be willing to allow Alexandra to practice her Orthodox faith in private—and with this shadow of an assurance Catherine proposed that a formal ceremony of betrothal take place, with the Orthodox clergy presiding.

The fragile compromise buoyed Catherine's spirits enormously. She felt her old powers returning, she began to envision great things. Alexandra would marry Gustavus, keeping her religious beliefs intact. The Swedes, now firm allies of Russia, would guard the Baltic while the Russian armies would dash across Europe to conquer France and restore the Bourbon monarchy. Catherine would become the Savior of Europe, the destroyer of the dreaded Jacobins. A heroine greater than all previous heroines. The iron age, the eighteenth century, would become in truth the Century of Catherine II.

Feeling invincible, Catherine received Gustavus's representative Count Markov. The count presented her with a formal letter from the young king in which he stated his final position on the subject of Alexandra's religion. He would not agree in writing to her retaining Orthodox worship, Gustavus said, but he was willing to make an informal oral promise to that effect.

Catherine was astonished. She turned beet red. Her mouth dropped open and one side of her face suddenly sagged, her mouth twisting grotesquely. Her servants rushed forward in concern, yet there was little they could do but watch in alarm while their mistress slowly revived. It was several minutes before her high color abated and she was able to speak.

She had suffered a stroke. Her women told the footmen, who

told the chamberlains, who spread the terrible news throughout the palace. Within an hour all Petersburg knew of the empress's affliction. She was very ill. Another stroke might come at any time. She might not last a day, a week. Surely the end was near.

The guards regiments were put in readiness for an imminent change of reigns. Frightened courtiers met in secret to make plans for how to handle the crisis of the empress's death, which they felt must come soon. Factions formed, strategies were plotted. Zubov, terrified about his future, wrung his hands and said his prayers.

The empress, recovering from her attack, felt dizzy and groggy, yet she was determined to carry on with her plans. The betrothal ceremony that was to unite Alexandra and Gustavus was not canceled, despite Gustavus's intractability. Catherine wanted to see Alexandra betrothed, to assure herself that she had not been bested.

On the appointed evening, September 11, the courtiers gathered at six o'clock in the throne room. Catherine made her way slowly to her throne, her obesity draped in brocade. The glittering stars of three Orders gleamed on her chest. On her head was a small crown. Something in her gait, and the swift, sudden shifts between pallor and ruddiness in her sunken cheeks betrayed her recent severe illness. Alexandra, uneasy but smiling and arrayed in bridal robes, sat beside her grandmother, awaiting her husband-to-be.

But Gustavus never came. Hours passed. Enraged at what she considered to be a monstrous insult, the empress sat stonily on her throne, her anger steadily mounting, her cheeks alternately pale and crimson. Finally, realizing that the king was never going to arrive, she stumbled out of the room and had the courtiers dispersed.

In coarse, vulgar language Catherine abused the Swedes, reserving her choicest insults for the vain, stiff young king. Gossip said she lashed out at one of the Swedes with her scepter, not once but twice.

The violence and vulgarity were unlike Catherine, and in all probability they were a result of brain damage following her stroke. She was not herself. Over the next weeks insomnia dogged her, she felt ill and confused at times. It was difficult for her to think clearly. She tried to carry on as usual but could not. She missed meals, did not attend mass, fell asleep at odd and inconvenient times. Her government functioned but just barely; Zubov was incapable of taking over, and the other officials, while dismayed by the empress's condition, and gravely concerned about the succession, were gratified at the thought that her unworthy minion would soon be ousted.

On the morning of November 5, the empress got up and put on her white silk dressing gown. She looked rested, and joked with her maid that she felt twenty years younger, and might even plan another tour of the Crimea when the weather improved.

She ordered her morning coffee and went to sit at her worktable, where she began reading documents concerning the French invasion of Italy and a young general named Bonaparte. The evening before, she had learned of an Austrian victory over the French, so her hopes were high as she scratched away with the first of her daily supply of quill pens. Probably she had a dog beside her, or in her lap. Perhaps she paused to feed the birds outside her window. She worked on, undisturbed, for several hours in the cold room, while above her head a candle burned under an icon of Our Lady of Kazan.

At nine-thirty or so the chamberlain Zotov began to wonder whether something might be wrong. The empress always rang her bell to summon him before nine. Could she have forgotten? Could she be in need of anything?

Cautiously he knocked at the door of her bedroom, and then, when there was no answer, he went inside. The room was empty. He called out, and quickly went to the water-closet that adjoined the main room. There, on the floor, was the empress, her gown crumpled immodestly around her legs, her face blood-red and her cap awry. Zotov called for help and, with the aid of several other

men, was able to heft the groaning old woman into the bedroom
and onto a leather mattress on the floor.

Doctors made futile efforts to revive the empress, who soon
lost consciousness. She was bled from her arm, medicines were
poured down her throat, other medicines administered rectally.
Her aged, fleshy body was pummeled and subjected to indignities
she would never have permitted had she been awake and alert.
Alexander took charge, as Paul was not at the palace but on his
estate at Gatchina several hours' ride away. A trusted messenger
was sent to tell Paul what had happened, but he did not arrive in
the capital until nearly nine o'clock that evening.

By then the doctors had declared that the empress would not
survive. The palace chaplain placed the holy wafer on her tongue
and anointed her convulsing body with holy oil on face and
hands. He intoned the solemn prayer for the dying, as everyone in
the room knelt to add their own prayers to his.

The empress, Mother of the Fatherland, was passing. Only a
miracle could save her. Those who had served her for decades,
even those who had felt the sting of her irascibility, were greatly
saddened. Weeping servants and officials filled the long, chill corridors of the Winter Palace, waiting for news from the doctors.

All night Catherine lay on her mattress, her breathing rough
and raw. Her family gathered around her, Alexander and Constantine, Paul and Maria, the younger children allowed in for a
few moments at a time. Paul began giving orders, and was
obeyed. The transfer of power had begun. Catherine's papers
were gathered up and given to her successor.

Hour by hour, throughout the day of November 6, the death-
watch went on. The empress's eyes were closed, she did not
speak, but her vital old body struggled mightily against death.
Spasms wrenched her belly, she gasped for breath like a great
beached fish. At times, a vile, stinking black liquid poured from
her mouth, filling the room with a terrible stench. Finally, just
before ten o'clock, a last, loud rattle came from her throat. Then
all was still, save for the sound of weeping.

Almost at once the thousand bells of Petersburg began to toll. Solemnly, reverently, their huge voices boomed out across the city, now in unison, now in random clangor, announcing the sad message that the great Catherine was with God. Hearing it, her subjects knelt and crossed themselves, their faces wet with tears. Most of them could remember no other ruler. Few of them looked forward to the reign of the Emperor Paul.

For three weeks Catherine's embalmed body lay in state in the throne room of the palace, covered in a gown of fine silk with an immensely long furlined train. A black velvet tent was erected over her casket, and soldiers and family members stood guard nearby while thousands of mourners filed past. Thousands more attended her lengthy public funeral in the first week of December, watching the imperial casket as it was conveyed across the ice-covered Neva to the Cathedral of Peter and Paul, traditional resting place of the sovereigns of Russia.

Catherine's casket did not make its final journey alone. Paul gave orders that Peter III's body, disinterred from its tomb in the Nevsky Monastery, be brought to the cathedral and reburied beside that of his late wife. It pleased the new emperor that his mother and putative father, so violently estranged in life, should lie side by side through eternity.

A Note on Sources

————————————◆————————————

T HE BIOGRAPHER SEEKING TO UNDERSTAND THE PERSONAL-
ity and inner life of Catherine II is unusually fortunate in
having at hand Catherine's own memoirs, in versions written at
different times in her life. A close reading of the memoirs, written
in indifferent but highly expressive and individualistic French,
reveals a great deal about their author, her tastes and views, her
priorities and outlook on life. Unfortunately, the memoirs cease
before Catherine became empress. For the period of her reign, the
biographer can draw on Catherine's other writings and letters, the
dispatches of visiting ambassadors, letters and memoirs of contemporaries, both Russian and European, contemporary de-
scriptions of Russian society and the Russian court by travelers,
and political and administrative documents.

For the reader in search of further reliable information about
Catherine there are few books in English that offer anything like
an authentic portrait of the empress; most either trivialize or
romanticize her achievements or echo the distorted image of her
invented by French revolutionary propagandists. John T.
Alexander's *Catherine the Great, Life and Legend* (Oxford University Press, 1989) is a sober and scholarly if somewhat dry political
history of Catherine's reign, with insights into her temperament.

Index